Nineteenth-Century Russian Literature in English
A Bibliography of Criticism and Translations

Compiled by Carl R. Proffer
and Ronald Meyer

Ann Arbor / Ardis

Ardis Publishers
2901 Heatherway
Ann Arbor, Michigan 48104

Library of Congress Cataloging-in-Publication Data

Proffer, Carl R.
Nineteenth-century Russian literature in English: a bibliography
of criticism and translations / compiled by Carl R. Proffer,
with Ronald Meyer.
        p.   cm.
    ISBN 0-88233-943-5 (alk. paper)
    1. Russian literature—19th century—History and criticism—
Bibliography.   2. Russian literature—19th century—Translations
into English—Bibliography.   3. English literature—19th century—
Translations from Russian—Bibliography.   I. Meyer, Ronald.
    II. Title.
        Z2503.P76   1990
    [PG3012]   89-18589
    891.709'003—dc20   CIP

CONTENTS

Acknowledgments

Carl R. Proffer (1938-1984), distinguished Slavist and co-founder of Ardis Publishers, was also a book collector and bibliographer. He perceived a need for a comprehensive bibliography of nineteenth-century Russian literature in English, which would include translations, critical studies and doctoral dissertations. Unfortunately, he did not live to see this project through to publication, but handed me the boxes of index cards with instructions on what needed to be added and verified. In completing the work on the bibliography I have almost doubled Carl's original number of entries.

The compilation of this volume would not have been possible without the fine bibliographies listed throughout. In addition, a number of people have taken time to verify entries and supply important missing items. I wish to thank especially Philip Frantz, Helena Goscilo, Barbara Heldt, David Lowe, James Rice, Christine Rydel and Sydney Schultze. Joseph Placek of The University of Michigan Libraries examined the entire volume, filled in hundreds of lacunae and gave advice on problematic details. Of course, any errors are my own.

Ronald Meyer

Introduction

Nineteenth-Century Russian Literature in English is the first encyclopedic and international bibliography devoted exclusively to this period. The bibliography, which catalogues items published from the 1890s through 1986, covers both general topics and 69 writers.

The bibliographies of the individual writers are divided into two sections: translations and criticism. The translations are listed in the following order: (1) collected works, (2) other book publications, arranged alphabetically by the title of the work, (3) translations published in anthologies and journals, arranged alphabetically by translator or editor. It was decided that it would be impractical to duplicate the bibliographies found in Richard C. Lewanski's indispensable *The Literatures of the World in English Translation: A Bibliography. Volume II: The Slavic Literatures* (NY: New York Public Library, 1967). For this reason emphasis, particularly in the case of the major writers, is placed on items that have been published since Lewanski's work.

The criticism sections of individual writers are divided as follows: (1) bibliographies, (2) monographs, (3) doctoral dissertations, (4) articles published in journals, Festschriften, conference proceedings, collected papers, as well as chapters or sections of monographs that deal with that writer. Items in each sub-section are arranged alphabetically by author. Review articles and reviews of theatrical productions (in the case of Chekhov, for example) are excluded. Again, space dictates that some sense of proportion be exercised in the selection of items. To include all references to Dostoevsky or Tolstoy would be impractical, whereas in the case of minor writers any reference at all can prove helpful. Finally, we assumed that D. S. Mirsky's magisterial *A History of Russian Literature* did not require indexing.

In those cases where an item proved unavailable for verification, the following bibliographies were consulted: *The Year's Work in Modern Language Studies, MLA International Bibliography of Books and Articles on the Modern Languages and Literatures,* as well as those bibliographies listed on pages 13-14 and the bibliographies of writers listed throughout.

The surnames of writers under each individual heading have been abbreviated to first initial. For example, Sergei Aksakov appears as Sergei A.

Journal references include volume number, year of publication and pagination. For example, *RLT* 1 (1971):22-42. A list of abbreviations of journal titles appears on page 11.

Abbreviations

ASEER—American Slavic and East European Review
BulDS—Bulletin of the International Dostoevsky Society
CalSS—California Slavic Studies
CASS—Canadian American Slavic Studies
CL—Comparative Literature
CLS—Comparative Literature Studies
CRCL—Canadian Review of Comparative Literature
CSP—Canadian Slavonic Papers
CSS—Canadian Slavic Studies
DostSt—Dostoevsky Studies
ESL—Etudes slaves et est-européennes
FMLS—Forum For Modern Language Studies
HSS—Harvard Slavic Studies
IJSLP—International Journal of Slavic Linguistics and Poetics
ISS—Indiana Slavic Studies
JRS—Journal of Russian Studies
MelbSS—Melbourne Slavonic Studies
MFS—Modern Fiction Studies
MLJ—Modern Language Journal
MLN—Modern Language Notes
MLR—Modern Language Review
MLS—Modern Language Studies
NZSJ—New Zealand Slavonic Journal
OSP—Oxford Slavonic Papers
PMLA—Publications of the Modern Language Association
PTL—PTL: A Journal for Descriptive Poetics & Theory of Literature
RLJ—Russian Language Journal
RLT—Russian Literature Triquarterly
RMS— Renaissance and Modern Studies
RusL—Russian Literature
RusR—Russian Review
SEEJ—Slavic and East European Journal
SEER—Slavonic and East European Review
SlavR—Slavic Review

BIBLIOGRAPHIES

Books

American Association for the Advancement of Slavic Studies (AAASS). *The American Bibliography for Slavic and East European Studies.* Annual publication, 1968-. [1957-67: *American Bibliography of Russian and East European Studies.*]

Bamborschke, U. & W. Werner, comps. *Bibliographie slavistischer Arbeiten aus den wichtigsten englischsprachigen Fach-zeitschriften sowie Fest- und Sammelschriften, 1922-1976.* Wiesbaden: Harrassowitz, 1981.

Breed, Paul F. & Florence M. Sniderman, comps. and eds. *Dramatic Criticism Index; a Bibliography of Commentaries from Ibsen to the Avant-Garde.* Detroit: Gale Research Press, 1972.

Dossick, Jesse J. *Doctoral Research on Russia and the Soviet Union.* NY: New York UP, 1960.

Ettlinger, Amrei & Joan M. Gladstone. *Russian Literature, Theatre and Art: A Bibliography of Works in English, Published 1900-1945.* London and NY: Hutchinson, 1947.

Horak, Stephan M., comp. *Russia, the USSR, and Eastern Europe: A Bibliographic Guide to English-Language Publications.* Vol.1:1964-74. Vol. 2: 1975-80. Vol. 3: 1981-85. Littleton, CO: Libraries Unlimited, 1978-87.

——. *The Soviet Union and Eastern Europe: A Bibliographic Guide to Recommended Books for Small and Medium-Sized Libraries and School Media Centers.* Littleton, CO: Libraries Unlimited, 1985.

Horecky, P. L. *Basic Russian Publications: An Annotated Bibliography on Russia and the Soviet Union.* Chicago: U Chicago P, 1962.

——. *Russia and the Soviet Union: A Bibliographic Guide to Western-Language Publications.* Chicago, 1965.

Hoskins, Janina W. *The USSR and East Central and Southeastern Europe. Periodicals in Western Languages.* 4th ed. Washington, D.C.: Library of Congress, 1979.

International Committee for Soviet and East European Studies. *European Bibliography of Soviet, East European and Slavonic Studies.* Vols. 1-2, Birmingham, 1975-76. Vols. 3-, Paris: Editions de l'Ecole des Hautes Etudes en Science Sociale & Institut d'Etudes Slaves, 1981-.

Lewanski, Richard C. *The Literatures of the World in English Translation. A Bibliography. Volume II, The Slavic Literatures.* NY: The New York Public Library & Frederick Ungar Publishing Co., 1967.

Line, Maurice B., et al. *Bibliography of Russian Literature in English Translation to 1945. Bringing Together Maurice B. Line, A Bibliography of Russian Literature in English Translation to 1900, and Amrei Ettlinger and Joan M. Gladstone, Russian Literature, Theatre and Art: A Bibliography of Works in English, Published Between 1900-1945.* Totowa, NJ: Rowman and Littlefield; London: Methuen, 1972.

Maichel, K. *Guide to Russian Reference Books.* Vol.1-. Stanford: Hoover Institution, 1962-.

Martianov, N. N., ed. *Books Available in English by Russians and on Russia Published in the United States.* 4th ed. New York, 1942.

Schanzer, George O., comp. *Russian Literature in the Hispanic World: A Bibliography.* Toronto: U Toronto P, 1972.

Simmons, J. S. G. *Russian Bibliography, Libraries and Archives: A Selective List of Bibliographical References for Students of Russian History, Literature, Political, Social and Philosophical Thought, Theology and Linguistics.* Twickenham: A. C. Hall, 1973.

Snow, Valentine. *Russian Writers: A Bio-Bibliographical Dictionary.* NY: International Book Service, 1946.

Terry, Garth M. *East European Languages and Literatures. A Subject Index to Articles in English-Language Journals, 1900-1977.* Oxford, England/ Santa Barbara, CA: Clio Press, 1978.

——. *East European Languages and*

Literatures II. A Subject and Name Index to Articles in Festschriften, Conference Proceedings, and Collected Papers in the English Language, 1900-1981, and Including Articles in Journals, 1978-1981. Nottingham, England: Astra Press, 1982.

Thompson, Anthony, comp. *Russia/ U.S.S.R. A Selective Annotated Bibliography of Books in English.* Oxford: Clio Press, 1979.

Yedlin, Tova & Jean Wilman, comps. *Women in Russia and the Soviet Union.* Ottawa: Carleton UP, 1985.

Zenkovsky, Serge & David L. Armbruster. *A Guide to the Bibliographies of Russian Literature.* Nashville, TN: Vanderbilt UP, 1970.

Articles and Dissertations

Boyer, Arline. A Description of Selected Periodicals in the First Half of the Nineteenth Century. *RLT* 3 (1972): 465-73.

Orel, Harold. Victorians and the Russian Novel. *Bulletin of Bibliography* 21 (Jan.-Apr., 1954):61-63; 21 (May-Aug., 1954): 78-81.

Phelps, G. The Early Phase of British Interest in Russian Literature. *SEER* 36 (1958):418-33.

Raphael, Jay E. An Annotated and Critical Bibliography of the Works Written in English since 1900 on the Pre-and Post-Revolutionary Russian Theatre. Ph.D. dissertation, Michigan State, 1971.

Rosenbaum, M. W. Slavonic Studies in America. Bibliography. *Journal of Higher Education.* 14 (1944):9-14.

Simmons, J. S. G. Theses in Slavonic Studies Approved for Higher Degrees by British Universities, 1907-1966. *OSP* 13 (1967).

Smith, G. S. A Bibliography of Soviet Publications on Russian Versification since 1958. *RLT* 6 (1973):679-94.

HISTORIES

Auty, Robert & Dimitri Obolensky. *An Introduction to Russian Language and Literature.* Cambridge: Cambridge UP, 1977.

Baring, Maurice. *Landmarks in Russian Literature.* NY: Barnes & Noble, 1960.

Brown, William Edward. *A History of Russian Literature of the Romantic Period.* 4 vols. Ann Arbor: Ardis, 1986.

Čiževskij, Dmytrij. *History of Nineteenth-Century Russian Literature.* Tr. Richard Porter. Ed. Serge A. Zenkovsky. Vol. I: The Romantic Period. Vol. II: The Realistic Period. Nashville: Vanderbilt UP, 1974; rpt. Westport, CT: Greenwood, 1986.

——— *On Romanticism in Slavic Literature.* The Hague: Mouton, 1957. (Musagetes, No. 1.)

——— *Russian Intellectual History.* Tr. J. Osborne. Ann Arbor: Ardis, 1978.

Fennell, John, ed. *Nineteenth-Century Russian Literature. Studies of Ten Russian Writers.* Berkeley & Los Angeles: U California P, 1973.

Freeborn, Richard. *The Rise of the Russian Novel. Studies in the Russian Novel from "Eugene Onegin" to "War and Peace."* Cambridge: Cambridge UP, 1973.

——— *The Russian Revolutionary Novel: Turgenev to Pasternak.* Cambridge: Cambridge UP, 1983.

Garrard, John, ed. *The Russian Novel from Pushkin to Pasternak.* New Haven: Yale UP, 1983.

Gifford, Henry. *The Novel in Russia: From Pushkin to Pasternak.* NY: Harper & Row, 1965.

Gregor, J. & R. Fülöp-Miller. *The Russian Theatre, Its Character and History.* Tr. P. England. London, 1930.

Hare, Richard. *Russian Literature from Pushkin to the Present Day.* London: Methuen, 1947.

Hingley, Ronald. *Russian Writers and Society 1825-1904.* NY: World University Library, 1967.

Karlinsky, Simon. *Russian Drama from its Beginnings to the Age of Pushkin.* Berkeley: California UP, 1985.

Lavrin, Janko. *From Pushkin to Maya-kovsky: A Study in the Evolution of a Literature.* London: Sylvan Press, 1948; rpt. Westport, CT: Greenwood, 1971.

____. *An Introduction to the Russian Novel.* London: Methuen, 1943.

____. *A Panorama of Russian Literature.* NY: Barnes & Noble, 1973.

____. *Russian Writers: Their Lives and Literature.* NY: D. Van Nostrand, 1954.

Lvov-Rogachevsky, V. *A History of Russian-Jewish Literature.* Ed. & tr. Arthur Levin. Ann Arbor: Ardis, 1979.

Magidoff, Robert. *A Guide to Russian Literature. Against the Background of Russia's General Cultural Development.* NY: New York UP, 1964.

Mersereau, John, Jr. *Russian Romantic Fiction.* Ann Arbor: Ardis, 1983.

Mirsky, D. S. *A History of Russian Literature.* Ed. Francis J. Whitfield. NY: Knopf, 1949.

Moser, Charles A. *The Russian Short Story: A Critical History.* Boston: Twayne, 1986.

Olgin, Moissaye. *A Guide to Russian Literature.* NY: Harcourt, Brace, Howe, 1920.

O'Toole, L. Michael. *Structure, Style and Interpretation in the Russian Short Story.* New Haven: Yale UP, 1982.

Reeve, F. D. *The Russian Novel.* London: F. Muller, 1967.

Simmons, Ernest J. *An Outline of Modern Russian Literature (1880-1940).* Ithaca, NY: Cornell UP, 1943.

Slonim, Marc. *The Epic of Russian Literature.* NY: Oxford UP, 1964.

____. *Modern Russian Literature from Chekhov to the Present.* NY: Oxford UP, 1953.

____. *Russian Theatre from the Empire to the Soviets.* Cleveland: World Pub. Co., 1961.

Stacy, Robert H. *Russian Literary Criticism: A Short History.* Syracuse: Syracuse UP, 1974.

Varneke, Boris V. *History of the Russian Theatre (Seventeenth Through Nineteenth Century).* Original tr. by Boris Brasol, rev. and ed. by Belle Martin. NY: Macmillan, 1951.

Vinogradov, V. *A History of the Russian Literary Language.* Tr. L. Thomas. Madison, U Wisconsin P, 1969.

Vogüé, E.-M., de. *The Russian Novel.* Tr. from the 11th French edition by H. A. Sawyer. NY: Knopf, 1916.

Welsh, David J. *Russian Comedy 1765-1823.* The Hague: Mouton, 1966.

Yarmolinsky, Avrahm. *The Russian Literary Imagination.* NY: Funk & Wagnalls, 1969.

ENCYCLOPEDIAS, DICTIONARIES

Berry, Thomas Edwin. *Plots and Characters in Major Russian Fiction.* 2 vols. Hamden, CT: Archon Books, 1977.

Brown, Archie, et al., eds. *The Cambridge Encyclopedia of Russia and the Soviet Union.* NY: Cambridge UP, 1982.

Harkins, William Edward. *Dictionary of Russian Literature.* NY: Philosophical Library, 1956.

Snow, Valentine. *Russian Writers: A Bio-Bibliographical Dictionary.* NY: International Book Service, 1946.

Terras, Victor, ed. *Handbook of Russian Literature.* New Haven: Yale UP, 1985.

Weber, Harry B. *The Modern Encyclopedia of Russian and Soviet Literature.* Gulf Breeze, FL: Academic International Press, 1977-.

GENERAL MONOGRAPHS & COLLECTED PAPERS

Andrew, Joe. *Writers and Society During the Rise of Russian Realism.* Atlantic Highlands: Humanities Press, 1980.

____, C. Pike & L. M. O'Toole, eds. *The Structural Analysis of Russian Narrative Fiction.* Keele: Keele UP, 1984.

Auty, Robert & Dimitri Obolensky. *An Introduction to Russian Language and Literature.* Cambridge: Cambridge UP, 1977.

Bann, S. & J. E. Bowlt, eds. *Russian Formalism: A Collection of Articles and Texts in Translation.* Edinburgh: Scottish Academic P, 1973.

Berry, Thomas E. *The Seasons through Russian Literature.* Minneapolis: Burgess, 1968.

Boyd, Alexander F. *Aspects of the Russian Novel.* Totowa, NJ: Rowman & Littlefield. 1972.

Chances, Ellen. *Conformity's Children: An Approach to the Superfluous Man in Russian Literature.* Columbus: Slavica, 1978.

Clardy, Jesse V. *The Superfluous Man in Russian Letters.* Washington, D.C.: University Press of America, 1980.

Clive, Geoffrey. *The Broken Icon: Intuitive Existentialism in Classical Russian Fiction.* NY: Macmillan, 1972.

Cockrell, R. R. *The Voice of a Giant: Essays on Seven Russian Prose Classics.* Exeter: Dept. of Russian, U Exeter, 1985.

Davies, Ruth. *The Great Books of Russia.* Norman: U Oklahoma P, 1968.

Debreczeny, Paul & Jesse Zeldin, eds. and trs. *Literature and National Identity: Nineteenth-Century Russian Critical Essays.* Lincoln: U Nebraska P, 1970.

Donskov, A. *Mixail Lentovskij and the Russian Theatre.* East Lansing, MI: Russian Language Journal, 1985.

Eikhenbaum, Boris & Yury Tynyanov, eds. *Russian Prose.* Tr. Ray Parrott. Ann Arbor: Ardis, 1985.

Fennell, John, ed. *Nineteenth-Century Russian Literature: Studies of Ten Russian Writers.* Berkeley: U California P, 1973.

Field, Andrew, comp. *The Complection of Russian Literature.* NY: Atheneum, 1971.

Freeborn, Richard. *The Rise of the Russian Novel: Studies in the Russian Novel from "Eugene Onegin" to "War and Peace."* NY: Barnes & Noble, 1973.

____ *Russian Literary Attitudes from Pushkin to Solzhenitsyn.* NY: Barnes & Noble, 1976.

____ *The Russian Revolutionary Novel: Turgenev to Pasternak.* NY: Cambridge UP, 1982.

Friedberg, Maurice. *Russian Classics in Soviet Jackets.* NY: Columbia UP, 1962.

Fuhrmann, J. T., E. C. Bock, L. I. Twarog. *Essays on Russian Intellectual History.* Austin: Texas UP, 1971.

Garrard, John, ed. *The Russian Novel from Pushkin to Pasternak.* New Haven: Yale UP, 1983.

Gifford, Henry. *The Hero of His Time. A Theme in Russian Literature.* London: Arnold, 1950.

____ *The Novel in Russia: From Pushkin to Pasternak.* London: Hutchinson, 1964.

Gleason, Abbott. *Young Russia. The Genesis of Russian Radicalism in the 1860s.* NY: Viking, 1980.

Goldberg, Leah. *Russian Literature in the Nineteenth Century.* Jerusalem: Magnes Press, 1976.

Gutsche, George J. & Lauren G. Leighton, eds. *New Perspectives on Nineteenth-Century Russian Prose.* Columbus: Slavica, 1982.

Hingley, Ronald. *Russian Writers and Society, 1825-1904.* NY: World U Library, 1968.

Jackson, Robert Louis. *Dostoevsky's Underground Man in Russian Literature.* Westport, CT: Greenwood, 1981.

Katz, M. R. *Dreams and the Unconscious in Nineteenth-Century Russian Fiction.* Hanover, NH: New England UP, 1984.

Kodjak, Andrej, Krystyna Pomorska & Stephen Rudy, eds. *Myth in Literature.* Columbus: Slavica, 1985.

Kropotkin, Petr. *Ideals and Realities in Russian Literature.* NY: Knopf, 1919.

____ *Russian Literature.* NY: B. Blom, 1967.

Kunitz, J. *Russian Literature and the Jew.* NY: Columbia UP, 1929.

Legters, L. H., ed. *Russia: Essays in History and Literature.* Leiden: Brill, 1972.

Leighton, Lauren. *Russian Romanticism.* The Hague: Mouton, 1975.

Lotman, Yury. *Analysis of the Poetic Text.* Tr. D. Barton Johnson. Ann Arbor: Ardis, 1976.

____ & B. A. Uspenskij. *The Semiotics of Russian Culture,* ed. Ann Shukman.

Ann Arbor: Dept. of Slavic Languages and Literatures, U Michigan P, 1984.

Matejka, Ladislav & Krystyna Pomorska, eds. *Readings in Russian Poetics: Formalist and Structuralist Views.* Cambridge: MIT Press, 1971.

Mathewson, Rufus Wellington, Jr. *The Positive Hero in Russian Literature.* Stanford: Stanford UP, 1975.

Mersereau, John, Jr. *Baron Delvig's "Northern Flowers" 1825-1832: Literary Almanac of the Pushkin Pleiad.* Carbondale: Southern Illinois UP, 1967.

Morson, Gary S. *Literature and History. Theoretical Problems and Russian Case Studies.* Stanford: Stanford UP, 1986.

Moser, Charles A. *Antinihilism in the Russian Novel of the 1860s.* The Hague: Mouton, 1964.

____. *Esthetics as Nightmare. Russian Literary Theory, 1855-1870.* Princeton: Princeton UP, 1989.

Nabokov, Vladimir. *Lectures on Russian Literature.* NY: Harcourt, 1981.

____. *Strong Opinions.* NY: McGraw-Hill, 1973.

Nakhimovsky, Alexander D. & Alice S. Nakhimovsky. *The Semiotics of Russian Cultural History: Essays by Iurii M. Lotman, Lidiia Ia. Ginsburg and Boris A. Uspenskii.* Intro. B. Gasparov. Ithaca: Cornell UP, 1985.

Neuhäuser, Rudolf. *Towards the Romantic Age. Essays on Sentimental and Preromantic Literature in Russia.* The Hague: Nijhoff, 1974.

Nilsson, N. A., ed. *Russian Romanticism: Studies in the Poetic Codes.* Stockholm: Almqvist & Wiksell, 1979.

Offord, Derek. *Portraits of Early Russian Liberals.* Cambridge: Cambridge UP, 1985. [Granovsky, Botkin, Annenkov, Druzhinin, Kavelin.]

O'Toole, L. Michael. *Structure, Style and Interpretation in the Russian Short Story.* New Haven: Yale UP, 1982.

Partridge, Monica. *Revolution and Nineteenth-Century Russian Literature.* Nottingham: U Nottingham, 1968.

Paul, J. V., ed. *Studies in Russian Literature.* Hyderabad: Central Institute of English and Foreign Languages, 1984.

Perlman, Louis. *Russian Literature and the Business Man.* NY: Columbia UP, 1937.

Phillips, Delbert D. *Spook or Spoof? The Structure of the Supernatural in Russian Romantic Tales.* Lanham, MD: University Press of America, 1982.

Poggioli, Renato. *The Phoenix and the Spider. A Book of Essays about Some Russian Writers and Their View of the Self.* Cambridge: Harvard UP, 1957.

____. *The Poets of Russia, 1890-1930.* Cambridge: Harvard UP, 1960.

Reeve, F. D. *The Russian Novel.* NY: McGraw-Hill, 1966.

Reid, Robert, ed. *Problems of Russian Romanticism.* Brookfield, VT: Gower, 1986.

Richards, David, ed. *The Voice of a Giant: Essays on Seven Russian Prose Classics.* Exeter: U Exeter, 1985.

Roberts, Spencer R. *Essays in Russian Literature: The Conservative View.* Athens: Ohio UP, 1968.

Rowe, Eleanor. *Hamlet: A Window on Russia.* NY: New York UP, 1976.

Rzhevsky, N. *Russian Literature and Ideology: Herzen, Dostoevsky, Leontiev, Tolstoy, Fadeev.* Urbana: U Illinois P, 1983.

Salaman, Esther. *The Great Confession: From Aksakov and DeQuincey to Tolstoy and Proust.* NY: St. Martin's, 1973.

Shukman, A., ed. *The Semiotics of Russian Culture.* Ann Arbor: Michigan Slavic Publications, 1984.

Simmons, E. J., ed. *Continuity and Change in Russian and Soviet Thought.* Cambridge: Harvard UP, 1955.

Simpson, Mark. *The Officer in Nineteenth-Century Russian Literature.* Washington, D.C.: University Press of America, 1981.

Stavrou, Theofanis G., ed. *Art and Culture in Nineteenth-Century Russia.* Bloomington: Indiana UP, 1983.

Thompson, Ewa M. *Understanding Russia: The Holy Fool in Russian Culture.*

Lanham, MD: University Press of America, 1987.

Thomson, Clive, ed. Special Issue on Mikhail Bakhtin. *Studies in Twentieth Century Literature* 9, 1 (1984).

Todd, William Mills III. *The Familiar Letter as a Literary Genre in the Age of Pushkin.* Princeton: Princeton UP, 1976.

——. *Fiction and Society in the Age of Pushkin.* Cambridge: Harvard UP, 1986.

——. *Literature and Society in Imperial Russia.* Stanford: Stanford UP, 1978.

Uspensky, Boris. *A Poetics of Composition.* Tr. V. Zavarin & S. Wittig. Berkeley: U California P, 1974.

Walicki, Andrzej. *The Slavophile Controversy.* Oxford: Oxford UP, 1975.

Wilson, Edmund. *A Window on Russia: For the Use of Foreign Readers.* NY: Farrar, Straus & Giroux, 1972.

Wilson, Reuel K. *The Literary Travelogue. A Comparative Study with Special Relevance to Russian Literature from Fonvizin to Pushkin.* The Hague, Nijhoff, 1973.

CONFERENCE PROCEEDINGS, FESTSCHRIFTEN

American Contributions to the Eighth International Congress of Slavists, 1978. Vol. 1: Linguistics and Poetics. Ed. H. Birnbaum. Vol. 2: Literature. Ed. V. Terras. Columbus: Slavica, 1978.

American Contributions to the Fifth International Congress of Slavists, 1963. Vol. 1: Linguistic Contributions. Vol. 2: Literary Contributions. The Hague: Mouton, 1963.

American Contributions to the Fourth International Congress of Slavists, 1958. 's-Gravenhage, Mouton, 1958.

American Contributions to the Ninth International Congress of Slavists: Kiev, September 1983. Vol. 2: Literature, Poetics, History. Ed. Paul Debreczeny. Columbus: Slavica, 1983.

American Contributions to the Seventh International Congress of Slavists, 1973. Vol. 1: Linguistics and Poetics. Ed. L. Matejka. Vol. 2: Literature and Folklore. Ed. V. Terras. The Hague: Mouton, 1973.

American Contributions to the Sixth International Congress of Slavists, 1968. Vol. 1: Linguistic Contributions. Ed. H. Kucera. Vol. 2: Literary Contributions. Ed. W. E. Harkins. The Hague: Mouton, 1968.

Amsenga, B. J., ed. *Miscellanea Slavica: To Honour the Memory of Jan M. Meijer.* Amsterdam: Rodopi, 1983.

Analecta Slavica: A Slavonic Miscellany Presented for His Seventieth Birthday to Bruno Becker. Amsterdam: De Bezige Bij, 1955.

Bartlett, R., ed. *Russian Thought and Society 1800-1917. Essays in Honor of Eugene Lampert.* Keele: Keele UP, 1984.

Bristol, Evelyn, ed. *Russian Literature and Criticism: Selected Papers from the Second World Congress for Soviet and East European Studies.* Berkeley: Berkeley Slavic Specialties, 1982.

Brostrom, Kenneth N. *Russian Literature and American Critics: In Honor of Deming B. Brown.* Ann Arbor: U Michigan, Dept. of Slavic Languages and Literatures, 1984. (Papers in Slavic Philology, 4.)

Canadian Contributions to the Eighth International Congress of Slavists, Zagreb-Ljubljana, ed. Z. Folejewski, et al. Ottawa: Canadian Association of Slavists, 1978.

Canadian Contributions to the Ninth International Congress of Slavists (Kiev 1983). Ed. Z. Folejewski, et al. Toronto: U Toronto P, 1983.

Canadian Contributions to the Seventh International Congress of Slavists, Warsaw, August 1973. Ed. Z. Folejewski. The Hague: Mouton, 1973.

Connolly, Julian W. & Sonia I. Ketchian, eds. *Studies in Russian Literature in Honor of Vsevolod Setchkarev.* Columbus: Slavica, 1986.

Demetz, P., et al, eds. *The Disciplines of Criticism: Essays in Literary Theory,*

Interpretation and History. For René Wellek on the Occasion of His 65th Birthday. New Haven: Yale UP, 1968.

Dutch Contributions to the Eighth International Congress of Slavists: Zagreb-Ljubljana, September 1978, ed. J. M Meijer. Amsterdam: Benjamins, 1979.

Dutch Contributions to the Fifth International Congress of Slavists, Sofia, 1963. The Hague: Mouton, 1963.

Dutch Contributions to the Ninth International Congress of Slavists, Literature, ed. A. G. F. van Holk. Amsterdam: Rodopi, 1983.

Dutch Contributions to the Seventh International Congress of Slavists, Warsaw, August 1973, ed. A. van Holk. The Hague: Mouton, 1973.

Dutch Contributions to the Sixth International Congress of Slavists. The Hague: Mouton, 1968.

Eekman, Thomas & Dean S. Worth, eds. *Russian Poetics: Proceedings of the International Colloquium at UCLA, September 22-26, 1975.* Columbus: Slavica, 1983.

Folejewski, Zbigniew, et al., eds. *Studies in Russian and Polish Literature in Honor of Waclaw Lednicki.* 's-Gravenhage: Mouton, 1962.

Freeborn, R., R. Milner-Gulland, C. A. Ward, eds. *Russian and Slavic Literature: Papers from the First International Slavic Conference, Banff, Sept. 4-7, 1974.* Cambridge: Slavica, 1976.

Gribble, C. E., ed. *Studies Presented to Professor Roman Jakobson by His Students.* Cambridge: Slavica, 1968.

Halle, Morris, comp. *For Roman Jakobson: Essays on the Occasion of His Sixtieth Birthday.* The Hague: Mouton, 1956.

Harrison, William J. & Avril Pyman, eds. *Poetry, Prose and Public Opinion: Aspects of Russia, 1850-1970; Essays Presented in Memory of N. E. Andreyev.* Letchworth: Avebury, 1982.

Jackson, Robert L. & Stephen Rudy, eds. *Russian Formalism: A Retrospective Glance: A Festschrift in Honor of Victor Erlich.* New Haven: Yale Center for International and Area Studies, 1985.

Jakobson, Roman, C. H. van Schooneveld, D. S. Worth, eds. *Slavic Poetics: Essays in Honor of Kiril Taranovsky.* The Hague: Mouton, 1973.

Kleberg, Lars & Richard Stites, eds. *Utopia in Russian History, Culture, and Thought: A Symposium.* Special issue of *Russian History* 11, 2 (1984). Irvine, CA: Charles Schlacks, 1984.

Kodjak, A., M. J. Connolly, K. Pomorska, eds. *The Structural Analysis of Narrative Texts: Conference Papers.* Columbus: Slavica, 1980.

Leighton, Lauren G., ed. *Studies in Honor of Xenia Gasiorowska.* Columbus: Slavica, 1983.

Lencek, R. L. & B. O. Unbegaun, eds. *Xenia Slavica: Papers Presented to Gojko Ružičić on the Occasion of His Seventy-Fifth Birthday.* The Hague: Mouton, 1975.

Magidoff, R., ed. *Studies in Slavic Linguistics and Poetics in Honor of Boris O. Unbegaun.* NY: New York UP, 1968.

Markov, V. & D. Worth, eds. *From Los Angeles to Kiev: Papers on the Occasion of the Ninth International Congress of Slavists.* Columbus: Slavica, 1983.

Paul, J. V., ed. *Studies in Russian Literature.* Hyderabad: Central Institute of English and Foreign Languages, 1984.

Shukman, A., ed. *The Semiotics of Russian Culture.* Ann Arbor: Michigan Slavic Publications, 1984.

Stolz, Benjamin A. *Papers in Slavic Philology, I: In Honor of James Ferrell.* Ann Arbor: Dept. of Slavic Languages and Literatures, U Michigan, 1977.

——, I. R. Titunik, Lubomir Dolezel, eds. *Language and Literary Theory: In Honor of Ladislav Matejka.* Ann Arbor: Dept. Slavic Languages and Literatures, U Michigan, 1984.

Strelka, Joseph P., ed. *Literary Theory and Criticism Festschrift Presented to René Wellek in Honor of His Eightieth Birthday.* NY: P. Lang, 1984, 2 vols.

Van Baak, J. J., ed. *Continuity and Change. Some Remarks on World Pictures in Russian Literature. Signs of*

Friendship to Honour A.-G.F. van Holk. Amsterdam: Rodopi, 1984.

Whiton, J. & H. Loewen, eds. *Crisis and Commitment. Studies in German and Russian Literature in Honour of J. W. Dyck*. Waterloo: U Waterloo P, 1983.

Worth, D. S., ed. *The Slavic Word: Proceedings of the International Slavistic Colloquium at UCLA*, Sept. 11-16, 1970. The Hague: Mouton, 1972.

GENERAL TOPICS DISSERTATIONS

Anderson, Margaret Louise. The Russian Character in the Russian Short Story. Kansas, 1949.

Armstrong, Judith M. The Novel of Adultery in the Second Half of the 19th Century in French, Russian, English and American Literature. Melbourne, 1974.

Blumberg, Edwina J. The Physiology of Petersburg: Russian Literature in the 1840s. Columbia, 1972.

Bohart, Eugene. An Exploration in Novel Form of the Literary Theme of Spiritual Rebirth. New York, 1976. [Tolstoy, Dostoevsky.]

Brailer, Kathryn Anne. Absurdist Features in Russian Drama: Nineteenth and Twentieth Centuries. Illinois, 1976.

Brueck, Katherine Trace. Treatments of Poverty in Realistic Fiction. Illinois, 1979. [Turgenev, Dostoevsky, Tolstoy].

Busch, Robert Louis. Freneticist Literature in the Russian Romanticist Period: Narrative Prose of the Early 1830s. Michigan, 1972.

Choldin, Marianna Tax. A Fence Around the Empire: The Censorship of Foreign Books in Nineteenth-Century Russia. Chicago, 1979.

Coleman, Arthur P. Humour in the Russian Comedy from Catherine to Gogol. Columbia, 1925.

Deutsch, Judith E. The Cossack Hero in Russian Literature: *Topoi* and Change. Columbia, 1985.

Donskov, Andrew. The Changing Image of the Peasant in Nineteenth-Century Russian Drama. Helsinki, 1972.

Duda, Sadik Tufan. The Theme of the Caucasus in Russian Literature of the XVIII-XIX Centuries. Vanderbilt, 1971.

Freeborn, R. H. Trends of Development in the Russian Nineteenth-Century Realistic Novel (1830-1880). Oxford, 1957-58.

Glasse, Antonia. The Poet in Search of an Audience: Russian Poetry in the Alexandrine Period. Columbia, 1972.

Glickman, Rose Burns. The Literary *Raznochintsy* in Mid-Nineteenth Century Russia. Chicago, 1967.

Glouberman, Emanuel. Fedor Dostoevsky, Vladimir Soloviev, Vasilii Rozanov and Lev Shestov on Jewish and Old Testament Themes. Michigan, 1974.

Gogolewski, Judith Ann (Hansleit). The Theme of "Vanishing Petersburg" in Russian Literature. Vanderbilt, 1969.

Golubov, Alexander S. Patterns of Religious Imagery: The Post-Gogolian Russian Realistic Novel, 1859-1881. Rochester, 1978.

Gregory, Paul. The Theme of Moscow in Russian Literature of the 19th Century. Vanderbilt, 1973.

Grzebieniowska, Xenia Z. Peter the Great in Russian Historical Novels. California, 1949.

Hill, B. M. The Growth of the Russian Psychological Novel. London, 1931.

Hopkins, William Hugh. The Development of "Pornographic" Literature in Eighteenth- and Early Nineteenth-Century Russia. Indiana, 1977.

Horowitz, Arthur Glenn. The Rebellious Hero in Russian Nineteenth-Century Literature. Northwestern, 1979.

Karapinka, Orysia. The Idea of the City in Russian Letters from Pushkin to Tolstoy. California, Berkeley, 1972.

Karkavelas, Sigrid Martha. The Visual Artist in Russian Literature of the First Half of the Nineteenth Century. California, Berkeley, 1980.

Kunitz, Joshua. Russian Literature and the Jew: A Sociological Inquiry into the Nature and Origin of Literary Patterns. Columbia, 1928.

Levy, Constance Andrea. Nineteenth-Century Novels of Introversion. New York, 1981. [Dostoevsky, Goncharov.]

MacGrath, M. A. The Servant in Nineteenth-Century Russian Prose Fiction. Durham, 1979.

Moser, Charles Arthur. Antinihilism in the Russian Novel of the 1860s. Columbia, 1962.

Neuenschwander, Dennis Bramwell. Themes in Russian Utopian Fiction: A Study in the Utopian Works of M. M. Shcherbatov, A. Ulybyshev, F. V. Bulgarin, and V. F. Odoevskij. Syracuse, 1974.

Osborne, David L. Russian Physiological Sketches and the "Natural School": Man and Environment in the 1840's. Ohio State, 1981.

Phillips, Delbert Darwal. The Supernatural Tale: An Analysis of Supernatural Elements in Russian Short Fiction of the First Three Decades of the Nineteenth Century. New York, 1977.

Pomar, Mark G. Russian Historical Drama of the Early Nineteenth Century. Columbia, 1978.

Reed, Phyllis Ann. The *Rusalka* Theme in Russian Literature. California, Berkeley, 1973.

Reifsnyder, Irene Pennington. A Comparative Study of the Problems of Adolescent Heroes and Heroines in Russian and Soviet Literature. New York, 1963.

Rosenbush, Michael. The Personality of Peter the Great in Nineteenth-Century Russian Literature. Montreal, 1970.

Rowe, Eleanor D. Hamlet and Hamletism in the Literature of Russia. New York, 1974.

Simpson, Mark Sherman. The Officer in Nineteenth-Century Russian Literature. California, Riverside, 1981.

Spitzer, Catherine Anne. The Image of the City in the Novels of Gogol, Dostoevsky and Bely. McGill, 1982.

Titunik, Irwin R. The Problem of *Skaz* in Russian Literature. Berkeley, 1963.

Todd, William Mills III. The Familiar Letters of *Arzamas* as a Literary Genre. Columbia, 1973.

Tsvetkov, Olga Samilenko. Aspects of the Russian Society Tale of the 1830s. Michigan, 1984.

Ware, R. J. A Russian Literary Journal and Its Public: *Otechestvennye Zapiski* 1868-1884. Oxford, 1980.

Weston, Bruce Louis. The Russian Polemic of 1846-1866 on the Function of Literature. Michigan, 1967.

Zelenak, Jan. The Epigraph in Russian Poetry: Its Chronological Development from Its Origins to the End of the Nineteenth Century. California, Los Angeles, 1977.

GENERAL TOPICS
CRITICAL ARTICLES

Alexeyev, M. William Ralston and Russian Writers of the Later Nineteenth Century. OSP 11:83-93.

Armstrong, J. M. True Origins of the Superfluous Man. RusL 12 (1985):279-96.

Austin, P. M. The Exotic Prisoner in Russian Romanticism. RusL 16 (1984): 217-74.

Bradley, J. The Writer and the City in Late Imperial Russia. SEER 64 (1986):321-38.

Brooks, J. Russian Nationalism and Russian Literature: The Canonization of the Classics. In Nations and Ideology: Essays in Honor of Wayne S. Vucinich, ed. I. Banac, et al. Boulder: East European Quarterly, 1981.

Browning, G. L. Russian Ornamental Prose. SEEJ 23 (1979):346-52.

Busch, R. Russian Freneticism. CASS 14 (1980):269-83.

Cruise, Edwina. The Natural School in Satirical Criticism. Ulbandus Review 2, 2 (1982):39-51.

Debreczeny, Paul. The Beginnings of Mass Literature in Russia: Early Imitations of Pushkin's Narrative Poems. CSS 5(1971): 1-21.

Egeberg, E. "Night" and "Day" in Russian Romantic Poetry. In *Russian Romanticism: Studies in the Poetic Codes,* ed. N. A. Nilsson. Stockholm, 1979, pp. 186-203.

Fanger, Donald. Influence and Tradition in the Russian Novel. In *The Russian Novel from Pushkin to Pasternak,* ed. J. Garrard. New Haven: Yale UP, 1983, pp. 29-50.

——. The Peasant in Literature. In *The Peasant in Nineteenth-Century Russia,* ed. W. S. Vucinich. Stanford: Stanford UP, 1968, pp. 231-62.

Fasting, S. Between Historical and Normative Aesthetics: N. I. Nadezhdin—A Comparative Study. *CASS* 14 (1980): 197-219.

Foote, I. P. Firing a Censor: The Case of N. V. Elagin, 1857. *OSP* 19 (1986):116-31.

Frank, Joseph. The Rise of the *Raznochintsy* in Russian Literature. In *Horizons of a Philosopher: Essays in Honor of David Baumgardt,* ed. Joseph Frank, et al. Leiden: Brill, 1964, pp. 93-102.

Garrard, John. The Rise of the Novel in Russia. In *The Russian Novel from Pushkin to Pasternak,* ed. J. Garrard. New Haven: Yale UP, 1983, pp. 1-28.

Glickman, Rose. An Alternative View of the Peasantry: The *Raznochintsy* Writers of the 1860s. *SlavR* 32 (1973): 693-704.

Grossman, Joan D. Genius and Madness: The Return of the Romantic Concept of the Poet in Russia at the End of the Nineteenth Century. In *American Contributions to the Seventh International Congress of Slavists,* vol. 2, ed. V. Terras. The Hague: Mouton, 1973, pp. 247-60.

Harper, Kenneth E. Criticism of the Natural School of the 1840s. *ASEER* 15 (1956):400-14.

Heldt, Barbara. Women's Studies in Russian Literature: Opportunities for Research and Publication with a Selective Bibliography. In *Women in Print I: Opportunities for Women's Studies Research in Language and Literature,* ed. Joan E. Hartman. NY: MLA, 1982, pp. 149-57.

Hippisley, Anthony R. The Emblem in Russian Literature. *RusL* 16, 3 (1984): 289-304.

Hollingsworth, Barry. *Arzamas:* Portrait of a Literary Society. *SEER* 44 (1967):306-26.

Karlinsky, Simon. The Alogical and Absurdist Aspects of Russian Realist Drama. *Comparative Drama* 3 (1969): 147-55.

Kjetsaa, G. A Quantitative Norm for the Use of Epithets in the Age of Pushkin. In *Russian Romanticism: Studies in the Poetic Codes,* ed. N. A. Nilsson. Stockholm: Almqvist & Wiksell, 1970, pp. 204-26.

Leighton, Lauren G. A Romantic Idealist Notion in Russian Romantic Criticism. *CASS* 7 (1973):285-95.

——. Romanticism, Marxism-Leninism, Literary Movement. *RusL* 14, 2 (1983): 183-220.

Lotman, Ju. M. The Theatre and Theatricality as Components of Early Nineteenth-Century Culture. In *The Semiotics of Russian Culture,* ed. A. Shukman. Ann Arbor: Dept. Slavic Languages, U Michigan, 1984, 141-64.

——. Theme and Plot: The Theme of Cards and the Card Game in Russian Literature of the Nineteenth Century. *PTL* 3 (1978): 455-92.

Luckett, R. Prerevolutionary Army Life in Russian Literature. In *War, Economy and the Military Mind,* ed. G. Best & A. Wheatcroft. London: Croom Helm, 1976, pp. 19-31.

McGrew, R. E. The Russian Intelligentsia: Radishchev to Pasternak. *Antioch Review* 23 (1963):425-37.

McNally, R. T. The Image of Ivan IV "The Terrible" in the Works by Petr Chaadaev, Ivan Kireevskii and Aleksei Khomiakov. In *Russian and Slavic History: Papers of the 1st International Slavic Conference,* ed. D. K. Rowney & G. E. Orchard. Columbus: Slavica, 1977, pp. 91-103.

Maichel, Karol. The Collected Works of Russian Classical Writers. *ASEER* 27 (1958):216-33.

Malnick, Bertha. Russian Serf Theatres. *SEER* 30 (1952):393-411.

———. The Theory and Practice of Russian Drama in the Early 19th Century. *SEER* 34 (1955):10-33.

Mathewson, Rufus W., Jr. The Hero and Society: The Literary Definitions (1855-1865, 1934-1939). In *Continuity and Change in Russian and Soviet Thought*, ed. E. J. Simmons. Cambridge: Harvard UP, 1955, pp. 255-76.

Matich, Olga. A Typology of Fallen Women in Nineteenth-Century Russian Literature. In *American Contributions to the Ninth International Congress of Slavists*, vol. 2, ed. P. Debreczeny. Columbus: Slavica, 1983, pp. 325-44.

Mersereau, John Jr. The Chorus and Spear Carriers of Russian Romantic Fiction. In *Russian and Slavic Literature: Papers from the First International Slavic Conference*, ed. R. Freeborn, et al. Columbus: Slavica, 1976, pp. 38-62.

——— Normative Distinctions of Russian Romanticism and Realism. In *American Contributions to the Seventh International Congress of Slavists*, vol. 2, ed. V. Terras. The Hague: Mouton, 1973, pp. 393-417.

———. Toward a Normative Definition of Russian Realism. *CalSS* 6: 131-43.

———. Yes, Virginia, There Was a Russian Romantic Movement. *RLT* 3 (1972): 128-47.

Monter, Barbara Heldt. *Rassvet* and the Woman Question. *SlavR* 36 (1977):76-85.

Moser, Charles A. Poets and Poetry in an Antipoetic Age. *SlavR* 28 (1969):48-62.

Muchnic, Helen. Russian Poetry and Methods of Translation. *RusR* 29:403-10.

Nepomnyashchy, Catharine Theimer. Katkov and the Emergence of the *Russian Messenger*. *Ulbandus Review* 1 (1977):59-89.

Partridge, Monica. Romanticism and the Concept of Communication in a Slavonic and a Non-Slavonic Literature. *RMS* (1973):62-82.

Pearson, I. Raphael as Seen by Russian Writers from Zhukovsky to Turgenev. *SEER* 59 (1981):346-69.

Picchio, Riccardo. On Russian Romantic Poetry of Pushkin's Era. *Slavic and East European Studies* 15 (1970): 16-30.

Poggioli, Renato. Realism in Russia. *CL* 3 (1950):253-67.

Pyziur, Eugene. Mikhail N. Katkov: Advocate of English Liberalism in Russia, 1856-1863. *SEER* 45:439-56.

Reeve, Helen S. Utopian Socialism in Russian Literature: 1840's-1860's. *ASEER* 18 (1959): 374-93.

Richards, D. Pistols for Two: Duelling in Nineteenth-Century Russian Literature. *JRS* 49 (1985):37-41.

Schaarschmidt, Gunter. The Lubok Novels: Russia's Immortal Best Sellers. *CRCL* 9, 3 (1982):424-36.

Seeley, Frank Friedeberg. The Heyday of the "Superfluous Man" in Russia. *SEER* 31 (1953):92-112.

Segel, H. B. Censorship and Literature: Russia, Poland, and the Ukraine. *SEEJ* 16 (1958):222-30.

Sendich, Munir. Problems of Literary Translation. *RLJ* 90 (1971):21-40.

Setchkarev, V. From the Golden to the Silver Age (1820-1917). In *An Introduction to Russian Language and Literature*, ed. R. Auty & D. Obolensky. Cambridge: Cambridge UP, 1977, pp. 133-84.

Shepard, E. C. The Society Tale and the Innovative Argument in Russian Prose Fiction of the 1830s. *RusL* 10 (1981): 111-61.

Siegel, George. The Fallen Woman in Nineteenth-Century Russian Literature. *HSS* 5:81-107.

Sova, Miloš. Sir John Bowring (1792-1872) and the Slavs. *SEER* 21 (1944): 128-44.

Stilman, Leon. Freedom and Repression in Prevrevolutionary Russian Literature. In *Continuity and Change in Russian and Soviet Thought*, ed. E. J. Simmons. Cambridge: Harvard UP, 1955, pp. 417-32.

Strakhovsky, Leonid I. Problems in Translating Russian Poetry into English. *SEER* 35 (1956):258-67.

Todd, William Mills III. Institutions of Literature in Early Nineteenth-Century Russia: Boundaries and Transgressions. In *Literature and History: Theoretical Problems and Russian Case Studies,* ed. G. S. Morson. Palo Alto: Stanford UP, 1986, pp. 57-89.

____. A Russian Ideology. *Stanford Literature Review* 1, 1 (1984):85-118.

Trensky, Paul I. The Year 1812 in Russian Poetry. *SEEJ* 10 (1967):283-302

Wasiolek, Edward. Design in the Russian Novel. In *The Russian Novel from Pushkin to Pasternak,* ed. J. Garrard. New Haven: Yale UP, 1983, pp. 51-66.

____. Nineteenth-Century Russian Criticism and Soviet Literary Policy. *Modern Age* 14 (1970):190-98.

Weeks, A. & R. Knecht. The Theme of the Chinovnik and the Antinomies of Order and Law in Nineteenth-Century Russian Literature. *RusL* 4 (1982):309-32.

Wellek, René. Social and Aesthetic Values in Russian Nineteenth-Century Literary Criticism (Belinskii, Chernyshevskii, Dobroliubov, Pisarev). In *Continuity and Change in Russian and Soviet Thought,* ed. E. J. Simmons. Cambridge: Harvard UP, 1955, pp. 381-97.

Ziolkowski, Margaret. Hagiography and History: The Saintly Prince in the Poetry of the Decembrists. *SEEJ* 30, 1 (1986):29-44.

COMPARATIVE STUDIES

Books and Dissertations

Barsch, Karl-Heinrich. Origin and Development of the Nineteenth-Century Short Story in Germany, France, Russia, and the USA. Ph.D. diss., Colorado, 1977.

Chyzhevsky, Dmitri. *On Romanticism in Slavic Literature.* The Hague: Mouton, 1957. (Musagetes, No. 1.)

Craven, Kenneth. "Laurence Sterne and Russia: Four Case Studies." Ph.D. diss., Columbia, 1967.

Cross, A. G. *The Russian Theme in English Literature. From the Sixteenth Century to 1980. An Introductory Survey and a Bibliography.* Oxford: Meeuws, 1985.

Davie, Donald Alfred. The English Idea of Russian Fiction Since 1828. Ph.D. diss., Cambridge, 1951.

____, ed. *Russian Literature and Modern English Fiction. A Collection of Critical Essays.* Chicago: Chicago UP, 1965.

Delaney, Joan. Edgar Allan Poe's Tales in Russia: Legend and Literary Influence, 1847-1917. Ph.D. diss., Harvard, 1967.

Futrell, M. H. Dickens and Three Russian Novelists: Gogol, Dostoevsky, Tolstoy. Ph.D. diss., London, 1955.

Gibian, George J. Shakespeare in Russia. Ph.D. diss., Harvard, 1951.

Goldman, Hannah S. American Slavery and Russian Serfdom: A Study in Fictional Parallels. Ph.D. diss., Columbia, 1955.

Goscilo, Margaret Bozenna. The Bastard Hero in the Novel. Ph.D. diss., Illinois, 1984. [Turgenev, Dostoevsky among others.]

Green, Melitsa. Some Aspects of Scottish Authors in Russian Literature in the First Half of the Nineteenth Century. Ph.D. diss., Edinburgh, 1955.

Hemmings, F. W. J. *The Russian Novel in France, 1844-1914.* NY: Oxford UP, 1950.

Herman, Lesley Singer. George Sand and the Nineteenth-Century Russian Novel: The Quest for a Heroine. Ph.D. diss., Columbia, 1979.

Ingham, Norman. *E.T.A. Hoffmann in Russia, 1822-1845.* Würzburg: Jal-Verlag, 1974.

Kostka, Edmund. *Glimpses of Germanic-Slavic Relations from Pushkin to Heinrich Mann.* Bucknell UP, 1975.

____. *Schiller in Russian Literature.* Philadelphia: U Pennsylvania P, 1965.

LeBlanc, Ronald D. *The Russianization of Gil Blas: A Study in Literary Appropriation.* Columbus: Slavica, 1986.

____. The Transplantation of Gil Blas: Problems in the Rise of the Russian Novel. Ph.D. diss., Washington, Seattle, 1984.

Lednicki, Waclaw. *Russia, Poland and the West.* NY, 1954.

Matthews, W. The Influence of Byron on Russian Poetry. Ph.D. diss., London, 1926.

Mlikotin, A. M., ed. *Western Philosophical Systems in Russian Literature: A Collection of Critical Studies.* Los Angeles: U Southern California P, 1980.

Orel, Harold. The Russian Novel in Victorian England: 1831-1917. Ph.D. diss., Michigan, 1953.

Passage, Charles E. The Influence of Goethe, Schiller and E.T.A. Hoffmann in Russia, 1800-1840. Ph.D. diss., Harvard, 1942.

——. *The Russian Hoffmannists.* The Hague: Mouton, 1963.

Phelps, Gilbert. *The Russian Novel in English Fiction.* London: Hutchinson, 1956.

Pushchin, Helen A. German and English Influences on the Russian Romantic Literary Ballad. Ph.D. diss., New York, 1976.

Redy, L. D. Russian Realism and the Development of the English Novel, 1880-1914—A Study in Literary Influence. Ph.D. diss., Trinity (Dublin), 1938.

Rosenthal, Bernice G., ed. *Nietzsche in Russia.* Princeton: Princeton UP, 1986.

Rowe, Eleanor. *Hamlet: A Window on Russia.* NY: NYU Press, 1976.

Schulz, Robert K. *The Portrayal of the German in Russian Novels—Gončarov, Turgenev, Dostoevskij, Tolstoj.* München: Sagner, 1969.

Seely, K. G. Dostoevsky and French Criticism from the Beginnings to 1960. Ph.D. diss., Columbia, 1966.

Simpson, M. S. *The Russian Gothic Novel and Its British Antecedents.* Columbus: Slavica, 1986.

Stahl, Sandra Gail. Byron's Influence on the Lives and Works of Representative Russian Poets of the Romantic Period, 1815-1825. Ph.D. diss., Northwestern, 1978.

Turkevich, Ludmilla. Cervantes in Russia. Ph.D. diss., Columbia, 1950.

Ugrinsky, Alexej. Heinrich von Kleist in Russia: 1892-1976/77. Ph.D. diss., New York, 1981.

Urbanic, Allan Joseph. In the Manners of the Times: The Russian Society Tale and British Fashionable Literature, 1820-1840. Ph.D. diss., Brown, 1983.

Von Gronicka, André. *The Russian Image of Goethe: Goethe in Russian Literature of the First Half of the Nineteenth Century.* Philadelphia: U Pennsylvania P, 1968.

——. *The Russian Image of Goethe. 2. Goethe in the Russian Literature of the Second Half of the Nineteenth Century.* Philadelphia: U Pennsylvania P, 1985.

Weiner, Jack. The Spanish Golden Age Theater in Tsarist Russia (1672-1917). Ph.D. diss., Indiana, 1968.

Zytaruk, George J. D. H. Lawrence's Response to Russian Literature. Ph.D. diss., Washington, Seattle, 1965.

Articles

Barratt, Glynn R. Chateaubriand in Russia, 1800-1830. *CLS* 9 (1972): 152-72.

Bida, Constantine. Shakespeare in Polish and Russian Classicism and Romanticism. *ESL* 6 (1962):188-95.

Bristol, Evelyn. From Romanticism to Symbolism in France and Russia. *American Contributions to the Ninth International Congress of Slavists,* ed. P. Debreczeny. Columbus: Slavica, 1983, vol. 2, pp. 69-80.

Busch, R. L. Victor Hugo's Narrative Prose Debut in Russia. In *Russian and Slavic Literature: Papers from the First International Slavic Conference,* ed. R. Freeborn, et al. Columbus: Slavica, 1976, pp. 17-37.

Chamberlain, John L., Jr. Notes on Russian Influences on the Nineteenth-Century French Novel. *MLJ* 33 (1949): 374-83.

Chapman, R. & E. Gottlieb. A Russian View of George Eliot. *Nineteenth Century Fiction* 33 (1978):348-65.

Cross, A. G. Russian Perceptions of England and Russian National Awareness at the End of the Eighteenth and the Beginning of the Nineteenth Centuries. *SEER* 61 (1983):89-106.

Jakobson, Roman. The Kernel of Comparative Slavic Literature. *HSS* 1 (1953):1-71.

Miller, A. Rousseau and Russia: Some Uses of the *Contrat social. Essays in Literature* 5, 1 (1978):119-28.

Neuhäuser, Rudolf. Notes on Early Russian-American Cultural Relations. *CSS* 1:461-73.

Nilsson, N. A. The Challenge from the Periphery. *Scando-Slavica* 27 (1981): 93-103.

Passage, Charles. The Influence of Schiller in Russia, 1800-1840. *ASEER* 5 (1946): 111-37.

Rubenstein, Roberta. Virginia Woolf and the Russian Point of View. *CLS* 9 (1972):196-206.

Wegner, Michael. The Russian Novel: Essence and Influence of a Literary Tradition. In *Adjoining Cultures as Reflected in Literature and Language,* ed. J. X. Evans. Tempe: Arizona State U, 1983, pp. 99-106.

West, J. Walter Scott and the Style of Russian Historical Novels of the 1830s and 1840s. In *American Contributions to the Eighth International Congress of Slavists,* vol. 1, ed. H. Birnbaum. Columbus: Slavica, 1978, pp. 757-73.

Zytaruk, George J. D. H. Lawrence's Reading of Russian Literature. *D. H. Lawrence Review* 2 (1969):120-37.

LANGUAGE AND VERSIFICATION

Bailey, James. The Evolution and Structure of the Russian Iambic Pentameter from 1880 to 1922. *IJSLP* 16 (1973): 119-46.

Burgi, Richard T. *A History of the Russian Hexameter.* Hamden, CT: Shoe String Press, 1954.

Eagle, Herbert Jay. The Structure of Russian and Czech Free Verse: A Comparative Analysis. Ph.D. dissertation, Michigan, 1973.

Erlich, Victor. *Russian Formalism: History—Doctrine.* 2d rev. ed. The Hague: Mouton, 1965.

Lotman, Yury. *Analysis of the Poetic Text.* Tr. D. Barton Johnson. Ann Arbor: Ardis, 1976.

Mandelker, Amy. Russian Formalism and the Objective Analysis of Sound in Poetry. *SEEJ* 27 (1983):327-38.

Matejka, Ladislav and Krystyna Pomorska, eds. *Readings in Russian Poetics: Formalist and Structuralist Views.* Cambridge: MIT P, 1971.

Scherr, B. P. *Russian Poetry: Meter, Rhythm and Rhyme.* Berkeley: California UP, 1986.

Stone, Gerald & Dean Worth, eds. *The Formation of the Slavonic Literary Languages.* Columbus: Slavica, 1985.

Suino, Mark Edward. Rhythm and Meter in Russian Iambic Tetrameters. Ph.D. diss., Michigan, 1966.

Taranovski, Kiril. The Sound Texture of Russian Verse. *IJSLP* 9 (1965):114-24.

Unbegaun, B. O. *Russian Versification.* Oxford: Oxford UP, 1956.

Vinogradov, V. V. *The History of the Russian Literary Language from the Seventeenth Century to the Nineteenth.* Tr. & intro. L. L. Thomas. Madison: U Wisconsin P, 1969.

ANTHOLOGIES OF TRANSLATIONS INTO ENGLISH

Bannikov, N., comp. *Three Centuries of Russian Verse.* Bilingual. Moscow: Progress, 1980.

Cooper, Joshua, ed. & tr. *Four Russian Plays.* NY: Penguin, 1972.

Coulson, Jessie, ed. *Russian Short Stories, XIXth Century.* Oxford: Clarendon Press, 1953.

Daniels, Guy, ed. & tr. *Russian Comic Fiction.* NY: Schocken, 1986.

Edie, James M., James P. Scanlan & Mary-Barbara Zeldin, eds. *Russian Philosophy.* 3 vols. Chicago: Quadrangle, 1965.

Fetzer, Leland, ed. & tr. *Pre-Revolutionary Russian Science Fiction: An Anthology (Seven Utopias and a Dream).* Ann Arbor: Ardis, 1982.

Gangulee, N. *The Russian Horizon. An Anthology.* London: Allen & Unwin, 1943.

Goscilo, Helena, ed. *Russian and Polish Women's Fiction.* Knoxville: U Tennessee P, 1985.

Leighton, Lauren Gray, ed. *Russian Romantic Criticism. An Anthology.* NY: Greenwood P, 1987.

Magarshack, David, tr. *The Storm and Other Russian Plays.* NY: Hill & Wang, 1960.

Noyes, George Rapall, ed. & tr. *Masterpieces of the Russian Drama.* 2 vols. NY, Dover, 1960-61.

Obolensky, Dimitri, ed. *The Heritage of Russian Verse. With Plain Prose Translations of Each Poem.* Bloomington: Indiana UP, 1976. [Previously published as *The Penguin Book of Russian Verse.*]

Proffer, Carl R., ed. *From Karamzin to Bunin.* Bloomington: Indiana UP, 1969.

——. *Russian Romantic Prose.* Ann Arbor: Translation Press, 1979.

Raffel, B., ed. *Russian Poetry Under the Tsars.* NY: SUNY P, 1971.

Reeve, F. D. *An Anthology of Russian Plays.* 2 vols. NY: Vintage, 1963.

Richards, David. *The Penguin Book of Russian Short Stories.* NY: Penguin, 1981.

Riha, Thomas, ed. *Readings in Russian Civilization.* 3 vols. in 1. Chicago: U Chicago P, 1964.

Rydel, Christine, ed. *The Ardis Anthology of Russian Romanticism.* Ann Arbor: Ardis, 1984.

Yarmolinsky, Avrahm. *An Anthology of Russian Verse: 1812-1960.* Garden City, NY: Doubleday, 1962.

——, ed. *Two Centuries of Russian Verse: An Anthology from Lomonosov to Voznesensky.* NY: Random House, 1966.

Zheleznova, Irina, ed. *Russian 19th Century Verse.* Moscow: Raduga, 1983.

SERGEI AKSAKOV

Translations

Chronicles of a Russian Family. Tr. M. C. Beverly, intro. D. S. Mirsky. London: G. Routledge & Sons, 1924. [The Family Chronicle, Years of Childhood, Recollections, 3 sketches. This is the fullest volume of A in translation, but parts of Years are cut and the volume is arranged to be read as one chronological whole.]

The Family Chronicle. Tr. M. C. Beverly, intro. Ralph E. Matlaw. NY: E. P. Dutton, 1961.

A Russian Gentleman (A Family Chronicle). Tr. J. D. Duff, foreword by Carl Van Doren. NY: Readers Club, 1943. [1st ed.—NY: Longmans, 1917.]

A Russian Schoolboy [Memoirs, part 3]. Tr. J. Duff. Oxford: Oxford UP, 1924; rpt. intro. J. Bayley. Oxford: Oxford UP, 1983.

Years of Childhood. Tr. Alex Brown. NY: Vintage, 1961.

Years of Childhood. Tr. J. D. Duff, intro. David Cecil. Oxford: Oxford UP, 1983.

The Little Scarlet Flower. Tr. James Riordan. Moscow: Progress, 1976.

Ransome, Arthur M. *Rod and Line.* London: Cape, 1929, pp. 244-86. [A on Fishing, Notes on Angling (Excerpts).]

Criticism

Durkin, Andrew. *Sergei A and the Russian Pastoral.* New Brunswick: Rutgers UP, 1983.

Carr, Nonna Hordowsky. S. T. A in Russian Literary Criticism Before 1917. Ph.D. diss., Colorado, 1976.

Cohen, Elliot Franklin. The Genre of the Autobiographical Account of Childhood—Three Test Cases: The Trilogies of Tolstoy, A and Gorky. Ph.D. diss., Yale, 1973.

Durkin, Andrew Robert. The Art of S. T. A. Ph.D. diss., Columbia, 1975.

Evans, Pamela. The Portrayal of Childhood. Ph.D. diss., Toronto, 1980.

Gauntt, Marsha Gayle. S. T. A's *The Family Chronicle:* An Exceptional Novel. Ph.D. diss., California, Los Angeles, 1975.

Rinkus, Jerome Joseph. The World View of Sergej A. Ph.D. diss., Brown, 1971.

Wreath, Patrick Joseph. A Critical Study of S. T. A. Ph.D. diss., Cornell, 1969.

Barksdale, E.C. A: Myth and Memoir. In *The Dacha and the Duchess,* NY: Philosophical Library, 1974, pp. 95-104.

Coe, R. N. *Reminiscences of Childhood: An Approach to a Comparative Mythology.* Leeds: Leeds Phil. & Literary Society, 1984.

Durkin, Andrew R. Pastoral in A: The Transformation of Poetry. *Ulbandus Review* 2 (1979):62-75.

Feuer, Kathryn B. *Family Chronicle:* The Indoor Art of Sergei A. *Ulbandus Review* 2 (1979):86-102.

Glowacki-Prus, X. The Biographical Sketches of S. T. A. *NZSJ* 2 (1977): 1-12.

＿ Sergey A as a Biographer of Childhood. *NZSJ* 2 (1974):19-38.

Prichett, V. S. A Russian Cinderella. In his *The Living Novel.* London: Chatto & Windus, 1954, pp. 248-54.

YEVGENY BARATYNSKY

Translations

Selected Letters. Tr. G. R. Barratt. The Hague: Mouton, 1973.

Coxwell, C., ed. *Russian Poems.* London: Daniel, 1929.
[Death; In Days of Insatiate Transports; Phillida; The Death of Heine; Rome; Has Time a Use?; Grief and Pleasure.]

Fuller, Jamie, tr. Poems. *RLT* 3 (1972):46-50.

Myers, A., tr. [3 poems.] *Modern Poetry in Translation* 40 (1980):26-29.
[Disillusion; The Muse; Desolation.]

Rydel, Christine, ed. *The Ardis Anthology of Russian Romanticism.* Ann Arbor: Ardis, 1984.
[Eda; Hopelessness; My gift is humble; Death; What reason has the captive spirit; The Last Poet; A thought when it appears anew; Autumn; Signs; The mass of men; Rhyme; Poor Craftsmen; Complaint; About Delusions and Truth.]

Wiener, L. *Anthology of Russian Literature.* NY: Putnam, 1902-3, vol. 2.
[Finland; Spring; Truth.]

Yarmolinsky, Avrahm & C. Cowdrey, eds. *A Treasury of Russian Verse.* NY: Macmillan, 1949.
[Phyllida; Blessed Are They; Of What Use Are Your Days?; Prayer; The Road of Life.]

Criticism

Dees, Benjamin. *Evgeny B.* NY: Twayne, 1972.

Burton, Dora. B: The Evolution of His Style and Poetic Themes. Ph.D. diss., Washington, Seattle, 1975.

Dees, Joseph Benjamin. Content and Expression in the Poetry of B. Ph.D. diss., Princeton, 1967.

Harvie, Jones A. The Passionate Skeptic: The Poetry of E. A. B. Ph.D. diss., Otago, 1971.

Kovalenko, Tatyana I. The Rhythmic and Syntactic Structure of the Sumerki Cycle of E. A. B. Ph.D. diss., New York, 1973.

Liapunov, Vadim. Poet in the Middest: Studies in the Poetics of E. B. Ph.D. diss., Yale, 1969.

Pratt, Sarah. The Metaphysical Poetry of F. I. Tiutchev and E. A. B.: Alternatives in Russian Romanticism. Ph.D. diss., Columbia, 1978.

Rolich, A. M. The Stanzaic Forms of K. N. Batjushkov and E. A. B. Ph.D. diss., Wisconsin, 1981.

Andreevsky, Sergei. On Evgeny B. In *The Complection of Russian Literature,* ed. A. Field. NY: Atheneum, 1971, pp. 13-19.

Barratt, G. B. In Soviet Publications: A Review Article. *SEEJ* 14 (1970):352-58. 84.

＿ I. S. Turgenev's Article on B. *Slavic and East European Studies* 13 (1968): 62-66.

＿ B in Soviet Publications: A Review Article. *SEEJ* 14 (1970):352-58.

＿ Borghese, B and the Ideal Italy. *Forum Italicum* 3 (1968):270-76.

＿. Eighteenth-Century Neoclassical Influences on E. A. B. and on Pushkin. *CLS* 6 (1969): 435-61.

___ A Note on B's Elegiac Verse. *SEER* 55 (1977):172-84.

Brown, William Edward. Poets of the Pushkin Pleiad: E. A. B. In his *A History of Russian Literature of the Romantic Period,* Ann Arbor: Ardis, 1986, vol. 3, pp. 311-38.

Grau, R. M. "Persten'":B's Fantastic Tale. *CSP* 26 (1984):296-306.

Harvie, J. A. The Demonic Element in Gogol' and B. *NZSJ* 6 (1970):77-85.

___. The Eclipse of the Golden Age (Wordsworth and B). *FMLS* 12 (1976): 176-88.

___ Poet of Nirvana. *NZSJ* 1 (1967):10 pp.

___ Russia's Doomsday Poet. *FMLS* 9 (1973):170-81.

___ Time and Eternity in B's "Zapustenie." *Scando-Slavica* 20 (1974):67-75.

Mersereau, John J., Jr. *Baron Delvig's "Northern Flowers."* Carbondale: So. Illinois UP, 1967, pp. 23-42, 65-67, 78-81, 249-52.

Nilsson, N. A. B's Elegiac Code. In *Russian Romanticism,* ed. N. Nilsson. Stockholm: Amlqvist & Wiksell, 1979, pp. 144-66.

Pratt, Sarah. Points of Contact: Two Russian Poets and Their Links to Schelling. *Germano-Slavica* 4 (1982):3-16.

Struve, Gleb. Evgeny B, 1800-44. *SEER* 23 (1945):107-15.

Woodward, J. B. The Enigmatic Development of B's Art. *OSP* 3 (1970):32-44.

KONSTANTIN BATYUSHKOV

Translations

Bowring, J. *Specimens of the Russian Poets.* London, 1821-23.
[Love in a Boat; The Prisoner; To the Rhine.]

Coxwell, C. *Russian Poems.* London: Daniel, 1929.
[To Bacchante; A Jovial Hour.]

Rydel, C., ed. *The Ardis Anthology of Russian Romanticism.* Ann Arbor: Ardis, 1984.
[My Penates; The Shade of My Friend.]

Wiener, L. *Anthology of Russian Literature.* NY: Putnam, 1902-3, vol. 2.
[The Dying Tasso; The Friend's Shadow.]

Criticism

Serman, Ilya. *Konstantin B.* NY: Twayne, 1974.

Brendel, Erica M. The Poetry of K. B. Ph.D. diss., Berkeley, 1969.

Johnson, Doris Verna. The Comparison in the Poetry of B and Zhukovsky. Ph.D. diss., Michigan, 1973.

Rolich, A. The Stanzaic Forms of K. N. B. and E. A. Baratynsky. Ph.D. diss., Wisconsin, 1981.

Brown, William Edward. The Older Innovators: Konstantin B. In his *A History of Russian Literature of the Romantic Period.* Ann Arbor: Ardis, 1986, vol. 1, pp. 227-55.

Johnson, Doris. The Simile in B and Zhukovsky. *RLT* 7 (1973):407-22.

Mersereau, John J., Jr. *Baron Delvig's "Northern Flowers."* Carbondale: So. Illinois UP, 1967, pp. 42-45, 156-58, 164-65.

Todd, William Mills III. *The Familiar Letter as a Literary Genre in the Age of Pushkin.* Princeton: Princeton UP, 1976, pp. 62-63, 82-83, 86-87, 97-98, 150-55, 160-63.

VISSARION BELINSKY

Translations

Selected Philosophical Works. Moscow: Foreign Languages Publishing House, 1948.
[Literary Reveries; The Idea of Art; A View of the Principle Aspects of Russian Literature in 1943; Eugene Onegin; Thoughts and Notes on Russian Literature; A Survey of Russian Literature in 1846; A Survey of Russian Literature in 1847; Letters to Botkin; Letter to Gogol.]

Matlaw, Ralph E., ed. *B, Chernyshevsky, Dobroliubov: Selected Criticism.* Bloomington: Indiana UP, 1976. [Thoughts and Notes on Russian Literature; A Survey of Russian Literature in 1847: Part 2; Letter to N. V. Gogol.]

Senelick, Laurence, ed. *Russian Dramatic Theory from Pushkin to the Symbolists.* Austin: U Texas P, 1981. [Dramatic Poesy.]

Criticism

Bowman, Herbert E. *Vissarion B (1811-1848). A Study in the Origins of Social Criticism in Russia.* Cambridge: Harvard Studies in Comparative Literature, 1954.

Proctor, T. *Dostoevskij and the B School of Criticism.* The Hague: Mouton, 1969.

Terras, Victor. *B and Russian Literary Criticism: The Heritage of Organic Aesthetics.* Madison, U Wisconsin P, 1974.

Dunn, Patrick B. B: The Road to Reality, 1811-1841. Ph.D. diss., Duke, 1969.

Hill, William Holoway II. Vissarion Grigorevich B, 1811-1840. Ph.D. diss., Berkeley, 1972.

Schillinger, Jack Arthur. The Evolution of Artistic Criteria in the Criticism of Vissarion B. Ph.D. diss., Wisconsin, 1973.

Yatzeck, Richard L. Schiller and B's Aesthetics. Ph.D. diss., Wisconsin, 1966.

Andrew, Joe. Vissarion B. In his *Writers and Society During the Rise of Russian Realism,* Atlantic Highlands: Humanities Press, 1980, pp. 114-52.

Berlin, Isaiah. Vissarion B. In his *Russian Thinkers,* NY: Penguin, 1978, pp. 150-85.

Brown, Edward J. Stankevič and B. In *American Contributions to the 4th International Congress of Slavists.* 's-Gravenhage: Mouton, 1958, pp. 19-37.

Chernyshevsky, Nikolai. B. In his *Selected Philosophical Essays.* Moscow: Foreign Languages Publishing House, 1953, pp. 454-503.

Christoff, Peter K. B and Gogol. In his *K. S. Aksakov: A Study in Ideas,* Princeton: Princeton UP, 1982, pp. 64-87.

Cloutier, H. Handley. B—Advocate of Liberty. *RusR* 8 (1949):20-33.

Cornwell, Neil. B and V. F. Odoevsky. *SEER* 62 (1984):6-24.

Forsyth, J. Pisarev, B. and *Yevgeniy Onegin. SEER* 48 (1970):163-80.

Genereux, George. Botkin's Collaboration with B on the Pushkin Articles. *SEEJ* 21 (1977):470-82.

——. The Crisis in Russian Literary Criticism: 1859—The Decisive Year. *RLT* 17 (1982):116-40.

Gifford, Henry. B: One Aspect. *SEER* 27 (1948):250-58.

Grosshans, Henry. Vissarion B and the Problems of the Russian Literary Critic in the Eighteen Forties. *Research Studies* 23 (1955):50-61.

Hare, Richard. B. In his *Pioneers of Russian Social Thought.* London: Oxford UP, 1951.

Kostka, Edmund. V. G. B's War on German Idealism. *Rivista di Letterature Moderne e Comparate* 16 (1963): 5-19.

Kresky, Elizabeth. Soviet Scholarship on B. *ASEER* 7 (1948):269-75.

Malnick, Bertha. V. G. B. *SEER* 27 (1949):363-80.

Mann, Iu. Gogol in the Context of Aesthetic Controversies: V. G. B's Polemic with Konstantin Aksakov. *Soviet Review* 26, 2 (1985):39-61.

Ponomareff, C. V. Configurations of Poetic Vision. B as an Idealist-Critic. *SEEJ* 14 (1970): 145-59.

——. V. G. B's Romantic Imagination. *CASS* 7 (1973):314-73.

Scherer, J. L. B and the Hegelian Dialectic. *SEEJ* 21 (1971):30-45.

Struve, Gleb. A B Centenary Bibliography: An Annotated List of 1948 Publications. *SEER* 27 (1949):546-55.

Swoboda, Victor. Shevchenko and B. *SEER* 94 (1962):168-83.

Swoboda, V. and R. Martin. Shevchenko and B Revisited. *SEER* 56 (1978):546-62.

Turgenev, Ivan. Reminiscences of B. In his *Literary Reminiscences and Autobiographical Fragments.* NY: Farrar, Straus & Cudahy, 1958, pp. 117-59.

Weber, Harry B. B and the Aesthetics of Utopian Socialism. *SEEJ* 15 (1971): 293-304.

Wellek, René. Social and Aesthetic Values in Russian Nineteenth-Century Literary Criticism (B, Chernyshevskii, Dobroliubov, Pisarev). In *Continuity and Change in Russian and Soviet Thought,* ed. E. J. Simmons. Cambridge: Harvard UP, 1959, pp. 381-97.

ALEXANDER BESTUZHEV-MARLINSKY

Translations

Ammalat Bek. In *Blackwood's Edinburgh Magazine* 53 (1843):281-301; 464-583; 568-89; 746-61.

The Tartar Chief; or, A Russian Colonel's Head for a Dowry. Tr. C. Hebbe. NY: W. H. Colyer, 1846.

Proffer, Carl R., ed. *Russian Romantic Prose.* Ann Arbor: Translation Press, 1979.
[An Evening on Bivouac; The Test.]

Rydel, Christine, ed. *The Ardis Anthology of Russian Romanticism.* Ann Arbor: Ardis, 1984.
[An Evening on Bivouac; *Ammalat Bek* (excerpts).]

Criticism

Leighton, Lauren. *Alexander B-M.* Boston: Twayne, 1975.

Bagby, Lewis. The Prose Fiction of Aleksandr Aleksandrovič B-M. Ph. D. diss., Michigan, 1972.

Leighton, Lauren Gray. Aleksandr B-M: The Romantic Prose Tale in Russia. Ph.D. diss., Wisconsin, 1968.

Bagby, Lewis. Aleksandr B-M's "Roman i Ol'ga": Generation and Degeneration. *SEEJ* 25 (1981):1-15.

———. B-M's "Mulla Nur": A Muddled Myth to Rekindle a Romance. *RusL* 11 (1982):117-28.

Brown, William Edward. Alexander B (M). In his *A History of Russian Literature of the Romantic Period.* Ann Arbor: Ardis, 1986, vol. 2, 119-32, 204-19.

Goodliffe, J. D. B-M as a Literary Critic. *NZSJ* 3 (1969):32-49.

Leighton, Lauren. B-M. *RLT* 3 (1972): 249-68.

———.B-M as a Lyric Poet. *SEER* 47 (1969):308-22.

———. B-M's "Ispytanie" [The Test]: A Romantic Rejoinder to "Evgenij Onegin." *SEER* 13 (1969):200-16.

———. B-M's "The Frigate *Hope*": A Decembrist Puzzle. *CSP* 22 (1980):173-86.

Mersereau, John J., Jr. *Russian Romantic Fiction.* Ann Arbor: Ardis, 1983, pp. 45-47, 53-63, 67-68, 120-26.

VASILY BOTKIN

Translation

A. A. Fet. Tr. G. Genereux. *RLT* 17 (1982):23-60.

Criticism

Motolanez, George R. B as Literary Critic. Ph.D. diss., New York, 1970.

Genereux, George. B's Collaboration with Belinsky on the Pushkin Articles. *SEEJ* 21 (1977):470-82.

———. The Crisis in Russian Literary Criticism: 1856—The Decisive Year. *RLT* 17 (1982):116-40.

Kostka, E. A Trailblazer of Russian Westernism. *CL* 18 (1966):211-24.

Offord, D. C. Vasily Petrovich B (1810-1869). *OSP* 16 (1983):141-63.

FADDEI BULGARIN

Translations

Ivan Vejeeghen, or Life in Russia. Philadelphia: Carey & Lea, 1832.
—— Tr. G. Ross. London: Whittaker, Treacher, 1831, 2 vols.
[Excerpts reprinted in *The Ardis Anthology of Russian Romanticism,* ed. C. Rydel. Ann Arbor: Ardis, 1984, pp. 242-51.]
Fetzer, Leland, ed. *Pre-Revolutionary Russian Science Fiction.* Ann Arbor: Ardis, 1982.
[Plausible Fantasies or a Journey in the 29th Century.]

Criticism

Alkire, Gilman H. The Historical Novels of Faddej B. Ph.D. diss., California, Berkeley, 1966.
Koepnick, Thomas Louis. The Journalistic Careers of F. V. B and N. I. Grech: Publicism and Politics in Tsarist Russia, 1812-1859. Ph.D. diss., Ohio, 1976.
Mocha, Frank. Tadeusz B (Faddej V. B), 1789-1859: A Study in Literary Maneuver. Ph.D. diss., Columbia, 1970.
Neuenschwander, Dennis Bramwell. Themes in Russian Utopian Fiction: A Study in the Utopian Works of M. M. Shcherbatov, A. Ulybyshev, F. V. B and V. F. Odoevsky. Ph.D. diss., Syracuse, 1974.
Vaslef, Nicholas P. Faddej V. B: Reevaluation of His Contribution to Nineteenth-Century Russian Prose. Ph.D. diss., Harvard, 1966.

Alkire, G. H. Gogol and B's *Ivan Vyzhigin. SlavR* 28 (1969):289-96.
Blaszczyk, L. Jezowski and B: A Case of Plagiarism or Collaboration? *Polish Review* 25 (1980):15-43.
Lubensky, Sophia. The First Russian Novel in English: B's *Ivan Vyzhigin. RLJ* 37 (1983):126-27.
Mersereau, John J., Jr. B. In his *Russian Romantic Prose,* Ann Arbor: Ardis, 1983, pp. 33, 86-88.

——.In his *Baron Delvig's "Northern Flowers."* Carbondale: So. Illinois UP, 1967, pp. 17-22, 52-56, 160-63.
Mocha, Frank. Tadeusz B, 1789-1859: A Study in Literary Maneuver. *Antemurale* 17 (1974).
Monas, S. Shishkov, B and the Russian Censorship. *HSS* 4 (1957):127-48.
Vaslef, Nicholas P. B and the Development of the Russian Utopian Genre. *SEEJ* 12 (1968):35-43.

PYOTR CHAADAEV

Translations

The Major Works. Tr. & commentary Raymond T. McNally, intro. Richard Pipes. Notre Dame UP, 1969.
Philosophical Letters and Apology of a Madman. Tr. & intro. Mary-Barbara Zeldin. Knoxville: U Tennessee P, 1969.

Criticism

Brun-Zejms, Julia. C and Pushkin. Ph.D. diss., Texas, 1973.
Moskoff, Eugene A. The Russian Philosopher C, His Ideas and His Epoch. Ph.D. diss., Columbia, 1938.
Tempest, R. V. Pyotr C: His Impact on Russian Society and Thought Between 1812 and 1856. Ph.D. diss., Oxford, 1981.

Gavin, William J. C and Emerson—Two Mystic Pragmatists. *RusR* 32 (1973): 119-30.
Koyré, Alexander. Russia's Place in the World: Peter C and the Slavophils. *Slavonic Review* 5 (1927):594-608.
Lavrin, Janko. C and the West. *RusR* 22 (1963):274-88.
McNally, Raymond T. C vs. Xomjakov in the Late 1830's and the 1840's. *Journal of the History of Ideas* 27 (1967):73-91.
—— C's Evaluation of Peter the Great. *SlavR* 23 (1964):31-44.
—— C's Evaluation of Western Christian

Churches. *SEER* 42 (1964):370-87.
———. The Significance of C's *Weltan-schauung. RusR* 23 (1964):352-61.
Tempest, Richard. Madman or Criminal: Government Attitudes in Petr C in 1836. *SlavR* 43, 2 (1984):281-87.
Zeldin, Mary-Barbara. C as Russia's First Philosopher. *SlavR* 37 (1978):473-80.

ANTON CHEKHOV

Bibliographies

Heifetz, A. Bibliography of C's Works Translated into English and Published in America. *Bulletin of Bibliography* (Boston) 13 (1929):172-76.
———. C in English: A Bibliography of Works By and About Him. *Bulletin of the New York Public Library* 53 (1949):27-38.
Hingley, Ronald. Selected Bibliography. In his *The Oxford C,* vol. 4, London-NY: Oxford UP, 1980, pp. 283-87. [Bibliographies of translations and biographical and critical studies.]
Lantz, K. A. *Anton C: A Reference Guide to Literature.* Boston: G. K. Hall, 1985.
Meister, Charles W. English and American Criticism of C. Ph.D. dissertation, Chicago, 1949.
Sendich, Munir. Anton C in English: A Comprehensive Bibliography of Works About and By Him (1889-1984). In *Anton C Rediscovered: A Collection of New Studies with a Comprehensive Bibliography,* ed. Savely Senderovich & Munir Sendich. East Lansing, MI: *Russian Language Journal,* 1987.
Yachnin, Raissa. *C in English: A Selective List of Works By and About Him, 1949-1960.* NY: NY Public Library, 1960.

Translations

The Oxford C. Tr. & ed. Ronald Hingley. 9 vols. Plays and Stories. London-NY: Oxford UP, 1964-80. [The most authoritative collection of C in English translation.]

The Tales of Tchekhov. Tr. Constance Garnett. 13 vols. London: Chatto-Windus; NY: Macmillan, 1916-22.

Anton C: Four Plays. Tr. David Magarshack. NY: Hill & Wang, 1969. [The Seagull; Uncle Vanya; Three Sisters; The Cherry Orchard.]
Anton C's Plays. Tr. & ed. Eugene K. Bristow. NY: W. W. Norton, 1977. [The Sea Gull, Uncle Vanya, The Three Sisters, The Cherry Orchard, Backgrounds, Criticism.]
Anton C's Short Stories. Selected & ed. Ralph E. Matlaw. NY: W. W. Norton, 1979. [Chameleon; Oysters; A Living Chronology; The Huntsman; Misery; The Requiem; Anyuta; Agatha; Grisha; A Gentleman Friend; The Chorus Girl; Dreams; Vanka; At Home; The Siren's Song; Sleepy; The Grasshopper; In Exile; Rothschild's Fiddle; The Student; The Teacher of Literature; Whitebrow; Anna on the Neck; The House with the Mansard; The Pecheneg; A Journey by Cart; The Man in a Case; Gooseberries; About Love; A Doctor's Visit; The Darling; The Lady with the Dog; The Bishop; The Betrothed; selections from C's letters; selected criticism, bibliography.]
The Bishop and Other Stories. Tr. C. Garnett. NY: Ecco Press, 1985.
The Brute and Other Farces, ed. Eric Bentley. In new versions by E. Bentley & T. Hoffmann. NY: Applause Theatre Book, 1985.
The Chorus Girl and Other Stories. Tr. C. Garnett. NY: Ecco Press, 1985.
The Image of C: Forty Stories in the Order in Which They Were Written. Tr. & intro. by Robert Payne. NY: Knopf, 1963. [The Little Apples; St. Peter's Day; Green Scythe; Joy; The Ninny; The Highest Merits; Death of a Government Clerk; At the Post Office; Surgery; In the Cemetery; Where There is a Will, There is a Way; A Report; The Threat; The Huntsman; The Malefactor; A Dead Body; Sergeant Prishibeyev; A Blunder; Heartache; Anyuta;

The Proposal; Who is to Blame?; Typhus; Sleepyhead; The Princess; Gusev; The Peasant Women; After the Theater; A Fragment; In Exile; Big Volodya and Little Volodya; The Student; Anna Round the Neck; The House with the Mezzanine; In the Horsecart; On Love; The Lady with the Pet Dog; The Bishop; The Bride.]

The Kiss and Other Stories. Tr. & intro. Ronald Wilks. NY: Penguin, 1982.
[The Kiss; Peasants; The Bishop; The Russian Master; Man in a Case; Gooseberries; Concerning Love; A Case History; In the Gully; Anna Round the Neck.]

Peasants and Other Stories. Selected and preface by Edmund Wilson. NY: Macmillan, 1917.
[A Woman's Kingdom; Three Years; The Murder; My Life; Peasants; The New Villa; In the Ravine; The Bishop; Betrothed.]

The Portable C. Ed. & intro. Avrahm Yarmolinsky. NY: Viking, 1947.
[Vanka; The Privy Councilor; A Calamity; At the Mill; The Chameleon; The Siren; Sergeant Prishibeyev; The Culprit; Daydreams; Heartache; An Encounter; The Letter; The Kiss; The Name-Day Party; An Attack of Nerves; Gusev; Anna on the Neck; In the Cart; At Home; Peasants; The Man in a Shell; Gooseberries; About Love; The Darling; The Lady with the Pet Dog; At Christmas Time; On Official Business; In the Ravine; The Boor; The Cherry Orchard; selected letters.]

The Russian Master and Other Stories. Oxford: Oxford UP, 1984.

The Shooting Party. Tr. A. E. Chamot (revised by Julian Symons). Intro. J. Symons. Chicago: U Chicago P, 1987.

The Unknown Chekhov: Stories and Other Writings Hitherto Untranslated. Tr. & intro. Avrahm Yarmolinsky. NY: Noonday Press, 1954, 1959.
[Because of Little Apples; Two in One; Perpetuum Mobile; The Skit; Worse and Worse; Vint; Two of a Kind; Drowning; The Village Elder; Saintly Simplicity; Hydrophobia; Other People's Misfortune; Women Make Trouble; The Lodger; Boa Constrictor and

Rabbit; An Unpleasantness; A Fragment; Peasants; A Visit to Friends; Decompensation; On the Harmful Effects of Tobacco; Moscow Hypocrites; Good News; Across Siberia; Yegor's Story (from The Island of Sakhalin).]

The Witch and Other Stories. Tr. C. Garnett. NY: Ecco Press, 1985.

Letters of Anton C. Tr. Michael Henry Heim in collaboration with Simon Karlinsky. Selection, commentary & intro. by Simon Karlinsky. NY: Harper & Row, 1973.

Letters of Anton C. Ed. Avrahm Yarmolinsky. NY: Viking Press, 1973.

Letters on the Short Story, the Drama & Other Literary Topics. Ed. Louis S. Friedland. NY: Minton, Balch & Co., 1924.

Personal Papers of Anton C. Intro. by Matthew Josephson. NY: Lear, 1948.

Senelick, Laurence, ed. *Russian Dramatic Theory from Pushkin to the Symbolists.* Austin: U Texas P, 1981, pp. 83-88. [More about Sarah Bernhardt.]

See also *Lewanski,* pp. 210-26 and
Sendich, Munir. Anton C in English: A Comprehensive Bibliography of Works About and By Him (1889-1984). In *Anton C Rediscovered: A Collection of New Studies with a Comprehensive Bibliography,* ed. Savely Senderovich & Munir Sendich. East Lansing, MI: Russian Language Journal, 1987, pp. 299-340.

Criticism-Books

Anton C. Anniversary issue, 120th Year since the Birth of Anton C. *Soviet Literature* 1 (1980).

Avilova, Lydia A. *C in My Life, A Love Story.* Tr. & intro. David Magarshack. London: J. Lehmann, 1950.

Barricelli, Jean-Pierre, ed. *Chekhov's Great Plays: A Critical Anthology.* NY: New York UP, 1981.

Bill, Valentine Tschebotarioff. *C. The Silent Voice of Freedom.* NY: Philosophical Library, 1986.

Bitsilli, Peter M. *C's Art: A Stylistic Analysis.* Tr. Toby Clyman & Edwina

Cruise. Ann Arbor: Ardis, 1983.

Brahms, Caryl. *Reflections in a Lake: A Study of C's Four Greatest Plays.* London: Weidenfeld & Nicolson, 1976.

Bruford, W. H. *C.* New Haven: Yale UP, 1957.

___ *C and His Russia.* Hamden, CT: Archon, 1971.

Bunin, Ivan. *About C.* An Unfinished manuscript. Intro. Mark Aldanov. NY: Walden Press, 1955.

Carey, Constance. *The C Proposal.* NY: Putnam, 1975.

Chekhova, Mariya Pavlovna. *The Chekhov Museum in Yalta.* Tr. Molly Perelman. Moscow: Foreign Languages Publishing House, 1958.

Chudakov, A. P. *C's Poetics.* Tr. Edwina Jannie Cruise & Donald Dragt. Ann Arbor: Ardis, 1983.

Debreczeny, Paul & Thomas Eekman, eds. *C's Art of Writing: A Collection of Critical Essays.* Columbus: Slavica, 1977.

Eekman, Thomas, ed. *Anton C, 1860-1960: Some Essays.* Leiden: E. J. Brill, 1960.

Egri, P. *C and O'Neill. The Uses of the Short Story in C's and O'Neill's Plays.* Budapest: Akadémiai Kiadó, 1986.

Emeljanov, V. *C: The Critical Heritage.* London: Routledge & Kegan Paul, 1981.

Eng, Jan dan der, Jan Meijer & Herta Schmid. *On the Theory of Descriptive Poetics: Anton P. C as Story-Teller and Playwright.* NY: Humanities Press, 1978.

Gerhardi, William. *Anton C: A Critical Study.* London: Duckworth, 1928.

Gillés, Daniel. *C: Observer Without Illusion.* Tr. C. L. Markmann. NY: Funk & Wagnalls, 1968.

Goldstone, Herbert, ed. *C's "The Cherry Orchard."* Boston: Allyn and Bacon, 1965.

Gottlieb, Vera. *C and the Vaudeville: A Study of C's One-Act Plays.* Cambridge: Cambridge UP, 1982.

Hahn, Beverly. *C: A Study of the Major Stories and Plays.* London: Cambridge UP, 1977.

Hingley, Ronald. *C: A Biographical and Critical Study.* NY: Barnes & Noble, 1966.

___ *A New Life of Anton C.* NY: Knopf, 1976.

Hulanicki, Leo and David Savignac, eds. *Anton C as a Master of Story-Writing.* The Hague: Mouton, 1976.

Jackson, Robert L., ed. *C: A Collection of Critical Essays.* Englewood Cliffs, NJ: Prentice-Hall, 1967.

Kirk, Irina. *Anton C.* Boston: Twayne, 1981.

Kramer, Karl D. *The Chameleon and the Dream: The Image of Reality in C's Stories.* The Hague: Mouton, 1970.

Lafite, Sophie. *C, 1860-1904.* Tr. from French by Moura Budberg & Gordon Latta. NY: Scribner, 1973.

Magarshack, David. *C: A Life.* Westport, CT: Greenwood, 1970.

___ *C the Dramatist.* NY: Hill & Wang, 1960.

___. *The Real C: An Introduction to C's Last Plays.* London: George Allen & Unwin, 1972; rpt. NY: Harper & Row, 1974.

Meijer, J. M. *On the Theory of Descriptive Poetics: Anton P. C as Story-Teller and Playwright.* Atlantic Highlands, NJ: Humanities Press, 1978.

Melchinger, Siegfried. *Anton C.* Tr. Edith Tarcov. NY: Ungar, 1972.

Moss, Howard. *C.* NY: Albondocani Press, 1972.

Nemirovsky, Irene. *A Life of C.* Tr. Erik de Mauny. London: Grey Walls P, 1950.

___ *C, The Dramatist.* London: Lehmann, 1952.

Nilsson, Nils Ake. *Studies in C's Narrative Technique: "The Steppe" and "The Bishop."* Stockholm: Almqvist & Wiksell, 1968.

Peace, Richard. *C. A Study of the Four Major Plays.* New Haven: Yale UP, 1983.

Pitcher, Harvey. *The C Play: A New Interpretation.* London: Chatto & Windus; NY: Barnes & Noble, 1973.

___ *C's Leading Lady: A Portrait of the Actress Olga Knipper.* London: Murray, 1979; rpt. NY: Franklin Watts, 1980.

Rayfield, Donald. *C: The Evolution of His Art*. NY: Barnes & Noble, 1975.

Schmid, Herta, Jan van der Eng, et al. *On the Theory of Descriptive Poetics: Anton P. C as Story-Teller and Playwright*. Atlantic Highlands, NJ: Humanities Press, 1978.

Senelick, Laurence. *Anton C*. London: Macmillan, 1985.

Shestov, Lev. *Anton Tchekhov and Other Essays*. Tr. S. Koteliansky & J. Middleton Murry. London: Maunsel, 1916.

____. *C and Other Essays*. Intro. Sidney Monas. Ann Arbor: U Michigan P, 1967.

Simmons, Ernest J. *C: A Biography*. Boston: Atlantic, Little, Brown, 1962.

Smith, Virginia L. *Anton C and "The Lady with the Dog."* London: Oxford UP, 1973.

Speirs, Logan. *Tolstoy and C*. Cambridge: Cambridge UP, 1971.

Stowell, H. Peter. *Literary Impressionism: James and C*. Athens: U Georgia P, 1980.

Styan, J. L. *C in Performance: A Commentary on the Major Plays*. Cambridge: Cambridge UP, 1971.

Troyat, Henri. *C*. Tr. Michael Henry Heim. NY: Dutton, 1986.

Tulloch, John. *C: A Structuralist Study*. NY: Barnes & Noble, 1980.

Valency, M. *The Breaking String. The Plays of Anton C*. NY: Oxford UP, 1967.

Wellek, René & Nonna D. Wellek, eds. *C. (New Perspectives)*. Englewood Cliffs, NJ: Prentice-Hall, 1984.

Winner, Thomas. *C and His Prose*. NY: Holt, Rinehart & Winston, 1966.

Worrall, N., comp. *C on File*. NY: Methuen, 1986.

Yermilov, V. V. *Anton Pavlovich C, 1860-1964*. Tr. Ivy Litvinov. Moscow: Foreign Languages Publishing House, 1957.

Dissertations

Baizer, Mary Martha. The Bloomsbury C. Ph.D., diss., Washington, St. Louis, 1985.

Berton, Luba. C Unbound: An Exploration of Untranslatable Material. Ph.D. diss., Michigan, 1975.

Bundala, E. The Structure of the Peasant Universe in C's Short Stories. Ph.D. diss., Ottawa, 1974.

Clyman, Toby W. Women in C's Prose Works. Ph.D. diss., New York, 1971.

Eisen, Donald Gilbert. The Art of Anton C: Principles of Technique in His Drama and Fiction. Ph.D. diss., Pittsburgh, 1982.

Eschliman, Herbert Ray. C in the English Short Story. Ph.D. diss., Minnesota, 1960.

Evans, Jack E. Structure and Style of Speech in the Drama of A. P. C. Ph.D. diss., Yale, 1970.

Forowa, Natalie Irene. Structural Irony in C's Stories. Ph.D. diss., Pennsylvania, 1978.

Frost, Edgar Lee. Concepts of Time in the Works of Anton C. Ph.D. diss., Ohio State, 1971.

Frydman, Anne. A Study of the Endings of Anton C's Short Stories. Ph.D. diss., Columbia, 1978.

Gamble, Christine Elizabeth. The English Chekhovians: The Influence of Anton C on the Short Story and Drama in England. Ph.D. diss., London, 1979.

Giles, S. R. The Problem of Action in Modern European Drama: A Comparative Study With Special References to Büchner, Ibsen, and C. Ph.D. diss., East Anglia, 1976.

Gotman, Sonia Kovitz. C's Use of Irony in His Fiction. Ph.D. diss., Ohio State, 1971.

Katsell, Jerome H. The Potential for Growth and Change: C's Mature Prose. Ph.D. diss., California, Los Angeles, 1972.

Kobler, Mary T. C as Moralist: The Man with the Hammer. Ph.D. diss., Texas, 1968.

Kramer, Karl David. The Chameleon and the Dream: A Study of Anton C's Shifting Perception of Reality in His Short Stories. Ph.D. diss., Washington, Seattle, 1964.

Lanz, Kenneth Alfred. Aspects of C's Comedy, 1880-1887. Ph.D. diss., Toronto, 1974.

Lindsey, Byron Trent. Early C: Development of Character and Meaning in the Short Stories, 1880-1887. Ph.D. diss., Cornell, 1975.

London, Todd. Incomplete Characters: Pirandello's "Father," C's "Colonel," and Brecht's "Good Woman." Ph.D. diss., American, 1985.

Majstorovic, Savka. The Motif of Loneliness in Selected Dramas by Gerhart Hauptmann and Anton C. Ph.D. diss., Florida State, 1980.

Maxwell, David Evans. The Role of Setting in the Prose of A. P. C: A Structural Approach. Ph.D. diss., Brown, 1974.

Narin, Sandra Carole. The Use of Irony in C's Stories. Ph.D. diss., Pennsylvania, 1973.

Palakiewicz, Leonard Anthony. The Image of the Doctor in C's Works. Ph.D. diss., Wisconsin, 1978.

Pervukhin, Natalia K. Incongruity as a Composition Device in the Prose of A. P. C. Ph.D. diss., Bryn Mawr, 1986.

Popkin, Cathy Lynn. The Pragmatics of Insignificance. Ph.D. diss., Stanford, 1985. [C, Zoshchenko, Gogol.]

Reifield, Beatrice Ann. A Theory of Tragi-Comedy in Modern Drama. Ph.D. diss., Penn State, 1976.

Rukalski, Zygmunt. Anton C and Guy de Maupassant: A Comparative Study. Ph.D. diss., Cambridge, 1958.

Saal-Losq, Christine. Literary Allusions in Anton C's Short Stories (1889-1904). Ph.D. diss., Stanford, 1978.

Schubert, P. Z. The Narratives of Čapek and C: A Typological Comparison of the Authors' World Views. Ph.D. diss., Alberta, 1985.

Scielzo, Carolina Anne Gray. The Doctor in C's Works. Ph.D. diss., New York, 1976.

Sklar, S. The Relationship Between Social Context and Individual Character in the Naturalist Drama, with Special Reference to C, D. H. Lawrence and David Storey. Ph.D. diss., London, 1975.

Stenberg, Douglas Graham. Characterization in C's Major Plays Through a Study of Time, Work and Language. Ph.D. diss., Bryn Mawr, 1987.

Stowell, H. Peter. The Prismatic Sensibility: Henry James and Anton C as Impressionists. Ph.D. diss., Washington, Seattle, 1972.

Strongin, Carol Diane. The Anguished Laughter of Shakespeare, C and Beckett: An Exploration of Their Tragicomedy Drama. Ph.D. diss., Brown, 1975.

Toumanova, Nina. Anton C, The Voice of Twilight Russia. Ph.D. diss., Columbia, 1937.

Tracy, Robert E. The Flight of the Seagull: C's Plays on the English Stage. Ph.D. diss., Harvard, 1960.

True, Warren Roberts. Chekhovian Dramaturgy in the Plays of Tennessee Williams, Harold Pinter, and Ed Bullins. Ph.D. diss., Tennessee, 1976.

Urbanski, Henry. C as Viewed by His Russian Literary Contemporaries. Ph.D. diss., New York, 1973.

Weingarten, Aaron. C and the American Director. Ph.D. diss., CUNY, 1972.

Williams, Lee John. Anton C: A Source for the Social Historian. Ph.D. diss., SUNY, Binghamton, 1981.

Articles

Aldanov, Marc. Reflections on C. *RusR* 14 (1955):83-92.

Andrew, Joe. Anton C. In his *Russian Writers and Society in the Second Half of the Nineteenth Century.* Atlantic Highlands, NJ: Humanities Press, 1982, pp. 152-93.

Artz, M. *The Red Flower* of V. M. Garshin and *The Black Monk* of A. P. C. A Survey of One Hundred Years of Literary Criticism. *RusL* 20 (1986): 267-95.

Babula, M. *Three Sisters,* Time and the Audience. *Modern Drama* 18 (1975): 365-70.

Balasubramanian, Kamakshi. Chekhovian Motifs in Roth's *Professor of Desire.* In *Studies in Russian Literature,* ed. J. V. Paul. Hyderabad: Central Institute of English & Foreign Languages, 1984, pp. 66-73.

Balukhatyi, S. D. *The Cherry Orchard:* A Formalist Approach. In *C: A Collection of Critical Essays,* ed. R. L. Jackson. Englewood Cliffs, NJ: Prentice-Hall, 1967, pp. 136-46.

Barricelli, J.-P. Counterpoint of the Snapping String: C's *The Cherry Orchard. CalSS* 10 (1977):121-36.

Basu, S. Russian Intelligentsia in the Works of Tolstoy and C at the End of the 19th Century. *Studies in Russian Literature,* ed. J. V. Paul. Hyderabad: Central Institute of English and Foreign Languages, 1984, pp. 47-52.

Bates, Herbert Ernest. Tchekov and Maupassant. In his *The Modern Short Story: A Critical Survey.* Boston: The Writer, 1941, pp. 72-94.

Bayuk, Milla. The Submissive Wife Stereotype in Anton C's *Darling. College Language Association Journal* 20 (1977):533-38.

Becker, George Joseph. Anton C. In his *Master European Realists of the Nineteenth Century.* NY: Ungar, 1982, pp. 202-38.

Beckerman, Bernard. The Artifice of "Reality" in C and Pinter. *Modern Drama* 21 (1978):153-61.

———. Dramatic Analysis and Literary Interpretation: *The Cherry Orchard* as Exemplum. *New Literary History* 2 (1971):391-406.

———. [*The Cherry Orchard.*] In his *Dynamics of Drama: Theory and Method Analysis.* NY: Knopf, 1970, pp. 101-12.

Beeson, B. Berker. Anton Tchekhov. *Annals of Medical History,* New Series 3 (1931):603-18.

Belgion, Montgomery. Verisimilitude in C and Dostoevsky. *Criterion* 16 (1936):14-32.

Bennett, John L. An Examination of C's Presentation of Characters and Themes in Act I of *Three Sisters.* In *Proceedings: Pacific Northwest Conference on Foreign Languages, 20th Annual Meeting, April 11-12, 1969,* ed. J. L. Mordaunt. Victoria, B.C.: University of Victoria, 20 (1969):94-102.

Bentley, Eric Russell. C as Playwright: Reconsiderations. *Kenyon Review* 11 (1949):226-50.

———. Craftsmanship in *Uncle Vanya.* In his *In Search of Theatre.* NY: Atheneum, 1946, pp. 342-64; rpt. in *Chekhov (New Perspectives),* ed. René and Nonna Wellek. Englewood Cliffs, NJ: Prentice-Hall, 1984, pp. 118-39.

Berdnikov, G. *Ivanov:* An Analysis. In *C: A Collection of Critical Essays,* ed. R. L. Jackson. Englewood Cliffs, NJ: Prentice-Hall, 1967, pp. 88-98.

Berlin, Normand. Waiting: *The Three Sisters* and *Riders to the Sea.* In his *The Secret Cause: A Discussion of Tragedy.* Amherst: U Massachusetts P, 1981, pp. 109-24.

Berthoff, A. E. Marvell's Stars, Schubert's Suns, C's Pipes: Recognizing and Interpreting Metaphor. *Sewanee Review* 89 (1981):57-82.

Bhatnagar, Y. C. C and His Theory of the Novel. In *Studies in Russian Literature,* ed. J. V. Paul. Hyderabad: Central Institute of English and Foreign Languages, 1984, pp. 53-65.

Bill, Valentine T. Nature in C's Fiction. *RusR* 23 (1974):153-66.

Bitsilli, Petr. From Chekhonte to C. In *Twentieth-Century Russian Literary Criticism,* ed. V. Erlich. New Haven: Yale UP, 1975, pp. 212-18.

Bordinat, Philip. Dramatic Structure in C's *Uncle Vanja. SEEJ* 16 (1958):195-210.

Borker, D. & O. Garnica. Male and Female Speech in Dramatic Dialogue: A Stylistic Analysis of Chekhovian Character Speech. *Language Sciences* 13 (1980):3-28.

Brandon, James R. Toward a Middle View of C. *Educational Theatre Journal* 7 (1960):270-75.

Brereton, Geoffrey. Imagination Dethroned: Ibsen, C. In his *Principles of Tragedy.* Coral Gables: U Miami P, 1969, pp. 189-222.

Brewster, Dorothy. C in America and England. *Masses and Mainstream* 7 (1954):35-41.

Brewster, Dorothy & Angus Burrell. Salvaging the Short Story: C and Mansfield Continued. In their *Dead Reckonings in Fiction.* NY: Longmans, Green & Co., 1924, pp. 71-100.

_____. Short Story and the Novelette: Anton C, Katherine Mansfield, A. E. Coppard & Others. In their *Modern Fiction.* NY: Columbia UP, 1934, pp. 348-403.

Bristow, Eugene K. Circles, Triads, and Parity in *The Three Sisters.* In *C's Great Plays. A Critical Anthology,* ed. J. Barricelli. NY: NY UP, 1981, pp. 76-95.

_____. On Translating C. *Quarterly Journal of Speech* 52 (1966):290-94.

Bruford, Walter Horace. Goethe and Tschechow as Liberal Humanists. In *Gestaltung-Umgestaltung. Festschrift zum 75. Geburtstag von Hermann August Korff,* ed. Joachim Muller. Leipzig: Koehler & Amelang, 1957, pp. 118-28.

Brustein, Robert Sanford. Anton C. In his *The Theatre of Revolt. An Approach to Modern Drama.* Boston: Little, Brown, 1964, pp. 135-79.

_____. [*The Cherry Orchard.*] Ibid, pp. 167-78.

Bunin, I. C. *Atlantic Monthly* 188 (July 1951):59-63.

Calder, Angus. Literature and Morality: Leskov, C, Late Tolstoy. In his *Russia Discovered: Nineteenth-Century Fiction from Pushkin to C.* NY: Barnes & Noble, 1976, pp. 238-63.

Chances, Ellen. C's *Seagull:* Ethereal Creature or Stuffed Bird? In *C's Art of Writing. A Collection of Critical Essays,* ed. P. Debreczeny & T. Eekman. Columbus: Slavica, 1977, pp. 27-33.

Chicherin, A. L. The Role of Adversative Intonation in C's Prose. In *Anton C as a Master of Story-Writing,* ed. L. Hulanecki & D. Savignac. The Hague: Mouton, 1976, pp. 187-92.

Chizhevsky, Dmitri. C in the Development of Russian Literature. In *Anton C: 1860-1960. Some Essays,* ed. T. Eekman. Leiden: E. J. Brill, 1960, pp. 293-310; also: *C: A Collection of Critical Essays,* ed. R. L. Jackson. Englewood Cliffs, NJ: Prentice-Hall, 1967, pp. 49-61.

Chudakov, Alexander. Newly-Discovered Works by the Young C. *Soviet Literature* 10 (1975):134-42.

_____. The Poetics of C: The Sphere of Ideas. *New Literary History* 9 (1978):353-80.

Chvany, Catherine V. Backgrounded Perfectives and Plot Line Imperatives: Toward a Theory of Grounding in Text. In *The Scope of Slavic Aspect,* ed. M. S. Flier. Columbus: Slavica, 1985, pp. 247-73.

Clarke, Charanna Carroll. Aspects of Impressionism in C's Prose. In *C's Art of Writing,* ed. P. Debreczeny & T. Eekman. Columbus: Slavica, 1977, pp. 123-33.

Clayton, J. Douglas. C's *Djadja Vanja* and Traditional Comic Structure. *RLJ* 40, 136-37 (1986):103-10.

Clyman, Toby. C's Victimized Women. *RLJ* 28 (1974):26-31.

_____. C's "Visiting Friends": A Satiric Parody. *MelbSS* 13 (1978):63-70.

Collins, H. P. C: The Last Phase. *Contemporary Review* 186 (1954):37-41.

Conrad, Joseph L. Anton C's Literary Landscapes. In *C's Art of Writing: A Collection of Critical Essays,* ed. P. Debreczeny & T. Eekman, Columbus: Slavica, 1977, pp. 82-99.

_____. C's "An Attack of Nerves." *SEEJ* 13 (1969):429-41.

_____. C's "The Man In a Shell": Freedom and Responsibility. *SEEJ* 10 (1966):400-10.

_____. C's "Verochka": A Polemical Parody. *SEEJ* 14 (1970):465-74.

_____. Sensuality in C's Prose. *SEEJ* 24 (1980):103-17.

_____. Unresolved Tension in C's Stories, 1886-1888. *SEEJ* 16 (1972):55-64.

Coope, J. Mania Sakhalina: An Episode in the Life of Dr. Anton C. *Medical History* 23 (1979):29-37.

Corrigan, Robert Willoughby. The Drama of Anton C. In *Modern Drama,* ed. Travis Bogard & William Irvin Oliver. NY: Oxford UP, 1965, pp. 73-98.

_____. The Plays of C. In his *The Theatre in Search of a Fix.* NY: Delacorte, 1973, pp. 125-46.

_____. Some Aspects of C's Dramaturgy. *Educational Theatre Journal* 7 (May 1955):107-14.

_____. Stanislavski and the Playwright. In *Theatre in the Twentieth Century,* ed. R. W. Corrigan. Freeport, NY: Books for Libraries Press, 1963, pp. 185-91.

Cross, A. G. The Breaking Strings of C and Turgenev. *SEER* 47 (1970):510-13.

Croyden, Margaret. "People Just Eat Their Dinner": The Absurdity of C's Doctors. *Texas Quarterly* 2, 3 (1968): 130-37.

Curtin, Constance. Bridging Devices in C's *The Bishop. CASS* 3, 4 (1969):705-11.

——. C's "Sleepy": An Interpretation. *SEEJ* 9 (1965):390-99.

Curtis, James M. Ephebes and Precursors in C's *The Seagull. SlavR* 44, 3 (1985):423-37.

——. Spatial Form in Drama: *The Seagull. CASS* 6, 1 (1972):13-37.

Davie, Donald. C and the English. In his *Russian Literature and Modern English Fiction: A Collection of Critical Studies.* Chicago: U Chicago P, 1965, pp. 203-35.

Davies, Ruth. C: The Axe to the Tree. In her *The Great Books of Russia.* Norman: U Oklahoma P, 1968, pp. 309-45.

Debreczeny, Paul. The Device of Conspicuous Silence in Tolstoy, C and Faulkner. *American Contributions to the Eighth International Congress of Slavists,* vol. 2, ed. V. Terras. Columbus: Slavica, 1978, pp. 124-45.

Deer, Irving. Speech as Action in C's *The Cherry Orchard. Educational Theatre Journal* 10 (1958):30-34.

Derman, A. The Essence of C's Creative Approach. In *Anton C as a Master of Story-Writing,* ed. L. Hulanecki & D. Savignac. The Hague: Mouton, 1976, pp. 23-38.

——. Structural Features in C's Poetics. In *C as a Master of Story-Writing,* ed. L. Hulanecki & D. Savignac. The Hague: Mouton, 1976, pp. 107-18.

Dessner, Lawrence J. Head, Heart, and Snout: Narrative and Theme in C's "Misery." *College Literature* 21, 3 (1985):246-57.

Dick, Gerhard. Anton C and Gerhardt. In *Anton C, 1860-1960: Some Essays,* ed. T. Eekman. Leiden: Brill, 1960, pp. 8-12.

Dobin, E. T. The Nature of Detail. In *C as a Master of Story-Writing,* ed. L. Hulanecki & D. Savignac. The Hague: Mouton, 1976, pp. 39-58.

Dobree, Bonamy. Tchekhov, King of Amateurs. *Theatre* (Winter 1945-46): pp. 5-12.

Duncan, P. A. C's "An Attack of Nerves" as Experimental Narrative. In *C's Art of Writing,* ed. P. Debreczeny & T. Eekman. Columbus: Slavica, 1977, pp. 112-22.

Durkin, Andrew R. C's Response to Dostoevskii: The Case of "Ward Six." *SlavR* 40 (1981):49-59.

——. *The Cherry Orchard* in English: An Overview. *Yearbook of Comparative and General Literature* 33 (1984):74-82.

Eekman, Thomas A. Anton C and the Classical Languages. *Slavia* 40 (1971): 48-60.

——. C—An Impressionist? *RusL* 15 (1984):203-22.

——. C and the Europe of His Day. In *Anton C, 1860-1960: Some Essays,* ed. T. Eekman. Leiden: Brill, 1960, pp. 13-38.

——. C, Melikhova and the Peasants. In *Analecta Slavica: A Slavonic Miscellany Presented for His 70th Brithday to Bruno Becker.* Amsterdam: De Bezige Bij, 1955, pp. 119-32.

——. The Frame Story in Russian Literature and in A. P. C. In *Signs of Friendship to Honour A. G. F. van Hold,* ed. J. J. van Baak. Amsterdam: Rodopi, 1984, pp. 401-18.

——. The Narrator and the Hero in C's Prose. *CalSS* 8 (1975):93-129.

——. A Recurrent Theme in C's Works. *Scando-Slavica* 8 (1962):3-25.

Egri, Peter. The Reinterpretation of the Chekhovian Mosaic Design in O'Neill's *Long Day's Journey into Night. Acta Litteraria Academiae Scientiarum Hungaricae* 22 (1980):29-72.

Ehre, Milton. The Symbolic Structure of Chekhov's "Gusev." *Ulbandus Review* 2 (1979):76-85.

Ehrenburg, Ilia. On Re-Reading C. In *C, Stendahl and Other Essays,* selected with intro. by H. E. Salisbury. Tr. Anna Bostock, et al. NY: Knopf, 1963, pp. 3-79.

Eikhenbaum, Boris. C at Large. In *C: A Collection of Critical Essays,* ed. R. L.

Jackson. Englewood Cliffs, NJ: Prentice-Hall, 1967, pp. 21-31.

Elton, Oliver. *C. The Taylorian Lecture.* Oxford: The Clarendon Press, 1929.

Epstein, Joseph. C's Lost Souls. *New Criterion* 4, 9 (1986).

Ermilov, V. C the Realist. *Masses and Mainstream* 7 (July 1954):11-26.

Fagin, N. Bryllion. Anton C. The Master of the Gray Short Story. *Poet Lore* 32 (Sept. 1921):416-24.

____ . In Search of an American *Cherry Orchard. Texas Quarterly* 1, 3 (1958): 132-41.

Farrell, James Thomas. On the Letters of Anton C. In his *The League of Frightened Philistines, and Other Papers.* NY: Vanguard, 1945, pp. 60-71.

Fasting, S. C's Story "The Kiss": An Analysis. *Slavica* 16 (1979):65-72.

Fergusson, Francis. *The Cherry Orchard:* A Theater-Poem of the Suffering of Change. In *C: A Collection of Critical Essays,* ed. R. L. Jackson. Englewood Cliffs, NJ: Prentice-Hall, 1967, 147-60.

____ . *Ghosts* and *The Cherry Orchard:* The Theatre of Modern Realism. In his *The Idea of a Theater, A Study of Ten Plays.* Princeton: Princeton UP, 1949, pp. 146-77.

Filipp, Valerie. Forms and Functions of Address in C's Plays: A Suggested Classification. *RLJ* 116 (1979):84-91.

Fiftieth Anniversary of C's Death and C in Foreign Countries. *Voks Bulletin* 86 (1954):26-68.

Filips-Juswigg, Katherina. Echoes of C's *The Cherry Orchard* in *Foxfire. Transactions Association of Russian-American Scholars* 18 (1985):303-6.

Finke, Michael. C's "Steppe": A Metapoetic Journey. *RLJ* 39, 132-34 (1985):79-119; rpt. in *Anton C Rediscovered: A Collection of New Studies with a Comprehensive Bibliography,* ed. S. Senderovich & M. Sendich. East Lansing: *RLJ,* 1987, pp. 93-133.

Fludas, John. Chekhovian Comedy: A Review Essay. *Genre* 6 (1973):333-45.

Fodor, Alexander. In Search of a Soviet C. *JRS* 21 (1971):9-19.

Freedman, Morris. C's Morality of Work. *Modern Drama* 5 (1962):83-93.

Freling, R. A New View of Dr. Dymov in C's Grasshopper. *Studies in Short Fiction* 16 (1979):183-87.

Frost, Edgar L. Characterization Through Time in the Works of C, with an Emphasis on *The Cherry Orchard. Studies in Language and Literature. Proceedings of the 23rd Mountain Interstate Foreign Language Conference,* ed. C. Nelson. Richmond: Dept. Foreign Languages, Eastern Kentucky U, 1976, pp. 169-73.

____ . The Search for Eternity in C's Fiction: The Flight from Time as a Source of Tension. *RLJ* 31, 108 (1977):111-20.

Frydman, Anne. "Enemies": An Experimental Story. *Ulbandus Review* 2 (1979): 103-19.

Ganz, Arthur. Arrivals and Departures: The Meaning of the Journey in the Major Plays of C. *Drama Survey* (Minneapolis) 5 (1966):5-23.

Garnett, Edward. Tchekhov and His Art. *Quarterly Review* 236 (Oct. 1921):257-69; rpt. in his *Friday Nights: Literary Criticism and Appreciations.* NY: Knopf, 1922, pp. 39-66.

Gaskell, Ronald. C: *The Cherry Orchard.* In his *Drama and Reality: The European Theatre Since Ibsen.* London: Routledge & Kegan Paul, 1972, pp. 94-98.

Gassner, John Waldhorn. C and the Russian Realists. In his *Masters of the Drama.* NY: Random House, 1940, pp. 495-525.

____ . The Duality of C. In *C: A Collection of Critical Essays,* ed. R. L. Jackson. Englewood Cliffs, NJ: Prentice-Hall, 1967, pp. 175-83.

Gerick, H. J. Tennessee Williams and Anton C. *Zeitschrift für Slavische Philologie* (Heidelberg) 39 (1976):157-65.

Gerould, Daniel Charles. *The Cherry Orchard* as Comedy. *Journal of General Education* 11 (1958):109-22.

Gifford, Henry. C the Humanist. In his *The Novel in Russia: From Pushkin to Pasternak.* NY: Harper, 1965, pp. 125-34.

____ . Russian Conscience. *FMLS* 12 (1976):263-75.

Gilliatt, Penelope. Hamlet the Husband. In her *Unholy Fools*. NY: Viking, 1973, pp. 336-38.

Gilman, Richard. C. In his *The Making of Modern Drama*. NY: Farrar, Straus & Giroux, 1974, pp. 116-56.

Glad, John. C Adapted. *CSP* 16 (1974):99-103.

Golomb, Harai. Communicating Relationships in C's *Three Sisters*. *RLJ* 39, 132-34 (1985):53-77; rpt. in *Anton C Rediscovered: A Collection of New Studies with a Comprehensive Bibliography*, ed. S. Senderovich & M. Sendich. East Lansing: *RLJ*, 1987, pp. 9-33.

——. Music as Theme and as Structural Model in C's *Three Sisters*. In *Semiotics of Drama and Theatre*, ed. Herta Schmid & A. Van Kesteren. Amsterdam: J. Benjamins, 1984, pp. 174-96.

Golubkov, V. V. C's Lyrico-Dramatic Stories. In *Anton C as a Master of Story-Writing*, ed. L. Hulanecki & D. Savignac. Columbus, OH: Slavica, 1976, pp. 135-68.

Goodliffe, John D. Time in C's Plays. *NZSJ* 7 (1971):32-41.

Gordon, Caroline. Notes on C and Maugham. *Sewanee Review* 57 (1949): 401-10.

Gorkii, Maksim. Reminiscences of Anton C. In his *Reminiscences of Tolstoy, C and Andreyev*. NY: Viking Press, 1959, pp. 67-126.

——. Reminiscences of Tchekhov. In *The Note-Books of Anton Tchekhov Together with Reminiscences of Tchekhov by Maksim Gorky*. London: Hogarth, 1964.

Gotman, Sonia K. The Role of Irony in C's Fiction. *SEEJ* 16 (1972):297-306.

Graaff, Frances de. Interpreting C to American Students. *AATSEEL Bulletin* 10 (1953):42-45.

Grossman, L. The Naturalism of C. In *C: A Collection of Critical Essays*, ed. R. L. Jackson. Englewood Cliffs, NJ: Prentice-Hall, 1967, pp. 32-48.

Hagan, John. C's Fiction and the Ideal of "Objectivity." *PMLA* 81 (1966):409-17.

——. "The Shooting Party," C's Early

Novel: Its Place in His Development. *SEEJ* 9 (1965):123-40.

——. The Tragic Sense in C's Earliest Stories. *Criticism* 7 (1965):52-80.

Hahn, Beverly. C: *The Three Sisters*. *Critical Review* 15 (1972):3-22.

——. C's *The Cherry Orchard*. *Critical Review* 16 (1973):56-72.

Hamburger, H. The Function of the Time Component in C's "Na podvode." In *Dutch Contributions to the Seventh International Congress of Slavists, Warsaw, 1973*, ed. A. van Holk. The Hague: Mouton, 1973, pp. 237-70.

——. The Function of the Verum Dicendi in C's "Smert' činovnika." In *Dutch Contributions to the Sixth International Congress of Slavists*. The Hague: Mouton, 1968, pp. 98-122.

——. The Function of the Viewpoint in C's "Griša." *RusL* 3 (1972):5-15.

Hanuszkiewicz, A. & V. Rozov. Dialogue about C. *Soviet Literature* 2 (1978): 161-65.

Harper, Kenneth E. Text Progression and Narrative Style. *American Contributions to the Eighth International Congress of Slavists*, vol. 2, ed. V. Terras. Columbus: Slavica, 1978, pp., 223-35.

Harris, W. B. C and Russian Drama. *Annual Reports and Transactions of Plymouth Institution and Devon and Cornwall Natural History Society* 21 (1947-49):141-50.

Harrison, John William. Symbolic Action in C's "Peasants" and "In the Ravine." *Modern Fiction Studies* 7, 4 (1961): 369-72.

Heim, Michael. C and the Moscow Art Theater. In *C's Great Plays: A Critical Anthology*, ed. J. Barricelli. NY: New York UP, 1981, pp. 133-43.

Heldt, Barbara. C (and Flaubert) on Female Devotion. *Ulbandus Review* 2 (1982):166-74.

Hellweg, J. D. & S. A. Hellweg. *Sea Gull*: A Communicative Analysis of Chekhovian Drama. *Communication Quarterly* 30 (1982):150-54.

Herling-Grudzinski, G. Yegor and Ivan Denisovich. In *Kultura Essays*, ed. L.

Tyrmand. NY: Free Press, 1970, pp. 192-97.

Hinchliff, Arnold. C's Early Tales. *Literary Review* 15 (1972):253-355.

Hodgson, Peter. Metaliterature: An Excerpt from the Anatomy of a Chekhovian Narrator. *Pacific Coast Philology* 7 (1972):36-42.

Holland, Peter. C and the Resistant Symbol. In *Drama and Symbolism*, ed. J. Redmond. NY: Cambridge UP, 1982, pp. 227-42.

Hollosi, Clara. C's Hungarian Story. *CSP* 27, 3 (1985):301-6.

____ C's Plays in Contemporary Soviet Criticism. *Les Littératures de langues européennes au tournant du siècle: lectures d'aujoud'hui, serie D.*, ed. Paul Varnai. Ottawa: Carleton UP, 1984, pp. 23-32.

____ C's Reactions to Two Interpretations of Nina. *Theater Studies* 24 (1983):117-26.

Holloway, John. Identity, Inversion and Density Elements in Narrative: Three Tales by C, James and Lawrence. In his *Narrative and Structure: Exploratory Essays*. Cambridge: Cambridge UP, 1979, 53-73.

Hubbs, Clayton. C and the Contemporary Theatre. *Modern Drama* 24, 3 (1981): 357-66.

____ The Function of Repetition in the Plays of C. *Modern Drama* 22 (1979): 115-24.

Hubbs, Clayton A. & Joanna T. Hubbs. The Goddess of Love and the Tree of Knowledge: Some Elements of Myth and Folklore in C's *The Cherry Orchard*. *South Carolina Review* 14 (1982):66-77.

Ivask, George. C and the Russian Clergy. In *Anton C, 1860-1960: Some Essays*, ed. T. Eekman. Leiden: E. J. Brill, 1960, pp. 83-92.

Jackson, Robert L. "The Betrothed": C's Last Testament. In *Anton C Rediscovered: A Collection of New Studies with a Comprehensive Bibliography*, ed. S. Senderovich & M. Sendich. East Lansing: *RLJ*, 1987, pp. 51-62.

____ C's "A Woman's Kingdom": A Drama of Character and Fate. *RLJ* 39, 132-34 (1985):1-11.

____ C's Garden of Eden, or The Fall of the Russian Adam and Eve: "Because of the Little Apples." *Slavica Hierosolymitana* 4 (1979):70-78.

____ The Garden of Eden in Dostoevsky's "A Christmas Party and a Wedding" and C's "Because of Little Apples." *Revue de Littérature Comparée* 45 (1981):331-41.

____ If I Forget Thee, O Jerusalem: An Essay on C's "Rothschild's Fiddle." *Slavica Hierosolymitana* 3 (1978):55-67; rpt. in *Anton C Rediscovered: A Collection of New Studies with a Comprehensive Bibliography*, ed. S. Senderovich & M. Sendich. East Lansing: *RLJ*, 1987, pp. 35-49.

____ *The Seagull:* The Empty Well, the Dry Lake and the Cold Cave. In *C: A Collection of Critical Essays*, ed. R. L. Jackson. Englewood Cliffs, NJ: Prentice-Hall, 1967, pp. 99-111.

Jarrell, Randall. Notes. In *The Three Sisters*. NY: Macmillan, 1969, pp. 101-60.

____ Six Russian Short Novels. In his *Third Book of Criticism*. NY: Farrar, Straus & Giroux, 1965, pp. 232-75.

Jones, W. Gareth. C's Undercurrent of Time. *MLR* 64 (1969):111-21.

____ *The Seagull's* Second Symbolist Play-Within-the-Play. *SEER* 53 (1975):17-26.

Karlinsky, Simon. C, Beloved and Betrayed. *Delos* 3 (1969):192-97.

____ Frustrated Artists and Devouring Mothers in C and Annenskij. In *Mnemozina. Studia Litteraria Russica in Honorem Vsevolod Setchkarev*, ed. J. T. Baer & N. W. Ingham. Munich: Fink, 1974, pp. 228-31.

____ Huntsmen, Birds, Forest, and *Three Sisters*. In *C's Great Plays: A Critical Anthology*, ed. J. Barricelli. NY: New York UP, 1981, pp. 144-60.

____ Nabokov and C: The Lesser Russian Tradition. *TriQuarterly* 17 (1970):7-16.

____ Russian Anti-Chekhovians. *RusL* 15 (1984):183-202.

Kaszkurewicz, Tamara. Development of the Psychological Theme in C's Story

Volodja Bol'šoj i Volodja Malen'kij. *RLJ* 30, 105 (1976):47-59.

Katayev, Vladimir. Understanding C's World. *Soviet Literature* 1 (1980):171-83.

Katsell, Jerome. Character Change in C's Short Stories. *SEEJ* 18 (1975):377-83.

—. C's *The Steppe* Revisited. *SEEJ* 22 (1978):313-23.

—. Mortality: Theme and Structure of C's Later Prose. In *C's Art of Writing. A Collection of Critical Essays,* ed. P. Debreczeny & T. Eekman. Columbus, OH: Slavica, 1977, pp. 54-67.

Kendle, Burton. The Elusive Horses in *The Seagull. Modern Drama* 13 (1970):63-66.

Kingsbury, Stewart A. Name Symbolism in C's *Uncle Vanya.* In *Festschrift in Honor of Virgil J. Vogel,* ed. E. Callary. Dekalb: Illinois Names Society, 1985, pp. 46-58.

Kircher, Cassie L. Trofimov's Galoshes: An Examination of a Čexovian Prop. *RLJ* 39, 132-34 (1985):51-52.

Kleine, D. W. The Chekhovian Source of "Marriage à la mode." *Philological Quarterly,* 42 (1963):284-88.

Klitko, Anatoli. C and the Short Story in the Soviet Union Today. *Soviet Literature* 1 (1980):143-48.

Knapp, S. H. Spencer in C's *Skučnaja istorija* and *Duel'.* The Love of Science and the Science of Love. *SEEJ* 29 (1986):279-96.

Korovin, Konstantin. My Encounters with C. *TriQuarterly* 28 (1973):561-69.

Korpan, B. C and Mann: An Overdue Debt. *Sovremennik* (Leeds) 9 (1965):4-17.

Kovitz, Sonia. A Fine Day to Hang Oneself: On C's Plays. In *C's Great Plays: A Critical Anthology,* ed. J Barricelli. NY: New York UP, 1981, pp. 189-200.

Kozhevnikova, I. Artists of C's Time. *Soviet Literature* 1 (1980):200-5.

Kramer, Karl D. C and the Seasons. In *C's Art of Writing. A Collection of Critical Essays,* ed. P. Debreczeny & T. Eekman. Columbus, OH: Slavica, 1977, pp. 68-81.

—. C at the End of the Eighties: The Question of Identity. *Slavic and East European Studies* 11 (1966):3-18.

—. C's "Gusev": A Study. *Studies in Short Fiction* 15 (1978):55-61.

—. Cycles in C Criticism: Impressionism Refurbished. In *Proceedings: Pacific Northwest Conference on Foreign Languages. 23rd Annual Meeting, 1972,* ed. W. C. Draft. Corvallis: Oregon State U, 1972, pp. 268-72.

Kronenberger, Louis. C: The Four Plays. In his *The Republic of Letters: Essays on Various Writers.* NY: Knopf, 1955, pp. 178-204.

—. Love and Comic Instability in *The Cherry Orchard.* In *Russian Literature and American Critics: In Honor of Deming B. Brown,* ed. K. Brostrom. Ann Arbor: Department of Slavic Languages, U Michigan, 1984, pp. 295-307.

—. *Three Sisters* or, Taking a Chance on Love. In *C's Great Plays: A Critical Anthology,* ed. J. Barricelli. NY: New York UP, 1981, pp. 61-75.

Kuhn, R. The Debasement of the Intellectual in Contemporary Continental Drama. *Modern Drama* 7 (1965):454-62.

Kus'muk, V. A. Vasilii Shukshin and the Early C: An Essay in Typological Analysis. *Soviet Studies in Literature* 3, 14 (1978): 61-78.

Lahr, John. Pinter and C: The Bond of Naturalism. *Tulane Drama Review* 13 (1968):137-45.

Lakshin, V. An Incomparable Artist. In *Anton C as a Master of Story-Writing,* ed. L. Hulanicki & D. Savignac. The Hague: Mouton, 1976, pp. 91-106.

—. The Literary Heritage of C. *Soviet Highlights (March 1960):1-13.*

—. An Unknown Note in the Hand of the Writer. *Soviet Literature* 1 (1980):128-31.

Lamm, Iudit. C's Art of Writing. *Studia Slavica Academiae Scientiarum Hungaricae* 26, nos. 3-4 (1980):425-56.

Lamm. Martin. Anton C. In his *Modern Drama.* Tr. Karin Elliott. Oxford: Blackwell, 1952, pp. 194-215.

Lantz, Kenneth Alfred. C and the *Scenka,* 1880-1887. *SEEJ* 19 (1975):377-87.

___. C's "Gusev": A Study. *Studies in Short Fiction* 15 (1978):55-62.

Latham, Jacqueline E. M. *The Cherry Orchard* as Comedy. *Educational Theatre Journal* 10 (1958):21-29.

Lau, Joseph Shiu-Ming. The Peking Man and *Ivanov:* Portraits of Two Super-fluous Men. *Contemporary Literature* 10 (1969): 85-102.

___. Ts'ao Yü, the Reluctant Disciple of C: A Comparative Study of *Sunrise* and *The Cherry Orchard. Modern Drama* 9, 4 (1967):358-72.

Lavrin, Janko. C and Maupassant. *SEER* 5 (1926):1-24.

___. The Dramatic Works of C. In his *Russian Writers. Their Lives and Literature.* NY: Van Nostrand, 1954.

Lawson, J. H. C's Drama: Challenge to Playwrights. *Masses and Mainstream* 7 (1954):11-26.

Le Fleming, L. S. K. The Structural Role of Language in C's Later Stories. *SEER* 48 (1970):323-40.

Lelchuk, Alan. An Analysis of Technique in C's "Anyuta." *Studies in Short Fiction* 6 (1969):609-18.

LeMaster, J. R. The Condition of Talk in C's *Three Sisters. New Laurel Review* 4, nos. 1-2 (1975):9-16.

Leong, Albert. Literary Unity in C's "Strakh." *JRS* 27 (1974):15-20.

Levertov, Denise. On C. In her *Light Up the Cave.* NY: New Directions, 1981, pp. 279-82.

Lewis, Allan. The Comedy of Frustration: C. In his *The Contemporary Theatre: The Significant Playwrights of Our Time.* NY: Crown, 1962, pp. 59-80.

Lucas, Frank Laurence. [C.] In his *The Drama of C, Synge, Yeats and Piran-dello.* London: Cassell, 1963, pp. 1-46.

MacCarthy, Sir Desmond. C. In his *Humanities.* NY: Oxford UP, 1954, pp. 71-82.

McConkey, James. In Praise of C. *Hudson Review* 20 (1967):417-28.

___. Two Anonymous Writers: E. M. Forster and Anton C. In *E. M. Forster: A Human Exploration: Centenary Essays,* ed. G. K. Das and J. Beer. NY: New York UP, 1979, pp. 231-44.

McLean, Hugh. C's "V Ovrage": Six Antipodes. *American Contributions to the Sixth International Congress of Slavists,* ed. W. E. Harkins. The Hague: Mouton, vol. 2, pp. 285-305.

McNamara, Brooks. Scene Design; 1876-1965: Ibsen, C, Strindberg. *Tulane Drama Review* 13 (1968):77-91.

Majdalany, Marina. Natasha Ivanova, the Lonely *Bourgeoise. Modern Drama* 26, 3 (1983):305-9.

Manderson, S. & D. M. Fiene. C's *Three Sisters. Explicator* 36 (1978):22-23.

Mann, Thomas. Anton C: An Essay. *Listener* (March 3, 1955):371-74.

___. Anton C: An Essay. In *Great Essays by Nobel Prize Winners,* ed. L. Hamalian & E. Loris Volpe. NY: Noonday, 1960, pp. 38-51.

___. Anton C. *Mainstream* 12, 3 (1959):2-21.

___. C. In *Russian Literature and Modern English Fiction,* ed. D. Davie. Chicago: Chicago UP, 1965.

___. Mann on C. In *Storytellers and Their Art,* ed. G. S. Trask & C. Burkhart. Garden City: Doubleday, 1963, pp. 313-38.

___. The Stature of Anton C. *New Republic* 132 (May 16, 1955):23-25.

Markov, Pavel. New Trends in the Interpretation of C. *World Theatre* 9 (1960):99-148.

Marshall, Richard H., Jr. C and the Russian Orthodox Clergy. *SEEJ* 7 (1963): 375-91.

Martin, D. Figurative Language and Concretism in C's Stories. *RusL* 8 (1980):125-49.

___. Historical References in C's Later Stories. *MLR* 71 (1976):595-606.

___. On the Structure of C's Stories. Back-Reference and Recapitulation. *Die Welt der Slaven* 30 (1985):100-18.

___. On Translation from Russian: C in English. *Durham University Journal* 76 (1984):235-48.

___. Philosophy in C's Major Plays. *Die Welt der Slaven* 23 (1978):122-39.

___. Realia and C's "The Student." *CASS* 12 (1978):266-73.

Massey, Irving. Escape from Fiction: Literature and Didacticism. *Georgia Review* 32 (1978):611-30.

Mathewson, Rufus W. Intimations of Mortality in Four C Stories. *American*

Contributions to the Sixth International Congress of Slavists, vol. 2, ed. W. E. Harkins. The Hague: Mouton: 1968, pp. 261-83.

——. Thoreau and C: A Note on The Steppe. Ulbandus Review 1 (1977):28-40.

Matlaw, Ralph E. C and the Novel. In Anton C: Some Essays, ed. T. Eekman, Leiden: Brill, 1960, pp. 148-67.

Matley, Ian M. C and Geography. RusR 31 (1972):376-82.

Matual, David. C's "Black Monk" and Byron's "Black Friar." International Fiction Review 5 (1978):46-51.

Maurois, André. The Art and the Philosophy of Anton Tchekhov. In his The Art of Writing. Tr. G. Hopkins. London: Bodley Head, 1960, pp. 224-64.

Maxwell, David. C's "Nevesta": A Structural Approach to the Role of Setting. RLT 6 (1974):91-100.

——. A System of Symbolic Gesture in C's "Step'." SEEJ 17 (1973):146-54.

——. The Unity of C's "Little Trilogy." In C's Art of Writing, ed. P. Debreczeny & T. Eekman. Columbus: Slavica, 1977, pp. 35-53.

Mays, Milton A. "Gooseberries" and C's Concreteness. Southern Humanities Review 6 (1972):63-67.

Meister, Charles W. C's Reception in England and America. ASEER 12 (1953): 109-21.

Mendelsohn, Michael J. The Heartbreak Houses of Shaw and C. Shaw Review 6 (1963):89-95.

Meyerhold, Vsevolod. Naturalistic Theater and Theater of Mood. In C: A Collection of Critical Essays, ed. R. L. Jackson. Englewood Cliffs, NJ: Prentice-Hall, 1967, pp. 62-68.

Miklashevsky, Mikhail. Without Wings: C and His Work. In The Noise of Change: Russian Literature and the Critics, 1891-1917, ed. S. Rabinowitz. Ann Arbor: Ardis, 1986, pp. 37-66.

Miller, J. William. Anton C. In his Modern Playwrights at Work. NY: S. French, 1968, pp. 114-59.

Miller, Jim Wayne. Stark Young, C and Method of Indirect Action. Georgia Review 18 (1964):98-115.

Mirković, Damir. Anton Pavlovich C and the Modern Sociology of Deviance. CSP 18 (1976):66-72.

Mirsky, D. S. C and the English. In Russian Literature and Modern English Fiction: A Collection of Critical Essays, ed. D. Davie. Chicago: Chicago UP, 1965, pp. 203-13.

Moravčevich, Nicholas. C and Naturalism: From Affinity to Divergence. Comparative Drama 6 (1970):219-40.

——. The Dark Side of the Chekhovian Smile. Drama Survey 5 (1967):237-51.

——. The Obligatory Scene in C's Plays. Drama Critique 9 (1966):97-104.

Morgan, Victor. C's Social Plays and their Historical Background. Papers of the Manchester Literary Club 114 (1939): 96-114.

Moss, H. Three Sisters. Hudson Review 30 (1977-78):525-43.

Mudford, Peter. Anton C. In his The Art of Celebration. Boston: Faber, 1979, pp. 110-22.

Mudrick, Marvin. Boyish Charmer and Last Mad Genius. Hudson Review 27 (1974):33-54.

——. C. In his The Man in the Machine. NY: Horizon Press, 1975, pp. 153-77.

Muller, Herbert Joseph. Realism of C. In his The Spirit of Tragedy. NY: Knopf, 1956, pp. 283-93.

Murdoch, Brian. Communication as a Dramatic Problem: Buchner, C, Hofmannsthal and Sesker. Revue de Littérature Comparée 45 (1971):40-59.

Nabokov, Vladimir. Anton C. In his Lectures on Russian Literature. NY: Harcourt Brace Jovanovich, 1981, pp. 245-96.

Nag, Martin. On the Aspects of Time and Place in Anton C's Dramaturgy. Scando-Slavica 16 (1970):23-34.

Nagle, John J. Idealism: The Internal Structure in Gogol's "Nevsky Prospect" and C's "An Attack of Nerves." West Virginia University Philological Papers 19 (1972):20-28.

Nazarenko, Vadim. Imagery in C. In Anton C as a Master of Story-Writing, ed. L. Hulanicki & David Savignac. The Hague: Mouton, 1976, pp. 131-34.

Nemirovich-Danchenko, Vladimir. Part One: Anton C. In his *My Life in the Russian Theatre*. Tr. J. Cournos. Boston: Little, Brown & Co., 1936, pp. 1-76.

Nevedomsky, M. P. Without Wings: C and His Work. In *The Noise of Change: Russian Literature and the Critics (1891-1917)*, ed. S. Rabinowitz. Ann Arbor: Ardis, 1986, pp. 37-66.

Newcombe, Josephine M. Was C a Tolstoyan? *SEEJ* 18 (1975):143-52.

Nicoll, Allardyce. The Poetic Realism of C. In *World Drama from Aeschylus to Anouilh*. London: G. Harrap, 1949, pp. 682-89.

Nilsson, Nils Ake. Intonation in Rhythm in C's Plays. In *Anton C: 1860-1960: Some Essays*, ed. T. Eekman. Leiden: E. J. Brill, 1960, pp. 168-80; rpt. *C: A Collection of Critical Essays*, ed. R. L. Jackson. Englewood Cliffs, NJ: Prentice-Hall, 1967, pp. 161-74.

——. Two Cs: Mayakovskii on C's "Futurism." In *C's Great Plays: A Critical Anthology*, ed. J. Barricelli. NY: New York UP, 1981, pp. 51-61.

Oates, Joyce Carol. C and the Theater of the Absurd. In her *The Edge of Impossibility*. NY: Fawcett, 1972, pp. 103-22.

O'Bell, Leslie. C's *Skazka:* The Intellectual's Fairy Tale. *SEEJ* 25 (1981):33-46.

Ober, William. C Among the Doctors: The Doctor's Dilemma. In *Boswell's Clap and Other Essays. Medical Analyses of Literary Men's Afflictions*. Carbondale: Southern Illinois UP, 1979, pp. 193-205.

O'Connor, Katherine Tiernan. C on C: Epistolary Self-Criticism. In *New Studies in Russian Language and Literature*, ed. A. Crone & C. Chvany. Columbus: Slavica, 1986, pp. 239-45.

O'Connor, Frank. The Slave's Son. *Kenyon Review* 25 (1963):40-54.

O'Faolain, Sean. Anton C, or the Persistent Moralist. In his *The Short Story*. NY: Devin-Adair, 1951, pp. 76-105.

O'Toole, L. M. "The Black Monk." In his *Structure, Style and Interpretation in the Russian Short Story*. New Haven: Yale UP, 1982, pp. 161-79.

——. Structure and Style in the Short Story: C's "Student." *SEER* 49 (1971): 44-67.

Pachmuss, Temira. Anton C in the Criticism of Zinaida Gippius. *Slavic and East European Studies* 11 (1966): 35-48.

Paperny, Zinovi. Truth and Faith: Reading C's Rough Drafts and Notebooks. *Soviet Literature* 1 (1980):104-11.

Parker, D. Three Men in C's *Three Sisters*. *Melbourne Critical Review* 21 (1979): 11-23.

Patrick, George Z. C's Attitude Towards Life. *SEER* 10 (1932):658-68.

Paul, Barbara. C's "Five Sisters." *Modern Drama* 14 (1971-72):436-40.

Pauls, John P. C's Humorous Names. *Literary Onomastics Studies* 1 (1974):53-65.

——. C's Meaningful Names. *Wiener Slavistisches Jarhbuch* 23 (1977):238-45.

——. C's Names. *Names* 23 (1975):67-73.

Pavis, Patrice. The Classical Heritage of Modern Drama: The Case of Postmodern Theatre. *Modern Drama* 29, 1 (1986):1-22.

Peacock, Ronald C. In his *Poet in the Theatre*. NY: Harcourt, Brace, 1946, pp. 94-104.

Pedrotti, Louis. C's Major Plays: A Doctor in the House. In *C's Great Plays: A Critical Anthology*, ed. J. Barricelli. NY: New York UP, 1981, pp. 233-50.

Perry, Henry Ten Eyck. Cross Currents in Russia: Gogol, Turgenev and C. In his *Masters of Dramatic Comedy and their Social Themes*. Cambridge: Harvard UP, 1939, pp. 338-58.

Phelps, Gilbert. Indifference in the Letters and Tales of Anton C. *Cambridge Journal* 7 (1954):208-20.

Pifer, Ellen. C's Psychological Landscape. *SEEJ* 17 (1973):273-78.

Pitcher, Harvey. Tolstoy and C. *FMLS* 8 (1972):237-42.

Poggioli, Renato. Storytelling in a Double Key. In his *The Phoenix and the Spider*. Cambridge: Harvard UP, 1957, pp. 109-30.

Polakiewicz, Leonard. C's *Tif:* An Analysis. *RLJ* 116 (1979):92-111.

——. Crime and Punishment in C. *Studies in Honor of Xenia Gasiorowska*, ed. L. Leighton. Columbus: Slavica, 1983, pp. 55-70.

Pomorska, Krystyna. On the Structure of Modern Prose: C and Solženicyn. *PTL: A Journal for Descriptive Poetics and Theory of Literature* 1 (1976):459-65.

Porter, R. N. Bunin's "A Sunstroke" and C's "The Lady with the Dog." *South Atlantic Bulletin* 42 (1977):51-56.

——. *Hamlet* and *The Seagull*. *JRS* 41 (1981):23-32.

Pospelov, G. N. The Style of C's Tales. In *Anton C as a Master of Story-Writing*, ed. L. Hulanicki & D. Savignac. The Hague: Mouton, 1976, pp. 119-30.

Pritchett, V. S. Anton C: A Doctor. In his *Myth Makers: Essays on European, Russian and South American Novelists*. NY: Random House, 1979, pp. 37-49.

Proffer, Carl R. "Heartache," "Gooseberries," "Anna on the Neck," "The Darling." In his *From Karamzin to Bunin*. Bloomington: Indiana UP, 1969, pp. 34-46.

Průšek, Jaroslav. Yeh Shao-chun and Anton C. In his *The Lyrical and the Epic*. Bloomington: Indiana UP, 1980, pp. 178-94.

Purdon, Liam. Time and Space in C's *Three Sisters*. *Publications of the Arkansas Philological Association* 2 (1976):47-53.

Quintus, John Allen. The Loss of Dear Things: C and Williams in Perspective. *English Language Notes* 18, 3 (1981): 201-6.

Rahv, Philip. The Education of Anton C. In his *The Myth and the Powerhouse*. NY: Farrar, Straus, Giroux, 1965, pp. 175-81.

Rayfield, Donald. What Did the Jews Mean to C? *European Judaism* 8 (1973-74):30-36.

Reed, W. L. *The Cherry Orchard* and *Hedda Gabler*. In *Homer to Brecht*, ed. M. Seidel and E. Mendelson. New Haven: Yale UP, 1977, pp. 317-35.

Reeve, F. D. Tension in Prose: C's *Three Years*. *SEEJ* 16 (1958):99-108.

Remaley, Peter B. C's *The Cherry Orchard*. *South Atlantic Bulletin* 38 (1973):16-20.

Rhys, Brinley. C. *Sewanee Review* 78 (1970):163-75.

Rinear, D. L. The Day the Whore Came out to Play Tennis: Kopit's Debt to C. *Today's Speech* 22 (1974):19-23.

Risso, Richard D. C: A View of the Basic Ironic Structures. In *C's Great Plays: A Critical Anthology*, ed. J. Barricelli. NY: New York UP, 1981, pp. 181-88.

Rosen, Nathan. C's Religion in "The Student." *Teoria e critica* 2-3 (1974):3-14.

——. The Life Force in C's "The Kiss." *Ulbandus Review* 2 (1979):175-85.

——. A Reading of C's "The Lady with the Dog." *RLJ* 39, 132-34 (1985):13-29.

——. The Unconscious in C's "Van'ka" (With a Note on "Sleepy"). *SEEJ* 15 (1971):441-54.

Rossbacher, Peter. C's Fragment "Solomon." *SEEJ* 12 (1968):27-34.

——. The Function of Insanity in C's "The Black Monk" and Gogol's "Notes of a Madman." *SEEJ* 13 (1969):191-99.

——. Nature and the Quest for Meaning in C's Stories. *RusR* 24 (1965):387-92.

——. The Thematic Significance of Four of C's Stylistic Devices. In *Proceedings: Pacific Northwest Conference on Foreign Languages, 21st Annual Meeting, April 3-4, 1970*. Victoria, B.C.: U Victoria, 21 (1970): 137-43.

Rowe, Eleanor. *Hamlet* in the Age of C and Blok. In her *Hamlet: A Window on Russia*. NY: New York UP, 1976, pp. 107-25.

Rowe, W. W. C. In his *Patterns in Russian Literature II: Notes on Classics*. Ann Arbor: Ardis, 1988, pp. 11-32.

Rubenstein, Roberta. Virginia Woolf and the Russian Point of View. *CLS* 9, 2 (1972):196-206.

Rukalski, Z. Anton C and Guy Maupassant: Their Views on Life and Art. *Slavic and East European Studies* 5 (1960)178-88.

——. Human Problems in the Works of Maupassant and C. *Slavic and East European Studies* 3 (1958):80-84.

____. Maupassant and C: Differences. *CSP* 13 (1971):374-402.

____. Maupassant and C: Similarities. *CSP* 11 (1969):346-58.

____. Russian and French Writers on Politics and Public Opinion. *Slavic and East European Studies* 6 (1961):188-96.

Rzepka, Charles J. C's *The Three Sisters,* Lear's Daughters and the Weird Sisters: The Arcana of Archetypal Influence. *MLS* 14 (1984):18-27.

Sagar, Keith. C's Magic Lake: A Reading of *The Seagull. Modern Drama* 15 (1973):441-48.

Saint-Denis, M. C and the Modern Stage. *Drama Survey* 3 (1965):77-81.

Saunders, Beatrice. Anton C. In her *Portraits of Genius.* London: J. Murray, 1959, pp. 200-9.

Savvas, Minas. C's Tragicomedy: Some Typical Examples. *Language Quarterly* 9, 1-2 (1970):54-56.

Schefski, Harold. C and Tolstoy on Philosophy. *NZSJ* (1985):81-88.

Schneider, Elizabeth. Katherine Mansfield and C. *Modern Language Notes* 50 (1935):394-97.

Schorer, Mark. ["Gooseberries."] In his *The Story: A Critical Anthology.* NY: Prentice-Hall, 1950, pp. 61-65.

Scott, V. Life in Art: A Reading of *The Seagull. Educational Theatre Journal* 30 (1978):357-67.

Seeley, F. F. On Interpersonal Relations in C's Fiction. *Annali dell'Istituto Universitario Orientale.* Naples, Sezione Germanica 15 (1972):59-90.

Senanu, K. E. Anton C and Henry James. *Ibadan Studies in English* 2 (1970):182-97.

Senderovich, M. C's "Kashtanka": Metamorphoses of Memory in the Labyrinth of Time (A Structural-Phenomenological Essay). In *Anton C Rediscovered: A Collection of New Studies,* ed. S. Senderovich & M. Sendich. East Lansing: *RLJ,* 1987, pp. 63-76.

____. The Symbolic Structure of C's Story "Ward No. 6" and Solzhenitsyn's *Cancer Ward.* In *C's Art of Writing,* ed. P. Debreczeny & T. Eekman. Columbus: Slavica: 1977, pp. 11-26.

Senderovich, Savely. Anton C and St. George the Dragonslayer (An Introduction to the Theme). In *Anton C Rediscovered: A Collection of New Studies,* ed. S. Senderovich & M. Sendich. East Lansing: *RLJ,* 1987, pp. 167-87.

____. C and Impressionism: An Attempt at a Systematic Approach to the Problem. In *C's Art of Writing,* ed. P. Debreczeny & T. Eekman. Columbus: Slavica, 1977, pp. 134-52.

____. The Poetic Structure of C's Short Story "On the Road." In *The Structural Analysis of Narrative Texts: Conference Papers,* ed. A. Kodjak, M. J. Connolly & K. Pomorska. Columbus: Slavica, 1980, pp. 44-81.

____. Poetics and Meaning in C's "On the Road." In *Anton C Rediscovered: A Collection of New Studies,* ed. S. Senderovich & M. Sendich. East Lansing: *RLJ,* 1987, pp. 135-66.

____. Towards C's Deeper Reaches. In *Anton C Rediscovered: A Collection of New Studies,* ed. S. Senderovich & M. Sendich. East Lansing: *RLJ,* 1987, pp. 1-8.

Senelick, Laurence. C's Drama, Maeterlinck, and the Russian Symbolists. In *C's Great Plays: A Critical Anthology,* ed. J. Barricelli. NY: New York UP, 1981, pp. 161-80.

____. C's Response to Bernhardt. In *Bernhardt and the Theatre of Her Time,* ed. Eric Salmon. Westport, CT: Greenwood, 1984, pp. 165-81.

____. The Lake-Shore of Bohemia: *The Seagull's* Theatrical Context. *Educational Theatre Journal* 29 (1977):199-213.

Senelick, Louis. C and the Irresistible Symbol. In *Drama and Symbolism,* ed. James Redmond. NY: Cambridge UP, 1982, pp. 243-51.

Seyler, Dorothy U. *The Sea Gull* and *The Wild Duck:* Birds of a Feather? *Modern Drama* 8 (1965):167-73.

Sheldon, Richard. Cathartic Disillusionment in *The Three Sisters.* In *Russian Literature and American Critics,* ed. K. Brostrom. Ann Arbor: Department of Slavic Langugaes, U Michigan, 1984, pp. 309-18.

Sherman, Stuart Pratt. C, Chekhovians, Chekhovism. In his *Critical Woodcuts.* NY: Scribner, 1926, pp. 122-37.

Shestov, Leo. Anton Tchekhov (Creation from the Void). In his *Penultimate Words & Other Essays.* Boston: Luce, 1916, pp. 3-60; rpt. Freeport, NY: Books for Libraries Press, 1966, pp. 3-60.

Shklovsky, Victor. A. P. C. In *Anton C as a Master of Story-Writing,* ed. L. Hulanicki & D. Savignac. The Hague: Mouton, 1976, pp. 59-90.

Shotton, M. H. C. In *Nineteenth-Century Russian Literature: Studies of Ten Russian Writers,* ed. J. Fennell. Berkeley: U California P, 1973, pp. 293-346.

Shugg, W. C's Use of Irony in "A Nervous Breakdown." *Studies in Short Fiction* 21 (1984):395-98.

Silverstein, Norman. C's Comic Spirit and *The Cherry Orchard. Modern Drama* 1 (1958):91-100.

Simmons, Ernest J. Tolstoj and C. *Midway* 8 (1968):91-103.

Skaftymov, A. Principles of Structure in C's Plays. In *C: A Collection of Critical Essays,* ed. R. L. Jackson. Englewood Cliffs, NJ: Prentice-Hall, 1967, pp. 69-87.

Smernoff, Susan. The Irony of the Doctor as Patient in C's "Ward No. 6" and in Solzhenitsyn's *Cancer Ward.* In *C's Art of Writing. A Collection of Critical Essays,* ed. P. Debreczeny & T. Eekman. Columbus: Slavica, 1977, pp. 167-79.

Smith, J. Oates [Joyce Carol Oates]. C and the Theater of the Absurd. *Bucknell Review* 14, 3 (1966):44-58. See also Oates.

Speirs, Logan. Tolstoy and C: The Death of Ivan Ilych and *A Dreary Story. OSP* 8 (1968):81-93.

Sperber, Michael A. The "As If" Personality and C's "The Darling." *Psychoanalytic Review* 58 (1971):14-21.

States, Bert O. C's Dramatic Strategy. *Yale Review* 61 (1966):212-24.

——. The Ironic Drama: C. In his *Irony and Drama: A Poetics.* Ithaca: Cornell UP, 1971, pp. 85-108.

Stewart, Maaja A. Scepticism and Belief in C and Anderson. *Studies in Short Fiction* 9 (1972):29-40.

Stowell, H. Peter. C and the *Nouveau Roman:*Subjective Criticism. In *C's Art of Writing. A Collection of Critical Essays,* ed. P. Debreczeny & T. Eekman. Columbus: Slavica, 1977, pp. 180-92.

——. C's "The Bishop": The Annihilation of Faith and Identity Through Time. *Studies in Short Fiction* 12 (1975): 117-26.

——. C's Prose Fugue "Sleepy." *RLT* 11 (1975):435-42.

——. C's "Steppe": A Journey Through Endless Change. In *Proceedings: Pacific Northwest Conference on Foreign Languages,* 24th Annual Meeting, May 1973, ed. W. C. Kraft. Corvallis: Oregon State U, 1973, 24, pp. 264-69.

Stroeva, M. N. *The Three Sisters* in the Production of the Moscow Art Theatre. In *C: A Collection of Critical Essays,* ed. R. L. Jackson. Englewood Cliffs, NJ: Prentice-Hall, 1967, pp. 121-35.

Strongin, Carol. Irony and Theatricality in C's *The Seagull. Comparative Drama* 15, 4 (1981-82):366-80.

Stroud, T. A. *Hamlet* and *The Seagull. Shakespeare Quarterly* 9 (1958):367-72.

Struve, Gleb. C and Communist Censorship. *SEER* 33 (1955):327-41.

——. On C's Craftsmanship: The Anatomy of a Story. *SlavR* 20 (1961):465-76.

Styan, J. L. C. In his *Dark Comedy: The Development of Modern Comic Tragedy.* Cambridge: Cambridge UP, 1962, pp. 82-119.

——. C's Contribution to Realism. In his *Modern Drama in Theory and Practice.* Cambridge: Cambridge UP, 1981, 81-91.

——. The Delicate Balance: Audience Ambivalence in the Comedy of Shakespeare and C. *Costerus* 2 (1972):159-84.

——. The Idea of a Definitive Production: C in and out of Period. *Comparative Drama* 4 (1970):117-96.

——. Shifting Impressions: *The Cherry Orchard.* In his *The Elements of Drama.* Cambridge: Cambridge UP, 1960, pp., 64-85.

Szewcow, Maria. Anatolij Efros Directs C's *The Cherry Orchard* and Gogol's *The Marriage. Theatre Quarterly* 7 (1977):34-47.

Szogyi, Alex. Aesthetic Structures (Molière and C). In *Proceedings of the 8th Congress of the International Comparative Literature Association.* Vol. 1, ed. B. Kopeczi & G. M. Vajda. Stuttgart: Kunst und Wissen, 1980.

Thompson, Alan Reynolds. C and Naturalism. In *The Anatomy of Drama.* Berkeley: U California P, 1946, pp. 330-38.

Timmer, Charles B. The Bizarre Element in C's Art. In *Anton C 1860-1960: Some Essays,* ed. T. Eekman. Leiden: Brill, 1960, pp. 277-92.

Tolstoi, Lev. An Afterword by Tolstoy to C's Story "Darling." In his *What Is Art? and Essays on Art.* Tr. Aylmer Maude. London: Oxford UP, 1930, pp. 323-27.

Tovstonogov, Georgii. C's *Three Sisters* at the Gorky Theatre. *The Drama Review* 13 (1968):146-55.

Tracy, Robert. A C Anniversary. *SEEJ* 4 (1960):25-34.

Trautmann, Joanne. Doctor C's Prison. In *Healing Arts in Dialogue: Medicine and Literature,* ed. J. Trautmann. Carbondale: So. Illinois UP, 1981, pp. 125-37.

Trilling, Lionel. Commentary to *Three Sisters.* In his *The Experience of Literature: A Reader with Commentaries.* Garden City: Doubleday, 1967, pp. 250-55.

Trofimov, M. V. C's Stories and Dramas. *Modern Language Teaching* (Nov. 1916): 176-86.

True, Warren Roberts. Ed Bullins, Anton C, and the "Drama of Mood." *College Literature Association Journal* 22 (1977): 521-32.

Tulloch, John. Critical Discourses: The Case of C. *Southern Review* 19, 3 (1986):291-318.

Turner, C. J. G. Time in C's *Tri sestry. CSP* 28, 1 (1986):64-79.

Untermeyer, Louis. Anton C. In his *Makers of the Modern World.* NY: Simon & Schuster, 1955, pp. 294-301.

Valency, Maurice. Vershinin. In *C's Great Plays: A Critical Anthology,* ed. J. Barricelli. NY: New York UP, 1981, pp. 218-32.

Vidaver, Doris & Maynard M. Cohen. Dr. A.P. C. *American Scholar* 55, 2 (1986): 227-33.

Vinogradov, V. V. On C's Style. In *Anton C as a Master of Story-Writing,* ed. L. Hulanecki & D. Savignac. The Hague: Mouton, 1976, pp. 169-86.

Vitins, Ieva. Uncle Vanya's Predicament. *SEEJ* 22 (1978):454-63; rpt. in *C's Great Plays: A Critical Anthology,* ed. J. Barricelli. NY: New York UP, 1981, pp. 35-46..

Wear, Richard. C's Trilogy: Another Look at "Ivan Ilych." *Revue Belge de Philologie et d'Histoire.* 55 (1977):897-906.

Welty, Eudora. Reality in C's Stories. In her *The Eye of the Story: Selected Essays and Reviews.* NY: Random House, 1978, pp. 61-81.

Werth, A. Anton C. *SEER* 3 (1924):622-41.

Willcocks, M. P. The Writings of Anton C. *English Review* 34 (1972):207-16.

Williams, Raymond. Anton C. In his *Drama from Ibsen to Eliot.* London: Chatto & Windus, 1965, pp. 126-37.

Wilson, A. The Influence of *Hamlet* upon C's *The Seagull. Susquehanna University Studies* (May 1952):309-16.

Wilson, Edmund. Seeing C Plain. *New Yorker* 28, no. 3 (Nov. 22, 1952):180-98; rpt. in his *A Window on Russia. For the Use of Foreign Readers.* NY: Farrar, Straus, Giroux, 1972, pp. 52-68.

Winner, Anthony. C's Characters: True Tears, Real Things. In his *Characters in the Twilight: Hardy, Zola, and C.* Charlottesville: UP Virginia, 1981.

Winner Thomas G. C and Scientism: Observations on the Searching Stories. In *Anton C: Some Essays,* ed. T. Eekman. Leiden: E. J. Brill, 1960, pp. 325-35.

——. The C Centennial Productions in the Moscow Theatres. *SEEJ* 5 (1961):255-62.

——. C's *Seagull* and Shakespeare's *Hamlet:* A Study of a Dramatic

Device. *ASEER* 15 (1956):103-111; rpt. *C: New Perspectives,* ed. R. & N. Wellek. Englewood Cliffs, NJ: Prentice-Hall, 1984, pp. 107-17.

——. C's *Ward No. 6* and Tolstoyan Ethics. *SEEJ* 17 (1959):321-34.

——. Myth as Device in the Works of C. In *Myth and Symbol: Critical Approaches and Applications,* ed. B. Slote. Lincoln: U Nebraska P, 1963, pp. 71-79.

——. The Poetry of C's Prose: Lyrical Structures in "The Lady with the Dog." In *Language and Literary Theory: In Honor of Ladislav Matejka,* ed. B. Stolz, I. R. Titunik, L. Dolezel. Ann Arbor: University of Michigan, Dept. of Slavic Languages and Literatures, 1984, pp. 609-22.

——. Syncretism in C's Art: A Study of Polystructural Texts. In *C's Art of Writing: A Collection of Critical Essays,* ed. P. Debreczeny & T. Eekman. Columbus: Slavica, 1977, pp. 153-66.

——. Theme and Structure in C's "The Betrothed." *Indiana Slavic Studies* 4 (1967):163-72.

Winslow, Joan. Language and Theme in C's "Misery." *RE: Artes Liberales* 2, 4 (1978):1-7.

Woods, L. C and the Evening Symbol: Cues and Cautions for the Plays in Performance. In *Drama and Symbolism,* ed. J. Redmond. Cambridge: Cambridge UP, 1982, pp. 253-58.

Woolf, Virginia. The Russian Point of View. In her *The Common Reader.* London: 1925, pp. 222-25.

Wright, A. C. Translating C for Performance. *Canadian Review of Comparative Literature* 7 (1980):174-82.

Yermilov, V. *Uncle Vanya:* The Play's Movement. In *C. A Collection of Critical Essays,* ed. R. L. Jackson. Englewood Cliffs, NJ: Prentice-Hall, 1967, pp. 112-20.

Young, Stark. Gulls and C. *Theatre Arts Monthly* 22 (1938):736-42.

Yurieff, Zoya. *Prishedshy:* A. Bely and A. C. In *Andrey Bely: A Critical Review,* ed. G. Janecek. Lexington: UP Kentucky, 1978, pp. 44-55.

Zamyatin, Yevgeny. C. In his *A Soviet Heretic: Essays by Yevgeny Zamyatin,* ed. & tr. M. Ginsburg. Chicago: Chicago UP, 1970, pp. 224-30.

NIKOLAI CHERNYSHEVSKY

Translations

Selected Philosophical Essays. Moscow: Foreign Languages Publishing House, 1953.

Vera Pavlovna's Fourth Dream (From the Novel What Can Be Done?). Tr. Leland Fetzer in his *Pre-Revolutionary Russian Science Fiction (Seven Utopias and a Dream).* Ann Arbor: Ardis, 1982, pp. 58-68.

What Is to Be Done? Tr. N. Dole & S. S. Skidelsky, intro. Kathryn Feuer. Ann Arbor: Ardis, Ann Arbor, 1986. [Reprint of *A Vital Question; or What Is to Be Done?* NY: T. Y. Crowell & Co., 1886.]

What's to Be Done? Tr. Benjamin R. Tucker. NY: Humboldt, 1883.

What Is to Be Done? Tr. Benjamin R. Tucker, revised by L. Turkevich, intro. E. H. Carr. NY: Vintage: 1961. [Abridged edition.]

What Is to Be Done? Tr. Benjamin R. Tucker, revised by L. Turkevich, "expanded" by Cathy Porter. London: Virago, 1982.

What Is to Be Done? Tr. Laura Beraha. Moscow: Raduga Publishers, 1983.

Matlaw Ralph E., ed. *Belinsky, C, Dobrolyubov: Selected Criticism.* Bloomington: Indiana UP, 1976. [Tolstoi's Childhood, Boyhood and Military Tales; The Russian at the Rendezvous.]

Edie, J., J. Scanlan, M. Zeldin, eds. *Russian Philosophy.* Chicago: Quadruple, 1965, vol. 2, pp. 11-60. [The Aesthetic Relations of Art to Reality; The Anthropological Principle in Philosophy.]

Criticism

Paperno Gasparov, I. *C and the Age of*

Realism. A Study in the Semiotics of Behavior. Stanford: Stanford UP, 1988.

Pereira, N. G. O. *The Thought and Teachings of N. G. C.* The Hague: Mouton, 1973.

Randall, Francis B. *N. G. C.* NY: Twayne, 1967.

Woehrlin, William B. *C, The Man and the Journalist.* Cambridge: Harvard UP, 1971.

Paperno Gasparov, Irina. The Individual in Culture: N. G. C. A Study in the Semiotics of Behavior. Ph.D. diss., Stanford, 1984.

Posin. Jack A. C, Dobrolyubov and Pisarev: The Ideological Forefunners of Bolshevism. Ph.D. diss., California, 1939.

Alissandratos, Julia. Hagiographical Commonplaces and Medieval Prototypes in N. G. C's *What Is to Be Done?"* *St. Vladimir's Theological Quarterly* 26, 2 (1982):103-17.

Baghoorn, F. C. The Philosophic Outlook of C: Materialism and Utilitarianism. *ASEER* 6 (1947): 42-56.

Barstow, J. Dostoevskij's *Notes from Underground* versus C's *What is to be Done? College Literature* 5 (1978):24-33.

Bowman, H. Revolutionary Elitism in C. *ASEER* 13 (1954):185-99.

Broyde, A. M. Conflicting Views of C and Dostoevsky on *The Newcomers* by W. Thackeray. *Scando-Slavica* 20 (1974): 39-50.

Davydov, S. Nabokov's Aesthetic Exorcism of C. *CSS* 19 (1985):357-74.

De Maegd-Soëp, Carolina. Women's Emancipation in the Works of C. In *The Emancipation of Women in Russian Literature and Society.* Ghent: Ghent State University, 1978, pp. 261-322.

Dryzhakova, E. Dostoevsky, C and the Rejection of Nihilism. *OSP* 13 (1980): 58-79.

Feuer, Kathryn. What Is to Be Done about *What Is to Be Done?* Intro. *What Is to Be Done?* Ann Arbor: Ardis, 1986, pp. v-xxxiii.

Frank, Joseph. N. G. C: A Russian Utopia. *Southern Review* 3 (1967):68-84.

Gronicka, A. von. Goethe and the Russian Radical N. G. C. *German Review* 49 (1974):29-43.

Hare, Richard. C. In his *Pioneers of Russian Social Thought.* London: Oxford UP, 1951, pp. 171-211.

Hecht, D. Two Classic Russian Publicists and the United States: 1. C and American Slavery; 2. Alexander Herzen and America. *ASEER* 4 (1945):1-32.

Heir, E. C's Lessing. In *Studies in Honour of Louis Shein,* ed. S. D. Cioran. Hamilton, Ont.: McMaster UP, 1983, pp. 55-64.

Katz, Michael. The Conclusion of *What Is to Be Done? RusR* 41 (1982):181-96.

Offord, D. C. Dostoevsky and C. *SEER* 57 (1979):509-30.

Paperno Gasparov, Irina. The Myth of Reality in N. G. C's Works and Life. In *Myth in Literature,* ed. A. Kodjak, K. Pomorska & S. Rudy. Columbus: Slavica, 1985, pp.154-69.

Pereira, N. G. O. N. G. C as Architect of the Politics of Anti-Liberalism in Russia. *RusR* 32 (1973):264-77.

Pogorelskin, A. E. Pypin and C: The "Prolog" Affair Reconsidered. *OSP* 14 (1981):107-20.

Reinhartz, Dennis P. Rakhmetov in C's *What Is To Be Done?* The Origins, Meaning, and Historical Impact of the Character. *Madison College Studies and Research* 29 (1971):5-14.

Scanlan, J. P. C and Rousseau. In *Western Philosophical Systems in Russian Literature: A Collection of Critical Studies,* ed. A. M. Mlikotin. Los Angeles: U Southern California P, 1980, pp. 103-20.

Struve, Gleb. *Monologue interieure:* The Origins of the Formula and the First Statement of Its Possibilities. *PMLA* 69 (1954):1101-11.

Venturi, Franco. C. In *Roots of Revolution,* trans. F. Haskell. NY: Knopf, 1960, pp. 129-86.

Zekulin, G. Forerunner of Socialist Realism: The Novel *What to Do?* by N. G. C. *SEER* 41 (1963):467-83.

VLADIMIR
DAL

Criticism

Baer, Joachim T. *Vladimir Ivanovič D as a Belletrist.* The Hague: Mouton: 1972.

——. The Artistic Work of Vladimir Ivanovič D. *SEEJ* 11 (1967):278-83.

——. Vladimir Ivanovich D: Collector and Recorder of Native Russian Culture. *Die Welt der Slaven* 22 (1977):225-41.

Mersereau, John J. Jr. D. In his *Russian Romantic Fiction.* Ann Arbor: Ardis, 1983, pp. 296-99.

DENIS
DAVYDOV

Translations

Rydel, Christine, ed. *The Ardis Anthology of Russian Romanticism.* Ann Arbor: Ardis, 1984, pp. 56-57.
[To a Pious Charmer; Song of an Old Hussar; Those Evening Bells; Dance.]

Criticism

Leighton, Lauren G. The Anecdote in Russia: Puškin, Vjazemskij, and D. *SEEJ* 10 (1966):155-63.

——. Denis D and *War and Peace.* In *Studies in Honor of Xenia Gasiorowska,* ed. L. Leighton. Columbus: Slavica, 1983, pp. 22-36.

——. Denis D's Hussar Style. *SEEJ* 7 (1963):349-60.

Rozov, Zoja. Denis D and Walter Scott. *SEER* 19 (1940):300-2.

ANTON
DELVIG

Translations

Bowra, C. M., ed. *Second Book of Russian Verse.* London: Macmillan, 1948.
[Romance; Russian Song; Russian Song (*sic*).]

Raffel, B., tr. *Russian Poetry Under the Tsars.* Albany: SUNY, 1971, pp. 104-7.
[Death; Cupid: A Sonnet; Death: An Aphorism.]

Rydel, Christine, ed. *Ardis Anthology of Russian Romanticism.* Ann Arbor: Ardis, 1984, pp. 58-60.
[Inspiration (A Sonnet); The Bathing Women (An Idyll).]

Wiener, L. *Anthology of Russian Literature.* NY: Putnam, 1902-3.
[Sang a Little Bird and Sang; Ah, You Night, You Little Night; Gloomy Thoughts.]

Wilson, C. T., ed. *Russian Lyrics in English Verse.* London: Truebner, 1887.
[The Cottage; Gloomy Thoughts; A Song.]

Criticism

Koehler, Ludmila. *Anton Antonovič D: A Classicist in the Time of Romanticism.* The Hague: Mouton, 1970.

Mersereau, John, Jr. *Baron Delvig's "Northern Flowers" 1825-1832: Literary Almanac of the Pushkin Pleiad.* Carbondale: Southern Illinois UP, 1967.

Barratt, G. R. An Unpublished Letter of A. A. D to Baratynski. *Slavic and East European Studies* 14 (1969): 113-16.

NIKOLAI
DOBROLYUBOV

Selected Philosophical Essays, tr. J. Fineberg. Moscow: Foreign Languages Publishing House, 1948.

Matlaw, Ralph E., ed. *Belinsky, Chernyshevsky, D: Selected Criticism.* Bloomington: Indiana UP, 1976.
[What is Oblomovitis?; When Will the Real Day Come?]

Criticism

Kuhn, Alfred R. The Literary Criticism of N. A. D. Ph.D. diss., Columbia, 1968.

Weinstein, Fred S. Nihilism and Death: A Study of the Life of N. A. D. Ph.D. diss., Berkeley, 1963.

Armstong, Judith. D, Dostoevsky, Injury and Insult. *MelbSS* 14 (1980):79-87.

Jackson, Robert L. Dostoevsky's Critique of the Aesthetics of D. *SlavR* 23 (1964): 258-74.

Kuhn, Alfred. D's Critique of *Oblomov:* Polemics and Psychology. *SlavR* 30 (1971):93-109.

Walicki, Andrzej. D and the Dispute over "Superfluous Men." In his *A History of Russian Thought from the Enlightenment to Marxism.* Stanford: Stanford UP, 1979, pp. 203-9.

FYODOR DOSTOEVSKY

Bibliographies

Dostoevsky Studies. 1980—.
International D Society. Bulletin. (1972)—

Allen, Robert V. D, in Full Measure. *Library of Congress Quarterly* 30 (1973): 229-39. [Bibliographic essay.]

Beebe, Maurice and Christopher Newton. D in English: A Selected Checklist of Criticism and Translations. *Modern Fiction Studies* 4, 3 (1958): 271-91.

Eddelman, Floyd E. D and *The Brothers Karamazov* in English, 1879-1959. Ph.D. diss., Arkansas, 1961.

Freeman, D., J. Pachuta, M. Rice, comps. Retrospective Bibliography: *Prestuplenie i nakazanie. BulDS* 8 (1978): 109-33.

Freeman, D., M. Schatoff, M. Rice, comps. Retrospective Bibliography: *Zapiski iz podpol'ia. BulDS* 5 (1975): 76-88.

Greenberg, Bette. FMD (1821-1888): Medico-Psychological and Psychoanalytic Studies in His Life and Writings: A Bibliography. *Psychoanalytic Review* 62 (1975-76):509-13.

Rice, Martin P. Current Research in the English Language on *Notes from Underground. BulDS* 5 (1975):24-34.

___. & M. Schatoff. The Young D. Selective Bibliography. *BulDS* 3 (1973):51-63.

Whitt, Joseph. The Psychological Criticism of D: 1875-1951, a Study of British, American and Chief European Critics. Ph.D. diss., Temple University.

Translations

The Novels. Tr. Constance Garnett. 12 vols. London: Heineman, 1912-20. [Garnett's translations have been reprinted in numerous editions. In the original 12-volume edition the works are arranged as follows: 1: The Brothers Karamazov 2: The Idiot 3: The Possessed 4: Crime and Punishment 5: The House of the Dead 6: The Insulted and the Injured 7: A Raw Youth 8: The Eternal Husband; The Double; A Gentle Spirit 9: The Gambler; Poor People; The Landlady 10: White Nights; Notes from Underground; A Faint Heart; A Christmas Tree and a Wedding; Polzunkov; A Little Hero; Mr. Prohartchin 11: An Honest Thief; Uncle's Dream; A Novel in Nine Letters; An Unpleasant Predicament; Another Man's Wife; The Heavenly Christmas Tree; The Peasant Marey; The Crocodile; Bobok; The Dream of a Ridiculous Man 12: A Friend of the Family; Nyetochka Nyezvanov.]

The Best Short Stories. Tr. David Magarshack. NY: Modern Library, 1955.
[White Nights; The Honest Thief; The Christmas Tree and a Wedding; The Peasant Marey; Notes from the Underground; A Gentle Creature; The Dream of a Ridiculous Man.]

The Brothers Karamazov. Tr. David Magarshack. London: Folio Society, 1964.

The Brothers Karamazov. Tr. Constance Garnett, revised by Ralph Matlaw; with backgrounds, sources and essays in criticism. NY: Norton, 1976.

Crime and Punishment. Tr. Jesse Coulson, ed. George Gibian with backgrounds, sources, essays in criticism. NY: Norton, 1975.

Crime and Punishment. Tr. Michael Scammell. NY: Washington Square, 1963.

The Crocodile. Tr. & intro. S. D. Cioran. Ann Arbor: Ardis, 1985.

The Devils. Tr. David Magarshack. Baltimore: Penguin, 1954.

The Diary of a Writer. Tr. Boris Brazol.

NY: Braziller, 1954.

The Double. Two Versions. Tr. Evelyn Harden. Ann Arbor: Ardis, 1984.

The Dream of a Queer Fellow, and *The Pushkin Speech.* Tr. S. Koteliansky & J. Middleton Murry. NY: Barnes & Noble, 1961.

The Friend of the Family, and *The Eternal Husband.* Tr. & intro. Philip Rahv. NY: Holt, 1963.

The Gambler; Bobok; A Nasty Story. Tr. Jessie Coulson. Baltimore: Penguin, 1967.

The Gambler, with Polina Suslova's Diary. Tr. Victor Terras. Chicago: U Chicago P, 1972.

The Idiot. Tr. H. & O. Carlisle, intro. H. Rosenberg. NY: New American Library, 1969.

Memoirs from the House of the Dead. Tr. Jessie Coulson. Oxford: Oxford UP, 1965.

Netochka Nezvanova. Tr. Ann Dunnigan. Englewood-Cliffs: Prentice-Hall, 1970.

Notebooks. Ed. Edward Wasiolek. Chicago: U Chicago P, 1967-71. [Crime and Punishment (1967); The Idiot (1967); The Possessed (1968); The Raw Youth (1969); The Brothers Karamazov (1971).]

Notes from Underground and *The Grand Inquisitor.* Selection, tr. & intro. Ralph E. Matlaw. NY: Dutton, 1961.

Notes from Underground. The Double. Tr. Jessie Coulson. Baltimore: Penguin, 1972.

Occasional Writings. Tr. & ed. David Magarshack. London: Vision, 1963.

Poor Folk. Tr. & intro. Robet Dessaix. Ann Arbor: Ardis, 1982.

Stavrogin's Confession, and the Plan of *The Life of a Great Sinner.* Tr. S. Koteliansky & V. Woolf. Richmond, England: L. & V. Woolf, 1922.

Uncle's Dream. Tr. Ivy Litvinov. Moscow: Foreign Languages Publishing House, 1956.

The Unpublished D: Diaries and Notebooks. Ed. Carl R. Proffer, intro. Robert Belknap. 3 vols. Ann Arbor: Ardis, 1973-76.

The Village of Stepanchikovo and Its Inhabitants. Tr. Ignat Avsey. London: Angel Classics, 1983.

Winter Notes on Summer Impressions. Tr. R. Renfield. NY: Criterion, 1954.

Complete Letters. Ed. & tr. David Lowe & Ronald Meyer. 5 vols. Ann Arbor: Ardis, 1988—.

Letters and Reminiscences. Tr. S. Koteliansky & J. Murry. London: Chatto & Windus, 1923.

Letters of D to His Wife. Tr. E. Hill & D. Mudie. London: Constable, 1930.

Letters of Fyodor M. D to His Family and Friends. Tr. E. Mayne. NY: Macmillan, 1914.

Letters of Fedor Mihailovich D. Tr. Ethel C. Mayne. NY: McGraw-Hill, 1964.

Letters of Fyodor Mikhailovich Dostoevsky to His Family and Friends. Tr. Ethel C. Mayne. NY: Horizon Press, 1961. [Tr. from German edition.]

New D Letters. Tr. S. Koteliansky. London: Mandrake, 1929.

Selected Letters of Fyodor D. Tr. Andrew R. MacAndrew. Ed. Joseph Frank & David I. Goldstein. New Brunswick: Rutgers UP, 1987.

Criticism

Anderson, Roger B. *D. Myths of Duality.* Gainesville: U Florida P, 1986.

Bakhtin, Mikhail. *Problems of D's Poetics.* Tr. R. W. Rotsel. Ann Arbor: Ardis, 1973.

——. *Problems of D's Poetics.* Ed. & tr. Caryl Emerson, intro. Wayne C. Booth. Minneapolis: U Minnesota P, 1984.

Belknap, Robert L. *The Structure of "The Brothers Karamazov."* The Hague: Mouton, 1967.

Berdyaev, Nicholas. *D.* Tr. Donald Attwater. NY: Meridian, 1957.

Brown, Nathalie B. *Hugo and D.* Intro. Robert Belknap. Ann Arbor: Ardis, 1978.

Burnett, L. *F. M. D (1821-1881). A Centenary Collection.* Colchester: Department of Literature, U Essex, 1981.

Carr, Edward Hallett. *D (1821-1881): A New Biography*. London: George Allen & Unwin, 1931.

Carroll, J. *Break-Out from the Crystal Palace: The Anarcho-Psychological Critique: Stirner, Nietzsche, D*. London: Routledge and Kegan Paul, 1974.

Cascardi, A. J. *The Bounds of Reason: Cervantes, D, Flaubert*. NY: Columbia UP, 1986.

Černý, Václav. *D and His Devils*. Tr. F. W. Galan. Ann Arbor: Ardis, 1975.

Chapple, Richard. *A D Dictionary*. Ann Arbor: Ardis, 1983.

Coulson, Jessie. *D: A Portrait*. Westport, CT: Greenwood, 1975.

———. *D: A Self-Portrait*. NY: Oxford, 1962.

Cox, Gary D. *Tyrant and Victim in D*. Columbus: Slavica, 1983.

Curle, R. *Characters of D: Studies from Four Novels*. London, 1950.

Dalton, Elizabeth. *Unconscious Structure in "The Idiot": A Study in Literature and Psychoanalysis*. Princeton: Princeton UP, 1979.

De Jonge, Alex. *D and the Age of Intensity*. NY: St. Martin's P, 1975.

Dolenc, Ivan. *D and Christ. A Study of D's Rebellion Against Belinsky*. Toronto: York, 1978.

Dostoevsky, Aimee. *Fyodor D: A Study*. New Haven: Yale UP, 1922.

Dostoevsky, Anna. *Dostoevsky: Reminiscences*. NY: Liveright, 1975.

Dowler, Wayne. *D, Grigor'ev and Native Soil Conservatism*. Toronto: Toronto UP, 1982.

Dunlop, John B. *Staretz Amvrosy: Model for D's Staretz Zossima*. Belmont, MA: Nordland, 1972.

Eng, Jan van der & J. M. Meijer. *The Brothers Karamazov by F. M. D. Essays*. The Hague: Mouton, 1971.

Fanger, Donald. *D and Romantic Realism: A Study of D in Relation to Balzac, Dickens and Gogol*. Cambridge: Harvard UP, 1965.

Frank, Joseph. *D. The Seeds of Revolt, 1821-1849*. Princeton: Princeton UP, 1976.

———. *D: The Stir of Liberation, 1860-1865*. Princeton: Princeton UP, 1986.

———. *D. The Years of Ordeal, 1850-1859*. Princeton: Princeton UP, 1983.

Fülöp-Miller, R. *D*. Madrid: Espasa, 1974.

Gibson, A. B. *The Religion of D*. Philadelphia: Westminster, 1973.

Gide, André. *D*. NY: New Directions, 1961.

Goldstein, David. *D and the Jews*. Austin: U Texas P, 1981.

Gorodetzky, N. *Saint Tikhon of Zadonsk: Inspirer of D*. Crestwood, NY: St. Vladimir's Seminary P, 1976. [Reprint of 1951 edition.]

Grishin, D. *D's Speech in Honor of Pushkin*. Melbourne: U Melbourne, 1974.

Grossman, Leonid. *Balzac and D*. Tr. Lena Karpov. Ann Arbor: Ardis, 1973.

———. *D. His Life and Work*. Indianapolis: Bobbs-Merrill, 1975.

Guérard, A. *The Triumph of the Novel: Dickens, D and Faulkner*. London: Oxford UP, 1976.

Hingley, Ronald. *D. His Life and Work*. NY: Scribners, 1978.

———. *The Undiscovered D*. London: H. Hamilton, 1962.

Holquist, Michael. *D and the Novel*. Princeton: Princeton UP, 1977.

Ivanov, Vyacheslav. *Freedom and the Tragic Life: A Study in D*. Tr. Norman Cameron, foreword by Sir Maurice Bowra. NY: Noonday Press, 1957.

Jackson, Robert Louis. *The Art of D: Deliriums and Nocturnes*. Princeton: Princeton UP, 1981.

———. *D's Quest for Form. A Study of His Philosophy of Art*. Bloomington: Physsardt, 1978.

———. *D's Underground Man in Russian Literature*. The Hague: Mouton, 1958.

———, ed. *D: New Perspectives*. Englewood Cliffs, NJ: Prentice-Hall, 1984.

Johnson, Leslie A. *The Experience of Time in "Crime and Punishment."* Columbus: Slavica, 1985.

Jones, John. *D*. Oxford: Clarendon Press, 1983.

Jones, Malcolm V. & Terry M. Garth. *New Essays on D*. Cambridge: Cambridge UP, 1983.

Jones, Malcolm. *D. The Novel of Discord*. NY: Barnes & Noble, 1976.

Kabat, Geoffrey. *Ideology and Imagination: The Image of Society in D*. NY: Columbia UP, 1978.

Kent, Leonard J. *The Subconscious in Gogol' and D, and Its Antecedents.* The Hague: Mouton, 1969.

Kirk, Irina. *D and Camus.* Munich: Fink, 1974.

Kjetsaa, Geir. *D and His New Testament.* Atlantic Highlands, NJ: Humanities Press, 1984.

Knapp, Liza, ed. & tr. *D as Reformer: The Petrashevsky Case.* Ann Arbor: Ardis, 1987.

Kostovski, I. *D and Goethe. Two Devils, Two Geniuses: A Study of the Demonic in Their Work.* NY: Revisionist, 1974.

Krag, E. *D: The Literary Artist.* Tr. Sven Larr. Oslo: Universitetsforlaget, 1976.

Kuznetzov, B. *Einstein and D.* London: Hutchinson, 1972.

Lary, N. M. *D and Dickens.* London: Routledge Kegan Paul, 1973.

——. *D and Soviet Film.* Ithaca: Cornell UP, 1986.

Lavrin, Janko. *D. A Study.* London: Methuen, 1943.

Leatherbarrow, William. *Fedor D.* Boston: Twayne, 1981.

Linner, Sven. *D on Realism.* Stockholm: Almqvist & Wiksell, 1967.

——. *Starets Zosima in "The Brothers Karamazov": A Study in the Mimesis of Virtue.* Stockholm: Almqvist & Wiksell, 1975.

Lloyd, John A. *Fyodor D.* Darby, PA: Arden Library, 1978.

Lord, Robert T. *D: Essays and Perspectives.* Berkeley: U California P, 1970.

MacPike, L. *D's Dickens.* Totowa, NJ: Barnes & Noble, 1981.

Magarshack, David. *D.* London: Secker & Warburg, 1962.

Matlaw, Ralph E. *"The Brothers Karamazov": Novelistic Technique.* 's-Gravenhage: Mouton, 1957.

Meier-Graefe, Julius. *D. The Man and His Work.* Tr. H. H. Marks. NY: Haskell, 1972.

Meyer, Priscilla & Stephen Rudy, eds. *D and Gogol: Texts and Criticism.* Ann Arbor: Ardis, 1979.

Mikhailovsky, N. *D: A Cruel Talent.* Tr. S.

Cadmus. Ann Arbor: Ardis, 1978.

Miller, Robin Feuer. *Critical Essays on D.* Boston: Hall, 1986.

——. *D and "The Idiot": Author, Narrative and Reader.* Cambridge: Harvard UP, 1981.

Mochulsky, Konstantin. *D: His Life and Work.* Tr. M. Minihan. Princeton: Princeton UP, 1967.

Morson, Gary Saul. *The Boundaries of Genre: D's "Diary of a Writer" and the Traditions of Literary Utopia.* Austin: U Texas P, 1981.

Muchnic, Helen: *D's English Reputation, 1881-1936.* NY: Octagon, 1969. [Reprint of 1939 edition.]

Nuttall, A. D. *D's "Crime and Punishment": Murder as Philosophic Experiment.* Sussex: Sussex UP, 1978.

Obolensky, Alexander & Nadine Natov, eds. *Transactions of the Association of Russian-American Scholars in the USA,* vol. 14, Dostoevsky Commemorative volume. NY, 1981.

Pachmuss, Temira. *F. M. D: Dualism and Synthesis of the Human Soul.* Carbondale: Southern Illinois UP, 1963.

Panichas, George A. *The Burden of Vision: D's Spiritual Art.* Grand Rapids: Eerdmans, 1977.

Passage, Charles E. *Character Names in D's Fiction.* Ann Arbor: Ardis, 1982.

——. *D the Adapter: A Study in D's Use of the Tales of Hoffman.* Chapel Hill: U of North Carolina P, 1954.

Payne, Robert. *D: A Human Portrait.* NY: Knopf, 1961.

Peace, Richard. *D: An Examination of the Major Novels.* NY: Cambridge UP, 1971.

Perlina, Nina. *Varieties of Poetic Utterance: Quotation in "The Brothers Karamazov."* Lanham, MD: University Press of America, 1985.

Powys, John Cowper. *D.* London: Village P, 1974. [Reprint of 1946 ed.]

Proctor, Thelwall. *D and the Belinskij School of Literary Criticism.* The Hague: Mouton, 1969.

Rice, James L. *D and the Healing Art. An Essay in Literary and Medical History.*

Ann Arbor: Ardis, 1985.

Rosenshield, Gary. *"Crime and Punishment": The Techniques of the Omniscient Author.* Lisse: P. de Ridder P, 1978.

Rowe, W. W. *D: Child and Man in His Works.* NY: New York UP, 1968.

Rozanov, Vasily. *D and the Legend of the Grand Inquisitor.* Tr. & afterword Spencer E. Roberts. Ithaca: Cornell UP, 1972.

Sajkovic, M. *F. M. D: His Image of Man.* Philadelphia: U Pennsylvania P, 1962.

Sandoz, E. *Political Apocalypse: A Study of D's Grand Inquisitor.* Baton Rouge: Louisiana State UP, 1971.

Seduro, V. *D in Russian and World Theatre.* North Quincey, MA: Christopher, 1977.

___ *D in Russian Literary Criticism. 1846-1956.* NY: Columbia UP, 1957.

___ *D's Image in Russia Today.* Belmont, MA: Nordland, 1975.

Shestov, Lev. *D, Tolstoy and Nietzsche.* Tr. B. Martin & S. Roberts; intro. B. Martin. Athens: Ohio UP, 1969.

Shneidman, N. N. *D and Suicide.* NY: Mosaic Press, 1984.

Simmons, Ernest J. *D: The Making of a Novelist.* Gloucester, MA: P. Smith, 1965 [rpt. 1940 edition].

___ *Feodor D.* NY: Columbia UP, 1968.

Slattery, Dennis Patrick. *"The Idiot": Dostoevsky's Fantastic Prince. A Phenomenological Approach.* NY: P. Lang, 1983.

Slonim, Marc. *Three Loves of D.* NY: Rinehart & Co., 1955.

Soloviev, Evgenii. *D, His Life and Literary Activity; A Biographical Sketch.* Tr. C. J. Hogarth. Folcroft, PA: Folcroft Library, 1973.

Soviet Literature (Moscow). "D and Today's World." 100th Anniversary Issue, no. 12 (1981).

Steinberg, A. *D.* London: Bowes & Bowes, 1967.

Steiner, George. *Tolstoy or D: An Essay in the Old Criticism.* NY: Knopf, 1959.

Stock, Irvin. *Fiction as Wisdom: From Goethe to Bellow.* University Park: Pennsylvania State UP, 1980.

Terras, Victor. *F. M. D. Life, Works and Criticism.* Fredericton, New Brunswick: York P, 1984.

___ *A Karamazov Companion. Commentary on the Genesis, Language, and Style of D's Novel.* Madison: U Wisconsin P, 1981.

___ *The Young D (1846-1849): A Critical Study.* The Hague: Mouton, 1969.

Troyat, Henri. *Firebrand: The Life of D.* NY: Roy Publishers, 1946.

Ugrinsky, Alexej, Frans S. Lambasa & Valija K. Ozolins, eds. *D and the Human Condition after a Century.* NY: Greenwood P, 1986.

Villadsen, P. *The Underground Man and Raskolnikov.* Odense: Odense UP, 1981.

Vladiv, S. B. *Narrative Priciples in D's "Besy". A Structural Analysis.* Berne: P. Lang, 1979.

Wasiolek, Edward, ed. *"The Brothers Karamazov" and the Critics.* Belmont: Wadsworth, 1967.

___ ed. *"Crime and Punishment" and the Critics.* San Francisco: Wadsworth, 1960.

___ *D: The Major Fiction.* Cambridge: MIT P, 1964.

Weisberger, Jean. *Faulkner and D. Influence and Confluence.* Tr. D. McWilliams. Athens: Ohio UP, 1974.

Wellek, René, ed. *D: A Collection of Critical Essays.* Englewood Cliffs, NJ: Prentice-Hall, 1962.

Yarmolinsky, Avrahm. *D: His Life and Art.* 2d ed., compl. rev. & enl. NY: Criterion, 1959.

___ *D: Works and Days.* NY: Funk & Wagnalls, 1971.

Dissertations

Adler, Judith Lowitz. Spatial Configuration in Late D. Pennsylvania, 1976.

Arenberg, Carol Rakita. The Double as an Initiation Rite: A Study of Chamisso, Hoffmann, Poe and D. Washington, St. Louis, 1979.

Banerjee, Maria N. The Religious and Metaphysical Interpretation of D from

Vladimir Solov'ev to Berdjaev: A Study of Six "Great Commentaries." Radcliffe, 1962.

Belknap, Robert L. The Structure of *The Brothers Karamazov*. Columbia, 1960.

Bergman, Eugene. The Divided Self in Hawthorne and D. George Washington, 1978.

Beveridge, Nancy Lourie. The Composition of D's Novel *The Devils*. Michigan, 1979.

Boll, R. W. D and the English Novel. Bristol, 1983.

Brand, H. E. Extreme Forms of Reality as an Expression of Religious Convictions in Heinrich Von Kleist and Fedor M. D. Waterloo,1969.

Bricker, Emil S. Duality in the Novels of William Faulkner and Fyodor D. Michigan, 1971.

Brown, Natalie Babel. A Structural and Thematic Analysis of Fyodor D's *Crime and Punishment* in Relation to Victor Hugo's *Les Miserables*. Columbia, 1971.

Cardaci, Paul F., Jr. Demon, Daimon, and Devil: A Study of the Demonic Element in D, Gide, and Mann. Maryland, 1972.

Carey, Marjorie Ann. Slavic Roots in D and Conrad: A Study in Themes and Narrative Conventions. Notre Dame, 1977.

Cassie, Kenneth Robert. The Narrative Technique in D's *Besy*. New York, 1972.

Chances, Ellen Bell. The Ideology of "Počvenničestvo" in D's Journals *Vremja* and *Epokha*. Princeton, 1972.

Clews, Hetty June. The Teller, Not the Tale: Studies in the Monologue Novel. Saskatchewan, 1979.

Cooper, David Jay. The Oscillations of the Double: Shakespeare and D. SUNY, Buffalo, 1978.

Dalton, Elizabeth Carville. Unconscious Structure in D's *The Idiot*. Columbia, 1975.

Danow, David Kevin. Structural Principles of *The Brothers Karamazov*. Brown, 1977.

Daugherty, Howard A. A Study of the Buffoon in the Novels of D. Washington, Seattle, 1968.

De Alvarez, Helen Canniff. The Augustinian Basis of D's *The Brothers Karamazov*. Dallas, 1977.

Devrnja, Milutin P. The Conceptions of Human Existence in the Early Works of F. M. D. Syracuse, 1972.

Dodd, W. J. Kafka and D: Influence and Affinities. Leeds, 1982.

Donahue, Bruce Elliot. From Despair to Irrational Faith: A Study of Kleist, Byron and D. Oregon, 1979.

Eddleman, Floyd E. D and *The Brothers Karamazov* in English, 1879-1959. Arkansas, 1961.

Estrada, Charles. Freedom and the Personality in the Thought of André Gide, Albert Camus and Fyodor D. Fordham, 1965.

Fayer, Mischa H. Gide, Freedom and D. Columbia, 1946.

Fitzgerald, Gene D. Antithetic Stylistic Elements in D's Narrative. Wisconsin, 1971.

Frank, Joseph. D and Russian Nihilism: A Context for *Notes From Underground*. Chicago, 1961.

French, Bruce Arnold. An Analysis of D's Novel *The Idiot*. New York, 1985.

Frucht-Levy, Michele. The Generic Coherence of Motifs in D and D. H. Lawrence. North Carolina, 1980.

Gasster, Susan C. Point of View in the Novels of Zola, Galdós, D, and Tolstoy: A Study in the Development of the Novel. George Washington, 1969.

Ginsburg, Carl. The Reception and Early Influence of D in France. Harvard, 1940.

Gransar, Fereshteh Nazerzadeh Kermani. The Interpretation of D's *Crime and Punishment* as It Applies to a Philosophy of Leadership for the Educator/Administrator. North Dakota, 1982.

Gregory, Serge Vladimir. The Literary Milieu of D's *The Possessed*. Washington, Seattle, 1977.

Grigorieff, Dmitry Felix. D and the Russian Orthodox Church. Pennsylvania, 1958.

Hafrey, Leigh Gidal. Parabola: The Interpolated Tale as Parable in Diderot, Goethe and D. Yale, 1978.

Hamilton, Robert M., Jr. Uses of the Pastoral in Dickens and D. Columbia, 1974.

Hardie, Frances Isley. D as Crime Writer: The Dangerous Edge. Vanderbilt, 1980.

Hetfield, Edwin Lambert. Language and Politics: A Study of the Relationship Between Literary Representation and Political Theory in the Novels of D and Conrad. SUNY, Buffalo, 1980.

Holquist, James M. Non-Realistic Modes in the Prose Fiction of Gogol and D. Yale, 1968.

Hucko, Grace Miriam. The Uses of the Narrator in D's *The Devils*. Yale, 1974.

Jackson, Robert Louis. Studies on D's *Notes from the Underground* in Russian Literature. California, 1956.

Jones, Anne Hudson. The Plight of the Modern Outsider: A Comparative Study of D's *Crime and Punishment*, Camus's *L'Etranger* and Wright's *The Outsider*. North Carolina, 1974.

Keller, Howard Hughes. D's Buffoon: A Study in Alienation. Georgetown, 1967.

Kent, Leonard Joseph. The Subconscious in Gogol and D and its Antecedents. Yale, 1965.

Kesarcodi-Watson, Ihita. F. M. D's Soteriology Related to Some Female Types in His Fiction. Northwestern, 1978.

King, Don Wayne. Exile in the Fiction of Joseph Conrad and Fyodor D. North Carolina, Greensboro, 1985.'

King, Henry H. D and Andreyev: Gazers Upon the Abyss. Columbia, 1936.

Kirk, Irene. Polemics, Ideology, Structure, and Texture in A. Camus' *The Fall* and F. D's *Notes from Underground*. Indiana, 1968.

Klotz, Kenneth. Comedy and the Grotesque in Dickens and D. Yale, 1973.

Knapp, Liza Atkinson. D and the Annihilation of Inertia: The Metaphysics of Physics in His Works. Columbia, 1985.

Knight, S. C. The Function of Quotation in D. Essex, 1976.

Koprince, Ralph Gordon. The Episode in *Crime and Punishment*. Michigan, 1977.

Levinsky, Ruth. Between Dream and Reality: A Study of Nathalie Sarraute and Fedor D. Southern California, 1969.

Levy, Constance Andrea. Nineteenth-Century Novels of Introversion. New York, 1981.

Livermore, Gordon Dexter. D's *Devils:* The Unifying Conflicts. Yale, 1978.

Logan, Richard M. D's *Djadjuškin son.* Los Angeles, 1985.

Lynch, Michael Francis. D, Richard Wright, and Ralph Ellison: The Choice of Individual Freedom and Dignity. Kent State, 1985.

Magretta, Joan Barbara Gorin. The Iconography of Madness: A Study in Melville and D. Michigan, 1976.

Mairs, Tanya E. Nihilism as Crime and Punishment: A Study of D's Anti-Nihilism in the 1860's. Columbia, 1982.

Makinen, Robert Samuel. D's Underground Man in Zamjatin's Single State. Pittsburgh, 1974.

Mara, William P. The Forerunner of Communism as Seen in the Major Works of Fyodor D. Fordham, 1953.

Martin, Thomas Scott. D's Concept of a Nation. Missouri, 1985.

Mead, Alfred D. D in Detail: A Study of the Artistic and Literary Contributions of His Descriptions of Living Quarters. Vanderbilt, 1971.

Miller, Robin Feuer. The Multi-Voiced Narrator of *The Idiot:* An Approach to Understanding the Narrative Methods in D's Novels. Columbia, 1977.

Minihan, Michael Allen. Mochulsky's *D.* Brown, 1984.

Mondry, Henrietta. The Evaluation of Recent Trends in Soviet D Scholarship (1970s-1980s). Witwatersrand (South Africa), 1984.

Morrison, Susan Leslie. F. M. D's *The Insulted and Injured:* A Transitional Novel. Vanderbilt, 1984.

Morson, Gary Saul. D's *Diary of a Writer:* Threshold Art. Yale, 1974.

Mosca, Frank K. The Tradition of the Apocalypse in D. New York, 1971.

Muchnic, Helen. D's English Reputation. Bryn Mawr, 1937.

Murav-Lavigne, Harriet Lisa. Scandalous

Folly: The Discourse of *Iurodstvo* in the Works of D. Stanford, 1985.

Murdoch, David Douglas. D as a Comic Novelist. Occidental College, 1963.

Murphy, Terry Wade. D and Tolstoy on Dickens' Christianity. Kent State, 1973.

Nakeeb, Diana Gosselin. The Earliest D: Style and Meaning in His Translation of *Eugénie Grandet*. Columbia, 1972.

Oliver, Donna S. The Disease of Consciousness in the Dostoevskian Hero: The Adverse Effects of Heightened Self-Awareness. Northwestern, 1985.

Olivero, Antonio. Fyodor D, Psychologist and Teacher: A Psychologico-Philosophical Study of *The Brothers Karamazov* and Its Implications. Texas, 1968.

Padunov, Vladimir. D's *The Devils* and the Form of Tendentious Narration. Cornell, 1983.

Palumbo, Donald Emmanuel. Faith, Identity, and Perception—Three Existential Crises in Modern Fiction and Their Artistic Reconciliation: A Comparison of the Fiction of D, Joyce, Kafka, and Faulkner from the Perspective of the Works of Sartre and Camus. Michigan, 1976.

Perelmuter, Joanna Elizabeth. The Substandard Lexical Features in D's Post-Exile Literary Works. McGill, 1971.

Phillips, Roger William. D's *Underground* Narrator: A Study in the Psychology and Structure of Contradiction. Illinois, 1970.

Pisani, Assunta Sarnacchiaro. The Raging Impotence: Humor in the Novels of D, Faulkner and Beckett. Brown, 1976.

Popluiko-Natov, Nadine N. Camus and D: A Comparative Study. Michigan, 1969.

Pribic, Rado. Bonaventura's *Nachtwachen* and D's *Notes from the Underground:* A Comparison in Nihilism. Vanderbilt, 1973.

Proctor, Thelwall True. D and the Belinskij School of Literary Criticism. California, Berkeley, 1962.

Rawlings, Carl D. Prophecy in the Novel. Washington, 1973.

Ries, Joachim Schutmann. Camus the Adapter: An Analysis of Camus' Dramatization of D's Novel *The Possessed*. Washington, Seattle, 1965.

Roberts, Christina H. Gide and D. Toronto, 1969.

Rogers, Elizabeth Lee. A Study of Multiplicity Manifested in the Protagonists of Five Novels by Fyodor D, James Joyce, Herman Hesse and Max Frisch. North Carolina, 1974.

Rogers, Joseph Aloysius. Moral Freedom as the Key to D's Major Novels. St. Louis, 1957.

Rosenshield, Gary. The Narrator in *Crime and Punishment*. Wisconsin, 1972.

Rowe, William Woodin. The Child in D. New York, 1968.

Rysten, Felix Simon Anton. False Prophets in Fiction: Camus, D, Melville, and Others. Southern California, 1969.

Sattin, Jerry Paul. Allegory in Modern Fiction: A Study of *Moby Dick, The Brothers Karamazov* and *Die Verwandung*. Illinois, 1978.

Scheinman, Marc Noel. The Morality of Violence: An Investigation of D, Malraux, and Camus. Indiana, 1974.

Schwab, Gweneth Boge. Theological Implications of Suffering Children in Teaching Four Novels by D, Camus, Golding, Greene. Illinois State, 1982.

Sheade, Carole Ann. D: A Hermeneutical Interpretation of *Crime and Punishment*. Northwestern, 1979.

Simon, Leslie A. J. Subjective Time in *Crime and Punishment*. New York, 1980.

Slater, A. J. D's Attitude to Institutionalized Religion. Liverpool, 1983.

Slattery, Dennis Patrick. *The Idiot:* D's Fantastic Prince. Dallas, 1976.

Smith, Jeremy. Religious Feeling and Religious Commitment in Faulkner, Werfel, and Bernanos. Indiana, 1985.

Smith, Leslie Wright. The Exclusive Confessant: A Study of Author and Character in D, Mauriac, and O'Connor. Texas, 1986.

Spiegel, John. Laughter in *Crime and Punishment:* Its Forms, Functions and Implications. Columbia, 1986.

Stewart, Marilyn Gump. The Festive Irony of Carnival: Comic Affirmation in *Don Quixote, The Brothers Karamazov*, and *The Rievers*. Dallas, 1980.

Stanton, Leonard Joseph. Optina Pustyn' in Russian Secular Literature: Backgrounds, Sources and Legacy: A Study of the Monastery, Its Elders, and Monks in D's *The Brothers Karamazov* and Works by Konstantin Leont'ev, Kliment Zedergol'm, Vasilij Rozanov, Lev Tolstoj, and Vladimir Solouxin. Kansas, 1984.

Sugden, John Neil. Thomas Mann and D: A Study of *Doctor Faustus* in Comparison with *The Brothers Karamazov*. Cambridge, 1981-82.

Szczepanska, K. *The Double* and Double Consciousness in D. Stanford, 1978.

Terras, Victor. The Stylistic Craftsmanship of the Young D, 1846-1849. Chicago, 1963.

Thompson, Diane Ella Oenning. *The Brothers Karamazov* and the Poetics of Memory. Cambridge, 1986.

Toews, Gurney Dwight. A Study of the Relationship Between the Human Will and the Learning Process: An Examination of Stavrogin, a Character in D's *The Possessed*. North Dakota, 1981.

Troncate, Joseph Charles. D's Use of Scripture in *The Brothers Karamazov*. Cornell, 1979.

Vacquier, Tatiana. D and Gide, A Comparison. Wisconsin, 1927.

Vaux, Sara Catherine Anson. The Fool and the Two Kingdoms: Radical Revolution in *King Lear, Little Dorrit,* and *The Brothers Karamazov*. Rice, 1974.

Ward, Bruce Kinsey. D's Critique of the West. McMaster, 1981.

Webb, Donald A. The Life and Works of D: A Theological and Depth-Psychological Study. Drew, 1967.

Weisberg, Richard H. Literature as Negativity: *Ressentiment* in D and Flaubert. Cornell, 1970.

Whitt, Joseph. Psychological Criticism of D, 1875-1951. Temple, 1953.

Williams, Michael Gary. Politics Without Love: Anarchism in Turgenev, D, and James. Michigan, 1974.

Yarmolinsky, Avrahm. D: A Study in His Ideology. Columbia, 1921.

Zahniser, R. W. The Autobiographical Hero of Gustav Sack and the Tradition of the Dostoevskian Underground Man. Arkansas, 1974.

Zbilut, Joseph Peter. Dostoevskian Romanticism: From Irony to Existentiality. Northwestern, 1973.

Articles

Abel, Lionel. A Taste for D. *Commentary* 78, 5 (Nov. 1984):36-41.

Adair, W. *Portnoy's Complaint:* A Comparative Version of *Notes from Underground*. *Notes on Contemporary Literature* 7, 3 (1977):9-10.

Adams, B. B. Sisters under Their Skins: The Women in the Lives of Raskolnikov and Razumov. *Conradiana* 6 (1974):113-24.

Alexandrov, V. E. The Narrator as Author in D's *Besy*. *RusL* 15, 2 (1984):243-54.

Allen, Robert V. D in Full Measure. *Quarterly Journal of the Library of Congress* 30 (1973):229-39.

Alm, B. M. The Four Horsemen and the Lamb: Structure and Balance in *Crime and Punishment*. *McNeese Review* 21 (1974-75):72-79.

Amend, Victor E. Theme and Form in *The Brothers Karamazov*. *MFS* 4 (1958): 240-52.

Anderson, Roger B. *Crime and Punishment:* Psychomyth and the Making of a Hero. *CASS* 11, 4 (1977):523-38.

——. D's Hero in *The Double:* A Reexamination of the Divided Self. *Symposium* 26 (1972):101-13.

——. The Meaning of Carnival in *The Brothers Karamazov*. *SEEJ* 23 (1979): 458-78.

——. Mythical Implications of Father Zosima's Religious Teachings. *SlavR* 38 (1979):272-89.

——. Raskol'nikov and the Myth Experience. *SEEJ* 20 (1976):1-17.

Annas, J. Action and Character in D's *Notes from Underground. Philosophy and Literature* 1 (1977):257-75.

Argus, M. K. Dostoevskian Tolerance. *Saturday Review* 41 (Oct. 9, 1965): 6,12.

Arisian, Khoren, Jr. The Grand Inquisitor Revisited: An Inquiry into the Character of Human Freedom. *Crane Review* 9 (1967):149-58.

Armstrong, J. Dobroliubov, D, Injury and Insult. *MelbSS* 14 (1980):79-87.

Arseniev, Nicholas. The Central Inspiration of D. *Transactions of the Association of Russian-American Scholars in the USA* 5 (1971):7-17.

Astrov, V. D on Edgar Allan Poe. *American Literature* 14 (1942):70-74.

———. Hawthorne and D as Explorers of the Human Conscience. *New England Quarterly* 15 (1942):296-319.

Bagby, Lewis. On D's Conversion: The Introduction to *Notes from a Dead House. Symposium* 39, 1 (1985):3-18.

Bakhtin, M. D's Dialogue. *Soviet Literature* 2 (1971):127-40.

Banerjee, Maria. "The American Revolver": An Essay on D's *The Devils. MFS* 27 (1981):278-83.

———. Rozanov on D. *SEEJ* 15 (1971):411-24.

Barksdale, E. D and Euripedes: A New Humanism in Christian Tragedy. *Révue belge de philologie et d'histoire* 52, 2 (1974):626-35.

Barran, Thomas. Dark Uses of Confession: Rousseau and D's Stavrogin. *Mid-Hudson Language Studies* (Poughkeepsie) 1 (1978):97-112.

Barry, Catherine A. Some Transpositions of D in *Les faux-monnayeurs. French Review* 45 (1972):580-87.

Barstow, Jane. D's *Notes from Underground* versus Chernyshevsky's *What Is to Be Done? College Literature* 5 (1978):24-33.

Batchelor, R. D and Camus: Similarities and Contrasts. *Journal of European Studies* 5 (1975):111-51.

———. Literature, Society and the Concept of Revolt. *European Studies Review* 5, 4 (1975):395-427.

Baumgarten, Murray. The Extraordinary Events of *The Devils. Western Humanities Review* (Utah) 22 (1968):23-33.

Beardsley, Monroe C. D's Metaphor of the "Underground." *Journal of the History of Ideas* 3 (1942):265-90.

Beatty, J. From Rebellion and Alienation to Salutary Freedom: A Study in *Notes from Underground. Soundings* 61 (1978): 182-205.

Beebe, Maurice. The Three Motives of Raskolnikov: A Reinterpretation of *Crime and Punishment. College English* 17 (1955):151-58.

Behrendt, Patricia F. The Russian Iconic Representation of the Christian Madonna: A Feminine Archetype in *Notes from Underground.* In *D and the Human Condition after a Century,* ed. A. Ugrinsky, et al. NY: Greenwood P, 1986, pp. 133-43.

Belknap, Robert L. D's Nationalist Ideology and Rhetoric. *Review of National Literatures* 3 (1972):89-100.

———. Memory in *The Brothers Karamazov.* In *American Contributions to the Eighth International Congress of Slavists,* vol. 2, ed. V. Terras. Columbus: Slavica, 1978, pp. 21-40.

———. The Origins of Alëša Karamazov. In *American Contributions to the Sixth International Congress of Slavists,* vol. 2, ed. W. E. Harkins. The Hague: Mouton: 1968, pp. 7-27.

———. The Origins of Mitja Karamazov. In *VII Międzynarodowy Kongres Slawistów w Warszawie 1973: Streszczenia referatów i komunikatów.* Warsaw: PAN, 1973, p. 435.

———. Recent Soviet Scholarship and Criticism on D: A Review Article. *SEEJ* 11 (1967):75-86.

———. The Rhetoric of an Ideological Novel. In *Literature and Society in Imperial Russia, 1800-1914,* ed. W. M. Todd III. Stanford: Stanford UP, 1978, pp. 173-201.

———. The Sources of Mitja Karamazov. In *American Contributions to the Seventh International Congress of Slavists,* vol. 2, ed. V. Terras. The Hague: Mouton, 1973, pp. 39-51.

Bell, G. "The Child is Father to the Man": A Brief Study on D's Knowledge of Children, Exemplified by His Story "A Little Hero." *NZSJ* 8 (1971):32-48.

Bell, Linda. A. Dialectic in D's *Notes from Underground. Journal of Thought* 12 (1977):136-46.

Belov, Sergei. D's Last Love: Notes of a Biographer. Tr. R. Daglish. *Soviet Literature* 9 (1986):66-94.

Bem, A. L. "The Nose" and "The Double."

Tr. P. B. Stetson. In *Dostoevsky and Gogol: Texts and Criticism,* ed. P. Meyer & S. Rudy. Ann Arbor: Ardis, 1979, pp. 229-48.

——. The Problem of Guilt. In *Twentieth Century Interpretations of "Crime and Punishment": A Collection of Critical Essays,* ed. R. L. Jackson. Englewood Cliffs: Prentice-Hall, 1974, pp. 77-80.

Bercovitch, S. Dramatic Irony in *Notes from the Underground. SEEJ* 8 (1964): 284-95.

Berdyaev, N. The Problem of Evil. In *Twentieth Century Interpretations of "Crime and Punishment": A Collection of Critical Essays,* ed. R. L. Jackson. Englewood Cliffs: Prentice-Hall, 1974, pp. 71-76.

Berry, T. E. D and Spiritualism. *DostSt* 2 (1981):43-49.

Bertensson, Sergei. *The Brothers Karamazov* at the Moscow Art Theater. *ASEER* 16 (1957):74-78.

Besançon, A. Michelet and Dostoyevskism in History. *Clio* 6 (1977):131-47.

Beyer, Thomas R., Jr. D's *Crime and Punishment. Explicator* 41, 1 (1982): 33-36.

Bizans, A. The "Grand Inquisitor" Motif in Samuel Butler's *Erewhon Revisited. Révue de Littérature Comparée* 47, 3 (1973):369-83.

Blackmur, R. P. *Crime and Punishment:* A Study. *Chimera* 1, 3 (1943):7-28; rpt. *Modern Literary Criticism,* ed. I. Howe. Boston: Beacon Press, 1958, pp. 219-38.

Blanchard, Margaret. D's *The Idiot. Explicator* 21 (1963): item 41.

Bortnes, J. The Function of Hagiography in D's Novels. *Scando-Slavica* 24 (1978): 27-33.

——. Polyphony in *The Brothers Karamazov:* Variations on a Theme. *CASS* 17 (1983):402-11.

Bourgeois, P. L. D and Existentialism— An Experiment in Hermeneutics. *Journal of Thought* 15, 2 (1980):29-38.

Brantley, Daniel. Charisma in Literature: An Examination of Fictional Charismatic Leadership. *West Georgia College Review* (1982):16-24.

Braun, Maximilian. *The Brothers Karamazov* as an Expository Novel. *CASS* 6 (1972):199-208.

Brodsky, Joseph. D. *Stand* 22 (1981):7-9.

——. The Power of the Elements. In his *Less Than One.* NY: Farrar, Straus, Giroux, 1986, pp. 157-63.

Brody, E. C. The Liberal Intellectual in *The Possessed. Germano-Slavica* 2 (1977): 253-72.

——. Meaning and Symbolism in the Names of D's *Crime and Punishment* and *The Idiot. Names* 27 (1979):117-40.

Brown, E. J. Pisarev and the Transformation of Two Russian Novels. In *Literature and Society in Imperial Russia, 1800-1914,* ed. W. M. Todd III. Stanford: Stanford UP, 1978, pp. 151-72.

Brumfield, W. C. "Thérèse philosophe" and D's Great Sinner. *CL* 32 (1980):238-52.

Burgin, Diana L. Prince Myškin, the True Lover and "Impossible Bridegroom": A Problem in Dostoevskian Narrative. *SEEJ* 27 (1983):158-75.

Burnett, L. D, Poe and the Discovery of Fantastic Realism. In *F. M. D (1821-1881): A Centenary Collection,* ed. L. Burnett. Colchester: Dept. of Literature, U Essex, 1981, pp. 58-86.

Bursov, B. The Unknown D. *Soviet Studies in Literature* 7, 1 (1970-71):41-52.

Busch, Robert L. D's Major Novels and the European Gothic Tradition. *RLJ* 40, 136/137 (1986):57-74.

——. D's Translation of Balzac's *Eugénie Grandet. CSP* 25 (1983):73-89.

——. D's Translation of Balzac's *Eugénie Grandet.* In *Canadian Contributions to the IX International Congress of Slavists,* ed. Z. Folejewski, et al. Toronto: U Toronto, 1983, pp. 73-89.

——. Humor in D's *Crime and Punishment. CASS* 9 (1975):54-68.

——. The Myshkin-Ippolit-Rogozhin Triad. *CASS* 17 (1983):372-83.

Byrnes, Robert F. D and Pobedonostsev. In *Essays in Russian and Soviet History,* ed. J. S Curtiss. Leiden, 1963, 85-102.

Campbell, Magda. D and Psychoanalysis. *Transactions of Assoc. of Russian-American Scholars in USA* 5 (1971):18-28.

Cardacci, P. F. D's Underground Man as Allusion and Symbol. *Symposium* 28

(1974):248-57.

Cash, E. A. The Narrators in *Invisible Man* and *Notes from Underground:* Brothers in Spirit. *College Language Association Journal* 16 (1973):505-7.

Cassedy, S. Daniil Kharms' Parody of D: Anti-Tragedy as Political Comment. *CASS* 18 (1984):268-84.

____. The Formal Problem of the Epilogue in *Crime and Punishment:* The Logic of Tragic and Christian Structures *DostSt* 3 (1982):171-90.

Cazzola, P. The Humour of the Young D—An Anticipation of the Tragic Nature of His Mature Works. *BulDS* 4 (1974):69-70.

Černý, Václav. The Devils. *Cross Currents* 5 (1986):485-92.

Chaitin, Gilbert D. Religion as Defense: The Structure of *The Brothers Karamazov. Literature and Psychology* 22 (1972):69-87.

Chances, Ellen. Literary Criticism and the Ideology of "Pochvennichestvo" in D's Thick Journals. *RusR* 34 (1975):151-64.

____. "Pochvennichestvo": Ideology in D's Magazines. *Mosaic* 7 (19174):71-88.

____. Pochvennichestvo—Evolution of an Ideology. *Modern Fiction Studies* 20, 4 (1974-75):543-51.

Chapple, R. L. Character Parallels in *Crime and Punishment* and *Sanctuary. Germano-Slavica* 2 (1976):5-14.

Chavkin, Allan. Ivan Karamazov's Rebellion and Bellow's "The Victim." *Papers on Language and Literature* 16 (1980): 316-20.

____. The Problem of Suffering in the Fiction of Saul Bellow. *CLS* 21 (1984):161-74.

Chirkov, N. M. A Great Philosophical Novel. In *Twentieth Century Interpretations of "Crime and Punishment": A Collection of Critical Essays,* ed. R. L. Jackson. Englewood Cliffs: Prentice-Hall, 1974, pp. 49-70.

Chizhevsky, D. The Theme of the Double in D. In *D: A Collection of Critical Essays,* ed. R. Wellek. Englewood Cliffs: Prentice-Hall, 1972, pp. 112-29.

Christensen, Peter G. D and Jean-Luc Godard: Kirillov's Return to *La Chinoise.* In *D and the Human Condition after a Century,* ed. A. Ugrinsky, et al. NY: Greenwood P, 1986, pp. 145-54.

Chulkov, Georgy. D's Technique of Writing. In *Crime and Punishment,* ed. G. Gibian. NY: Norton, 1975, pp. 487-92.

Church, Margaret. D's *Crime and Punishment* and Kafka's *The Trial. Literature and Psychology* 19 (1969):47-55.

____. Spatial Patterns in *The Brothers Karamazov.* In *Structure and Theme—Don Quixote to James Joyce.* Columbus: Ohio State UP, 1983, pp. 81-101.

Cipolla, J. D and Free-Will. *Forum (I)* 1 (1976):91-98.

Clark, Katerina. M. M. Bakhtin's *Problemy tvorchestva Dostoevskogo. MelbSS* 14 (1980):33-40.

Clayton, J. Douglas. Soviet Views of Parody: Tynianov and Morozov. *CASS* 7 (1973):485-93.

Coleman, S. M. The Phantom "Double": Its Psychological Significance. *British Journal of Medical Psychology* 14 (1934): 254-73.

Consigny, S. The Paradox of Textuality: Writing as Entrapment and Deliverance in *Notes from Underground. CASS* 12 (1978):341-52.

Cornwell, Neil. V. F. Odoevsky's Ridiculous Dream About That? Themes and Ideas in Works by V. F. Odoevsky, D, and Mayakovsky. *Quinquere* 2, 1 (1979):75-86; 2, 2 (1979):246-55.

Corrigan, Kevin. Ivan's Devil in *The Brothers Karamazov* in the Light of a Traditional Platonic View of Evil. *FMLS* 22, 1 (1986):1-9.

Corten, I. S. The Influence of D on Majakovskij's Poem "Pro eto". In *Studies Presented to Profesor Roman Jakobson by His Students,* ed. C. Gribble. Cambridge: Slavica, 1968, pp. 76-83.

Cox, G. D. D. H. Lawrence and F. M. D: Mirror Images of Murderous Aggression. *MFS* 29 (1983):175-82.

Cox, Roger L. D's Grand Inquisitor. *Cross Currents* 17 (1967):427-44.

____. Kirillov, Stavrogin and Suicide. *D and the Human Condition after a*

Century, ed. A. Ugrinsky, et al. NY: Greenwood P, 1986, pp. 79-86.

___. Stavrogin and Prince Hal. *CSP* 26 (1984):121-26.

___. Time and Timelessness in D.'s Fiction. *Forum International* 3 (1980):3-9.

Crone, A. L. Unamuno and D: Some Thoughts on Atheistic Humanitarianism. *Hispanofila* 64 (1978):43-59.

Curtis, James M. Shestov's Use of Nietzsche in His Interpretation of Tolstoy and D. *Texas Studies in Language and Literature* 17 (1975): 289-302.

___. Solzhenitsyn and D. *MFS* 23 (1977):133-52.

___. Spatial Form as the Intrinsic Genre of D's Novels. *MFS* 18 (1972):135-54.

Curtis, M. S. The Murder of Alyosha: A Question of Crime or Design? A Structural Study of *Crime and Punishment. Massachusetts Studies in English* 4, 4-5 (1974):57-63.

Dalton, Elizabeth. Myshkin's Epilepsy. *Partisan Review* 45 (1978):595-610.

Danow, David K. Dialogic Structure in *Crime and Punishment. RusL* 19, 3 (1986):291-314.

___ A Note on the Internal Dynamics of the Dostoevskian Conclave. *DostSt* 2 (1981):61-68.

___. Notes on Generating a Text: *The Brothers Karamazov. MLS* (1980-81):75-95.

___. Semiotics of Gesture in Dostoevskian Dialogue. *RusL* 8 (1980):41-75.

___. Subtexts of *The Brothers Karamazov. RusL* 12 (1982):173-82.

Darring, Gerald & Walter. D's Prophetic *Notes. Genre* 6 (1973):388-403.

Davison, R. Camus' Attitude to D's Kirillov and the Impact of the Engineer's Ideas on Camus' Early Work. *Orbis Litterarum* 30 (1975):225-40.

___ D's *The Devils:* The Role of Stepan Trofimovich Verkhovensky. *FMLS* 16 (1980):109-19.

___. Moral Ambiguity in D. *SlavR* 27 (1968):313-16.

___. The Translation of Surnames in D. *JRS* 30 (1975):102-7.

Debreczeny, Paul. D's Use of *Manon Lescaut* in *The Gambler. CL* 28 (1976):1-18.

DeMott, Benjamin. Mobile Souls: *The Brothers Karamazov* Maps a Multitude of Transfigurations. *Harpers* (Oct. 1984):87-89.

Deveau, Daniel P. D's *Crime and Punishment. Explicator* 40, 3 (1982):36-38.

Dilman, Ilham. D: Psychology and the Novelist. In *Philosophy and Literature,* ed. A. Phillips Griffiths. Cambridge: Cambridge UP, 1984, pp. 95-114.

___ D as Philosopher: A Short Note. *Philosophy and Literature* 43 (1968): 280-84.

Dirscherl, Dennis. D and the Catholic Pax Romana. In *D and the Human Condition after a Century,* ed. A.Ugrinsky,et al. NY: Greenwood P, 1986, pp. 171-79.

Dolan, P. D: The Political Gospel. In his *War and Alarms.* NY: Free Press, 1975, pp. 36-69.

Doody, T. The Underground Man's Confession and His Audience. *Rice University Studies* 61 (1975):27-38.

Dukas, Vytas & Richard Lawson. Goethe in D's Critical Works. *German Quarterly* 39 (1967):348-57.

Dunlop, John B. D's *Poor Folk* Reconsidered. *Transactions of the Association of Russian American Scholars in the USA* 5 (1971):29-37.

Eastman, Richard M. Idea and Method in a Scene by D. *College English* 17 (1955): 143-50.

Edgerton, William. Cosmic Farce or Transcendental Vision: Modern Manifestations of the Absurd in Slavic and Non-Slavic Literature. In *American Contributions to the Seventh International Congress of Slavists,* vol. 2, ed. V. Terras. The Hague: Mouton, 1973, pp. 119-46.

Engelberg, Edward. Some Versions of Consciousness and Egotism: Hegel, D's Underground Man, and *Peer Gynt.* In his *The Unknown Distance: From Consciousness to Conscience. Goethe to Camus.* Cambridge: Harvard UP, 1972, pp. 87-116.

Erlich, Victor. Gogol' and Kafka: A Note on "Realism" and "Surrealism." In *For Roman Jakobson: Essays on the Occasion of His Sixtieth Birthday*, ed. M. Halle, et al. The Hague: Mouton, 1956, pp. 100-8.

——. Two Concepts of the D Novel. *IJSLP* 25-26 (1982):127-36.

Falen, James E. The Meaning of Dostoevskian Narrative. *BulDS* 8 (1978): 42-55.

Fanger, Donald. D Today: Some Recent Critical Studies. *Survey* 36 (1961):13-19.

Farakos, M. The Narrator in *The Idiot*. *NZSJ* 11 (1973):123-32.

Fasting, S. D and George Sand. *RusL* 15 (1976):309-22.

——. The Hierarchy of "Truths" in the Structure of *The Brothers Karamazov*. *Forum International* 3 (1980):99-111.

Feldman, A. B. D and Father-Love Exemplified by *Crime and Punishment*. *Psychoanalysis and the Psychoanalytic Review* 45, 4 (1958):84-98.

Fiene, D. M. Elements of D in the Novels of Kurt Vonnegut. *DostSt* 2 (1981): 129-42.

——. Pushkin's "Poor Knight": The Key to Perceiving D's *Idiot* as Allegory. *BulDS* 8 (1978):10-21.

——. Vonnegut's Quotations from D. *Notes on Modern American Literature* 1 (1977): item 29.

Fitzgerald, G. D. Anton Lavrent'evič G-v: The Narrator as Recreator in D's *The Possessed*. In *New Perspectives on Nineteenth-Century Prose*, ed. G. J. Gutsche & L. G. Leighton. Columbus: Slavica, 1982, pp. 121-24.

——. The Chronology of F.M.D's *The Possessed*. *SEEJ* 27 (1983):19-46.

——. The Mysterious Appearance of Mar'ja Šatova: An Examination of Motivation in *The Possessed*. *Forum at Iowa* 2 (1977):33-48.

Florance, E. C. The Neurosis of Raskolnikov: A Study in Incest and Murder. *Archives of Criminal Psychodynamics* 1 (1955):344-96.

Florovsky, A. D and the Slavonic Question. *SEER* 9 (1930):411-23.

Folejewski, Z. Murder Mystery or Christian Tragedy: Remarks on Some Structural Elements of *The Brothers Karamazov*. *Forum International* 3 (1980): 111-18.

Fortin, R. E. Responsive Form: D's *Notes from Underground* and the Confessional Tradition. *Essays in Literature* 7 (1980): 225-45.

Foy, J. L. & S. J. Rojcewicz. D and Suicide. *Confinia Psychiatrica* 22, 2 (1979):65-80.

Frank, Joseph. D and Russian Populism. In *The Rarer Action: Essays in Honor of Francis Fergusson*, ed. A. Cheuse & R. Koffler. New Brunswick: Rutgers UP, 1970, pp. 301-19.

——. D and the Socialists. *Partisan Review* 32 (1965):409-22.

——. D as Journalist: 1847. *Boston University Journal* 23, 2 (1975):12-18.

——. D: The Encounter with Europe. *RusR* 22 (1963):237-52.

——. D: *The House of the Dead*. *Sewanee Review* 74 (1966):779-803.

——. D's Discovery of "Fantastic Realism". *RusR* 27 (1968):286-95.

——. The Masks of Stavrogin. *Sewanee Review* 77 (1969):660-91.

——. Men and Ideas: D's Realism. *Encounter* 40 (1973):31-38.

——. Nihilism and *Notes from Underground*. *SlavR* 48 (1961):1-33.

—— Ralph Ellison and a Literary "Ancestor": D. *New Criterion* 2, 1 (1983):11-21.

——. A Reading of *The Idiot*. *Southern Review* 5 (1969):303-31.

——. The World of Raskolnikov. *Encounter* 26 (1966):30-35.

Freud, Sigmund. D and Parricide. *Partisan Review* 12 (1945):530-44.

Fridlender, G. D: A Definitive Edition. *Soviet Literature* 4 (1976):155-63.

Friedman, Maurice. Martin Buber's *For the Sake of Heaven* and F.M.D's *The Brothers Karamazov*. *CLS* 3 (1966): 155-67.

Fuchs, D. Saul Bellow and the Example of D. In *The Stoic Strain in American Literature*, ed. D. J. MacMillan.

Toronto: U Toronto P, pp. 157-76.

Fülöp-Miller, R. D's Literary Reputation. *Rus R* 10 (1950):46-54.

——. The Lost D Manuscripts. *RusR* 10 (1950):268-82.

——. The Posthumous Life of D. *RusR* 15 (1956):259-65.

Furst, L. D's *Notes from Underground* and Salinger's *The Catcher in the Rye*. *Canadian Review of Comparative Literature* 5 (1978):72-85.

Futrell, M. Buddhism and *The Brothers Karamazov*. *DostSt* 2 (1981):155-62.

——. D and Dickens. *English Miscellany* (Rome) 7 (1956):41-89.

——. D and Islam. *SEER* 57 (1979):16-31.

Geha, Richard, Jr. D and *The Gambler:* A Contribution to the Psychogenesis of Gambling. *Psychoanalytic Review* 57 (1970):95-123, 289-302.

Gibian, George. D's Use of Russian Folklore. *Journal of American Folklore* 69 (1956):239-53.

——. The Forms of Discontent in D and Tolstoy. In *Comparatists at Work: Studies in Comparative Literature*, ed. S. G. Nichols & R. B. Vowles. Waltham, MA: Blaisdell, 1968, pp. 126-45.

——. The Grotesque in D. *MFS* 4 (1958): 262-70.

——. Traditional Symbolism in *Crime and Punishment. PMLA* 70 (1955):979-96.

Gibson, A. Boyce. Napoleon III in Russia (D's *Crime and Punishment* and Tolstoi's *War And Peace). MelbSS* 7 (1972):4-13.

——. The Riddle of the Grand Inquisitor. *MelbSS* 4 (1970):45-56.

Gill, Richard. The Bridges of St. Petersburg: A Motif in *Crime and Punishment. DostSt* 3 (1982):145-55.

Girard, R. Superman in the Underground: Strategies of Madness—Nietzsche, Wagner and D. *MLN* 91, 4 (1976): 1161-85.

Glazov, Yuri. *The Devils* by D and the Russian Intelligentsia. *Studies in Soviet Thought* 17, 4 (1977):309-30.

Glicksberg, Charles I. D and the Problem of Religion. *Bucknell Review* 8 (1959): 202-17.

Goerner, Tatyana. Art and Aesthetics in D's *The Idiot. Ulbandus Review* 2 (1982):79-95.

Goldstein, Martin. The Debate in *The Brothers Karamazov. SEEJ* 14 (1970): 326-40.

——. Rewriting D's Letters. *ASEER* 10 (1961):279-88.

Golosovker, Ya. The Words "Secret" and "Mystery." In *The Brothers Karamazov,* ed. R. Matlaw. NY: Norton, 1976, pp. 857-60.

Golubov, Alexander. Religious Imagery in the Structure of *The Brothers Karamazov*. In *Russian and Slavic Literature,* ed. R. Freeborn, et al. Cambridge: Slavica, 1976.

Gordon, H. D and Existentialist Education: Father Zosima as a Religious Educator. *Religious Education* 74, 2 (1979):272-89.

Gould, J. A. The Concepts of Freedom in the Grand Inquisitor. *Dialogos* 14 (1980): 171-77.

Greenberg, B. F.M.D (1821-81): Medico-Psychological and Psychoanalytic Studies on His Life and Writing. A Bibliography. *Psychoanalytic Review* 62 (1975):509-13.

Greenway, J. L. Kierkegaardian Doubles in *Crime and Punishment. Orbis Litterarum* 33 (1978):45-60.

Gregg, Richard. Apollo Underground: His Master's Still, Small Voice. *RusR* 32 (1973):64-71.

——. D's Upside-Down Fairy Tale; The Place of "A Little Hero" in the Pre-Siberian Oeuvre. *CASS* 18 (1984):285-97.

——. Two Adams and Eve in the Crystal Palace: D, the Bible and *We. SlavR* 24 (1965):680-87; rpt. *Zamyatin's "We": A Collection of Critical Essays,* ed. G. Kern. Ann Arbor: Ardis, 1988, pp. 61-69.

Gregory, Serge. D's *The Devils* and the Anti-nihilist Novel. *SlavR* 38 (1979): 444-55.

Grigorieff, Dimitry F. D's Elder Zosima and the Real Life Father Amvrosy. *St. Vladimir's Seminary Quarterly* 11 (1967): 22-34.

——. The Last Year, Death and Burial of Fedor M. D. *St. Vladimir's Theological Quarterly* 25 (1981):147-58.

——. Pasternak and D. *SEEJ* (1959):335-42.

Grishin, N. *The Diary of a Writer. Twentieth Century* 15 (1961):151-64.

Grossman, Joan. D and Stendahl's Theory of Happiness. In *American Contributions to the Eighth International Congress of Slavists,* vol. 2, ed. V. Terras. Columbus: Slavica, 1978, pp. 204-20.

Grossman, Leonid. The Stylistics of Stavrogin's Confession: A Study of the New Chapter of *The Possessed.* Tr. K. T. O'Connor. In *Critical Essays on Dostoevsky,* ed. R. F. Miller. Boston: Hall, 1986, pp. 148-58.

Guardini, R. The Legend of the Grand Inquisitor. *College English* 3 (1952):58-85.

Gubler, D. V. D's Women. *Proceedings of the Pacific Northwest Conference on Foreign Languages* 29 (1978):130-35.

Guerard, A. On the Composition of D's *The Idiot. Mosaic* 8 (1974):201-15.

Hackel, Sergei. F. M. D (1821-1881): Prophet Manqué? *DostSt* 3 (1982):5-25.

——. Raskolnikov Through the Looking-Glass: D and Camus's *L'Etranger. Wisconsin Studies in Comparative Literature* 9 (1968):189-209.

Hacker, A. D's Use of French as a Symbolic Device in *The Brothers Karamazov. CLS* 2 (1965):171-74.

Haltresht, M. Symbolism of Rats and Mice in D's *Notes from Underground. South Atlantic Bulletin* 39, 4 (1974):60-62.

Hamill, Pete. Introduction. D and the Human Condition after a Century: The Poet and the City. In *D and the Human Condition after a Century,* ed. A. Ugrinsky, et al. NY: Greenwood P, 1986, pp. 1-9.

Hamilton, Morse. Pastoral in *The Possessed: Existe-t-elle? Ulbandus Review* 2 (1979):120-27.

Hamilton, William. Banished from the Land of Unity: A Study of D's Religious Vision Through the Eyes of Ivan and Alyosha Karamazov. *Journal of Religion* 39 (1959):245-62.

Hanak, Miroslav J. D vs. Tolstoy: A Struggle Against Subjective Idealism. *CASS* 12 (1978):371-76.

——. D's Metaphysics in the Light of Nietzsche's Psychology. *NZSJ* 9 (1972):20-37.

——. D's Novel-Biography. *BulDS* (1975): 18-23.

——. D's *Possessed:* The Epilepsy of Unreason in Men without a Transcendent Ground. In *Festschrift für Nikola R. Pribić,* ed. J. Matesic. Neuried: Hieronymus, 1983, pp. 139-48.

——. Hegel's "Frenzy of Self-Conceit" as Key to the Annihilation of Individuality in D's *Possessed. DostSt* 2 (1981):147-54.

——. Nietzsche, D, and Faulkner: Rebellion Against Society in the Light of the New Left. In *Proceedings of the 6th Congress of the International Comparative Literature Association,* ed. M. Cadot. Stuttgart: Bieber, 1975, pp. 739-43.

Hanan, David. *Crime and Punishment:* The Idea of the Crime. *Critical Review* 12 (1969):15-28.

Harap, L. Poe and D: A Case of Affinity. In *Weapons of Criticism: Marxism in America and the Literary Tradition,* ed. N. Rudich. Palo Alto: Ramparts, 1976, pp. 271-85.

Hardesty, W. H. III. The "Femme Fatale" in *The Idiot* and *The Arrow of Gold. Research Studies* 44 (1976):175-82.

Harries, Richard. Ivan Karamazov's Argument. *Theology* 81 (1978):104-11.

Harris, Harold J. D: The Writer as Anti-Semite. *Midstream* 28, 2 (1982):50-53.

Hart, John A. Underground Man and Saint in D. In *Six Novelists: Stendhal, D, Tolstoy, Hardy, Dreiser, Proust,* ed. W. M. Schutte et al. Pittsburgh: Carnegie Institute of Technology, 1959, pp. 17-28.

Hart, Pierre R. Looking Over Raskolnikov's Shoulder: The Narrator in *Crime and Punishment. Criticism* 13 (1971):166-79.

——. Schillerean Themes in D's "Malen'kij geroj." *SEEJ* 15 (1971):305-15.

Haugh, R. D and Hawthorne? *Transactions of the Association of Russian-American Scholars in the USA* 5 (1971): 38-59.

Hernández, Francis. D's Prince Myshkin as a *jurodivij. Bulletin of the Rocky Mountain Modern Language Association* 26 (1972):16-21.

Hesse, Hermann. *The Brothers Karamazov,* or the Downfall of Europe: Thoughts on Reading D. *Western Review* 17 (1953):185-95.

Hodgson, Peter. Awakenings to Nightmare. In *The Anxious Subject: Nightmares and Daymares in Literature and Film,* ed. M. Lazar. Malibu: Undena, 1983, pp. 41-50.

Hoffmann, Frederick J. The Friends of God: D and Kazantzakis. In *The Imagination's New Beginning: Theology and Modern Literature.* Notre Dame: U Notre Dame P, 1967, pp. 43-72.

——. The Scene of Violence; D and Dreiser. *MFS* 6 (1960):91-105.

Hoffmeister, C. *William Wilson* and *The Double:* A Freudian Insight. *Coranto* 9, 2 (1974):24-27.

Hollander, R. The Apocalyptic Framework of D's *Idiot. Mosaic* 7, 2 (1974):123-39.

Holquist, Michael. Dostoievskian Standard Time. *Diacritics* 3 (1973):10-13.

——. Plot and Counter-Plot in *Notes from Underground. CASS* 6 (1972):225-38.

Hope, A. D. D and Nietzsche. *MelbSS* 4 (1970):38-45.

Horsman, Dorothea. *Crime and Punishment:* A Study in Technique. *NZSJ* 6 (1970):34-52.

Howard, Barbara. The Rhetoric of Confession: D's *Notes from Underground* and Rousseau's *Confessions. SEEJ* 25 (1981):16-32.

Howe, Irving. The Struggle for Creation: A View of D's Notebooks. In *The Critical Point: On Literature and Culture.* NY: Horizon, 1973, pp. 77-86.

Hutzler, J. Family Pathology in *Crime and Punishment. American Journal of Psychoanalysis* 38 (1978):335-42.

Ivanits, L. J. Folk Beliefs about the Unclean Force in D's *The Brothers Karamazov.* In *New Perspectives on Nineteenth-Century Russian Prose,* ed. G. Gutsche and L. Leighton. Columbus: Slavica, 1982, pp. 135-40.

——. D's Mar'ja Lebjadkina. *SEEJ* 22 (1978):127-40.

Ivask, George. D's Wit. *RusR* 21 (1962): 154-64.

Jackson, Robert L. Chateaubriand and D: The Posing of a Problem. *Scando-Slavica* 12 (1966):28-37.

——. Dmitrij Karamazov and the "Legend." *SEEJ* 9 (1965):257-67.

——. D and the Marquis de Sade. *RusL* 13 (1976):27-46.

——. A Footnote to *Selo Stepančikovo. Richerche slavistische* 17-19 (1970-72):247-57.

——. The Narrator in D's *Notes from the House of the Dead.* In *Studies in Honor of Waclaw Lednicki,* ed. Z. Folejewski, et al. 's-Gravenhage: Mouton, 1956, pp. 192-216.

——. Nietzsche and D: Counterpoint. *Comparatist* 6 (1982):24-34.

——. Philosophical Pro and Contra in Part I of *Crime and Punishment.* In *Twentieth-Century Interpretations of "Crime and Punishment": A Collection of Critical Essays,* ed. R. L. Jackson. Englewood Cliffs: Prentice-Hall, 1974, pp. 26-40.

——. The Root and the Flower, D and Turgenev. A Comparative Esthetic. *Yale Review* 63 (1974):228-50.

——. The Testament of F.M.D. *RusL* 4 (1973):87-99.

——. Tolstoy's "Kreutzer Sonata" and D's *Notes from Underground.* In *American Contributions to the Eighth International Congress of Slavists,* vol. 2, ed. V. Terras. Columbus: Slavica, 1978, pp. 281-91.

——. Triple Vision: D's "The Peasant Marey." *Yale Review* 67 (1978):225-35.

Jarrett, James L. D: Philosopher of Freedom, Love, and Life. *Review of Religion* 21 (1956):17-30.

Jitkoff, A. & J. Thomas. "Floor" and "Storey" in the Garnett *Crime and Punishment. American Speech* 31 (1956): 160-70.

Johae, A. Idealism and the Dialectic in *The Brothers Karamazov.* In *F.M.D (1821-1881): A Centenary Collection,* ed. L. Burnett. Colchester: Dept. of Literature, U Essex, 1981, pp. 109-18.

Jones, G. V. "Agape"and "Eros": Notes on D (Analysis of Love in *The Brothers Karamazov*). *Expository Times* 66 (1954): 3-7.

Jones, Malcolm V. An Aspect of Romanticism in D: Netochka Nezvanova and Eugène Sue's *Mathilde*. *Renaissance and Modern Studies* 17 (1973):38-61.

———. D and an Aspect of Schiller's Psychology. *SEER* 52 (1974):337-54.

———. D and Europe: Travels in the Mind. *Renaissance and Modern Studies* 24 (1980):38-57.

———. D, Tolstoy, Leskov and *Redstokizm*. *JRS* 23 (1972):3-20.

———. D's Conception of the Idea. *Renaissance and Modern Studies* 13 (1969):106-31.

———. Raskolnikov's Humanitarianism. *CASS* 8 (1974):370-80.

———. Some Echoes of Hegel in D. *SEER* 49 (1971):500-20.

Justman, S. The Strange Case of D and Freud: A Lesson in the Necessity of Imagination. *Gypsy Scholar* (East Lansing) 2 (1975):94-101.

Kanzer, Mark. D's Matricidal Impulse. *Psychoanalytic Review* 35 (1948):115-25.

———. D's "Peasant Marey." *American Imago* 4 (1947)78-88.

———. The Vision of Father Zossima. *American Imago* 8 (1951):329-35.

Karyakin, Yu. F. Toward Regeneration. In *Twentieth-Century Interpretations of "Crime and Punishment": A Collection of Critical Essays,* ed. R. L. Jackson. Englewood Cliffs: Prentice-Hall, 1974, pp. 94-102.

Katkov, G. Steerforth and Stavrogin on the Sources of *The Possessed. SEER* 27 (1949):469-89.

Katz, Michael R. *Dreams and the Unconscious in Nineteenth-Century Russian Fiction.* Hanover: UP of New England, 1984, pp. 84-116.

Kavanagh, Thomas M. D's *Notes from Underground:* The Form of the Fiction. *Texas Studies in Literature and Language* 14 (1972):491-507.

Keller, Howard H. Prince Myshkin: Success or Failure? *JRS* 24 (1972):17-23.

Kesich, Veselin. Some Religious Aspects of D's *Brothers Karamazov. St. Vladimir's Seminary Quarterly* 9 (1965):83-99.

Ketchian, Sonia. The Theme of Suggestion in D's *Slaboe serdtse.* In *Mnemozina: Studia litteraria russica in honorem Vsevolod Setchkarev,* ed. J. T. Baer & N. W. Ingham. Munich: Wilhelm Fink, 1974, pp. 232-42.

Kim, Chrysostom, O.S.B. Ivan's Devil in D's *The Brothers Karamazov. American Benedictine Review* 16 (1965):291-309.

Kiraly, G. Hamlet and Raskolnikov: Renaissance and the Nineteenth Century. *Acta Litteraria Academiae Scientiarum Hungarica* 21 (1979):15-43.

Kiremidjian, D. Crime and Punishment: Matricide and the Woman Question. *American Imago* 33 (1976):403-33.

Kirilloff, A. The "Outsider" Figure in D's Works. *Renaissance and Modern Studies* 18 (1974):126-40.

Kirk, Irina. Buddhistic Elements in *The Idiot. Studia Slavica Academiae Scientiarum Hungaricae* 1-2 (1972):1123-26.

——— Dramatization of Consciousness in Camus and D. *Bucknell Review* 16 (1968):96-104.

——— Polemics and Art in D and Camus. *NZSJ* 8 (1971):49-74.

Kjetsaa, G. Written by D? *Scando-Slavica* 26 (1980):19-31.

Knapp, Shoshana M. The Dynamics of the Idea of Napoleon in *Crime and Punishment.* In *D and the Human Condition after a Century,* ed. A. Ugrinsky, et al. NY: Greenwood P, 1986, pp. 31-40.

———. The Morality of Creation: D and William James in Le Guin's "Omelas." *Journal of Narrative Technique* 15, 1 (1985):75-81.

Koehler, Ludmila. The Grotesque Poetry of D. *SEEJ* 14 (1970):11-23.

——— "The Little Hero" of a Great Writer. *BulDS* 8 (1978):22-30.

——— A Metaphysical Vision of Graveyard Debauchery. *CASS* 8, 3 (1974):427-33.

——— Renan, D, and Fedorov. *CASS* 17 (1983):362-71.

Koening, A. E. D's Testament: *The Diary*

of a Writer. South Atlantic Quarterly 53 (1954):10-23.

Kogan, G. Sketches of Familiar Faces: Drawings in D's Rough Drafts. *Soviet Literature* 10 (1975):82-85.

Kohlberg, Lawrence. Moral Psychology and the Study of Tragedy. In *Directions in Literary Criticism: Contemporary Approaches to Literature. Festschrift for Henry W. Sams,* ed. S. Weintraub & P. Young. University Park: Pennsylvania State UP, 1973, pp. 24-52.

Kohlberg, Lawrence. Psychological Analysis and Literary Forms: A Study of the Doubles in D. *Daedalus* 92 (1963):345-63.

Kohn, Hans. D and Danilevsky: Nationalist Messianism. In *Continuity and Change in Russian and Soviet Thought,* ed. E. J. Simmons. Cambridge: Harvard UP, 1955, pp. 500-15.

Koprince, Ralph. Background Characters and *The Brothers Karamazov. RLT* 10 (1974):343-50.

———. D's Petraševskij Deposition as a Biographical Source. *SEEJ* 28 (1984):310-23.

———. The Question of Raskolnikov's Suicide. *CASS* 16 (1982):73-81.

Kovács, A. The Narrative Model of the Novel of "Awakening": D. *Acta Litteraria Academiae Scientiarum Hungaricae* 25 (1983):359-74.

———. The Poetics of *The Idiot:* On the Problem of D's Thinking about Genre. In *Critical Essays on D,* ed. R. F. Miller. Boston: Hall, 1986, pp. 116-26.

Kozhinov, V. V. The First Sentence in *Crime and Punishment.* In *Twentieth-Century Interpretations of "Crime and Punishment": A Collection of Critical Essays,* ed. R. L. Jackson. Englewood Cliffs: Prentice-Hall, 1974, pp. 17-25.

Krag, Erik. The Riddle of the Other Goljadkin: Some Observations on D's *Double.* In *For Roman Jakobson: Essays on the Occasion of His Sixtieth Birthday,* comp. M. Halle, et al. The Hague: Mouton, 1956, pp. 265-72.

Kreyling, M. *Crime and Punishment:* The Pattern Beneath the Surface of Percy's *Lancelot. Notes on Mississippi Writers* 11 (1978):36-44.

Krieg, R. A. Narrative as a Linguistic

Rule: Fyodor D and Karl Barth. *International Poetry Review* 8 (1977):190-205.

Krieger, M. D's *Idiot:* The Curse of Saintliness. In *D: A Collection of Critical Essays,* ed. R. Wellek. Englewood Cliffs: Prentice-Hall, 1962, pp. 39-52.

Kudryavtsev, Y. D and His *Diary of a Writer. MelbSS* 8 (1973):58-63.

Kuhn, Alfred. A Note on Raskolnikov's Hats. *SEEJ* 15 (1971):425-32.

Kuznetsov, Boris. Einstein and D. Tr. Paul Grigorieff. *Diogenes* 54 (1967):1-16.

Laing, R. O. The Counterpoint of Experience. In *Crime and Punishment,* ed. G. Gibian. NY: Norton, 1975, pp. 612-22.

Lampert, E. D. In *Nineteenth-Century Russian Literature: Studies of Ten Writers,* ed. J. Fennell. London: Faber & Faber, 1973, pp. 225-60.

Langbaum, Robert. Thoughts for Our Time: Three Novels on Anarchism. *American Scholar* 42 (1973):227-50.

Lavine, Thelma Z. The Legend of the Grand Inquisitor: The Death Struggle of Ideologies. In *D and the Human Condition after a Century,* ed. A. Ugrinsky, et al. NY: Greenwood P, 1986, pp. 13-21.

Lavrin, Janko. D and Proust. *SEER* 5 (1926):609-27.

———. A Note on Nietzsche and D. *RusR* 28 (1969):160-70.

Lawrence, D. H. On D and Rozanov. In *Russian Literature and Modern English Fiction,* ed. D. Davie. Chicago: Chicago UP, 1965, pp. 99-103.

———. Preface to D's "The Grand Inquisitor." In *D: A Collection of Critical Essays,* ed. R. Wellek. Englewood Cliffs: Prentice-Hall, 1962, pp. 90-97.

Leatherbarrow, W. J. Aesthetic Louse: Ethics and Aesthetics in D's *Prestupleniye i nakazaniye. Modern Language Review* 71 (1976):857-66.

———. Apocalyptic Imagery in *The Idiot* and *The Devils. DostSt* 3 (1982):43-51.

———. D's Treatment of the Theme of Romantic Dreaming in "Khozyayka" and "Belye nochi." *MLR* 69 (1974)584-95.

———. Pushkin and the Early D. *MLR* 74

(1979):368-85.

——. The Rag with Ambition: The Problem of Self-Will in D's "Bednye lyudi" and "Dvoynik." *MLR* 68 (1973):607-18.

——. Raskolnikov and the "Enigma of His Personality." *FMLS* 9 (1973):153-65.

Leer, Norman. The Double Theme in Malamud's Assistant: D with Irony. *Mosaic* 4, 3 (1971):89-102.

——. Stavrogin and Prince Hal: The Hero in Two Worlds. *SEEJ* 6 (1962):99-116.

Leighton, Lauren. The Crime and Punishment of Monstrous Coincidence. *Mosaic* 12 (1978):93-106.

Lerner, Laurence. Psychoanalysis and Art. In *The Literary Imagination: Essays on Literature and Society.* Totowa, NJ: Barnes & Noble, 1982, pp. 60-77.

Leshinsky, Tania. D—Revolutionary or Reactionary? *ASEER* 4 (1945):98-107.

Lesser, Simon O. The Role of Unconscious Understanding in Flaubert and D. *Daedalus* 92 (1963):363-82; rpt. *The Whispered Meanings: Selected Essays of Simon O. Lesser.* Amherst: Mass. UP, 1977, pp. 86-104.

——. Saint and Sinner—D's *Idiot. MFS* 4 (1958):211-24.

Lethcoe, J. Self-Deception in D's *Notes from Underground. SEEJ* 10 (1966):9-21.

Levitsky, Igor. Dreams of a Golden Age: A Recurrent Theme in D's Later Fiction. In *Crisis and Commitment: Studies in German and Russian Literature in Honour of J. W. Dyck,* ed. J. Whiton & H. Loewen. Waterloo, Ontario: U Waterloo P, 1983, pp. 148-55.

Levy, Michele. Trouble in Paradise: The Failure of Flawed Vision in D's *Idiot. South Central Review* 2, 2 (1985):49-59.

Light, J. F. Violence, Dreams and D: The Art of Nathanael West. *College English* 19 (1958):208-13.

Lindenmeyr, A. Raskolnikov's City and the Napoleonic Plan. *SlavR* 35 (1976):1-17.

Linner, S. Bishop Tichon in *The Possessed. RusL* 4, 15 (1976):273-84.

——. D's Moral Authority. *CASS* 17 (1983):412-21.

Lloyd, J. A. T. D and Flaubert. *Fortnightly Review* 110 (1921):1017-26.

Loewen, Harry. Freedom and Rebellion in D's "The Grand Inquisitor" and Nietzsche's *The Antichrist.* In *Crisis and Commitment: Studies in German and Russian Literature in Honour of J. W. Dyck.* ed. J. Whiton & H. Loewen. Waterloo, Ontario: U Waterloo P, 1983, pp. 156-67.

LoGatto, E. Genesis of D's "Uncle's Dream." *SEER* 26 (1948):452-67.

Lord, R. D and N. F. Fyodorov. *SEER* 40 (1962):409-31.

——. D and Vladimir Solov'ev. *SEEJ* 42 (1964):415-26.

——. A Reconsideration of D's Novel *The Idiot. SEER* 45 (1967):30-46.

Louria, Yvette. An Analysis of D's Nastasia Filippovna. *Newsletter: Teaching Language Through Literature* 11 (1971): 35-46.

——. D and Goncharov. *MLN* 88 (1973): 1325-28.

Lower, R. B. "Dedoublement" in D and Camus. *MLR* 56 (1961):82-83.

——. On Raskolnikov's Dreams in *Crime and Punishment. Journal of the American Psychoanalytic Association* 17 (1969):728-42.

Lucow, B. Art and Reality in D's "The Peasant Marey." *Studies in Short Fiction* 2 (1965):185-86.

Lukács, G. D. In *D: A Collection of Critical Essays,* ed. R. Wellek. Englewood Cliffs: Prentice Hall, 1962, pp. 146-58.

McDonald, Walter R. D's *Crime and Punishment. Explicator* 26 (1968): item 53.

McDowall, A. *The Possessed* and Bolshevism. *London Mercury* 17 (1927):52-61.

Maceina, Antanas. The Metaphysical Meaning of the Legend from the Grand Inquisitor. *Lituanas* 15 (1969):14-26.

McKinney, D. *Notes from Underground:* A Dostoevskian Faust. *CASS* 12 (1978): 189-229.

MacPike, Loralee. Dickens and D: The Technique of Reverse Influence. In *The Changing World of Charles Dickens,* ed. R. Giddings. Totowa, NJ: Barnes & Noble, 1983, pp. 196-215.

McSweeny, Kerry. Alyosha's Sacred Memory. *Dalhousie Review* 56 (1976-

77):663-70.

Madaule, J. Raskolnikov. In *Twentieth-Century Interpretations of "Crime and Punishment": A Collection of Critical Essays,* ed. R. L. Jackson. Englewood Cliffs: Prentice-Hall, 1974, pp. 41-48.

Madeline, Sister M. Mauriac and D: Psychologists of the Unconscious. *Renascence* 5 (1952):7-14.

Magistrale, Tony. Between Heaven and Hell: The Dialectic of D's Tragic Vision. *D and the Human Condition after a Century,* ed. A. Ugrinsky, et al. NY: Greenwood P, 1986, pp. 191-97.

___. From St. Petersburg to Chicago: Wright's *Crime and Punishment. CLS* 23, 1 (1986):59-70.

Magretta, J. Radical Disunities: Models of Mind and Madness in *Pierre* and *The Idiot. Studies in the Novel* 10 (1978):234-50.

Malenko, Z. & James Gebhard. The Artistic use of Portraits in *The Idiot. SEEJ* 5 (1961):243-54.

Mann, R. Elijah the Prophet in *Crime and Punishment. CSP* 23 (1981):261-72.

___. The Faustian Patterns in *The Devils. CSP* 24 (1982):239-44.

Manning, Clarence Augustus. Alyosha Valkovsky and Prince Myshkin. *MLN* 57 (1942):182-85.

___. The *Double* of D. *MLN* 59 (1944): 317-21.

___. The Grand Inquisitor. *American Theological Review* 15 (1933):16-26.

___. Hawthorne and D. *SEER* 14 (1936): 417-24.

Marchant, P. The Mystery of Lizaveta. *Modern Language Studies* 4, 2 (1974): 5-13.

Martin, M. A. The Last Shall Be First: A Study of Three Russian Short Stories. *Bucknell Review* 6 (1956):13-23.

Marullo, T. G. Transcending "Urban" Romanticism: D's *Netočka Nezvanova. RusL* 12 (1985):297-317.

Marx, Paul. A Defense of the Epilogue to *Crime and Punishment. Bucknell Review* 10 (1961):57-74.

Maslenikov, Oleg A. The Ludicrous Man-of-the-Family: A Recurrent Type in D.

CalSS 6 (1971):29-36.

Mathewson, Rufus W., Jr. D and Malraux. *American Contribuitions to the Fourth International Congress of Slavists.* 's-Gravenhage: Mouton, 1958, pp.211-23.

Matich, Olga. *The Idiot:* A Feminist Reading. *D and the Human Condition after a Century,* ed. A. Ugrinsky, et al. NY: Greenwood P, 1986, pp. 53-60.

Matlaw, Ralph E. D and Conrad's Political Novels. *American Contributions to the Fifth International Congress of Slavists.* The Hague: Mouton, 1963, pp. 213-31.

___. Recurrent Imagery in D. *Harvard Slavic Studies* 3 (1957):201-26.

___. Structure and Integration in *Notes from Underground. PMLA* 73 (1958):101-9.

___. Thanatos and Eros: Approaches to D's Universe. *SEEJ* 4 (1960):17-24.

Matual, David. Fate in *Crime and Punishment. International Fiction Review* 3, 2 (1976):12-125.

___.The Number "Four" in D's *Crime and Punishment* and Jung's Theory of Quaternity. *RLJ* 115 (1979)54-62.

Maximoff, N. Future of Russia: Marx, Tolstoi, or D? *Religion in Life* 24 (1954-55):44-55.

Meijer, J. M. The Author of *Bratja Karamazovy.* In *The Brothers Karamazov by F. M. D: Essays,* ed. J. van der Eng, J. M. Meijer. The Hague: Mouton, 1971, pp. 7-27.

___. The Development of D's Hero. *RusL* 4, 3 (1976):257-72.

___. A Note on Time in *Bratja Karamazovy.* In *The Brothers Karamazov by F.M.D: Essays,* ed. J. van der Eng, J. M. Meijer. The Hague: Mouton, 1971, pp. 47-62.

___ Situation Rhyming in a Novel of D. *Dutch Contributions to the Fourth International Congress of Slavists.* The Hague: Mouton, 1958, pp. 115-28.

___. Some Notes on D and Russian Realism. *RusL* 4 (1973):5-17.

___. Some Remarks on D's *Besy. Dutch*

Contributions to the Fifth International Congress of Slavists. The Hague: Mouton, 1963, pp. 125-44.

Mercier, V. From Jane Austen to D. In *The New Novel. From Queneau to Pinget.* NY: Farrar, Straus, Giroux, 1971, pp. 104-64.

Merezhkovsky, D. S. D and Tolstoy. In *Russian Literature and Modern English Fiction: A Collection of Critical Essays,* ed. D. Davie. Chicago: Chicago UP, 1965, pp. 75-98.

Merrill, Reed. Brain Fever in the Novels of D. *Texas Quarterly* 19, 3 (1976):29-50.

____. The Demon of Irony: Stavrogin the Adversary at Tihon's. *D and the Human Condition after a Century,* ed. A. Ugrinsky, et al. NY: Greenwood P, 1986, pp. 87-97.

____. The Mistaken Endeavor: D's *Notes from Underground. MFS* 18 (1973): 505-16.

Meyer, Priscilla. D, Naturalist Poetics and "Mr. Prokharchin." *RusL* 10 (1981): 163-90.

Meyers, J. Holbein and *The Idiot.* In *Painting and the Novel.* NY: Barnes & Noble, 1975, pp. 136-47.

Miller, C. The Nihilist as Tempter-Reedemer: D's "Man-God" in Nietzsche's Notebooks. *Nietzsche-Studien* 4 (1975): 165-226.

Miller, Richard C. The Biblical Story of Joseph in D's *The Brothers Karamazov. SlavR* 41 (1982): 653-65.

Miller, Robin Feuer. D and the Tale of Terror. *The Russian Novel from Pushkin to Pasternak,* ed. J. Garrard. New Haven: Yale UP, 1983, pp. 103-21.

____. The Function of Inserted Narratives in *The Idiot. Ulbandus Review* 1 (1977):15-27.

____. The Role of the Reader in *The Idiot. SEEJ* 23 (1979):190-202.

Milosz, Czeslaw. D and Swedenburg. *SlavR* 34 (1975):302-18.

____. D and Western Intellectuals. *Cross Currents* 5 (1986):493-505.

____ and Carl R. Proffer. A Conversation about D. *Michigan Quarterly Review* 22 (1983):541-51.

Mindess, Harvey. Reappraisals: Freud on D. *American Scholar* 36 (1967):446-52.

Mochulsky, K. D's Search for Motives in the Notebooks of *Crime and Punishment.* In *Twentieth-Century Interpretations of "Crime and Punishment": A Collection of Critical Essays,* ed. R. L. Jackson. Englewood Cliffs: Prentice-Hall, 1974, pp. 11-16.

Monter, Barbara H. The Quality of D's Humor: *The Village of Stepančikovo. SEEJ* 17 (1973):33-41.

Moore, Gene M. The Voices of Legion: The Narrator of *The Possessed. DostSt* 6 (1985):51-65.

Moravcevich, Nicholas. Humor in D. *Bucknell Review* 14 (1967):59-77.

____. The Romantization of the Prostitute in D's Fiction. *RusL* 4, 15 (1976):299-308.

Moravia, **Alberto. The Marx-D Duel and** Other Russian Notes. *Encounter* 7 (Nov. 1956):3-12; rpt. in part in *Crime and Punishment,* ed. G. Gibian. NY: Norton, 1975, pp. 642-64.

Morson, Gary Saul. D's Anti-Semitism and the Critics: A Review Article. *SEEJ* 27 (1983):302-17.

____. D's *Writer's Diary* as Literature of Progress. *RusL* 4 (1976):1-14.

____. Literary Psychoanalysis and the Creative Process. *SEEJ* 25 (1981):62-75.

____. Reading Between the Genres: D's *Diary of a Writer. Yale Review* 68 (1978):224-34.

____. Verbal Pollution in *The Brothers Karamazov. PTL* 3 (1978):222-33.

Mortimer, Ruth. D and the Dream. *Modern Philology* 54 (1956):106-16.

Moser, Charles. D and the Aesthetics of Journalism. *DostSt* 3 (1982):377-88.

____. Nihilism, Aesthetics and *The Idiot. RusL* 11 (1982):377-88.

____. Svidrigajlov and Stavrogin. *Forum International* 3 (1980):88-98.

Moss, Kevin. A Typology of Embedded Texts in *The Brothers Karamazov. SlavR* 42 (1983):253-57.

Mossman, Elliott D. D's Early Works: The More than Rational Distortion. *SEEJ* 10 (1966):268-78.

Muchnic, Helen. The Leap and the Vision: A Note on the Pattern of D's Novels. *SEEJ* 8 (1964):379-90.

Murdoch, David. D's Satiric Comedy. *Satire Newsletter* 3 (1965):3-12.

Murthy, V. *Crime and Punishment:* A Tragedy of the Dialectic. *Kurukshetra University Research Journal* 5, 2 (1971): 107-12.

Nabokov, Vladimir. Fyodor D. In his *Lectures on Russian Literature.* NY: Harcourt Brace, 1981, pp. 97-136.

Naginsky, Isabelle. D and George Sand: Two Opponents of the Anthill. *D and the Human Condition after a Century,* ed. A. Ugrinsky, et al. NY: Greenwood P, 1986, pp. 199-210.

——. The Serenity of Influence: The Literary Relationship of George Sand and D. In *George Sand: Collected Essays,* ed. J. Glasgow. Troy, NY: Whitson, 1985, pp. 110-25.

Natov, Nadine. Anticipation of the Major Action in D's Works as a Problem of Free Choice. *Forum International* 3 (1980):10-31.

——. D and Diderot: A Comparative Study. *BulDS* 4 (1974):29-31.

——. D in the Theatre: Stage Adaptations of *The Brothers Karamazov. CASS* 8, 3 (1974):434-53.

——. Pushkin and D: Some Thematic Affinities. *Transactions of the Association of Russian-American Scholars in the USA* 5 (1971):27-51.

——. Some Plot Invariants in the Works of F. M. D as a Means of Expression of His Ideas. *Transactions of the Association of Russian-American Scholars in the USA* 5 (1971):79-92.

Naumann, Marina T. Death in *The Brothers Karamazov. St. Vladimir's Theological Quarterly* 25 (1981):159-74.

——. Raskolnikov's Shadow: Porfirij Petrovič. *SEEJ* 16 (1972):287-96.

Neuhäuser, R. F. M. D. *CASS* 12 (1978):321-22.

——. "The Landlady": A New Interpretation. *CSP* 10 (1968):42-67.

——. Observations on the Structure of *Notes from Underground* with Reference to the Main Themes of Part II. *CASS* 6 (1972):239-55.

——. Recent D Studies and Trends in D Research. *Journal of European Studies* 2 (1972):355-73.

——. Re-Reading *Poor Folk* and *The Double. BulDS* 6 (1976):29-32.

——. Romanticism in the Post-Romantic Age: A Typological Study of D's Man From Underground. *CASS* 8 (1974): 333-58.

——. Social Reality and the Hero in D's Early Works: D and Fourier's Psychological System. *RusL* 4 (1973):18-36.

——. The Structure of "The Insulted and Humiliated." *Forum International* 3 (1980):46-60.

Neumann, Harry. Milton's Adam and D's Grand Inquisitor on the Problem of Freedom Before God. *Personalist* 48 (1967):317-27.

Niemi, Pearl C. The Art of *Crime and Punishment. MFS* 9 (1963):291-313.

Nilsson, N. A. D and the Language of Suspense. *Scando-Slavia* 16 (1970):35-44.

——. Rhyming as a Stylistic Device in *Crime and Punishment. RusL* 4 (1973):65-71.

Nisula, Dasha C. D and Richard Wright: From St. Petersburg to Chicago. *D and the Human Condition after a Century,* ed. A. Ugrinsky, et al. NY: Greenwood P, 1986, pp. 163-70.

Noble, A. D's Anti-Utopianism. In *The Victorians and Social Protest: A Symposium,* ed. J. Butt & I. Clarke. Hamden: Archon Books, 1973, pp. 133-55.

Oates, Joyce Carol. The Double Vision of *The Brothers Karamazov. Journal of Aesthetics and Criticism* 27 (1968):203-13.

——. Tragic and Comic Visions in *The Brothers Karamazov.* In her *The Edge of Impossibility.* NY: Fawcett, 1972, pp. 77-102.

——. The Tragic Vision of *The Possessed. Georgia Review* 32 (1978):868-93.

Obolensky, A. Solzhenitsyn's Alyosha the Baptist and Alyosha Karamazov.

Cross Currents 23 (1973):329-36.

Offord, D. C. D and Chernyshevsky. *SEER* 57 (1979):509-30.

Orr, John. The Demonic Tendency, Politics and Society in D's *The Devils.* In *The Sociology of Literature: Applied Studies,* ed. D. Laurenson. Keele: U Keele, 1978, pp. 271-83.

——. *Tragic Realism and Modern Society: Studies in the Sociology of the Modern Novel.* London: Macmillan, 1977, pp. 53-86.

Ortega y Gasset, José. D and Proust. In his *The Dehumanization of Art,* rev. ed. Princeton: Princeton UP, 1968, pp. 74-80.

O'Toole, Michael. The Scythian Factor: Non-Verbal Interaction in Tolstoy and D. *Melbourne Slavonic Studies* 17 (1983):1-20.

Ozolins, Valija K. The Concept of Beauty in *The Possessed.* In *D and the Human Condition after a Century,* ed. A. Ugrinsky, et al. NY: Greenwood P, 1986, pp. 99-111.

Pachmuss, Temira. D and Herman Hesse: Analogies and Congruences. *Orbis Litterarum* 30, 3 (1975):210-24.

——. D and Max Frisch: Identity in the Modern World. *NZSJ* 1 (1982):89-102.

——. D and T. S. Eliot: A Point of View. *Forum for Modern Language Studies* 12, 1 (1976):82-89.

——. D and Thomas Mann: Parallels and Consequences. *Wiener Slavistiches Jahrbuch* 23 (1977):226-37.

——. D, D. H. Lawrence, and Carson McCullers: Influences and Confluences. *Germano-Slavica* 4 (1974);59-68.

——. D in Soviet Criticism of the Early 1930's. *SEEJ* 6 (1962):322-33.

——. D in the Criticism of the Russian Radical Intelligentsia in the 1870's and 1880's. *RusR* 21 (1962):59-74.

——. D, Werfel and Virginia Woolf: Influence and Confluences. *CLS* 9 (1972): 416-28.

——. D's Porfiry: A New Socrates. *NZSJ* 1 (1980):17-24.

——. Prometheus and Job Reincarnated: Melville and D. *SEEJ* 23 (1979):25-37.

——. Soviet Studies of D, 1935-56. *SlavR* 21 (1962):707-21.

——. The Technique of Dream-Logic in the Works of D. *SEEJ* 4 (1960):220-42.

Palumbo, Donald. The Paradoxical and Constructive Uses of Irony in D's Novels. *Liberal and Fine Arts Review* 4, 2 (1984):25-36.

——. The Theme of the Fortunate Fall in D's *The Brothers Karamazov:* The Effective Counterargument to Ivan's Ambivalent Atheism. *CEA Critic* 43, 4 (1981):8-12.

Panichas, George A. D and Satanism. *Journal of Religion* 45 (1965):12-29.

——. D's Political Apocalypse. *Intercollegiate Review* 12, 2 (1976):89-98.

——. Fyodor D and Roman Catholicism. *The Greek Orthodox Theological Review* (1958):16-34.

——. In Sight of the Logos: D's *Crime and Punishment. St. Vladimir's Seminary Quarterly* 15, 3 (1971):130-50.

——. *The Reverent Discipline: Essays in Literary Criticism and Culture.* Knoxville: U Tennessee P, 1974, pp. 205-82.

——. The Spiritual Art of D. *St. Vladimir's Seminary Quarterly* (1958):20-36.

——. The World of D. *Modern Age* 22 (1978):346-57.

Panteli, C. D's Aesthetic: Dichotomy Between Reality and Transcendence in Ivan Karamazov's Nightmare. In *F.M.D: (1821-1881): A Centenary Collection,* ed. L. Burnett. Colchester: Dept. of Literature. U Essex, 1981, pp. 119-26.

Paris, Bernard J. *Notes from Underground:* A Horneyan Analysis. *PMLA* 88 (1973):511-22.

——. The Two Selves of Rodion Raskolnikov: A Horneyan Analysis. *Gradiva* 1 (1978):316-28.

——. The Withdrawn Man: *Notes from Underground.* In his *Psychological Approach to Fiction.* Bloomington: Indiana UP, 1974, pp. 190-214.

Pascal, R. D and the Flux of Experience: The Idiot: In his *The Dual Voice: Free Indirect Speech and Its Functioning in the Nineteenth-Century Novel.* Totowa, NJ: Rowman & Littlefield, 1977, pp. 123-34.

Patterson, David. D's *Dvoinik* per Lacan's

"Parole." *Essays in Literature* 10 (1983): 299-308.

___. Unity of Existential Philosophy as Revealed by Shestov's Approach to D. *Studies in Soviet Thought* 19 (1979):219-31.

Peace, Richard. D and "The Golden Age." *DostSt* 3 (1982):61-78.

___. D's "The Eternal Husband" and Literary Polemics. *Essays in Poetics* 3, 2 (1978):22-40.

Pekurovskaya, Asya. The Nature of Referentiality in *The Double*. In *D and the Human Condition after a Century*, ed. A. Ugrinsky, et al. NY: Greenwood P, 1986, pp. 41-51.

Perlina, Nina. Herzen in *The Brothers Karamazov*. *CASS* 17 (1983):349-61.

___. & A. Forman. The Role and Function of Quotation in D. *Forum International* 3 (1980):33-47.

Perring, R. E. The Grand Inquisition. *Studies in the Humanities* 7, 2 (1979):52-57.

Pervushin, N. V. D's Foma Opiskin and Gogol. *CSP* 14 (1972):87-91.

___. Tolstoy, Rousseau, G. Sand and D. *Transactions of the Association of Russian-American Scholars in the USA* 11 (1978):164-73.

Peterson, D. D's Mock Apocalypse. *The Centennial Review* 18 (1974):76-90.

Peterson, R. E. Johan Borgen and D: Some Remarks. *Germano-Slavica* 4 (1982):101-8.

Petro, Peter. D the Satirist. *RLJ* 40, 136-137 (1986):95-102.

Peyre, Henri. The French Face of D. In *D and the Human Condition after a Century*, ed. A. Ugrinsky, et al. NY: Greenwood P, 1986, pp. 115-30.

___. The French Literary Imagination and D. In his *The French Literary Imagination and D and Other Essays*. Tuscaloosa: U Alabama P, 1975, pp. 1-56.

Pfohl, I. Knowing, Doing and Foreknowing: A Philosophical Re-Interpretation of *Crime and Punishment*. *Undergraduate Journal of Philosophy* 6, 2 (1974):1-9.

Phillips, Roger W. D's "Bobok": Dream of a Timid Man. *SEEJ* 18 (1974):132-42.

___. D's "Dream of a Ridiculous Man": A Study in Ambiguity. *Criticism* 17 (1975): 355-63.

Poggioli, Renato. D, or Reality and Myth. In his *The Phoenix and the Spider*. Cambridge: Harvard UP, 1957, pp. 16-32.

Pomar, Mark. Aleša Karamazov's Epiphany: A Reading of "Cana of Galilee." *SEEJ* 27 (1983):47-56.

Pomerants, Grigory. Euclidean and Non-Euclidean Reasoning in the Works of D. Tr. M. Dewhirst. *Kontinent* (English edition) 3 (1978):143-83.

Pope, J. C. Prufrock and Raskolnikov. *American Literature* 17 (1945):213-30; 18 (1946):319-21.

Porter, L. M. The Devil as Double in Nineteenth-Century Literature: Goethe, D, and Flaubert. *CLS* 15 (1978):316-35.

Pratt, Branwen. The Role of the Unconscious in *The Eternal Husband*. *Literature and Psychology* 22 (1972):13-25.

Pribic, Rado. *Notes from the Underground:* One Hundred Years after the Author's Death. In *D and the Human Condition after a Century*, ed. A. Ugrinsky, et al. NY: Greenwood P, 1986, pp. 71-77.

Pritchett. V. S. D. In *The Myth Makers: Essays on European, Russian and South American Novelists*. London: Chatto & Windus, 1979, pp. 63-76.

Pyman, A. D's Influence on Religious Thought in the Russian Silver Age. *CASS* 17 (1983):287-324.

Rabinowitz, P. J. The Click of the Spring: The Detective Story as Parallel Structure in D and Faulkner. *Modern Philology* 76 (1979):355-69.

Radoyce, L. Writer in Hell: Notes on D's Letters. *CalSS* 9 (1976):71-122.

Rae, S. H. D and the Theological Revolution in the West. *RusR* 29 (1970): 74-80.

Rahv, Phillip. D In *Crime and Punishment*. In *D: A Collection of Critical Essays*, ed. R. Wellek. Englewood Cliffs: Prentice-Hall, 1962, pp. 16-38.

___. D in *The Possessed*. In his *Essays on Literature and Politics*. Boston: Houghton-Mifflin, 1978, pp. 107-27.

___. The Other D. *New York Review of Books* April 20, 1972: 30-38.

Ramm, B. *The Double* and Romans 7. *Christianity Today* 15, 9 (April 1971):14-18.

Rayfield, D. D's *Eugénie Grandet. FMLS* 20 (1984):133-42.

Reeve, F. D. In the Stinking City: D's *Crime and Punishment. SEEJ* 4 (1960): 127-36.

Reid, Stephen. D's Kirilov and Freedom of the Will. *Hartford Studies in Literature* 3 (1971):197-208.

Rice, James. Raskol'nikov and Tsar Gorokh. *SEEJ* 25 (1981):38-53.

Rice, M. Current Research in the English Language on *Notes from Underground. BulDS* 5 (1975):24-34.

——. D's *Notes from Underground* and Hegel's *Master and Slave. CASS* 8 (1974):359-69.

Riemer, A. P. The Charter City: A Reading of *Crime and Punishment. Balcony* 1 (1965):15-22.

Riemer, N. Some Reflections on the Grand Inquisitor and Modern Democratic Theory. *Ethics* 67 (1957):249-56.

Richards, D. Four Utopias. *SEER* 40 (1962):220-28.

Richards, I. A. The God of D. *Forum* 78 (1927):88-97.

Roodkowsky, Nikita D. D: Seer of Modern Totalitarianism. *Thought* 47 (1972):587-98.

Roseberry, R. L. Schillerean Elements in the Works of D. *Germano-Slavica* 3 (1974):17-35.

Rosen, Nathan. Apollon in *Notes from Underground. Forum International* 3 (1980):77-78.

——. "Breaking Out of the Underground: The "Failure" of *A Raw Youth. MFS* 4 (1958):225-39.

——. Chaos and D's Women. *Kenyon Review* 20 (1958):257-77.

——. The Defective Memory of the Ridiculous Man. *CASS* 12 (1978):323-38.

——. D's Notebooks. *SlavR* 27 (1968):625-35.

——. Style and Structure in *The Brothers Karamazov. RLT* 1 (1971):352-65.

——. The Relation of Part I to Part II in *Notes from Underground. BulDS* 4 (1974):59-61.

——. Why Dmitri Karamazov Did Not Kill His Father. *CASS* 6 (1972):209-24.

Rosenshield, Gary. Artistic Consistency in *Notes from the Underground*—Part One. In *Studies in Honor of Xenia Gasiorowska,* ed. L. Leighton. Columbus: Slavica, 1983, pp. 11-21.

——. First- versus Third-Person Narration in *Crime and Punishment. SEEJ* 17 (1973):399-407.

——. Gorshkov in *Poor Folk:* An Analysis of an Early Dostoevskian "Double." *SEEJ* 26 (1982):149-62.

——. Point of View and Imagination in D's "White Nights." *SEEJ* 21 (1977):191-203.

Rosenthal, Richard J. D's Experiment with Projective Mechanisms and the Theft of Identity in *The Double.* In *The Anxious Subject: Nightmares and Daymares in Literature and Film,* ed. M. Lazar. Malibu: Undena, 1983, pp. 13-40.

Ross, Rochelle H. Who Is Ivan Karamazov? *Forum* (Houston) 8 (1970):39-43.

Rossbacher, Peter. Schiller's Poem "Resignation" and D's *Bratja Karamazovy. Wiener Slavistiches Jahrbuch* 23 (1977): 245-54.

Rowe, William W. *Crime and Punishment* and *The Brothers Karamazov:* Some Comparative Observations. *RLT* 10 (1974):33-42.

——. Dostoevskian Patterned Antinomy and Its Function in *Crime and Punishment. SEEJ* 16 (1972):287-96.

Rubenstein, R. Genius of Translation. *Colorado Quarterly* 22 (1974):359-68.

Rudicina, Alexandra F. Crime and Myth: The Archetypal Pattern of Rebirth in Three Novels of D. *PMLA* 87 (1972):1065-74.

Rzhevsky, L. D's *Besy:* Its Language and the Author's Image. *RLJ* 117 (1980):101-08.

Rzhevsky, N. D: The Christian Ego. In his *Russian Literature and Ideology.* Urbana: U Illinois P, 1983, pp. 66-98.

Saintsbury, G. Turgenev, D, and Tolstoy. In *Russian Literature and Modern English Fiction: A Collection of Critical Essays,* ed. D. Davie. Chicago:

Chicago UP, 1965, pp. 23-30.

Samchuk, U. D on Leninism. *Ukrainian Quarterly* 6 (1950):299-305.

Sandoz, Ellis. Philosophical Anthropology and "The Legend of the Grand Inquisitor." *Review of Politics* 26 (1964): 353-77.

____. Philosophical Dimensions of D's Politics. *Journal of Politics* 40, 3 (1978): 648-74.

Sandstrom, G. The Roots of Anguish in Conrad and D. *Polish Review* 20, 2-3 (1975):71-77.

Santangelo, G. The Five Motives of Raskolnikov. *Dalhousie Review* 54 (1975): 710-10.

Savage, D. S. D: The Idea of "The Gambler." *Sewanee Review* 58 (1950):281-98.

Schmeck, J. M. D and Freud on Criminal Psychopathology. *Psychiatric Quarterly Supplement* 40 (1966):278-82.

Schmid, Wolf. Narration and Narrative Content in *The Brothers Karamazov.* In *Miscellanea Slavica: To Honour the Memory of Jan M. Meijer,* ed. B. J. Amsenga, et al. Amsterdam: Rodopi, 1983, pp. 389-402.

Schmidl, F. Freud and D. *Journal of the American Psychoanalytic Association* 13 (1965):518-32.

Schoenl, W. J. From the Crystal Palace to D's Grand Inquisitor. *Journal of Thought* 15 (1980):19-28.

Schultze, Sydney. Settings in *Brat'ja Karamazovy. RusL* 19, 3 (1986):315-22.

Seduro, V. The Fate of Stavrogin's Confession. *RusR* 25 (1967):397-404.

Seeley, F. Aglaja Epančina. *SEEJ* 18 (1974):1-11.

____. D's Women. *SEER* 39 (1961):291-312.

____. The Two Faces of Svidrigailov. *CASS* 12 (1978):413-17.

Seiden, Melvin. Nabokov and D. *Contemporary Literature* 12 (1972):423-44.

Seifrid, Thomas. Theatrical Behavior Redeemed: D's *Belye nochi. SEEJ* 26 (1982):174-86.

Seliwoniuk, J. On Reading D with a Proustian "I." In *Studies in Honor of Louis Shein,* ed. S. Cioran, et al. Hamilton, Ontario: McMaster UP, 1983, pp. 117-24.

Sewall, Richard B. *The Brothers Karamazov.* In his *The Vision of Tragedy.* New Haven: Yale UP, 1959, pp. 106-26.

____. The Tragic World of the Karamazovs. In *Tragic Themes in Western Literature,* ed. Cleanth Brooks. New Haven: Yale UP, 1955, pp. 107-27.

Shahovskoy, Z. The Actuality of *The House of the Dead. Contemporary Review* (September 1944):161-64.

Shaw, J. Thomas. Raskol'nikov's Dreams. *SEEJ* 17 (1973):131-45.

Shein, L. The Concept of Good in Relation to Justice in D's Ethics. *CASS* 17 (1983):422-31.

____. An Examination of the Kantian Antinomies in *The Brothers Karamazov. Germano-Slavica* 2 (1973):49-60.

____. Kantian Elements in D's Ethics. In *Literature and National Identity: Nineteenth-Century Russian Critical Essays.* Tr. & ed. P. Debreczeny & J. Zeldin. Lincoln: Nebraska UP, 1970, pp. 59-69.

Shestov, Lev. D and Nietzsche: The Philosophy of Tragedy. In *Essays in Russian Literature,* ed. S. Roberts. Athens: Ohio UP, 1969, pp. 3-183.

Shneidman, N. Norman. Murder and Suicide in *The Brothers Karamazov:* The Double Rebellion of Pavel Smerdiakov. In *D and the Human Condition after a Century,* ed. A. Ugrinsky, et al. NY: Greenwood P, 1986, pp. 23-29.

Siefken, H. Man's Inhumanity to Man— Crime and Punishment: Kafka's Novel *Der Prozess* and Novels by Tolstoy, D, and Solzhenitsyn. *Trivium* 7 (1972):28-40.

Silbajoris, Rimvydas. The Children in *The Brothers Karamazov. SEEJ* 7 (1963): 26-38.

Simmons, E. J. D in Soviet Russia. *American Quarterly on the Soviet Union* 1 (1938):22-30.

Simmons, J.S.G. F.M.D and A. K. Tolstoy: Two Letters. *OSP* 9 (1960):64-72.

Simons, J. D. The Grand Inquisitor in Schiller, D and Huxley. *NZSJ* 8 (1971):20-31.

____. The Myth of Progress in Schiller and D. *CL* 24 (1972):328-37.

Simpson, P. The Rejection of the World: D, Ivanov, Camus. In *F. M. D (1821-1881): A Centenary Collection,* ed. l. Burnett. Colchester: Dept. of Literature, U Essex, 1981, pp. 97-108.

Slattery, D. P. The Frame Tale: Temporality, Fantasy and Innocence in *The Idiot. BulDS* 9 (1979):6-25.

——. The Icon and the Spirit of Comedy: D's *The Possessed.* In *The Terrain of Comedy,* ed. L. Cowan. Dallas: Dallas Institute of Humanities and Culture, 1984, pp. 195-219.

——. Narcissus Inverted: Fantastic-Realism as a Way of Knowing in *The Idiot.* In *D and the Human Condition after a Century,* ed. A. Ugrinsky, et al. NY: Greenwood P, 1986, pp. 61-69.

——. The Nature of Suffering in Schiller and D. *CL* 19 (1967):160-73.

——. Pan, Myth and Fantasy in D's *The Idiot. CASS* 17 (1983):384-401.

——. Panic in Petersburg: D's Mythical Method. *Publications of the Arkansas Philological Association* 5, 2-3 (1979):48-57.

Slochower, Harry. Incest in *The Brothers Karamazov. The American Imago* 16 (1959):127-45.

Slonim, Marc. D under the Soviets. *RusR* 10 (1951):118-30.

Smalley, Barbara. The Compulsive Patterns of D's Underground Man. *Studies in Short Fiction* 10 (1973):389-96.

Smith, C. M. Theology and the Human Story: The Redemptive Passage Through Human Suffering in D's *Crime and Punishment. Encounter* 42 (1981):29-44.

Smyth, Sarah. The "Lukovka" Legend in *The Brothers Karamazov. Irish Slavonic Studies* 7 (1986):41-51.

Snipes, K. Intellectual Villains in D, Chaucer and Albert Camus. *Discourse* 13 (1970):240-50.

Snodgrass, W. D. Crime for Punishment: The Terror of Part I. *Hudson Review* 13 (1960):202-53.

Solovev, V. In Memory of D. In *Literature and National Identity: Nineteenth-Century Russian Critical Essays,* tr. &

ed. P. Debreczeny & J. Zeldin. Lincoln: Nebraska UP, 1970, pp. 169-80.

Sorokin, Boris. D on Tolstoy: The Immoral Message of *Anna Karenina. Connecticut Review* 2 (1973):25-33.

Spencer, F. Form and Disorder in D's *A Raw Youth.* In *F. M. D (1821-1881): A Centenary Collection,* ed. L. Burnett. Colchester: Dept. of Literature, U Essex, 1981, pp. 37-57.

Spilka, Mark. Human Worth in *The Brothers Karamazov. Minnesota Review* 5 (1965):38-49.

——. Kafka's Sources for the Metamorphosis. *CL* 11 (1959):289-307.

——. Playing Crazy in the Underground. *Minnesota Review* 6 (1966):233-43.

Spoonhour, C. D and Freedom. *Duns Scotus Philosophical Association* 28 (1964):30-52.

Squires, P. C. D's Master-Study of the "Protest." *Science Monthly* June 1937: 555-57.

——. D's Raskolnikov: The Criminalistic Protest. *Journal of Criminal Law* 28 (1937):478-94.

Stacy, R. Tolstoy and D. In his *Russian Literary Criticism: A Short History.* Syracuse: Syracuse UP, 1974, pp. 80-104.

Stammler, H. D's Aesthetics and Schelling's Philosophy of Art. *CL* 7 (1955): 313-23.

Steinberg, A. Z. The Death of Svidrigailov. In *Twentieth-Century Interpretations of "Crime and Punishment": A Collection of Critical Essays,* ed. R. L. Jackson. Englewood Cliffs: Prentice Hall, 1974, pp. 103-5.

Stenbock-Fermor, Elisabeth. Lermontov and D's Novel *The Devils. SEEJ* 17 (1959):215-30.

——. Stavrogin's Quest in *The Devils* of D. In *To Honor Roman Jakobson. Essays on the Occasion of His Seventieth Birthday.* The Hague: Mouton, 1967, pp. 1926-34.

Stern, J. P. The Testing of the Prince: On the Realism of D's *The Idiot.* In *Gorski Vijenac: A Garland of Essays Offered to Professor Elizabeth Hill,* ed. R. Auty, et al. Cambridge: Modern Humanities Research Assn., 1970, pp. 252-67.

Stern, Lawrence. Freedom and Love in *Notes from Underground. Philosophy Research Archives* 4, (1978):no. 1248.

Stock, Irvin. *Fiction as Wisdom: From Goethe to Bellow.* University Park: Penn State UP, 1980.

Stief, C. D's *The Possessed:* From a Political Pamphlet to a Work of Art. In *Expression, Communication and Experience in Literature and Language,* ed. R. G. Popperwell. London: Modern Humanities Research Association, 1972, pp. 127-28.

Stolnitz, Jerome. "You Can't Separate the Work of Art from the Artist." *Philosophy and Literature* 8 (1984): 209-21.

Strauss, G. The Prophet: D's "Grand Inquisitor" and Gide's "El Hadj." *Australian Journal of French Studies* 14 (1977):88-104.

Streetman, R. F. The Table of Rational Desires? Underground Man, The Overman, and Dionysius Encounter the Computer. In *Proceedings of Apollo Agonistes: The Humanities in a Computerized World,* ed. M. E. Grenander. Albany: SUNYA, 1979, pp. 394-402.

Strelsky, Katharine. D in Florence. *RusR* 23 (1964):149-63.

____. D's Early Tale, "A Faint Heart." *RusR* 30 (1971):146-53.

Struc, Roman. D's "Confessions" as Critique of Literature. *Research Studies* 46 (1978):79-89.

____. Kafka and D as "Blood Relatives." *DostSt* 2 (1981):111-17.

____. Madness as Existence: An Essay on a Literary Theme (On Works by Hoffmann, Büchner, Kafka and D). *Research Studies* 38 (1970):75-94.

____. Petty Demons and Beauty: Gogol, D, Sologub. In *Essays in European Literature in Honor of Liselotte Dieckmann,* ed. P. U. Hohendahl, et al. St. Louis: Washington UP, 1972, pp. 61-82.

Sutherland, D. Language and Interpretation in *Crime and Punishment. Philosophy and Literature* 3 (1978):223-36.

Sutherland, Stewart. Death and Fulfillment, Or Would the Real Mr. D Stand Up? In *Philosophy and Literature,* ed.

A. Phillips Griffiths. Cambridge: Cambridge UP, 1984, pp. 15-27.

____. D and the Grand Inquisitor: A Study in Atheism. *Yale Review* 66 (1977):364-73.

Tate, Allen. D's Hovering Fly: A Causerie on the Imagination and the Actual World. *Sewanee Review* 51 (1943):353-69.

Terras, Victor. Dissonances and False Notes in a Literary Text. In *The Structural Analysis of Narrative Texts: Conference Papers,* ed. A. Kodjak, et al. Columbus: Slavica, 1980.

____. D the Humorist: 1846-1849. *ISS* 3 (1963):152-80.

____. D's Organic Aesthetics in Its Relation to Romanticism. *RusL* 4, 1 (1976):15-26.

____. Turgenev and the Devil in *The Brothers Karamazov. CASS* 6 (1972):265-71.

Todd, William Mills III. The Anti-Hero with a Thousand Faces: Saltykov-Shchedrin's Porfiry Petrovich. *Studies in the Literary Imagination* (Georgia State College) 9, 1 (1976):87-105.

Toporov, V. N. On D's Poetics and Archaic Patterns of Mythological Thought. *New Literary History* 9 (1978):333-52.

Trahan, Elizabeth. The Golden Age— Dream of a Ridiculous Man?: A Concentric Analysis of D's Short Story. *SEEJ* 17 (1959):349-71.

Traschen, I. D's *Notes from Underground. Accent* 16 (1956): 255-64.

____. Existential Ambiguities in *Notes from Underground. South Atlantic Quarterly* 73 (1974):363-76.

Trubeckoj, Nikolaj S. The Style of *Poor Folk* and *The Double. ASEER* 7 (1948): 150-70.

Turner, J. Neville. Dostoevsky and the Judicial Process. *MelbSS* 14 (1980):3-32.

Tynyanov, Y. D and Gogol: Toward a Theory of Parody. Part One: Stylization and Parody. In *D and Gogol: Texts and Criticism,* ed. Priscilla Meyer & Stephen Rudy. Ann Arbor: Ardis, 1979, pp. 101-17.

Tyrras, N. On D's Funeral. *SEEJ* 30 (1986):271-77.

Updike, John. Polina and Aleksei and Anna and Losnitsky. *The New Yorker* 49 (April 14, 1973):145-54; reprinted in his *Picked-Up Pieces*. NY: Knopf, 1975, pp. 132-40.

Vacquier, T. D and Gide: A Comparison. *Sewanee Review* 37 (1929):478-89.

Van Holk, A. Verbal Aggression and Offended Honour in D's *Selo Stepanchikovo i ego obitateli*. *RusL* 4, 13 (1976):67-107.

Vinograde, Ann C. *The Gambler*: Prokofev's Libretto and D's Novel. *SEEJ* 16 (1972):414-18.

Vinogradov, V. V. The School of Sentimental Naturalism: D's Novel *Poor Folk* Against the Background of the Literary Evolution of the 1840s. In *D and Gogol: Texts and Criticism*, ed. Priscilla Meyer & Stephen Rudy. Ann Arbor: Ardis, 1979, pp. 161-215.

——. Towards a Morphology of the "Naturalist Style." In *D and Gogol: Texts and Criticism*, ed. Priscilla Meyer & Stephen Rudy. Ann Arbor: Ardis, 1979, pp. 217-28.

Vladiv, S. D's Major Novels as Semiotic Models. In *Proceedings of the Russian Colloquium*, University of Melbourne, 1976, ed. N. Christensen & J. Scarfield. Melbourne: U Melboune, 1977, pp. 47-57.

——. D's *The Idiot* and Existential Psychology. *MelbSS* 14 (1980):41-55.

——. The Use of Circumstantial Evidence in D's Works. *CASS* 12 (1978):353-70.

Voge, Noel. D as a Translator. *SEEJ* 15 (1957):251-59.

Walker, H. Observations on Fyodor D's *Notes from the Underground*. *American Imago* 15 (1962):195-210.

Walsh, Harry. The Book of Job and the Dialectic of Theodicy in *The Brothers Karamazov*. *South Central Bulletin* 37, 4 (1977):161-64.

——. D's Andrej Versilov as Counterfeit Holy Man. *RLJ* 37, 126-27 (1983):69-76.

——. The Permutations of a Complex Metaphor: D's Sunsets. *SEEJ* 27 (1983): 293-301.

Warrick, P. Sources of Zamiatin's *We* in D's *Notes from Underground*. *Extrapolation* 17 (1975):63-77.

Wasiolek, Edward. *Aut Caesar, Aut Nihil*: A Study of D's Moral Dialectic. *PMLA* 78 (1963):89-97.

——. D, Camus, and Faulkner: Transcendence and Mutilation. *Philosophy and Literature* 1 (1977):131-46.

——. D's Notebooks for *Crime and Punishment*. *Psychoanalytic Review* 55 (1968):349-59.

——. Eclecticisms and Pluralisms: Trying to Find D and Tolstoy. *Studies in the Novel* 4 (1972):86-92.

——. On the Structure of *Crime and Punishment*. *PMLA* 74 (1959):131-36.

——. Raskolnikov's Motives: Love and Murder. *American Imago* 31 (1974): 252-69.

Watson, Ihita. D's Theory of Salvation. *Melbourne Slavonic Studies* 11 (1976):33-51.

Webster, Alexander. The Exemplary Kenotic Holiness of Prince Myshkin in D's *The Idiot*. *St. Vladimir's Theological Quarterly* 28, 3 (1984):189-216.

Weintraub, W. Two Parallels. 1. D. 2. Claudel. In *Adam Mickiewicz: Księga w stulecie zgonu*. London, 1957, pp. 499-508.

Weisberg, Richard H. *The Failure of the Word: The Protagonist as Lawyer in Modern Fiction*. Part 2. The Failure of the Christian Narrative Vision: D's Legal Novels (*Crime and Punishment, Brothers Karamazov*). New Haven: Yale UP, 1984, pp. 43-81.

Weisberger, Jean. Faulkner's Monomaniacs: Their Indebtedness to Raskolnikov. *CLS* 5 (1968):181-93.

Weiss, Daniel. Freedom and Immortality: Notes from the Dostoevskian Underground. In his *The Critic Agonistes: Psychology, Myth and the Art of Fiction*. Seattle: U Washington P, 1985, pp. 229-43.

Welch, L. M. Luzhin's Crime and the Advantages of Melodrama in D's *Crime and Punishment*. *Texas Studies in Language and Literature* 18 (1976):135-46.

Wellek, René. Bakhtin's View of D: "Polyphony" and "Carnivalesque." *DostSt* 1 (1980):31-40; rpt. in *Russian Formalism: A Retrospective Glance: A*

Festschrift for Victor Erlich, ed. R. L. Jackson & S. Rudy. New Haven: Yale Center for International and Area Studies, 1985, pp. 231-41.

Werge, T. Word as Deed in *Crime and Punishment. Renascence* 27 (1975): 207-19.

Westbrook, F. A. On Dreams, Saints, and Fallen Angels: Reality and Illusion in *Dreams of the Red Chamber* and *The Idiot. Literature East & West* 15 (1971): 371-91.

Whalen, S. The Pronouns of Address in D's *Besy:* A Socio-linguistic Sketch. *CSP* 24 (1982):67-72.

Wharton, Robert V. D's Defense of Christ in *The Brothers Karamazov:* Part Two. *Cithara* 24, 1 (1984):59-70.

____. Evil Man, Earthly Paradise: D's Theodicy. *Thomist* 41 (1977):567-84.

____. Roads to Happiness in *The Brothers Karamazov:* D's Defense of Christ. *Cithara* 23, 2 (1984):3-15.

Wienhorst, S. E. Vision and Structure in *The Possessed. Religion in Life* 45 (1976):490-8.

Wierzbicki, J. E. Remarks on the Notebooks to *The Idiot. MelbSS* 14 (1980):88-98.

Willett, Maurita. The "Ending" of *Crime and Punishment. Orbis Litterarum* 25 (1970):244-58.

Wilson, A. C. The Soviet Critique of D, 1953-1983, and Its Links with Soviet Aesthetics. *MelbSS* 19 (1985):71-106.

Wilson, R. Raskolnikov's Dream in *Crime and Punishment. Literature and Psychology* 26, 4 (1976):159-66.

Winfield, W. Reflection/Negation/Reality: D and Hegel. *CLS* 17 (1980):399-409.

Woodhouse, C. M. The Two Russians. *Essays by Divers Hands* 29 (1958):18-36.

Woodward, J. Overlapping Portraits in D's *The Idiot. Scando-Slavica* 26 (1980): 115-27.

____. "Transferred Speech" in D's "Vechnyi muzh." *CASS* 8 (1974):398-407.

Yakushev, H. The Trial Scenes in *The Brothers Karamazov* and *Resurrection* as a Reflection of the Author's *Weltanschauung. Forum International* 3 (1980): 119-32.

Yarwood, Edmund. A Comparison of Selected Symbols in *Notes from the Underground* and *We. Proceedings of the Pacific Northwest Conference of Foreign Languages* 21 (1970):144-49.

Žekulin, G. On the Language and Style of "Skvernyj anekdot." *Forum International* 3 (1980):61-76.

Zellar, Leonard. Conrad and D. In *The English Novel in the Nineteenth Century: Essays on the Literary Mediation of Human Values,* ed. George Goodin. Urbana: U Illinois P, 1972, pp. 214-23.

Zohrab, Irene. F. M. D and A. N. Ostrovsky. *MelbSS* 14 (1980):56-79.

ALEXANDER DRUZHININ

Criticism

Curtis, Glenn Eldon. D's *Biblioteka dlia chteniia:* Resurrection and Demise of a Literary Journal. Ph.D. diss., Indiana, 1980.

Genereux, George Alfred. Alexander D's Writings on English Literature. Ph.D. diss., California, Los Angeles, 1968.

Schulak, Helen Szyrman. Aleksandr D and His Place in Russian Criticism. Ph.D. diss., California, Berkeley, 1967.

Brojde, A. D's View of American Life and Literature. *CASS* 10 (1976):382-99.

Genereux, George. The Crisis in Russian Literary Criticism: 1859—The Decisive Year. *RLT* 17 (1982):116-40.

NADEZHDA DUROVA

Translations

The Cavalry Maid. The Memoirs of a Woman Soldier of 1812. Tr. & intro. John Mersereau and David Lapeza. Ann Arbor: Ardis, 1988.

The Cavalry Maiden. Journals of a Russian Officer in the Napoleonic Wars. Tr. & intro. Mary Fleming Zirin. Bloomington: Indiana UP, 1988.

Zirin, Mary Fleming. My Childhood Years: A Memoir by the Czarist Cavalry Officer, Nadezhda Durova. *New York Literary Forum* 12-13 (1984):119-41. [Includes translation into English.]

AFANASY FET

Translations

I Have Come to Greet You: Selected Poems. Tr. James Greene. London: Angel Books, 1983.
[57 poems.]

Arndt, Walter, tr. *RLT* 11 (1975):283-84. [Willows and Birches; No, I decline to go where a perfidious boulder; How fresh at the dawn's first glimmers.]
Nabokov, Vladimir, tr. Three Poems. *RusR* 3 (1943):31-33.
Obolensky, D., ed. *The Heritage of Russian Verse.* Bloomington: Indiana UP, 1976, pp. 190-94.
[I have come to you with greeting; Willows and Birches; The rapture of fragrant spring; On a southern night; How beautiful, in the faintly glimmering morning; The September Rose.]
Raffel, B., ed. & tr. *Russian Poetry under the Tsars.* Albany: SUNY P, 1971, pp. 145-52.
[On a Southern Night; Here I Am; Dark Sky; Spring Will Be Coming; Amphitrite; Like Gnats at Dawn.]

Criticism

Gustafson, Richard F. *The Imagination of Spring: The Poetry of Afanasy F.* New Haven: Yale UP, 1967.
Lotman, Lydia. *Afanasy F.* Tr. M. Wettlin. Boston: Twayne, 1976.

Buck, Christopher David. Duality in A. A. F: Conflict and Transcendence. Ph.D. diss., Yale, 1978.
Gustafson, Richard Polke. The Imagination of Spring: The Poetry of Afanasij F. Ph.D. diss., Columbia, 1963.

Laferriere, Daniel A. Psycholinguistic Studies Primarily in the Lyric Poetry of Afanasij F. Ph.D. diss., Brown, 1972.
Maurer, Sigrid Helga. Schopenhauer in Russia: His Influence on Turgenev, F, and Tolstoy. Ph.D. diss., California, Berkeley, 1966.
Van Tuyl, Jo Anne. The Aesthetic Immediacy of Selected Lyric Poems of Keats, Fet and Verlaine. Ph.D. diss., North Carolina, 1986.

BinyonT. J. Lermontov, Tyutchev and F. In *Nineteenth-Century Russian Literature,* ed. J. Fennell. Berkeley: U California P, 1973, pp. 168-224.
Botkin, Vasily. A. A. F. Tr. G. Genereux. *RLT* 17 (1982):23-63.
Briggs, Anthony D. Annualarity as a Melodic Principle in F's Verse. *SlavR* 28 (1969):591-603.
—— The Metrical Virtuosity of Afanasy F. *SEER* 52 (1974):355-65.
Fitzlyon, A. A Weekend in the Country. *Listener* (Dec. 9, 1965):951-53.
Goy, E. D. The First Translations of Fet in Serbian. *SEER* 37 (1959):236-42.
Klenin, Emily. Emotion and Serenity in a Late Poem by Fet. *IJSLP* 31-32 (1985): 225-34.
—— On the Sources of F's Aesthetics of Music: Wackenroder, Schopenhauer and Ševyrev. *Die Welt der Slaven* 30 (1985): 319-44.
Silbajoris, Rimvydas. Dynamic Elements in the Lyrics of F. *SlavR* 26 (1967):217-26.
Stammler, H. Metamorphoses of the Will: Schopenhauer and F. In *Western Philosophical Systems in Russian Literature,* ed. A. Mlikotin. Los Angeles: U Southern California P, 1979, pp. 35-58.

VSEVOLOD GARSHIN

Bibliography

Yarwood, Edmund, comp. A Bibliography of Works By and About Vsevolod M. Garshin. *RLT* 17 (1982):227-41.

Translations

From the Reminiscences of Private Ivanov and Other Stories. Tr. Peter Henry, et al. London: Angel Books, 1988.
[Four Days, An Incident, A Very Brief Romance, An Encounter, The Coward, Artists, *Attalea princeps,* A Night, Order and Officer, What Never Was, From the Reminiscences of Private Ivanov, The Red Flower, The Tale of the Toad and the Rose, The Legend of Haggai the Proud, The Travelling Frog, The Signal.]

A Red Flower. Philadelphia: Brown Bros., 1911.

The Scarlet Flower. Stories. Tr. B. Isaac. Moscow: Foreign Languages Publishing House, 1959.

The Signal and Other Stories. Tr. R. Smith. NY: Knopf, 1915; reprinted: Freeport, NY: Books for Libraries P, 1971.

The Dangerous Desire for Growth in a Glass House. Tr. V. Romberg. *Poet Lore* 12 (1900):327-34.

Colorado Quarterly. Boulder, CO, 1980.
[The Coward; Reminiscences of Private Ivanov; Nadezhda Nikolaevna.]

See also Edmund Yarwood, A Bibliography of Works By and About Vsevolod M. Garshin. RLT 17 (1982):227-41.

Criticism

Henry, Peter. *Vsevolod G: The Man, his Works, and his Milieu.* Oxford: Meeuws, 1983. [Bibliography.]

Parker, F. *Vsevolod G—A Study of a Russian Conscience.* Morningside Heights, NY: King's Crown, 1946.

Yarwood, Edmund. *Vsevolod G.* Boston: Twayne, 1981.

Parker, Fan. V. G: A Study of a Russian Conscience. Ph.D. diss., Columbia, 1946.

Penny, Bernard. Vsevolod Mikhailovich G: A Study of the Dynamics of Guilt. Ph.D. diss., Georgetown, 1977.

Siegel, George. The Art of Vsevolod G. Ph.D. diss., Harvard, 1958.

Varnai, Paul. The Prose of V. G. Ph.D. diss., Michigan, 1970.

Yarwood, Edmund John. Hero and Foil: Structure in the Stories of V. G. Ph.D. diss., North Carolina, 1974.

Brodal, Jan. The Pessimism of V. M. G. *Scando-Slavica* 19 (1973):17-30.

Fetzer, Leland. Art and Assasination: G's "Nadezhda Nikolaevna. *RusR* 34 (1975): 55-66.

Henry, Peter. Imagery of *Podvig* and *Podvizhnichestvo* in the Works of G and the Early Gorky. *SEER* 61 (1983):139-59.

Kallaur, Constantine H. Imagery in Vsevolod G's *The Scarlet Flower. Nassau Review* 2, 3 (1972):16-20.

Kramer, Karl D. Impressionist Tendencies in the Work of Vsevolod G. In *American Contributions to the Seventh International Congress of Slavists,* vol. 2, ed. V. Terras. The Hague: Mouton, 1973, pp. 339-56.

Lejins, Hamilkars. Suicide in G's Life and Stories. *South Central Bulletin* 27, 4 (1967):34-44.

Manning, C. A. The Guilty Conscience of G. *SEER* 10 (1931):255-92.

Varnai, Paul. Structural and Syntactic Devices in G's Stories. *RLJ* 94-95 (1972): 61-71.

NIKOLAI GOGOL

Bibliographies

Frantz, Philip, comp. *G. A Bibliography.* Ann Arbor: Ardis, 1989.

Proffer, Carl R., ed. *Letters of Nikolai G.* Ann Arbor: U Michigan P, 1967, [Bibliography of works about Gogol in West European languages to 1966.]

Translations

Arabesques. Tr. Alexander Tulloch, intro. Carl R. Proffer. Ann Arbor: Ardis, 1982.
[Preface; Sculpture, Painting and Music; On the Middle Ages; On the

Teaching of World History; The Portrait (1835 version); A Glance at the Composition of Little Russia; A Few Words about Pushkin; On Present-Day Architecture; Al-Mamun; Life; Schlözer, Müller and Herder; Nevsky Prospect; The Songs of the Ukraine; Thoughts on Geography; The Last Day of Pompeii; On the Movements of Peoples at the End of the Fifth Century; The Diary of a Madman.]

The Collected Tales and Plays, ed. L. J. Kent. (The Constance Garnett translations revised by the editor.) NY: Pantheon, 1964.

[Evenings on a Farm Near Dikanka; Mirgorod; Nevsky Prospect; Diary of a Madman; The Nose, The Coach; The Portrait (1842 version); The Overcoat; The Inspector General; Marriage; The Gamblers. The best anthology—recommended for any works not singled out as better elsewhere in this section.]

The Complete Tales of Nikolai G, ed. Leonard J. Kent. Intro., notes. Chicago: U Chicago P, 1985, 2 vols.

Dead Souls.

[The novel has been translated anonymously, by Isabel Hapgood, C. Hogarth, Constance Garnett, B. G. Guerney, George Reavey, Andrew MacAndrew, Helen Michailoff, and David Magarshack. The first three and the MacAndrew and Michailoff versions are to be avoided. Of the others Guerney's is obviously the best, with Magarshack's the runner-up. However, as I pointed out in my article "*Dead Souls* in Translation" (*SEEJ* 8 [1964]:420-33), Guerney's version contains a whole chapter (chapter 11 in his version) which does not belong in the novel and there are other minor textual irregularities.—C.R.P.]

Dead Souls: The Reavey Translation, Backgrounds and Sources, Essays in Criticism, ed. George Gibian. NY: W. W. Norton, 1985.

Evenings Near the Village of Dikanka. Moscow: Foreign Languages Publishing House, 1957.

[The Fair at Sorochintsi; Saint John's Eve; A May Night, or the Drowned Maiden; The Lost Letter; Christmas Eve; A Terrible Revenge; Ivan Fyodorovich Shponka and His Aunt; A Place Bewitched. The translations are an edited version of Constance Garnett.]

Hanz Kuchelgarten, Leaving the Theater and Other Works. Ed. Ronald Meyer. Ann Arbor: Ardis, forthcoming.

Mirgorod. Tr. David Magarshack. NY: Noonday Press, 1962.

[The Old-World Landowners, Taras Bulba; Viy; The Story of How Ivan Ivanovich Quarrelled with Ivan Nikiforovich. Recommended translations of all 4 tales.]

Selected Passages from Correspondence with Friends. Tr. J. Zeldin. Nashville: Vanderbilt UP, 1969.

The Theater of Nikolay Gogol: Plays and Selected Writings. Ed. & intro. Milton Ehre, Chicago: U Chicago P, 1980.

[The Government Inspector, Marriage, The Gambler. The translations are different if not necessarily superior to the revised Garnett version in the Kent anthology.]

An Author's Confession. Tr. David Lapeza. *RLT* 10 (1974):101-28.

Petersburg Notes of 1836. Tr. Linda Germano. *RLT* 7 (1973): 177-86.

Meyer, Priscilla & Stephen Rudy, eds. *Dostoevsky and G: Texts and Criticism.* Ann Arbor: Ardis, 1979.

[The Diary of a Madman; The Nose.]

Senelick, Laurence, tr. & ed. *Russian Dramatic Theory from Pushkin to the Symbolists.* Austin: U Texas P, 1981, pp. 16-59.

[Petersburg Notes for 1836; A Theater Lets Out after the Performance of a New Comedy.]

Letters of Nikolai Gogol. Ed. Carl R. Proffer. Ann Arbor: U Michigan P, 1967.

See also Philip Frantz, *Gogol. A Bibliography.* Ann Arbor: Ardis, 1989.

Criticism

Bogojavlensky, Marianna. *Reflections on Nikolai G.* Jordanville, NY: Holy Trinity Monastery, 1969.

Debreczeny, Paul. *G and His Contemporary Critics.* Philadelphia, 1966. (Transactions of the American Philosophical Society 56, 3 [1966]:5-68.)

Driessen, Frederick Christoffel. *G as a Short-Story Writer: A Study of His Technique of Composition.* Tr. Ian F. Finlay. The Hague: Mouton, 1965.

Erlich, Victor. *G.* New Haven: Yale UP, 1969.

Fanger, Donald. *The Creation of Nikolai G.* Cambridge: Harvard UP, 1979.

___. *Dostoevsky and Romantic Realism: A Study of Dostoevsky in Relation to Balzac, Dickens and G.* Cambridge: Harvard UP, 1956.

Gippius, V. V. *G.* Tr. Robert Maguire. Ann Arbor: Ardis, 1981.

Hodgson, Peter. *From G to Dostoevsky: Jakov Butkov, a Reluctant Naturalist in the 1840's.* Munich: Fink, 1976.

Karlinsky, Simon. *The Sexual Labyrinth of Nikolai G.* Cambridge: Harvard UP, 1976.

Kent, L. J. *The Subconscious in G and Dostoevsky and Its Antecedents.* The Hague: Mouton, 1969.

Lavrin, Janko. *Gogol.* NY: Haskell House, 1973.

___. *Nikolai G: 1809-1852.* London: Sylvan P, 1951.

Lindstrom, Thais. *Nikolay G.* NY: Twayne, 1974.

Little, T. E. *The Fantasts.* Amersham, England: Avebury, 1982.

Luckyj, George Stephen Nestor. *Between G and Shevchenko. Polarity in the Literary Ukraine: 1798-1847.* Munich: Wilhelm Fink, 1971.

Magarshack, David. *G: A Life.* NY: Grove, 1957.

Maguire, Robert, ed. *G from the Twentieth Century: Eleven Essays.* Princeton: Princeton UP, 1974.

Meyer, Priscilla & Stephen Rudy, eds. *Dostoevsky and G: Texts and Criticism.* Ann Arbor: Ardis, 1979.

Muchnic, Helen. *The Unhappy Consciousness: G, Poe, Baudelaire.* Baltimore: Smith College, 1967.

Nabokov, Vladimir. *Nikolai G.* NY: New Directions, 1961.

Obolensky, Alexander P. *Food-Notes on G.* Winnipeg: Trident P, 1972.

Ovcharenko, Maria M. *G (Hohol') and Os'machka.* Winnipeg: UVAN, 1969.

Passage, Charles. *The Russian Hoffmannists.* The Hague: Mouton, 1963.

Peace, Richard. *The Enigma of G: An Examination of the Writings of N. V. G and Their Place in the Russian Literary Tradition.* Cambridge: Cambridge UP, 1981.

Proffer, Carl R. *The Simile and G's "Dead Souls."* The Hague: Mouton, 1968.

Rancour-Laferriere, Daniel. *Out from Under G's Overcoat: A Psychoanalytic Study.* Ann Arbor: Ardis, 1982.

Rowe, W. W. *Through G's Looking-Glass.* NY: New York UP, 1976.

Setchkareff, Vsevolod. *G: His Life and Works.* Tr. Robert Kramer. NY: New York UP, 1965.

Sobel, Ruth. *G's Forgotten Book: "Selected Passages" and Its Contemporary Readers.* Washington, D.C.: University Press of America, 1981.

Stromecky, Ostap. *The How of G.* Huntsville, Alabama: U Alabama Huntsville Press, 1975.

Taylor, P. *Gogolian Interludes: G's Story "Christmas Eve" as the Subject of the Operas by Tchaikovsky and Rimsky-Korsakov.* London: Collets, 1984.

Trahan, Elizabeth, ed. *G's "Overcoat": An Anthology of Critical Essays.* Ann Arbor: Ardis, 1982.

Troyat, Henri. *Divided Soul: The Life of G.* Tr. Nancy Amphoux. Garden City, NY: Doubleday, 1973.

Vinogradov, V. V. *G and the Natural School.* Tr. Debra K. Erickson & Ray Parrott. Ann Arbor: Ardis, 1987.

Woodward, James. *G's "Dead Souls."* Princeton: Princeton UP, 1978.

___. *The Symbolic Art of G: Essays on His Short Fiction.* Columbus: Slavica, 1982.

Worrell, N. *Nikolai G and Ivan Turgenev.* London: Macmillan, 1982.

Zeldin, Jesse. *Nikolai G's Quest for Beauty*. Lawrence, KS: Regents' Press of Kansas, 1978.

Dissertations

Ages, Rose Shoshana. G's Correspondence and *Selected Passages from Correspondence with Friends*. Ph.D. diss., Toronto, 1980.

Barrett, Constance McClintock. Artist as Missionary: A History of G's Literary Development in Terms of His Attitude Toward the Reading Public. Ph.D. diss., Stanford, 1975.

Bogojavlensky, Marianna. On the Development and Concept of G's Religious Thought. Ph.D. diss., Pennsylvania, 1959.

Byrns, Richard. Memory and Myth in Thomas De Quincey, Gérard De Nerval and Nikolai G. Ph.D. diss., California, Berkeley, 1973.

Christensen, Julie Ann. The Shaping of the Russian Philosophical Heroine: Feminine Images of Beauty in Russian Philosophical Aesthetics and the Heroines of Nikolai G. Ph.D. diss., California, Berkeley, 1978.

Cosman, Tatiana M. The Letter as a Literary Device in the Fiction of Puškin, Lermontov and G. Ph.D. diss., New York U, 1973.

Cox, Gary Duane. A Study of G's Narrators. Ph.D. diss., Columbia, 1978.

Debreczeny, Paul. A Study of G's Style. Ph.D. diss., London, 1960.

Edmunds, Catherine J. Puškin and G as Sources for the Librettos of the Fantastic Fairy Tale Operas of Rimskij-Korsakov. Ph.D. diss., Harvard, 1985.

Fusso, Susanne Grace. Čičikov on G: The Structure of Oppositions in *Dead Souls*. Ph.D. diss., Yale, 1984.

Futrell, M. A. Dickens and Three Russian Novelists: G, Dostoevsky, Tolstoy. Ph.D. diss., London, School of Slavonic and East European Studies, 1954.

Harussi, Yael. G's *Dead Souls:* A Reading. Ph.D. diss., Columbia, 1974.

Hasenclever, Nora. G and Dostoevsky. Ph.D. diss., Bennington, 1951.

Holquist, James Michael. Non-Realistic Modes in the Prose Fiction of G and Dostoevsky. Ph.D. diss., Yale, 1968.

Hrishko, Wasyl. G's Ukrainian-Russian Bilingualism. Ph.D. diss., Washington, Seattle, 1973.

Karriker, Alexandra W. The Grotesque Metamorphosis: G's Anthroponyms and Toponyms. Ph.D. diss., Brown, 1970.

Kent, Leonard Joseph. The Subconscious in G and Dostoevsky and Its Antecedents. Ph.D. diss., Yale, 1965.

Kirkoff, M. D. The Impact of G Upon the Works of Milovan Glisic, Steven Serenac and Branislav Nusic. Ph.D. diss., Toronto, 1974.

Lefevre, Carl A. G's First Century in England and America. Ph.D. diss., Minnesota, 1944.

Markov-Belaeff, Olga. *Dead Souls* and the Picaresque Tradition: A Study in the Definition of Genre. Ph.D. diss., California, Berkeley, 1982.

Nebolsine, Arcadi. Poshlost [A Study of the Writings of G, Dickens, Dostoevsky and Annensky]. Ph.D. diss., Columbia, 1972.

Nordby, Edward L. G's Comic Theory and Practice in *The Inspector General*. Ph.D. diss., Stanford, 1971.

Olson, Kenneth J. G and the Natural School. Ph.D. diss., Illinois, 1972.

Pickle, Charles DeWitt. Nikolaj G and Black Humor. Ph.D. diss., Colorado, 1974.

Pikulyk, Romana Myroslawa Bahrij. *Taras Bul'ba* and *The Black Council:* The Adherence to and Divergence from Walter Scott's Historical Novel Pattern. Ph.D. diss., Toronto, 1978.

Proffer, Carl R. The Comparisons in G's *Dead Souls*. Ph.D. diss., Michigan, 1963.

Shapiro, Gavriel. N. V. G and the Baroque. Ph.D. diss., Illinois, 1984.

Snyder, Harry Charles, Jr. The Airborne Imagery in G's *Dead Souls*. Ph.D. diss., Brown, 1974.

Sobel, R. G's *Selected Passages* and Its Contemporary Critics: An Analysis of Its Content and the Reactions of the Literary Critics and the Readers of the

Time. Leeds, 1977.

Stahlberg, Lawrence. The Grotesque in G and Poe. Ph.D. diss., SUNY, Binghamton, 1978.

Stevenson, Joan Nabseth. Literary and Cultural Patterns in G's *Arabeski*. Ph.D. diss., Stanford, 1984.

Stilman, Leon. Nikolai G: Historical and Biographical Elements in His Creative Personality. Ph.D. diss., 1953.

Vasilaky, Ludmila Jakowenko. Irony as Device in G's Short Stories. Ph.D. diss., New York, 1983.

Vuchich, Olga V. Stylistic Contrasts in G's Artistic Works: An Analysis. Ph.D. diss., Pittsburgh, 1969.

Weiss, Robert Mark. The Hidden World of G: A Study of the Irrational in *Dead Souls*. Ph.D. diss., California, Los Angeles, 1985.

Young, Donald Allen. N. V. G in Russian and Western Psychoanalytic Criticism. Ph.D. diss., Toronto, 1977.

Yurieff, Zoya. G as Interpreted by the Russian Symbolists. Ph.D. diss., Radcliffe, 1956.

Zaslove, Jerald. The Ideology and Poetics of "Poshlost'": The Work of Nikolai G and Its Importance in Our Time. Ph.D. diss., U of Washington, 1968.

Articles

Alexander, Alex. The Two Ivans' Sexual Underpinnings. *SEEJ* 25 (1981):24-37.

Alkire, Gilman H. G and Bulgarin's *Ivan Vyzhigin*. *SlavR* 28 (1969):289-96.

Andrew, Joe. Nikolay G. In his *Writers and Society during the Rise of Russian Realism*. Atlantic Highlands, NJ: Humanities P, 1980, pp. 76-113.

Annenkov, Pavel Vasil'evich. *The Extraordinary Decade. Literary Memoirs*. Tr. I. R. Titunik, ed. A. P. Mendel. Ann Arbor: U Michigan P, 1968, pp. 5-6, 39-44, 50-51, 56, 67-70, 106-8, 112-17, 119, 121, 204-5, 207-8, 223-214, 231, 233, 241, 245-55.

Annensky, I. The Aesthetics of G's *Dead Souls* and Its Legacy. In *Twentieth-Century Russian Literary Criticism*, ed. V. Erlich. New Haven: Yale UP, 1975, pp. 51-60.

Asch, Laurie. The Censorship of Nikolai G's "Diary of a Madman." *RLT* 14 (1976):20-35.

Bahrij-Pikulyk, Romana Myroslawa. Superheroes, Gentlemen or Pariahs? The Cossack in Nikolai G's *Taras Bulba* and Panteleimon Kulish's *Black Council*. *Journal of Ukrainian Studies* 5, 2 (1980): 30-47.

Bailey, James. Some Remarks about the Structure of G's *Overcoat*. In *Mnemozina: Studia Litteraria Russica in Honorem Vsevolod Setchkarev*, ed. J. T. Baer & N. W. Ingham. Munich: Fink, 1974, pp. 13-22.

Barksdale, E. G: The Descent into Dreams. In his *Daggers of the Mind*. Lawrence, KS: Coronado P, 1979, pp. 84-95.

——. G: The Myth and the Grotesque. In *The Dacha and the Duchess*. NY: Philosophical Library, 1974, pp. 105-11.

Barratt, A. Plot as Paradox: The Case of G's *Shinel'*. *NZSJ* 2 (1979):1-24.

Baumgarten, Murray. G's *The Overcoat* as a Picaresque Epic. *Dalhousie Review* 46 (1966):186-99.

Belinsky, Vissarion. Letter to N. V. G. In *Belinsky, Chernyshevsky and Dobrolyubov*, ed. R. Matlaw. Bloomington: Indiana UP, 1976.

Bely, Andrei. G. Tr. Elizabeth Trahan. *RLT* 4 (1972):131-44.

Bem, A. L. "The Nose" and "The Double." Tr. P. B. Stetson. In *Dostoevsky and G: Texts and Criticism*, ed. Priscilla Meyer & Stephen Rudy. Ann Arbor: Ardis, 1979, pp. 229-48.

Bernheimer, C. C. Cloaking the Self: The Literary Space of G's *Overcoat*. *PMLA* 90 (1975):53-61.

Berry, Thomas E. *Plots and Characters in Major Russian Fiction*, volume 2: G, Goncharov, Dostoevsky. Hamden, CT: Shoe String, 1978.

Bertensson, Sergei. The Première of *The Inspector General*. *RusR* 7 (1947):88-95.

Besoushko, Volodymyr. Nicholas G and Ukrainian Literature. *Ukrainian Quarterly* 16 (1960):162-68.

Beyer, Thomas R. Belyj's *Serebrjanyj golub'*: G in Gugolevo. *RLJ* 107

(1976):79-88.

Billington, James H. *The Icon and the Axe: An Interpretive History of Russian Culture.* NY: Knopf, 1966; NY: Random House, 1970. [Consult index.]

Birkhead, A. Russian Pickwick. *Living Age* 287 (1915):312-15.

Blankoff-Scarr, Goldie. The Use of Person in G's *Revizor. Equivalences* 10 (1979):71-88.

Bonnet, Gail. Deity to Demon: G's Female Characters. In *Proceedings: Pacific Northwest Conference on Foreign Languages.* (23rd Annual Meeting, April 28-29, 1972.) Corvallis: Oregon State U, 1973, pp. 253-67.

Börtnes, Jostein. G's *Revizor:* A Study in The Grotesque. *Scando-Slavica* 15 (1969): 47-63.

Bowen, C. M. *Dead Souls* and *Pickwick Papers. Living Age* 280 (1916):369-73.

Bowman, Herbert. "The Nose." *SEER* 31 (1952):204-11.

Brasol, Boris. *The Mighty Three: Pushkin—G—Dostoevsky.* NY: Payson, 1934.

Brodiansky, Nina. G and his Characters. *SEER* 31 (1952):36-57

Brown, Clarence. The Not Quite Realized Transit of G. In *Mnemozina: Studia Litteraria Russica in Honorem Vsevolod Setchkarev,* ed. J. T. Baer & N. W. Ingham. Munich: Fink, 1974, pp. 41-45.

Bryner, Cyril. G, Dickens and the Realistic Novel. *Etudes slaves et est-européennes* 8 (1963):17-42.

——. G's *The Overcoat* in World Literature. *SEER* 32 (1954):499-509.

Bryusov, V. Burnt to Ashes. In *G from the Twentieth Century: Eleven Essays,* ed. R. A. Maguire. Princeton: Princeton UP, 1974, pp. 103-32.

Busch, Robert L. G and the Russian Freneticist Cycle of the Early 1820s. *CSP* 22 (1980):28-42.

Byrns, Richard. G and the Feminine Myth. *Etudes slaves et est-européennes* 20-21 (1975-76): 44-60.

Charques, R. D. Nikolay G. *Fortnightly Review* 130 (1931):230-42.

Chizhevsky, Dmitry. About G's "Overcoat." In *G from the Twentieth Century: Eleven Essays,* ed. R. A. Maguire. Princeton: Princeton UP, 1974, pp. 293-322.

——. The Composition of G's *Overcoat.* Tr. E. V. Lawler & E. W. Trahan. *RLT* 14 (1976):378-401.

——. G: Artist and Thinker. *Annals of the Ukrainian Academy of Arts and Sciences in the USA* 2 (1952):261-79.

——. On G's *The Overcoat.* In *Dostoevsky and G: Texts and Criticism,* ed. & tr. P. Meyer & S. Rudy. Ann Arbor: Ardis, 1979, pp. 137-60.

——. The Unknown G. *SEER* 30 (1952): 476-93.

—— and P. Hofer. An Illustrated Manuscript of G. *Harvard Library Bulletin* 6 (1952):397-400.

Christoff, Peter K. G. In his *K. S. Aksakov: A Study in Ideas.* Princeton: Princeton UP, 1981, pp. 64-98.

Clayton, J. Douglas. Soviet Views of Parody: Tynianov and Morozov. *CASS* 6 (1973):485-93.

Clyman, T. W. The Hidden Demons in G's "Overcoat." *RusL* 7 (1979):601-10.

Coleman, A. P. *Humor in Russian Comedy from Catherine to G.* NY: Columbia UP, 1925 (Columbia U Slavonic Studies, vol. 2).

Cook, Albert. Reflexive Attitudes: Sterne, G, Gide. *Criticism* 2 (1960):164-74.

Corbett, G. G. A Note on Grammatical Agreement in Šinel'. *SEER* 59 (1981): 59-61.

Cox, Gary. Geographic, Sociological and Sexual Tension in G's Dikanka Stories. *SEEJ* 24 (1980):219-32.

——. The Writer as Stand-Up Comic: A Note on G and Dickens. *Ulbandus Review* 2 (1979):45-61.

Debreczeny, Paul. The Effect of the Style on the Theme in G's Works. *Kent Foreign Language Quarterly* 11, 3 (1964):126-33.

——. G's Mockery of Romantic Taste: Varieties of Language in "The Tale of the Two Ivans." *CASS* 7 (1973):327-41.

DeJonge, A. G. In *Nineteenth-Century Russian Literature: Studies of Ten Russian Writers,* ed. J. Fennell. Berkeley: U California P, 1973, pp. 69-129.

Edgerton, William B. Leskov's Parody on G: *Otbornoe zerno.* In *Lingua viget.* Helsinki: Suomalaisen Kirjallisnuden Kirjapaini, 1965; item 306, pp. 38-43.

Ehre, Milton. G's "Gamblers": Idea and Form. *SEEJ* 25 (1981):13-20.

——. Laughing through the Apocalypse: The Comic Structure of G's *Government Inspector. RusR* 39 (1980):137-49.

Eikhenbaum, Boris. How G's "Overcoat" Is Made. In *G's "Overcoat": An Anthology of Critical Essays,* ed. Elizabeth Trahan. Ann Arbor: Ardis, 1982, pp. 21-36.

——. How G's "Overcoat" Is Made." In *G from the Twentieth Century: Eleven Essays,* ed. Robert A. Maguire. Princeton: Princeton UP, 1974, pp. 267-92.

——. The Structure of G's "The Overcoat." *RusR* 22 (1963):377-99.

Emerson-Topronin, A. E. "Shinel'"—The Devil's Ovals—Motif of the Doubles. *Forum at Iowa on Russian Literature* 1 (1976):34-56.

Erlich, Victor. G and Kafka: A Note on "Realism" and "Surrealism." In *For Roman Jakobson: Essays in Honor of His Sixtieth Birthday,* comp. M. Halle, et al. The Hague: Mouton: 1956, pp. 100-8.

——. The Masks of Nikolaj G. In *The Disciplines of Criticism: Essays in Literary Theory, Interpretation, and History,* ed. P. Demetz, T. Greene, N. Lowry. New Haven: Yale UP, 1968, pp. 229-39.

——. A Note on the Grotesque. G: A Test Case. In *To Honor Roman Jakobson on the Occasion of His Seventieth Birthday.* The Hague: Mouton, 1967, pp. 630-33.

——. Some Western Interpretations of G. In *Proceedings of the Fifth Congress of the International Comparative Literature Association,* ed. N. Banašević. Amsterdam: Swets & Zeitlinger, 1969, pp. 595-602.

Ermakov, Ivan. "The Nose." Tr. R. A. Maguire. In *G from the Twentieth Century,* ed. R. Maguire. Princeton: Princeton UP, 1974, pp. 156-98.

Fanger, Donald. *Dead Souls:* The Mirror and the Road. *Nineteenth-Century Fiction* 33 (1978):24-47.

——. Dickens and G: Energies of the Word. In *Veins of Humor,* ed. H. Levin. Cambridge: Harvard UP, 1972, pp. 131-45.

——. G and His Reader. In *Literature and Society in Imperial Russia, 1800-1914,* ed. W. M. Todd III. Stanford: Stanford UP, 1978, pp. 61-95.

——. G as a Man of Letters: Writer and Audience in 19th Century Russia. *Actes du VIe Congrès de l'Association Internationale de Littérature Comparée,* ed. M. Cadot, et al. Stuttgart: Bieber, 1975, pp. 421-25.

——. The G Problem: Perspectives from Absence. In *Slavic Forum: Essays in Linguistics,* ed. M. S. Flier. The Hague: Mouton, 1974, pp. 103-29.

——. Romanticism and Neo-Romanticism in the Literary Myth of Petersburg: G's Tales and Belyj's Novel In *VII Międzynarodowy Kongres Slawistów w Warszawie, 1973: Streszczenia referatów i komunikatów.* Warsaw: PAN, 1973, pp. 616-18.

Fedorenko, Eugen W. G's *Revizor:* A Reexamination of Language Characteristics. *RLJ* 106 (1976):39-50.

Fiene, D. M. "The Story of How Ivan Ivanovich Quarreled with Ivan Nikiforovich." *Explicator* 34 (1976), item 55.

Finch, Chauncey. Classical Influence on N. V. G. *Classical Journal* 48 (1953): 291-96.

Florovsky, Georges. Three Masters: The Quest for Religion in Nineteenth-Century Russian Literature. *CLS* 3 (1966):119-137.

Frank, Joseph. From G to Gulag Archipelago. *Sewanee Review* (Spring 1976): 314-33.

Freeborn, Richard. *Dead Souls:* A Study. *SEER* 49 (1971):18-44.

Friedberg Seeley, Frank. Notes on G's Short Stories. *Annali (Istituto Universitario Orientale. Sezione Slava, Napoli)* 19 (1976):3-44.

Friedman, Peter. "The Nose." *The American Imago* 8 (1951):337-50.

Futrell, M. G and Dickens. *SEER* 33 (1956):443-59.

Fylypovych, Pavlo. Hohol's Ukrainian

Background. *Slavistica* 13 (1952):5-27.

Gabrowicz, George. Three Perspectives on the Cossack Past: G, Shevchenko, Kulich. *Harvard Ukrainian Studies* 5 (1981):171-94.

Garrard, J. G. Some Thoughts on G's "Kolyaska." *PMLA* 90 (1975):848-59.

——. Worm's Eye View in G's Fiction. In *Expression, Communication and Experience in Literature and Language,* ed. R. G. Popperwell. London: Modern Humanities Research Association, 1973, p. 166.

Gifford, Henry. G's *Dead Souls.* In his *The Novel in Russia.* NY: Harper & Row, 1965, pp. 40-50.

Gippius, V. *The Inspector General:* Structure and Problems. In *G from the Twentieth Century,* ed. Robert A. Maguire. Princeton: Princeton UP, 1974, pp. 216-65.

Glass, Elliot S. *Dead Souls* and the Hispanic Picaresque Novel. *Revista de Estudios Hispánicos* (Univ. of Alabama) 11 (1977):77-90.

Goodliffe, J. D. *Dead Souls* and the Mock Epic. *Proceedings and Papers of the 16th Congress of the Australasian Universities Language and Literature Association, Held 21-21 August 1974 at the University of Adelaide, South Australia* [n.p.: n.d.], pp. 330-341.

Gregg, Richard. A la recherche du nez perdu: An Inquiry into the Genealogical and Onomastic Origins of "The Nose." *RusR* 40 (1981):365-77.

Gustafson, Richard. The Suffering Usurper: G's "Diary of a Madman." *SEEJ* 9 (1965):268-90.

Hallett, R. W. The Laughter of G. *RusR* 30 (1971):373-84.

Harper, Kenneth E. Dickens and G's "Šinel'." In *American Contributions to the Sixth International Congress of Slavists,* vol. 2, ed. W. E. Harkins. The Hague: Mouton, 1968, pp. 165-80.

——. Text Progression and Narrative Style. In *American Contributions to the Eighth International Congress of Slavists,* vol. 2, ed. V. Terras. Columbus: Slavica, 1978, pp. 223-35.

Hare, Richard. The Age of Pushkin, Lermontov and G. In *Russian Literature from Pushkin to the Present Day.* London: Methuen, 1947, pp. 26-49.

Hart, Pierre R. In Search of a Real Ideal: G's Critical Prose. *CASS* 7 (1973):342-49.

Harvie, J. A. The Demonic Element in G and Baratynsky. *NZSJ* 6 (1970):77-85.

Heier, E. The Process of Dehumanization in G's Literary Portraits. *RusL* 12 (1985):263-78.

Hippisley, A. G's "The Overcoat": A Further Interpretation. *SEEJ* 20 (1976): 121-29.

Hoisington, Sona. G's Nature Descriptions. *RLJ* 119 (1980):59-65.

Holquist, James M. The Burden of Prophecy: G's Conception of Russia. *Review of National Literatures* 3 (1972): 39-55.

——. The Devil in Mufti: The Märchenwelt in G's Short Stories. *PMLA* 82 (1967):352-62.

Hryshko, Wasyl I. Nikolai G and Mykola Hohol': Paris 1837. *Annals of the Ukrainian Academy of Arts and Sciences in the US* 12, 1-2 (1969-72):113-42.

Hughes, Olga. The Apparent and the Real in G's "Nevskij Prospekt. *CalSS* 8 (1975):77-92.

Hulanicki, L. "The Carriage" by N. V. G. *RusL* 12 (1975):61-77.

Hyde, G. M. Melville's *Bartleby* and G's "The Overcoat." *Essays in Poetics* 1 (1976):32-47.

Ivanov, Vyacheslav. G's *Inspector General* and the Comedy of Aristophanes. In *G from the Twentieth Century,* ed. Robert A. Maguire. Princeton: Princeton UP, 1974, pp. 199-214.

Jackson, Robert L. Two Views of G and the Critical Synthesis—Belinskij, Rozanov and Dostoevsky. *RusL* 15, 2 (1984):223-42.

Jakobson, Roman & Bayara Aroutunova. An Unknown Album Page by Nikolaj G. *Harvard Library Bulletin* 20 (1972):236-54.

Jamosky, Edward. G's *Evenings on a Farm near Dikanka:* A Commentary. *Proceedings of the Kentucky Foreign Language Conference: Slavic Section*

1, 1 (1983):74-80.

____. Romanticism or Realism: Which Predominates in G's *Taras Bulba? Proceedings of the Kentucky Foreign Language Conference: Slavic Section* 2, 1 (1984):53-63.

Jennings, Lee B. G's Dead-Soul Grotesqueries. In *Vistas and Vectors. Essays Honoring the Memory of Helmut Rehder,* ed. L. B. Jennings & G. Schulz-Behrend. Austin: Dept. of Germanic Langs, U Texas, 1979, pp. 136-41.

Johnson, Warren. Spontaneous Generation: The Rumor in G. *RLJ* 37, 126-127 (1983):87-95.

Juran, Sylvia. "Zapiski sumasšedšego": Some Insights into G's World. *SEEJ* 5 (1961):331-33.

Kanser, Mark. G: A Study in Wit and Paranoia. *Journal of the American Psychoanalytic Association* 3, 1 (1955): 110-29.

Karlinsky, Simon. The Alogical and Absurdist Aspects of Russian Realist Drama. *Comparative Drama* 3 (1969):147-55.

____. Portrait of G as a Word Glutton, with Rabelais, Sterne, and Gertrude Stein as Background Figures. *CalSS* 5 (1970):169-86.

Kaun, Alexander. Poe and G. *SEER* 25 (1937):389-99.

Keefer, Lubov. G and Music. *SEEJ* 14 (1970):160-81.

Kolb-Seletski, Natalia M. Gastronomy, G, and His Fiction. *SlavR* 29 (1970):35-57.

Konick, Willis. The Theme of Brotherhood in G's "The Overcoat." In *Proceedings: Pacific Northwest Conference on Foreign Languages* (24th Annual Meeting, May 1973). Corvallis: Oregon State U, 1973, pp. 253-58.

Landry, Hilton. G's *The Overcoat. Explicator* 19 (1961), item 54.

Lefevre, Carl. G and Anglo-Russian Literary Relations during the Crimean War. *ASEER* 8 (1949):106-25.

Leong, Albert. Idea and Technique in G's "Notes of a Madman." *Proceedings: Pacific Northwest Conference on Foreign Languages* (24th Annual

Meeting, May 1973). Corvallis: Oregon State U, 1973, pp. 247-53.

Little, Edmund. G's Town of NN and Peakes's Gormenghast: The Realism of Fantasy. *JRS* 34 (1977):13-18.

____. P. A. Vyazemsky as a Critic of G. *NZSJ* 1 (1978):47-58.

____. Some Observations on the Biography and Work of Lewis Carroll and Nicholas G. *FMLS* 11 (1975):74-92.

Little, T. E. G and Romanticism. In *Problems of Russian Romanticism,* ed. Robert Reid. Brookfield, VT: Gower, 1986, pp. 96-126.

Lotman, Ju. M. Concerning Khlestakov. In *The Semiotics of Russian Cultural History,* ed. A. D. Nakhimovsky & A. S. Nakhimovsky. Ithaca: Cornell UP, 1985, pp. 150-87.

____. G's Chlestakov: The Pragmatics of a Literary Character. In *The Semiotics of Russian Culture,* ed. A. Shukman. Ann Arbor: Michigan Slavic Publications, 1984, pp. 177-212.

____. G's Tale of Captain Kopejkin: Reconstruction of the Plan and Ideo-Compositional Function. In *The Semiotics of Russian Culture,* ed. A. Shukman. Ann Arbor: Michigan Slavic Publications, 1984, pp. 213-30.

Louria, Yvette. G Reconsidered. *CASS* 5 (1971):259-65.

Luckyj, George. G's Ukrainian Interests: A Reappraisal. *Symbolae in Honorem Georgii Shevelov,* ed. W. E. Harkins. Munich: Logos, 1971, pp. 285-96.

McFarlin, H. A. "The Overcoat" as a Civil Service Episode. *CASS* 13 (1979):235-53.

McLean, Hugh. G and the Whirling Telescope. In *Russia: Essays in History and Literature,* ed. L. H. Legters. Leiden: Brill, 1972, pp. 79-99.

____. G's Retreat from Love: Towards an Interpretation of *Mirgorod. American Contributions to the Fourth International Congress of Slavists.* 's-Gravenhage: Mouton, 1958, pp. 225-45.

Maguire, Robert. The Formalists on G. In *Russian Formalism: A Restrospective Glance,* ed. R. L. Jackson & S. Rudy. New Haven: Yale Center for International and Area Studies, 1985, pp. 213-30.

———. G's "Confession" as a Fictional Structure. *Ulbandus Review* 2 (1982):175-90.

——— The Legacy of Criticism. In his *G from the Twentieth Century.* Princeton: Princeton UP, 1974, pp. 3-54.

——— Some Stylistic Approaches to G's "Two Ivans." *Newsletter: Teaching Language through Literature* 15 (1976):25-39.

Malkiel, Yakov. Cervantes in Nineteenth-Century Russia. *CL* 3 (1951): 310-29.

Manning, Clarence. G and Ukraine. *Ukrainian Quarterly* 6 (1950):323-30.

———. The Neglect of Time in the Russian Novel. In *Slavic Studies,* ed. A. Kaun & E. J. Simmons. Ithaca: Cornell UP, 1943, pp. 99-116.

——— Nicholas G. *SEER* 4 (1926):573-87.

——— The Tragedy of G. *Russian Orthodox Journal* July 3-4 (1937).

Markov, Vladimir. The Poetry of Russian Prose Writers. *CalSS* 1 (1960):77-82.

Martin, Mildred. The Last Shall Be First: A Study of Three Russian Short Stories. *Bucknell Review* 6, 1 (1956):13-23.

Masson, E. Russia's G: A Centenary. *Pacific Spectator* 7, 3 (1953): 322-31.

Matthews, I. G's Early Satire. *Satire Newsletter* 1 (1971):6-17.

Maurois, André. Nicolas G. In *The Art of Writing.* NY: Dutton, 1960, pp. 265-95.

Merezhkovsky, D. G and the Devil. In *G from the Twentieth Century,* ed. Robert A. Maguire. Princeton: Princeton UP, 1974, pp. 55-102.

Mersereau, John, Jr. The Chorus and Spear Carriers of Russian Romantic Fiction. In *Russian and Slavic Literature,* ed. R. Freeborn, et al. Cambridge: Slavica, 1976.

——— Normative Distinctions of Russian Romanticism and Realism. In *American Contributions to the Seventh International Congress of Slavists,* vol. 2, ed. V. Terras. The Hague: Mouton, 1973, pp. 393-417.

Mills, J. O. G's "Overcoat": The Pathetic Passages Reconsidered. *PMLA* 89 (1974): 106-11.

Montagu-Nathan, M. G and Music. *Monthly Musical Record* (May 1952), pp. 92-98.

Moyle, N. K. Folktale Patterns in G's "Vij." *Harvard Ukrainian Studies* 2 (1978):211-34.

Nabokov, Vladimir. Nikolay G. In his *Lectures on Russian Literature.* NY: Harcourt, Brace, Jovanovich, 1981, pp. 15-63.

Nagle, John J. Idealism: The Internal Structure in G's "Nevsky Prospect" and Chekhov's "An Attack of Nerves." *West Virginia University Philological Papers* 19 (1972):20-28.

Nilsson, N. A. G's "The Overcoat" and the Topography of St. Petersburg. *Scando-Slavica* 21 (1975):5-18.

——— On the Origins of G's "Overcoat." In *G's "Overcoat": An Anthology of Critical Essays,* ed. Elizabeth Trahan. Ann Arbor: Ardis, 1982, pp. 61-72.

Noyes, George Rapall. G, A Precursor of Modern Realists in Russia. *Nation* 101 (Nov. 18, 1915):592-594.

Obolensky, Alexander P. Nicholas G and Hieronimous Bosch. *RusR* 32 (1973):158-72; rpt. Association of Russian-American Scholars in the USA. *Issue Dedicated in Part to Nikolai G on the 175th Anniversary of His Birth.* NY: Association of Russian-American Scholars, 1984, pp. 115-32.

Ohloblyn, Oleksander. Ancestry of Mykola G (Hohol). *Annals of the Ukrainian Academy of Arts and Sciences in the US* 12, 1-2 (1969-72):3-43.

Oinas, Felix J. Akakij Akakievič's Ghost and the Hero Orestes. *SEEJ* 20 (1976):27-33.

———. The Transformation of Folklore into Literature. In *American Contributions to the Eighth International Congress of Slavists,* vol. 2, ed. V. Terras. Columbus: Slavica, 1978, pp. 570-603.

Ostrander, Sheila & Lynn Schroeder. Off Stage with *The Inspector General* in the USSR. *Texas Quarterly* 11, 2 (1968):209-16.

O'Toole, L. M. "The Overcoat." In his *Structure, Style and Interpretation in the Russian Short Story.* New Haven:

Yale UP, 1982, pp. 20-36.

Oulianoff, Nicholas I. Arabesque or Apocalypse? On the Fundamental Idea of G's Story "The Nose." *CSS* 1 (1967):158-71.

Peace, Richard Arthur. G and Psychological Realism: "Shinel'." In *Russian and Slavic Literature*, ed. R. Freeborn, et al. Cambridge: Slavica, 1976, pp. 63-91.

____. The Logic of Madness. G's "Zapiski sumasŝedŝego." *OSP* 9 (1976):28-45.

Pedrotti, Louis. "The Architecture of Love in G's "Rome." *CalSS* 6 (1971):17-27.

Pereverzev, V. The Evolution of G's Art. In *G from the Twentieth Century*, ed. Robert A. Maguire. Princeton: Princeton UP, 1974, pp. 133-54.

Perry, Idris. Kafka, G and Nathanael West. In *Kafka*, ed. Ronald Gray. Englewood Cliffs, NJ: Prentice-Hall, 1962.

Pikulyk, R. B. Superheroes, Gentlemen or Pariahs? The Cossacks in Nikolai G's *Taras Bulba* and Panteleimon Kulish's *Black Council*. *Journal of Ukrainian Graduate Studies* (Toronto) 5, 2 (1980):30-47.

Plaskacz, Bohdan. The Story of Captain Kopejkin in the Structure of G's *Mertvye dushi*. *RLJ* 119 (1980):51-58.

Poggioli, Renato. G's "Old-Fashioned Landowners": An Inverted Eclogue. *ISS* 3 (1963):54-72.

Pomorska, Krystyna. On the Problem of Parallelism in G's Prose: "A Tale of the Two Ivans." In *The Structural Analysis of Narrative Texts: Conference Papers*, ed. A. Kodjak, et al. Columbus: Slavica, 1980, pp. 31-43.

Proffer, Carl R. *Dead Souls* in Translation. *SEEJ* 8 (1964):420-33.

____. G's *Arabesques:* Introduction. In *Arabesques*, tr. Alexander Tulloch. Ann Arbor: Ardis, 1982, pp. 6-10.

____. G's Definition of Romanticism. *Studies in Romanticism* 6, 2 (1967): 120-27.

____. G's *Taras Bulba* and the *Iliad*. *CL* 17, 2 (1965):142-50.

____. "The Overcoat." In his *From Karamzin to Bunin*. Bloomington: Indiana UP, 1969, pp. 12-17.

____. Washington Irving in Russia: Push-kin, G, Marlinsky. *CL* 20 (1968):329-42.

Proffitt, Edward. G's "Perfectly True" Tale. "The Overcoat" and Its Mode of Closure. *Studies in Short Fiction* 14 (1977):35-40.

Pursglove, M. Bird Imagery in *Taras Bulba*. *Irish Slavonic Studies* 2 (1981):16-21.

Rahv, Phillip. G as a Modern Instance. In his *Essays on Literature and Politics*. Boston: Houghton Mifflin, 1978, pp. 222-26.

Rancour-Laferriere, Daniel. All the World's a *Vertep:* The Personification/Depersonification Complex in G's *Soročinskaja jarmarka*. *Harvard Ukrainian Studies* 4, 3 (1982):339-71.

____. The Identity of G's "Vij." *Harvard Ukrainian Studies* 2 (1978):211-34.

Reeve, F. D. *Dead Souls*. In his *The Russian Novel*. NY, 1966, pp. 64-103.

Richards, S. L. F. The Eye and the Portrait: The Fantastic in Poe, Hawthorne and G. *Studies in Short Fiction* 20 (1983):307-16.

Rossbacher, Peter. The Function of Insanity in Chekhov's "The Black Monk" and G's "Notes of a Madman." *SEEJ* 13, 2 (1969):191-99.

Rowe, W. W. Gogolesque Perception—Expanding Reversals in Nabokov. *SlavR* 30 (1971):110-26.

____. Observations on Black Humor in G and Nabokov. *SEEJ* 18 (1974):392-99.

____. Paper Presented on Three Types of Soft, Round, Nonmasculine Men in Russian Literature from 1842 to 1927. *RLT* 10 (1974):446-50.

Rozanov, V. V. How the Character Akaky Akakiyevich Originated. In *Essays in Russian Literature. The Conservative View*, ed. Spencer Roberts. Athens: Ohio UP, 1968, pp. 369-83.

____. Pushkin and G. In *Essays in Russian Literature. The Conservative View*, ed. Spencer Roberts. Athens: Ohio UP, 1968, pp. 357-68.

Rudnitsky, K. [Meyerhold productions of *The Inspector General*.] In his *Meyerhold the Director*. Ann Arbor: Ardis, 1981, pp. 382-86, 415-22.

Saunders, D. B. Contemporary Critics of

G's *Vechera* and the Debate about Russian *Narodnost'*. *Harvard Ukrainian Studies* 5 (1981):66-82.

Schillinger, John. G's "The Overcoat" as a Travesty of Hagiography. *SEEJ* 16 (1972):36-41.

Selig, Karl Ludwig. Concerning G's *Dead Souls* and *Lazarillo de Tormes*. *Symposium* 8 (1954):138-40.

Shapiro, G. The Hussar: A Few Observations on G's Characters and Their "Vertep" Prototypes. *Harvard Ukrainian Studies* 9, 1 (1985):133-38.

____. Nikolai G and the Baroque Heritage. *SlavR* 45, 1 (1986):95-104.

____. The Role of *Facetiae* in G's Early Works. *Transactions of the Association of Russian-American Scholars in the USA* 38 (1984):115-32.

____. The Transformation of the Lost Pipe Motif: Nikolai G's *Taras Bulba* and Leo Tolstoy's "The Wood Felling." *Die Welt der Slaven* 31 (1986):174-82.

Shepard, Elizabeth. Pavlov's "Demon" and G's "The Overcoat." *SlavR* 33 (1974):288-301.

Sherry, C. The Fit of G's "Overcoat": An Ontological View of Narrative Form. *Genre* 7 (1974):1-29.

Shevyrev, Stepan. *The Adventures of Chichikov, or Dead Souls, A Narrative Poem by N. G*. In *Literature and National Identity*, ed. P. Debreczeny & J. Zeldin. Lincoln: U Nebraska P, 1970, pp. 17-64.

Simmons, E. J. G and English Literature. *MLR* 26 (1931):445-50.

Sirskyj, W. Ideological Overtones in G's *Taras Bulba*. *Ukrainian Quarterly* 35 (1979):279-87.

Slonimsky, A. The Technique of the Comic in G. In *G from the Twentieth Century*, ed. Robert A. Maguire. Princeton: Princeton UP, 1974, pp. 323-74.

Snyder, H. C. Airborne Imagery in G's *Dead Souls*. *SEEJ* 23 (1979):173-89.

Sobel, Ruth. G's "Rome": A Final Draft for a Utopia. *Essays in Poetics* 5, 1 (1980):48-70.

____. Time, Space and Genre in G's *Mirgorod*. *Essays in Poetics* 6, 1 (1981):1-21.

Spilka, Mark. Kafka's Sources for *The Metamorphosis*. *CL* 11 (1959):289-308.

Spycher, P.C. N.V.G's *The Nose:* A Satirical Comic Fantasy Born of an Impotence Complex. *SEEJ* 7 (1963): 361-74.

Stephen, Halina. Tynjanov's Film Theory in Practice: Tynjanov's Film of G's *The Overcoat*. In *Purdue University Fifth Annual Conference on Film*, ed. Maud Walther. Purdue University Dept. of Foreign Languages, 1980, pp. 193-99.

Stilman, Leon. Afterword. In *The Diary of a Madman and Other Stories*. Tr. A. MacAndrew. NY: New American Library, 1961, pp. 223-38.

____. The All-Seeing Eye in G. In *G from the Twentieth Century*, ed. Robert A. Maguire. Princeton: Princeton UP, 1974, pp. 375-89.

____. G's "Overcoat," Thematic Patterns and Origins. *ASEER* 11 (1952):138-48.

____. Men, Women, and Matchmakers. In *G from the Twentieth Century*, ed. Robert A. Maguire. Princeton: Princeton UP, 1974, pp. 390-403.

____. Nikolaj G and Ostap Hohol. *Orbis Scriptus* 92 (1966):811-25.

Strakhovsky, Leonid. The Historianism of G. *ASEER* 12 (1953):360-71.

Stromecky, Ostap. G's Reverse Symbolism. *Ukrainian Quarterly* 38, 2 (1982): 151-63.

____. Ukrainian Elements in Mykola Hohol's *Taras Bulba*. *Ukrainian Quarterly* 25, 4 (1969):350-61.

Strong, Robert L. The Soviet Interpretation of G. *ASEER* 14 (1955):528-39.

Struc, Roman. Categories of the Grotesque: G and Kafka. In *Proceedings of the Comparative Literature Symposium*, ed. W. Zyla, et al. Vol. 4. Lubbock: Interdepartmental Committee on Comparative Literature, Texas Tech U, 1971, pp. 135-54.

____. Kafka and the Russian Realists. *Newsletter of the Kafka Society of America* 1 (1979):11-15.

____. Petty Demons and Beauty: G, Dostoevsky, Sologub. In *Essays on European Literature in Honor of Liselotte Dieckman*, ed. P. Hohendahl.

St. Louis: Washington UP, 1972, pp. 61-82.

Tilley, A. G, the Father of Russian Realism. *Living Age* 202 (1894):489-97.

Timmer, Charles B. *Dead Souls* Speaking. *SEER* 45 (1967):273-91.

——. G. *Tirade* 8 (1964):722-23.

Titunik, Irwin Robert. The Problem of *Skaz.* (Critique and Theory.) Papers in *Slavic Philology,* ed. B. A. Stolz. Ann Arbor: U Michigan, 1977, pp. 276-301.

Todd, William M. [Gogol.] In his *The Familiar Letter as a Literary Genre in the Age of Pushkin.* Princeton: Princeton UP, 1976, pp. 192-96.

Tsanoff, Radoslav Andrea. The Russian Soil and Nikolai G. *Rice Institute Pamphlet* 4, 2 (1917):119-26.

Tschižewskij, D. The Composition of G's "Overcoat." In *G's "Overcoat": An Anthology of Critical Essays,* ed. Elizabeth Trahan. Ann Arbor: Ardis, 1982, pp. 37-60. [Reprinted from *RLT* 14 (1976):378-402.]

Tulloch, A. The Stories of *Arabesques.* In *N. Gogol, Arabesques,* tr. A. Tulloch. Ann Arbor: Ardis, 1982, pp. 11-20.

Turgenev, Ivan. G. In *Turgenev's Literary Reminiscences.* NY: Farrar, 1958, pp. 160-71.

Turner, Charles Edward. Life and Genius of G; The Works of G. *Studies in Russian Literature.* London: Sampson Low, Marston, Searle and Rivington, 1882, pp. 155-208; rpt. NY: Kraus, 1971.

Tynianov, Yury. Dostoevsky and G. In *Twentieth-Century Russian Literary Criticism,* ed. V. Erlich. New Haven: Yale UP, 1975, pp. 102-16.

——. Dostoevsky and G. Towards a Theory of Parody. Part One: Stylization and Parody. in *Dostoevsky and G. Texts and Criticism,* ed. P. Meyer & S. Rudy. Ann Arbor: Ardis, 1979, pp. 101-17.

Ulianov, Nikolai I. Arabesque or Apocalypse? On the Fundamental Idea of G's Story "The Nose. *CASS* 1 (1967):158-71.

Van der Eng, Jan. Bashmachkin's Character. In *G's "Overcoat": An Anthology of Critical Essays,* ed. Elizabeth Trahan. Ann Arbor: Ardis, 1982, pp. 73-85.

Van Schooneveld, C. H. G and the Romantics. In *Slavic Poetics: Essays in Honor of Kiril Taranovsky,* ed. R. Jakobson; C. H. van Schooneveld & D. S. Worth. The Hague: Mouton, 1973, pp. 481-84.

Vinogradov, V. The Language of G. In his *History of the Russian Literary Language.* Madison: U Wisconsin P, 1969, pp. 209-36.

——. The School of Sentimental Naturalism. Dostoevsky's Novel *Poor Folk* Against the Background of the 1840s. In *Dostoevsky and G. Texts and Criticism,* ed. P. Meyer & S. Rudy. Ann Arbor: Ardis, 1979, pp. 161-215.

——. Towards a Morphology of the "Naturalist Style." In *Dostoevsky and G: Texts and Criticism,* ed. Priscilla Meyer & Stephen Rudy. Ann Arbor: Ardis, 1979, pp. 217-28.

Vinokur, G. O. The Literary Language in the Nineteenth and Twentieth Centuries. *The Russian Language: A Brief History.* Tr. M. A. Forsyth. Cambridge: Cambridge UP, 1971, pp. 126-38.

Vogel, Lucy. G's "Rome." *SEEJ* 11 (1967):145-58.

Vroon, Ronald. G in Oblomovka. *RLT* 3 (1972):282-96.

Waszink, P. Mythical Traits in G's "The Overcoat." *SEEJ* 22 (1978):287-300.

Weathers, Winston. G's *Dead Souls:* The Degrees of Reality. *College English* 27 (1956):159-64.

Wellek, René. Introduction. In *Dead Souls.* Tr. B. Guerney. NY: Rinehart & Co., 1948, pp. v-x.

Wilson, Edmund. G: The Demon in the Overgrown Garden. In his *A Window on Russia.* NY: Farrar, Straus, Giroux, 1972, pp. 38-51.

Wilson, Reuel K. "A Marvelous Hangout," or *Dead Souls* Revisited. *World Literature Today* 54 (1980):376-81.

Wisseman, Heinz. The Ideational Content of G's "Overcoat." In *G's "Overcoat": An Anthology of Critical Essays,* ed. E. Trahan. Ann Arbor: Ardis, 1982, pp. 86-105.

Wittlin, Joseph. G's Inferno. *Polish Review* 7 (1962):5-19.

Wolterstorff, N. Characters and Their Names. *Poetics* 8 (1979):101-27.

Woodward, James B. Allegory and Symbol in G's Second Idyll. *MLR* 73 (1978):351-67.

——. G's *Mertvye duši:* The Epic as Analogue. *Die Welt der Slaven* 29 (1984):1-17.

——. The Threadbare Fabric of G's "Overcoat." *CSS* 1 (1964):95-104.

Worrall, Nick. [G's Plays.] In his *Nikolai Gogol and Ivan Turgenev.* London: Macmillan, 1982, pp. 31-116.

——. Meyerhold Directs G's *Government Inspector. Theatre Quarterly* 2, 7 (1972): 75-95.

Wright, A. Colin. Three Approaches to Russian Nineteenth-Century Literature, and the Purpose of Reading. *The Humanities Association Review* 30 (1979):322-27.

Žekulin, G. Rereading G's "Vii." *CSP* 25 (1983):301-6.

Zeldin, J. Foreword. In his trans. of G's *Selected Passages from Correspondence with Friends.* Nashville: Vanderbilt UP, 1969.

——. A Revaluation of G's *Selected Passages. RusR* 27 (1968):421-31.

Zoshchenko, Mikhail. [On G's Melancholia.] In his *Before Sunrise,* tr. Gary Kern. Ann Arbor: Ardis, 1974, pp. 270-82.

IVAN GONCHAROV

Bibliography

Terry, G. M. *Ivan G: A Bibliography.* Nottingham, England: Astra, 1986.

Translations

A Common Story. Tr. Constance Garnett. NY: Collier, 1894.

Oblomov. Tr. N. Duddington. NY: Macmillan, 1929.

Oblomov. Tr. Ann Dunnigan. NY: Signet, 1963.

Oblomov. Tr. David Magarshack. Baltimore: Penguin, 1967.

The Precipice. Tr. anon. (M. Bryant?). London: Hodder & Stoughton, 1915; reprinted Westport, CT: Hyperion, 1977. [Abridged by roughly 50% and poorly translated.]

The Same Old Story. Tr. Ivy Litvinov. Moscow: Foreign Languages Publishing House, 1957.

The Voyage of the Frigate Pallada. Ed. & tr. N. W. Wilson. London: Folio Society, 1965.

Ivan Savich Podzhabrin—Sketches. Tr. W. E. Brown. *RLT* 10 (1974):7-66.

Ivan Turgenev. In Andrew Field, *The Complection of Russian Literature.* NY: Atheneum, 1971, pp. 131-47.

Criticism

Ehre, Milton. *Oblomov and His Creator: The Life and Art of Ivan G.* Princeton: Princeton UP, 1973.

Lavrin, Janko. *G.* Cambridge: Bowes & Bowes, 1956.

Lyngstad, A. & S. *Ivan G.* NY: Twayne, 1971.

Schulz, Robert. *The Portrayal of the German in Russian Novels—G, Turgenev, Dostoevskij, Tolstoj.* Munich: Sagner, 1969.

Setchkarev, Vsevolod. *Ivan G: His Life and Works.* Würzburg: Jal-Verlag, 1974.

Barksdale, Ethelbert Courtland. G and the Pastoral Novel in Nineteenth-Century Russian Literature. Ph.D. diss., Ohio State, 1971.

Ehre, Milton H. The Fiction of Ivan G: A Literary Study. Ph.D. diss., Columbia, 1970.

Lorriman, Gabrielle T. Time in G's *Oblomov.* Ph.D. diss., McGill, 1971.

Rapp, H. Ivan G and His Relation to the Intelligentsia. Ph.D. diss., London, 1953.

Rosenbaum, Maurice W. Ivan Alexandrovich G and the Sociological Novel in Russia. Ph.D. diss., New York, 1946,

Wilson, Natalia Lopato. Women in G's Fiction Ph.D. diss., Alberta, 1981.

Barksdale, E. C. The Pastoral Myth and G. In his *The Dacha and the Duchess. An Application of Levi-Strauss's Theory of Myth to Works of Nineteenth-Century Russian Novelists.* NY: Philosophical Library, 1974, pp. 49-75.

Belinsky, V. G's *An Ordinary Story.* In his *Selected Philosophical Works.* Moscow: Foreign Languages Publishing House, 1956, pp. 478-501.

Chances, Ellen. On the Road to Ideology: Herzen, Turgenev and G. In her *Conformity's Children.* Columbus: Slavica, 1978, pp. 81-88.

De Maegd-Soëp, Carolina. Women's Emancipation in the Works of G. In her *The Emancipation of Women in Russian Literature and Society.* Ghent: Ghent State U, 1978, pp. 151-96.

Dobrolyubov, N. What Is Oblomovism? In *Belinsky, Chernyshevsky, and Dobrolyubov: Selected Criticism,* ed. R. E. Matlaw. NY: Dutton, 1962.

—— What Is Oblomovism? In his *Selected Philosophical Essays.* Moscow: Foreign Languages Publishing House, 1948, pp. 174-217.

Freeborn, Richard. The Novels of G. In his *The Rise of the Russian Novel.* Cambridge UP, 1973, pp. 135-57.

Giergielewicz, M. Prus and G. In *American Contributions to the Fifth International Congress of Slavists.* The Hague, Mouton, 1963, vol. 2, pp. 129-46.

Gifford, H. G. In *Nineteenth-Century Russian Literature,* ed. J. Fennell. Berkeley: U California P, 1973, pp. 130-42.

Hadfield, C. H. G. What is Oblomivism? A Sociological Approach. *NZSJ* 10 (1972): 106-13.

Hainsworth, J. D. *Don Quixote, Hamlet* and "Negative Capability": Aspects of G's *Oblomov. Journal of the Australian Universities Languages and Literatures Association* 53 (1980):42-53.

Harjan, G. Dobroliubov's "What Is Oblomovism?": An Interpretation. *CSP* 18 (1976):284-92.

Harper, Kenneth E. Under the Influence of Oblomov. In *From LA to Kiev,* ed. V. Markov & D. S. Worth. Columbus: Slavica, 1983, pp. 105-18.

Herrmann, Lesley Singer. Woman as Hero in Turgenev, G and George Sand's *Mauprat. Ulbandus Review* 2 (1979): 128-38.

Janecek, G. G. Some Comments on Character in *Oblomov. Scando-Slavica* 21 (1975):41-50.

Kuhn, Alfred. Dobroliubov's Critique of *Oblomov:* Polemics and Psychology. *SlavR* 30 (1971):93-109.

Lensen, G. A. Historicity of *Fregat Pallada. MLN* 68 (1953):462-66.

Louria, Y. Dostoevsky and G. *MLN* 88 (1973):1325-28.

Louria, Yvette & Morton I. Seiden. Ivan G's Oblomov: The Anti-Faust as Christian Hero. *CSS* 3 (1969):39-68.

Macauley, Robie. The Superfluous Man. *Partisan Review* 19, 2 (1952):169-82.

Manning, Clarence A. Ivan Aleksandrovich G. *The South Atlantic Quarterly* 26 (1927):63-75.

—— The Neglect of Time in the Russian Novel. In *Slavic Studies,* ed. Alexander Kaun & E. J. Simmons. Ithaca: Cornell UP, 1943.

Mays, Milton A. Oblomov as Anti-Faust. *Western Humanities Review* 21 (1967): 141-52.

Moser, Charles. *Antinihilism in the Russian Novel of the 1860's.* The Hague: Mouton, 1964.

Poggioli, Renato. On G and His *Oblomov.* In his *The Phoenix and the Spider.* Cambridge: Harvard UP, 1956, pp. 33-48.

Pritchett, V. S. G. The Dream of a Censor. In his *The Myth Makers.* NY: Random House, 1979, pp. 57-62.

—— The Great Absentee. In his *The Living Novel.* London: Chatto & Windus, 1946, pp. 233-40.

Rapp, Helen. The Art of Ivan G. *SEER* 36 (1958):370-95.

Reeve, F. D. *Oblomov.* In his *The Russian Novel.* NY: McGraw-Hill, 1966, pp. 103-18.

—— Oblomovka Revisited. *ASEER* 15 (1956):112-18.

Seeley, F. F. *Oblomov. SEER* 54 (1976): 335-54.

Setchkarev, Vsevolod. Andrej Štolc in G's *Oblomov:* An Attempted Reinterpretation. In *To Honor Roman Jakobson: Essays on the Occasion of His Seventieth Birthday*. The Hague: Mouton, 1967, pp. 1799-1805.

Stilman, Leon. Oblomovka Revisited. *ASEER* 7 (1948):45-77.

Vroon, Ronald. Gogol in Oblomovka. *RLT* 3 (1972):282-96.

Woodhouse, C. M. The Two Russians (The Russian Character as Revealed in Dostoevsky's *Possessed* and G's *Oblomov)*. *Essays by Divers Hands* 29 (1958):18-36.

ALEXANDER GRIBOEDOV

Translations

Chatsky, or The Meaning of Having a Mind. Tr. Joshua Cooper. In *Four Russian Plays*. NY: Penguin, 1972, pp. 125-214.

The Misfortune of Being Clever. Tr. S. Pring. London: Nutt, 1914.

The Trouble with Reason. In *An Anthology of Russian Plays*, ed. F. D. Reeve. NY: Vintage, 1961, vol. 1, pp. 85-163.

Wit Works Woe. Tr. Sir B. Pares. In *Masterpieces of the Russian Drama*, ed. G. R. Noyes. NY: Appleton, 1933, pp. 85-155.

Criticism

Harden, Evelyn. *The Murder of Griboedov. New Materials*. Birmingham: Birmingham Slavonic Monogrphs, no. 6, 1979.

Baratynskii, V. V. *The Misfortune of Being Clever: A Classical Comedy by Alexander G. Fortnightly Review* 89 (1911):113-21.

Brown, William Edward. Alexander G before 1823. Alexander G and *Woe from Wit*. In his *A History of Russian Literature of the Romantic Period*. Ann Arbor: Ardis, 1986, vol. 2, pp. 93-99, 105-15.

Chances, Ellen. First Steps Toward Superfluity: G, Pushkin, and Lermontov. In her *Conformity's Children*. Columbus: Slavica, 1978, pp. 32-35.

Costello, D. P. G in Persia in 1820: Two Diplomatic Notes. *OSP* 5 (1954):81-92.

____. The Murder of G. *OSP* 8 (1958):66-89.

____. A Note on "The Diplomatic Activity" of A. S. G by S. V. Shostakovich. *SEER* 40 (1962):235-44.

Dessaix, Robert. On Chatsky as Antihero. *FMLS* 10 (1974):379-87.

Giergielewicz, M. Structural Footnotes to G's *Woe from Wit*. *Polish Review* 24 (1979):3-21.

Harden, Evelyn. The Dependence of Apollo Korzeniowski's *Komedia* upon G's *Gore ot uma*. In *For Wiktor Weintraub: Essays in Polish Literature, Language and History Presented on the Occasion of His 65th Birthday*, ed. V. Erlich, et al. The Hague: Mouton, 1975, pp. 209-26.

____. G and the Willock Affair. *SlavR* 30 (1971):74-92.

____. G in Persia: December 1828. *SEER* 57 (1979):255-67.

Hoover, M. L. Classic Meyerhold: *Woe to Wit* by G. *RLT* 7 (1973):285-95.

Janecek, Gerald. A Defense of Sof'ja in *Woe from Wit*. *SEEJ* 21 (1977):318-31.

Jones, M. Andrew Hay and the G Affair. *JRS* 42 (1981):16-21.

Lang, David M. G's Last Years in Persia. *ASEER* 7 (1948):317-39.

Law, A. H. *Woe to Wit* (1828): A Reconstruction. *Drama Review* 18, 3 (1974):89-107.

Little, E. Vyazemsky, G and *Gore ot uma* (Woe from Wit): A Question of Heresy. *NZSJ* (1984):15-31.

Matlaw, R. E. The Dream in *Yevgeniy Onegin*, with a Note on *Gore ot Uma*. *SEER* 37 (1959):487-504.

Mirsky, D. S. Centenary of the Death of G. *SEER* 8 (1929):140-43.

Richards, D. J. Two Malicious Tongues— The Wit of Chatsky and Pechorin. *NZSJ* 11 (1973):11-28.

Rudnitsky, K. [Meyerhold's productions of *Woe from Wit*.] In his *Meyerhold the Director*. Ann Arbor: Ardis, 1981, pp. 421-35.

Varneke, B. V. G. In his *A History of the Russian Theater*, tr. B. Brasol. NY: Macmillan, 1951, pp. 200-10.

Veselovsky, Alexei. G. In *The Complection of Russian Literature*, ed. Andrew Field. NY: Atheneum, 1971, pp. 49-54.

APOLLON GRIGORIEV

Translations

My Literary and Moral Wanderings. Ed. & tr. Ralph E. Matlaw. NY: Dutton, 1962.
[Also includes: A Hopeless Situation; Sorrowful Thoughts about the Despotism and Voluntary Slavery of Thought; A Brief Record as a Keepsake.]

The Literary Work of Count L. Tolstoi. Tr. Paul Mitchell. *RLT* 17 (1982):7-18.
Bannikov, Nikolai, comp. *Three Centuries of Russian Poetry.* Moscow: Progress, 1980, pp. 211-12.
[The Comet; A mysterious power I wield over you.]
Debreczeny, P. & J. Zeldin, eds. *Literature and National Identity.* Lincoln: U of Nebraska P, 1970, pp. 65-118.
[*A Nest of Gentry* by Ivan Turgenev.]
Obolensky, D., ed. *The Heritage of Russian Verse.* Bloomington: Indiana UP, 1976, pp. 214-15.
[O you at least, speak to me.]

Criticism

Dowler, Wayne. *Dostoevsky, G and Native Soil Conservatism.* Toronto: Toronto UP, 1982.

Bowler, William Elliott. Apollon G's Poetry. Ph.D. diss., Michigan, 1981.
Czyzewski, Frank Joseph. The Aesthetics of Apollon G: Theory and Practice. Ph.D. diss., Wisconsin, 1976.
Jerkovich, George C. Apollon G as a Literary Critic. Ph.D. diss., Kansas, 1970.
Krupitsch, Victor S. Apollon A. G and His "Organic Criticism." Ph.D. diss., Pennsylvania, 1957.
Sahgal, Preeti. Aleskandr Blok and Apollon G: A Synthesized View of Life and Art. Ph.D. diss., Virginia, 1983.
Talbot, Elizabeth Mullen. Apollon G as Literary Critic. Ph.D. diss., Brown, 1973.
Whittaker, Robert T. Apollon Aleksandrovič G and the Evolution of Organic Criticism. Ph.D. diss., Indiana, 1970.

Chances, Ellen. Literary Criticism and the Ideology of *Pochvennichestvo* in Dostoevsky's Thick Journals *Vremja* and *Epokha. RusR* 34 (1975):151-64.
Dowler, Wayne. Herder in Russia: A. A. G and "Progressivist Traditionalism. *CSS* 19 (1977):167-80.
Grossman, Leonid. Apollon G. In *The Complection of Russian Literature,* ed. Andrew Field. NY: Atheneum, 1971, pp. 156-60.
Matlaw, Ralph E. Introduction. In Apollon G, *My Literary and Moral Wanderings.* NY: Dutton, 1962, pp. ix-xlvi.
Mitchell, Paul. G on Tolstoi. *RLT* 17 (1982):19-22.
Terras, Victor. Apollon G's Organic Criticism and Its Western Sources. In *Western Philosophical Systems in Russian Literature,* ed. A. Mlikotin. Los Angeles: U Southern California P, 1980, pp. 71-88.
Walicki, A. Critics of the "Enlighteners": Apollon G and Nikolai Strakhov. In *A History of Russian Thought.* Stanford: Stanford UP, 1979, pp. 215-21.
Whittaker, Robert. My Literary and Moral Wanderings: Apollon G and the Changing Cultural Topography of Moscow. *SlavR* 42 (1983):390-407.

DMITRI GRIGOROVICH

Translations

The Fishermen. Preface by A. Rappoport. Philadelphia: McKay; London: Paul, 1916.
Edwards, H. S., tr. *Tales from the Russian.* London: Railway and General Automatic Library, 1892.
[New Year's Eve.]

Criticism

Pursglove, M. D. V. G (1822-1899): "Derevenja" and "Anton Goremyka." *SEER* 51 (1973):505-16.
Strong, Robert L., Jr. G's "The Village":

An Etude in Sentimental Naturalism. *SEEJ* 12 (1968):169-75.

Woodhouse, J. A Landlord's Sketches?: D. V. G and Peasant Genre Fiction. *Journal of European Studies* 16 (1986): 271-94.

ALEXANDER HERZEN

Bibliography

Grosshans, Henry. Alexander H and the Free Russian Press in London, 1853-1865. *Research Studies* 26 (1958):17-36.

Translations

Childhood, Youth and Exile. Tr. J. D. Duff. Oxford: Oxford UP, 1979.
 [First two parts of *My Past and Thoughts* in a new translation.]

From the Other Shore and The Russian People and Socialism. Intro. by Isaiah Berlin. Oxford: Oxford UP, 1979.

My Past and Thoughts. Tr. Constance Garnett. London, 1924-27. 6 vols.
 [Revised by Humphrey Higgins. London, 1968, 4 vols. Abridged into 1 volume by Dwight MacDonald. London, 1974.]

Selected Philosophical Works. Tr. L. Navrozov. Moscow: Foreign Languages Publishing House, 1956.

Who Is to Blame? Tr. M. Wettlin. Preface by Ya. Elsberg. Moscow: Progress, 1978.

Who Is to Blame? Tr. Robert Busch & T. Yedlin. Edmonton, Alberta: Central and East European Studies of Alberta, 1982.

Who Is to Blame? Tr., annotation and intro. by Michael Katz. Ithaca: Cornell UP, 1984.

Criticism

Acton, Edward. *Alexander H and the Role of the Intellectual Revolutionary.* Cambridge: Cambrdige UP, 1979.

Carr, E H. *The Romantic Exiles.* Cambridge: MIT P, 1981.

Copleston, Frederick C. *Philosophy in Russia: From Herzen to Lenin and*

Berdyaev. Notre Dame: U Notre Dame 1986.

Lenin, Vladimir Ilich. *In Memory of Herzen.* Moscow: Progress, 1966.

Malia, Martin. *Alexander H and the Birth of Russian Socialism, 1812-1855.* Cambridge: Harvard UP, 1961.

Partridge, Monica, ed. *Alexander H and European Culture: Proceedings of an International Symposium, Nottingham and London, 1982.* Nottingham: Astra, 1984.
 [Contributors: J. Lothe, R. Freeborn, M. Partridge, K. Sharova, G. Ziegengeist, M. Cadot, A. Lehning, A. Gereben, M. Kun, R. Sliwowsky, M. Altshuller, E. Dryzhakova, G. Fridlender, K. Lomunov, I. Ptushkina, H. Rothe, A. Flaker. S. Marković.]

Acton, Edward Joseph Lyon-Dalberg. Alexander H and the Role of the Intellectual Revolutionary, 1847-1863. Ph.D. diss., Cambridge, 1976.

Bullitt, Margaret M. Voice of a Generation, Generation of a Voice: Childhood in H's *Byloe i dumy.* Ph.D. diss., Harvard, 1984.

Rzewsky, Nicolaes. H in Russian Literature. Ph.D. diss., Princeton, 1972.

Weidemaier, William C. The Anticipation of Nietzschean Themes in the Writings of Alexander H. Ph.D. diss., Arizona State, 1975.

Winter, Robert J. Narrative Devices in the Fiction of Alexander H. Ph.D. diss., Columbia, 1971.

Aikhenvald, Y. Alexander H. In *The Complection of Russian Literature,* ed. Andrew Field. NY: Atheneum, 1971, pp. 105-7.

Avineri, Shlomo. The Russian Question in the Nineteenth Century. *Dissent* 33, 1 (1986):79-83. [Letters by Moses Hess in response to Herzen's *From the Other Shore.*]

Belinsky, V. H's *Who's to Blame?* In his *Selected Philosophical Works.* Moscow: Foreign Languages Publishing House, 1956, pp. 465-78.

Berlin, Isaiah. Alexander H. In his *Russian Thinkers.* NY: Penguin, 1978, pp. 186-209.

___ H and Bakunin on Individual Liberty. Ibid., pp. 82-113.

Blackham, H. J. The Comparison of H with Kierkegaard: A Comment. *SlavR* 25 (1966):213-17.

Carr, E. Some Unpublished Letters of Alexander H. *OSP* 3 (1952):80-124.

Chances, Ellen. On the Road to Ideology: H, Turgenev, and Goncharov. In her *Conformity's Children*. Columbus: Slavica, 1978, pp. 50-63.

Davison, R. M. H and Kierkegaard. *SlavR* 25 (1967):191-209, 218-21.

Dziewanowski, M. K. H, Bakunin and the Polish Insurrection of 1863. *Journal of Central European Affairs* 8 (1948):58-78.

Gavin, W. J. H and James: Freedom as Radical. *Studies in Soviet Thought* 14 (1974):213-29.

Grosshans, H. Alexander H and the Defense of the Russian Literary Tradition. *Research Studies* 21 (1953): 310-23.

___ Alexander H and the Free Russian Press in London, 1853-65. *Research Studies* 26 (1958):17-36.

Hecht, D. Two Classic Russian Publicists: 1. Chernyshevski and Russian Slavery, 2. Alexander H and America. *ASEER* 4 (1945):1-32.

Kelly, A. The Destruction of Idols: Alexander H and Francis Bacon. *Journal of the History of Ideas* 61 (1980):635-62.

Partridge, Monica. Alexander H and the English Press. *SEER* 36 (1958):453-70.

___ Alexander H and the South Slav Liberation Movements of the Second Half of the Nineteenth Century: Some Observations and Comments. *SEER* 56 (1978): 360-70.

___ Alexander H and the Younger Joseph Cowen, M.P.: Some Unpublished Material. *SEER* 41 (1963):50-63.

___ H's Changing Concept of Reality and Its Reflection in His Literary Works. *SEER* 46 (1968):397-421.

___ The Young H: A Contribution to the Russian Period of the Biography of Alexander H. *Renaissance and Modern Studies* 1 (1957):154-73.

Pirumova, N. Bakunin and H: An Analysis of Their Ideological Disagreements. *CASS* 10 (1976):552-69.

Randall, Francis B. H's *From the Other Shore*. *SlavR* 27 (1968):91-101.

Rzhevsky, Nicholas. H's Fiction: An Affective Variety; Tolstoy's Ideological Order: H and *War and Peace*. In *Russian Literature and Ideology*. Urbana: U Illinois P, 1983, pp. 29-65, 116-32.

___ The Shape of Chaos: H and *War and Peace*. *RusR* 34 (1975):367-81.

Seeley, Frank Friedeberg. H's "Dantean" Period. *SEER* 33 (1955):44-74.

Slavutych, Y. Alexander H and Ukraine. *Ukrainian Quarterly* 16 (1960):342-48.

Stoehr, Taylor. Alexander H's *My Past and Thoughts*. *Southern Review: An Australian Journal of Literary Studies* 3 (1968):168-79.

Tregenza, J.M. C.H. Pearson on Russia and His Correspondence with H, Ogarev and Others, 1858-1863. *OSP* 11 (1964):69-82.

Weidemaier, William Cannon. H and the Existential World View: A New Approach to an Old Debate. *SlavR* 40 (1981):557-69.

ALEXEI KHOMYAKOV

Translations

Andrews, Larry, tr. Poems. *RLT* 8 (1974):72-83.

[Longing; The Poet; Dream; Inspiration; Two Hours; Two Songs; The Lark, the Eagle and the Poet; Thoughts; Vision; To I. V. Kireevsky; Night; To Russia.]

Rydel, Christine, ed. *The Ardis Anthology of Russian Romanticism*. Tr. Larry Andrews. Ann Arbor: Ardis, 1984, pp. 77-79.

[Dream; The Lark, the Eagle, and the Poet; Inspiration; Two Hours; Vision.]

Criticism

Bartenev, P.I. A.S.H. Tr. H. Frank. *Anglo-Russian Literary Society Proceedings* 39 (1904):109-11.

Lavrin, Janko. K and the Slavs. *RusR* 23 (1964):36-48.

Manning, C. K and the Orthodox Church. *Review of Religion* 6 (1942):169-78.

Marchant, F. P. The Life and Work of Alexei K. *Anglo-Russian Literary Society Proceedings* 17 (1914):36-52.

ALEXEI KOLTSOV

Translations

The Complete Poems of Aleksey Vasil'evich K. Tr. with an introduction & commentary by C. P. L. Dennis. London, 1922.

Bannikov, Nikolai, comp. *Three Centuries of Russian Poetry.* Moscow: Progress, 1980. Bilingual, pp. 171-79.
[A Village Feast; The Mower; Do Not Rustle, Rye.]

Obolensky, Dimitri, ed. *The Heritage of Russian Verse.* Bloomington: Indiana UP, 1976, pp. 150-53.
[Bitter Lot; Song.]

Rydel, Christine, ed. *The Ardis Anthology of Russian Romanticism.* Ann Arbor: Ardis, 1984, pp. 83-84.
[The Nightingale; Song; Song of a Ploughman; A Peasant's Meditation; Bitter Fate; Separation.]

Wiener, Leo, ed. *Anthology of Russian Literature.* NY: Putnam, 1902-3, vol. 2, pp. 176-81.
[First Love; The Abundant Harvest; The Forest; Betrayed by a Bride; The Mower.]

Zheleznova, Irina, ed. *Russian 19th-Century Verse.* Moscow: Raduga, 1983, pp. 155-75.
[A Village Feast; A Ploughman's Song; Do Not Rustle, Rye; Harvestime; The Reaper; The Mower; Thoughts of a Countryman; A Song; The Last Kiss; Peasant, why do you sleep?; Thoughts of a Young Man; A Russian Song (With what Passion, what force); A Russian Song (Fierce as flame blazed

my love).]

Criticism

Caffrey, Elena. K: A Study in Meter and Rhythm. Ph.D. diss., Harvard, 1968.

Bailey, J. The Trochaic Song Meters of K and Kashin. *RusL* 12 (1975):5-28.

Brown, William Edward. Alexei K. In his *A History of Russian Literature of the Romantic Period.* Ann Arbor: Ardis, 1986, vol. 4, pp. 82-96.

Manning, C. Aleksei K, A Peasant Poet. *SEER* 18 (1939):175-83.

Soskice, P. Imagery in Esenin and Some Comparisons with K and Nekrasov. *NZSJ* 2 (1968):41-49.

VLADIMIR KOROLENKO

Translations

Birds of Heaven and Other Stories. Tr. C. Manning. NY: Duffield, 1919.
[Birds of Heaven; Isn't It Terrible; Necessity; On the Volga; The Village of God.]

The Blind Musician. Tr. H. Altschuler. Moscow: Foreign Languages Publishing House, 1956.

Children of the Vaults. Moscow: Foreign Languages Publishing House, n.d.

The History of My Contemporary. Tr. & abridged by Neil Parsons. Oxford: Oxford UP, 1972.

In a Strange Land. Tr. G. Zilboorg. NY: Richards, 1925.

Makar's Dream and Other Stories. Tr. M. Fell. NY: Duffield, 1916.
[Makar's Dream; The Murmuring Forest; In Bad Company; The Day of Atonement.]

Selected Stories. Intro. by R. Bobrova. Moscow: Progress, 1978.
[In Bad Company, The Blind Musician; The Strange One; Makar's Dream; The Murmuring Forest; The River at Dawn; Lights.]

The Vagrant and Other Tales. Tr. A.

Delano. NY: Crowell, 1887.
[The Old Bell-Ringer; The Forest
Soughs; A Forest Legend; Easter
Night; A Saghalinian; The Tale of a
Vagrant.]

Makar's Dream. Tr. Carl R. Proffer. In his
From Karamzin to Bunin. Bloomington: Indiana UP, 1969, pp. 300-27.

My First Encounter with Dickens. In
*Russian Literature and Modern
English Fiction,* ed. D. Davie. Chi-
cago: U Chicago P,1965, pp. 107-16.

Criticism

Hastie, Ruth Gordon. Vladimir Galak-
tionovich K: The Writer and the
Liberation Movement 1853-1907.
Ph.D. diss., Washington, St. Louis,
1979.

Seletski, Natalia M. The Elements of Light
in the Life and Fiction of V. G. K.
Ph.D. diss., Pennsylvania, 1964.

Windle, Kevin McNeil. A Comparative
Study of Translations of Janko
Muzykant by Henryk Sienkiewicz,
with Special Reference to V. Koro-
lenko's Translation, J. Curtin's English
Translation, and N. Tasin's Spanish
Translation. Ph.D. diss., McGill, 1974.

Calderon, G. L. K. *Monthly Review* 4
(1901):115-28.

Christian, R.F. V.G.K (1853-1921): A
Centennial Appreciation. *SEER* 32
(1954): 449-63.

Gruzenberg, O.O. V.G.K. In his *Yesterday: Memoirs of a Russian-Jewish
Lawyer.* Berkeley: U California P,
1981, pp. 169-88.

Kolb-Seletski, Natalia M. Elements of
Light in the Fiction of K. *SEEJ* 16
(1972):173-83.

Leighton, Lauren G. K's Stories of Siberia.
SEER 49 (1971):200-13.

Moser, Charles A. K and America. *RusR*
28 (1969):303-14.

O'Toole, L. M. K: "Makar's Dream." In
his *Structure, Style and Interpretation
in the Russian Short Story.* New
Haven: Yale UP, 1982, pp. 84-98.

Perris, G. H. Vladimir K. *Temple Bar
Magazine* 1 (1906):1-13.

Proffer, Carl R. "Makar's Dream." In his
From Karamzin to Bunin. Bloomington: Indiana UP, 1969, pp. 32-34.

Shub, Vladimir. Lenin and Vladimir K.
RusR 25 (1966):46-53.

SOFYA KOVALEVSKAYA

Translations

Recollections of Childhood. Tr. I. Hapgood. Biography by Carlotta Leffler.
NY: Century, 1895.

A Russian Childhood. Intro. Beatrice
Stillman. NY: Springer-Verlag, 1978.

Sonya Kovalevsky. Tr. A. De Furnhjelm &
A. M. Clive Bayley. Biographical note
by Lily Wolfsohn. NY: T. Fisher
Unwin, 1895.

Criticism

Koblitz, Ann Hibner. *A Convergence of
Lives.* Basel-Boston, 1983.

Chapman, Raymond & E. Gottlieb. A
Russian View of George Eliot.
Nineteenth-Century Fiction 33
(1978):348-65.

Heldt, Barbara. [K.] In her *Terrible
Perfection. Women and Russian Literature.* Bloomington: Indiana UP, 1987,
p. 66.

Stillman, Beatrice. Sofya K: Growing up in
the Sixties. *RLT* 9 (1974):276-302.

IVAN KOZLOV

Translations

Rydel, Christine, ed. *Ardis Anthology of
Russian Romanticism.* Ann Arbor:
Ardis, 1984, pp. 118-24.
[The Monk. A Kievan Tale.]

Wiener, Leo, ed. *Anthology of Russian
Literature.* NY: Putnam, 1902-3, vol.2,
pp. 68-73.
[The Black Monk; Kiev; Solitude.]

Wilson, Charles, ed. *Russian Lyrics in
English Verse.* London: Truebner,

1887.
[Chernetz (The Black Monk); The Village Orphan; The Wreck; The Dream of the Betrothed.]

Criticism

Barratt, G. R. *Ivan K. A Study and a Setting.* Toronto: Hakkert, 1972.

——. I. I. K: Unpublished Correspondence. *SEEJ* 15 (1970):104-16.

——. Somov, K and Byron's Russian Triumph. *Canadian Review of Comparative Literature* 1 (1974):104-22.

Brown, William Edward. Ivan K. In his *Russian Literature of the Romantic Period.* Ann Arbor: Ardis, 1986, vol. 3, pp. 242-65.

Mersereau, John. [K.] In his *Baron Delvig's "Northern Flowers"* Carbondale: Southern Illinois UP, 1967, pp. 27-36, 81-84.

IVAN KRYLOV

Translations

Fables. Tr. with preface by B. Pares. NY: Harcourt, 1927.

Krilov and His Fables. Tr. W. Ralston. London: Strahan, 1869.

Krylov's Fables. Tr. C. Coxwell. London: Paul-Trench-Trubner, 1921.

Criticism

Stepanov, Nikolay. *Ivan K.* NY: Twayne, 1973.

Epifan, Tamara A. The Dictionary of I. A. K's Poetic Language. Ph.D. diss., New York, 1978.

Werchun, Zofia Janina. The Influence of La Fontaine on K. Ph.D. diss., Northwestern, 1973.

Brown, William Edward. Ivan K. In his *Russian Literature of the Romantic Period.* Ann Arbor: Ardis, 1986, vol. 1, pp. 124-35.

Cross, A. G. The English and K. *OSP* 16

(1983):91-140.

Hamburger, H. The Function of Concessive Construction in Some of K's Fables. In *Dutch Contributions to the Eighth International Congress of Slavists,* ed. J. M. Meijer. Amsterdam: Benjamins, 1979, pp. 249-78.

Hart, Pierre R. Ivan K and the Mock Eulogy. *Satire Newsletter* 9, 1 (1971):1-5.

IVAN KUSHCHEVSKY

Translation

Nikolai Negorev, or The Successful Russian. Tr. D. P. & B. Costello. London: Calder & Boyars, 1967.

Criticism

Mirsky, D. S. K (1847-76). In his *A History of Russian Literature.* NY: Knopf, 1958, pp. 287-88.

WILHELM KÜCHELBECKER

Translations

Rydel, Christine, ed. *The Ardis Anthology of Russian Romanticism.* Ann Arbor: Ardis, 1984, pp. 79-80.
[Tsarskoe selo; 19 October 1837.]

Selden, Elizabeth, ed. *The Book of Friendship: An International Anthology.* Boston: Houghton-Mifflin, 1947.
[To Alexander Griboyedóv.]

Criticism

Baxter, Norman Allen. The Early (1817-1825) Literary Criticism of Wilhelm K. Ph.D. diss., California, Berkeley, 1977.

Levin, Yu. D. K and Crabbe. *OSP* 12 (1965):99-113.

Malenko, P. Tieck's Russian Friends (K and Zhukovskii). *PMLA* 55 (1940): 1129-45.

IVAN
LAZHECHNIKOV

Translations

The Heretic. Tr. T. Shaw. NY: Harper 1844.

Wiener, Leo, ed. *Anthology of Russian Literature.* NY: Putnam, 1902-3, vol. 2, pp. 111-19.
[The Heretic (Excerpt).]

Criticism

Wowk, Vitaly. The Historical Novels of I. I. L. Ph.D. diss., Ohio State, 1972.

Brown, William Edward. Ivan L. In his *A History of Russian Literature of the Romantic Period.* Ann Arbor: Ardis, 1986, vol. 2, pp. 289-301.

Twarog, Leon. The Soviet Revival of a Nineteenth-Century Historical Novelist: I. I. L. *HSS* 4 (1957):107-26.

KONSTANTIN
LEONTIEV

Translations

Against the Current: Selections from the Novels, Essays, Notes and Letters of K. L. Tr. G. Reavey. NY: Weybright & Talley, 1969.

The Egyptian Dove: The Story of a Russian. Tr. G. Reavey. NY: Weybright & Talley, 1969.

The Novels of Count L. N. Tolstoy. In *Essays in Russian Literature,* ed. Spencer E. Roberts. Athens: Ohio UP, 1969, pp. 225-356.

Criticism

Berdiaev, N. A. *L.* Tr. G. Reavey. Orono: Academic International, 1968.

Lukashevich, Stephen. *Konstantin L (1831-1891): A Study in Russian "Heroic Vitalism."* NY: Pageant, 1967.

Obolensky, Alexander. Konstantin Nikolaevič L: An Expository Study and Analysis of His Thought as Reflected in His Life and His Writing. Ph.D. diss., Pennsylvania, 1967.

Ivask, G. Konstantin L's Fiction. *SlavR* 20 (1961):622-27.

Kurland, J. E. L's Views on the Course of Russian Literature. *ASEER* 16 (1957):260-74.

Rzhevsky, Nicholas. L's Prickly Prose. *SlavR* 35 (1976):258-68.

___ L's Prickly Prose. In his *Russian Literature and Ideology.* Urbana: U Illinois P, 1983, pp. 99-115.

MIKHAIL
LERMONTOV

Bibliography

Heifetz, Anna, comp. *L in English: A List of Works By and About the Poet.* NY: New York Public Library, 1942. [136 translation items; 72 critical items.]

Translations

The Demon and Other Poems. Tr. Eugene M. Kayden. Yellow Springs, OH: Antioch P, 1965.
[65 lyric poems; The Lay of Kalashnikov the Merchant; The Fugitive; The Novice; The Demon.]

A Hero of Our Own Times. Tr. E. and C. Paul. NY: Oxford UP, 1958.

A Hero of Our Time. Tr. Paul Foote. Harmondsworth: Penguin, 1974.

A Hero of Our Time. Tr. Philip Longworth. Afterword by William E. Harkins. London: New English Library, 1975.

A Hero of Our Time. Tr. Vladimir Nabokov in collaboration with Dmitri Nabokov. Intro. V. Nabokov. Garden City, NY: Anchor, 1958; rpt., Ann Arbor: Ardis, 1988.

A Hero of Our Time. Tr. Martin Parker. Moscow: Foreign Languages Publishing House, 1951.

A L Reader. Tr. Guy Daniels. NY: Macmillan, 1965.
[19 lyric poems, A Fairytale for Children; Songs about Kalashnikov; The Tambov Treasurer's Wife; The

Novice; Princess Ligovskaya; A Strange One.]

Major Poetical Works. Tr. Anatoly Liberman. Minneapolis: U Minnesota P, 1984.

Masquerade. Tr. Roger W. Phillips. *RLT* 7 (1973):67-116.

Mikhail L. Tr. C. E. L'Ami & A. Welikotny. Winnipeg: U Manitoba P, 1967.

Narrative Poems by Alexander Pushkin and Mikhail L. Tr. Charles Johnston. NY: Vintage, 1983.
[The Tambov Lady; The Novice; The Demon.]

The Prophet & Other Poems. Tr. E. M. Kayden. Sewanee: U of the South, 1942.

Selected Works. Tr. A. Pyman & Irina Zheleznova. Moscow: Progress, 1976.
[27 lyrics; Lay of Kalashnikov; Mtsyri; The Demon; A Panorama of Moscow; Asheek-Kerib; A Hero of Our Time.]

A Sheaf from L. Tr. J. J. Robbins. NY: Lieber & Lewis, 1923.
[23 lyrics.]

Vadim. Tr. with an introduction by Helena Goscilo. Ann Arbor: Ardis, 1984.

Guerney, B. G., ed. *A Treasury of Russian Literature*. NY: Vanguard, 1943.
[Ashik-Kerib (A Turkish Fairy Tale); The Chalice of Life; Lonely & Far Sea; White Sail Soars; The Angel; Testament; A Song of Kalashnikov.]

Nabokov, Vladimir, tr. *Three Russian Poets*. Norfolk, CT: New Directions, 1944.

Rydel, Christine, ed. *Ardis Anthology of Russian Romanticism*. Ann Arbor: Ardis, 1984.
[15 lyrics; The Lay of the Merchant Kalashnikov; The Demon; Shtoss.]

Criticism

Eikhenbaum, Boris M. *L. A Study in Literary-Historical Evaluation*. Tr. Ray Parrott & Harry Weber. Ann Arbor: Ardis, 1981.

Garrard, John. *Mikhail L*. Boston: Twayne, 1982.

Kelly, Lawrence. *L: Tragedy in the Caucasus*. NY: Braziller, 1977.

Lavrin, Janko. *L*. London: Bowes & Bowes; NY: Hillary House, 1959.

Mersereau, John Jr. *Mikhail L*. Carbondale: Southern Illinois UP, 1962.

Turner, C. J. G. *Pechorin: An Essay on L's "A Hero of Our Time."* Birmingham: Birmingham Slavic Monographs, 1978.

Cameron, Alan Harwood. Byronism in L's *A Hero of Our Time*. Ph.D. diss., British Columbia, 1974.

Cosman, Tatiana M. The Letter as a Literary Device in the Fiction of Pushkin, L and Gogol. Ph.D. diss., New York, 1973.

Goscilo, Helena. From Dissolution to Synthesis: The Use of Genre in L's Prose. Ph.D. diss., Indiana, 1976.

Henderson, I. Study of the Development of L as a Poet through His Different Versions of "The Demon" (written between 1829 and 1839). Ph.D. diss., Oxford, 1980.

Lemmon, Dallas Marion, Jr. The Novelle, or the Novel of Interrelated Stories: M. L, G. Keller, S. Anderson. Ph.D. diss., Indiana, 1970.

Mersereau, John, Jr. The Novel in the Literary Art of M. Y. L. Ph.D. diss., California, 1957.

Rathbone, C. Problems of Pattern in L's Verse and Prose. Ph.D. diss., Oxford, 1976.

Wilkinson, Joel Lynn. The Development of the Ballad in Russian Literature by Mixail Jur'evič L (1814-1841). Ph.D. diss., Kansas, 1977.

Angeloff, A. and Pr. Klingenburg. L's Uses of Nature in the Novel *Hero of Our Time*. *RLJ* 88 (1970):3-12.

Arian, I. Some Aspects of L's *A Hero of Our Time*. *FMLS* 4 (1968):22-32.

Austin, Paul M. New Light on L's "Bela." *RLJ* 40, 136-37 (1986):161-65.

Bagby, L. Narrative Double-Voicing in L's *A Hero of Our Time*. *SEEJ* 22 (1978):265-86.

Bikerman, J. J. Centenary. *Poetry Review* July-August 1941: 205-10.

Binyon, T. J. L, Tyutchev & Fet. In *Nineteenth-Century Russian Literature*, ed. John Fennell. Berkeley: U California P, 1973, pp. 168-224.

Bowra, Sir Maurice. L. *OSP* 3 (1953):1-20.

Briggs, A. D. P. "Pikovaya dama" and "Taman'": Questions of Kinship. *JRS* 37 (1979):13-20.

Brown, William Edward. L. In his *A History of Russian Literature of the Romantic Period.* Ann Arbor: Ardis, 1986, vol. 4, pp. 140-261.

Chistova, Irina. The First L Biography from England. *Soviet Literature* 7 (1986): 174-81.

Cox, Gary. Dramatic Genre as a Tool of Characterization in L's *A Hero of Our Time. RusL* 11-12 (1982):163-72.

Cross, S. H. Mikhail Yurevich L. *American Quarterly Review on the Soviet Union* 4, 4 (1941):25-51.

Debreczeny, Paul. Elements of the Lyrical Verse Tale in L's *A Hero of Our Time.* In *American Contributions to the Seventh International Congress of Slavists,* vol. 2, ed. V. Terras. The Hague: Mouton, 1973, pp. 93-118.

Dennis, C. P. L. Mikhayl Yurevich L: A Brief Account of His Life and Poetry. *Poetry Review* 16 (1925):304-12.

Eagle, Herbert. L's "Play" with Romantic Genre Expectations in *A Hero of Our Time. RLT* 10 (1974):299-315.

Eikhenbaum, B. Some Principles of Literary History: The Study of L. Tr. C. Pike. *Russian Poetics in Translation* 5 (1978):1-8.

Entwistle, William James. The Byronism of L's *A Hero of Our Time. CL* 1 (1949):140-46.

Faletti, H. Elements of the Demonic in the Character of Pechorin in L's *A Hero of Our Time. FMLS* 14 (1978):365-77.

Freeborn, Richard. *A Hero of Our Time.* In his *The Rise of the Russian Novel.* Cambridge: Cambridge UP, 1973, pp. 38-73.

Garner, M. Linguistics and Literature: The Web of Associations in L's "Parus." In *Proceedings of the Russian Colloquium, University of Melbourne, August, 1976.* Melbourne: Russian Dept. U Melbourne, 1977, pp. 34-39.

Goscilo, Helena. The First Pečorin En Route to *A Hero of Our Time:* L's *Princess Ligovskaya. RusL* 11-12 (1982):129-62.

____. Gilded Guilt: Confession in Russian Romantic Prose. *RusL* 14 (1983):149-82.

____. L's Debt to Lavater and Gall. *SEER* 59 (1981):500-15.

____. L's Sketches: From Poetic City to Prosaic Man. *CASS* 14 (1980):21-35.

Gregg, Richard. The Cooling of Pechorin: The Skull Beneath the Skin. *SlavR* 43 (1984):387-98.

Grigor'jan, K. N. Pechorin and Hamlet: Towards a Typology of Character. Tr. C. Roberts. *Canadian Review of Comparative Literature* 1 (1974):235-52.

Halpert, E. L and the Wolf Man. *American Imago* 32 (1975):315-28.

Harvie, J. A. L's "Demon." *AUMLA: Journal of the Australasian Universities Modern Languages and Literatures Association* 29 (1968):25-32.

____. The Vulture and the Dove. *CLS* 18 (1981):15-32.

Hecht, L. L and the German Poets. *CASS* 10 (1976):400-9.

Heier, E. The Second *Hero of Our Time. SEEJ* 11 (1967):35-43.

Hopkins, W. H. Lermontovian Elements in Leskov's Story "Deception." *NZSJ* 1 (1977):23-34.

____. L's Hussar Poems. *RLT* 14 (1976):36-41.

Katz, Michael. L's Literary Ballads. In his *The Literary Ballad in Early 19th-Century Russian Literature.* Oxford: Oxford UP, 1976, pp. 166-82.

Kostka, Edmund. The Influence of Schiller's Aesthetics on the Dramas of L. *Philological Quarterly* 30 (1951): 393-402.

____. L's Debt to Schiller. *Revue de Littérature Comparée* 37 (1963):68-88.

____. Schiller's Influence on L's Drama *The Two Brothers. Philological Quarterly* 35 (1956):186-90.

____. Schiller's Influence on the Early Dramas of L. *Philological Quarterly* 32 (1953):396-410.

Lavrin, Janko. Some Notes on L's Romanticism. *SEER* 36 (1958):69-81.

Manning. C. A. Dramas of Schiller and L. *Philological Quarterly* 8 (1929):11-20.

____. L and Spain. *Romanic Review* 22

(1931):126-29.

——. Mikhail Yurevich L. *South Atlantic Quarterly* 24 (1925):50-60.

——. Napoleon and L. *Romanic Review* 17 (1926):32-40.

——. The "Two Brothers" of L and Pechorin. *MLN* 63 (1948):149-53.

Maslenikov, O. M.Yu.L, 1814-1841: In Commemoration of the 125th Anniversary of His Birth. *Slavia* 14, 9-10 (1939):1-8.

Mersereau, John Jr. The Fatalist as a Keystone of L's *A Hero of Our Time*. *SEEJ* 4 (1960):137-46.

——. L and Balzac. In *American Contributions to the Fifth International Congress of Slavists*. The Hague: Mouton, 1963, pp. 233-58.

——. L's *Shtoss:* Hoax or Literary Credo? *SlavR* 21 (1962):280-95.

——. M. Yu. L's *The Song of the Merchant Kalashnikov:* An Allegorical Interpretation. *CalSS* 1 (1960):110-33.

Michailoff, Helen. The Death of L (The Poet and the Tsar). *RLT* 10 (1974):279-98.

——. The Vereshchagina Albums. *RLT* 10 (1974):363-407.

Milivojević, D. English Translations of L's "Vyxožu odin ja na dorogu": A Commentary. *RLJ* 118 (1980):169-78.

Milner-Gulland, R. Heroes of Their Time?: Form and Idea in Büchner's *Danton's Death* and L's *A Hero of Our Time*. In *Idea of Freedom, Essays in Honour of Isaiah Berlin*, ed. A. Ryan. Oxford: Oxford UP, 1979, pp. 115-37.

Nabokov, Vladimir. The L Mirage. *RusR* 1 (1941):31-39.

Ostoupe, N. Vigny's *Eloa* and L's *Demon*. *SEER* 34 (1956):311-37.

Parry, Albert. The "Deadly Game." *Army* 33 (Feb. 1983):59-61.

Peace, R. A. The Role of *Taman'* in L's *Geroy nashego vremeni. SEER* 4 (1967): 12-29.

Pervushin, Nicholas V. L's Poetic Apprenticeship. *SEER* 12 (1967):25-43.

Proffer, Carl R. The Similes of Pushkin and L. *RLT* 3 (1972):148-94.

Puterman, J. Notes on L (On the 125th Anniversary of His Birth). *Nineteenth Century* 127 (1940):349-57.

Reeve, F. D. *A Hero of Our Time*. In his *The Russian Novel*. London: Muller, 1967, pp. 45-63.

Reid, Robert. The Critical Uses of Translation (L's *A Hero of Our Time). Essays in Poetics* 11, 2 (1986):55-90.

——. Eavesdropping in *A Hero of Our Time. NZSJ* 1 (1977):13-22.

——. L's *Demon:* A Question of Identity. *SEER* 60 (1982):189-210.

——. L's *Mtsyri:* Themes and Structure. In *Problems of Russian Romanticism,* ed. Robert Reid. Brookfield, VT: Gower, 1986, pp. 127-68.

Richards, David. Pechorin and the Art of Seduction. *JRS* 22 (1971):3-9.

——. Two Malicious Tongues—The Wit of Chatsky and Pechorin. *NZSJ* 11 (1973):11-28.

Ripp, V. *A Hero of Our Time* and the Historicism of the 1830's. *MLN* 92 (1977):969-86.

Ross, R. H. L: A Hero of His Time. *South Atlantic Bulletin* 37 (1977):158-61.

Rowe, Eleanor. Pushkin, L and *Hamlet. Texas Studies in Literature and Language* 17 (1975):337-47.

Rowe, W. W. Duality and Symmetry in L's *A Hero of Our Time*. In his *Nabokov and Others: Patterns in Russian Literature*. Ann Arbor: Ardis, 1979, pp. 27-36.

Sengupta, N. An Introduction to L's *A Hero of Our Time*. In *Studies in Russian Literature,* ed. J. V. Paul. Hyderabad: Central Institute of English and Foreign Languages, 1984, pp. 19-27.

Shaw, J. Thomas. Byron: The Byronic Tradition of the Romantic Verse Tale in Russian, and L's Mtsyri. *ISS* 1 (1956):165-90.

——. L's *Demon* and the Byronic Oriental Verse Tale. *ISS* 2 (1958):163-80.

Simpson, Mark S. L's *The Demon* and Maturin's *Melmoth the Wanderer. RusL* 16, 3 (1984):275-88.

Sommer, T. The Imagery of Loneliness in L's Lyrics. *NZSJ* 1 (1977):1-11.

Spector, I. The Death of L. *Slavia* 16, 4 (1941):98-102.

Spence, L. Ercildoune in Muscovy: The Centenary of L. *Scots Magazine* 35 (1941):321-30.

Stenbock-Fermor, E. L and Dostoevskij's Novel *The Devils. SEEJ* 3 (1959):219-30.

Turner, C. J. G. The System of Narrators in Part I of *A Hero of Our Time. CSP* 17 (1975):617-28.

Tverskoy, P. A. M. J. L, 1814-1841. *RusR* 2 (1916):23-25.

Ulph, Owen. Unmasking the Masked Guardsman. *RLT* 3 (1972):269-81.

Vernadsky, N. L in Russian Music. *SEER* 22, 1 (1943):6-31.

Vinogradov, V. The Language of L. In his *A History of the Russian Literary Language.* Madison: U Wisconsin P, 1969, pp. 158-77.

Warner, N. O. The Footnote as a Literary Genre: Nabokov's Commentaries to L and Pushkin. *SEEJ* 30 (1986):167-82.

Weeks, A. Tiutchev, Schelling and the Question of Influence. *Germano-Slavica* 3 (1981):307-18.

Wen, C. From Glaring Cheat to Daring Feat: Two Episodes in the Reception of M. Yu. L in Victorian England. *NZSJ* 2 (1980):1-16.

Woodward, James B. Semantico-Syntactic Contrastive Schemes in the Lyric Poetry of L. *CalSS* 3, 3 (1969):516-27.

Yalom, M. K. *La chute* and *A Hero of Our Time. French Review* 36 (1962):138-45.

NIKOLAI LESKOV

Bibliography

Muller de Moragues, Ines. *L'oeuvre journalistique et littéraire de N. S. L: Bibliographie.* NY: P. Lang, 1984. (Slavica Helvetica; v. 23.)

Translations

The Amazon and Other Stories. Tr. David Magarshack. London: Allen-Unwin, 1949.

[The Amazon; A Little Mistake; The March Hare.]

The Cathedral Folk. Tr. Isabel Hapgood. NY: Knopf, 1924.

The Enchanted Pilgrim and Other Stories. Tr. David Magarshack. London: Hutchinson International, 1946; rpt. Westport, CT: Hyperion, 1977.

[The Enchanted Pilgrim; Iron Will; Deathless; Golovan; The Left-Handed Artificer; The Make-Up Artist.]

The Enchanted Wanderer and Other Stories. Tr. G. Hanna. Moscow: Foreign Languages Publishing House, 1958 (?).

[The Enchanted Wanderer; Lady Macbeth of the Mtsensk District; Lefty; The Make-Up Genius; The Sentry.]

Five Tales. Tr. M. Shotton. London: Angel Books, 1984.

The Musk-Ox and Other Tales. Tr. R. Norman. London: Routledge, 1944; rpt. Westport, CT: Hyperion, 1977.

[The Musk-Ox; Kotin and Platonida; The Spirit of Madame de Genlis; The Stinger; A Flaming Patriot; The Clothes-Mender; The Devil Chase; The Alexandrite.]

Satirical Stories. Tr. William B. Edgerton. NY: Pegasus, 1969.

[The Steel Flea; The Archbishop and the Englishman; Single Thought; A Journey with a Nihilist; Deception; Choice Grain; Notes from an Unknown Hand; About the Rooster and His Children; Fish Soup without Fish; Figura; Night Owls; A Product of Nature.]

The Sealed Angel and Other Stories. Ed. & tr. K. A. Lantz. Knoxville: U Tennessee P, 1984.

Selected Tales. Tr. David Magarshack, intro. V. S. Pritchett. NY: Noonday Press, 1961.

[Lady Macbeth of the Mtsensk District; The Enchanted Wanderer; The Left-Handed Craftsman; The Sentry; The White Eagle.]

The Sentry and Other Stories. Tr. A. Chamot. London: Bodley Head, 1922.

[Lady Macbeth of Mzinsk District; The Toupee Artist; On the Edge of the World.]

The Steel Flea. Tr. Isabel Hapgood. Boston: Merrymount Press, 1916.

The Wild Beast. Tr. Guy Daniels. NY, 1968.

Criticism

Lantz, K. A. *Nikolay L.* Boston: Twayne, 1979.

McLean, Hugh. *Nikolai L. The Man and His Art.* Cambridge: Harvard UP, 1977.

Muckle, James Y. *Nikolai L and the "Spirit of Protestantism."* Birmingham: Birmingham Slavic Monographs, 1978.

Revue des études slaves. 58, 3 (1986). Special Leskov issue.

Aman, Thomas L. Structural Features of L's "Soboryane" and His Stories of the 1860's. Ph.D. diss., Toronto, 1968.

Barsom, Valentina K. The Misunderstood and Misinterpreted Leskov: (Leskov in Radical Pre-Revolutionary and Soviet Literary Criticism). Ph.D. diss., Pittsburgh, 1969.

Bowers, Catherine. L's Ukrainian Stories. Ph.D. diss., Bryn Mawr, 1979.

Burago, Alla. L's *Cathedral Folk:* A Russian Apocalypse. Ph.D. diss., Texas, 1976.

Dragt, Donald Jay. The Righteous Man: A Study of Positive Heroes in the Works of N. S. L. Ph.D. diss., Michigan State, 1975.

Edgerton, William B. Nikolai L: The Intellectual Development of a Literary Nonconformist. Ph.D. diss., Columbia, 1955.

Ferry, Marjorie Anne. N. S. L's Tales about the Three Righteous Men: A Study in the Positive Type. Ph.D. diss., Yale, 1977.

Keenan, William Laurence. The Early Work of N. S. L. A Study of the Writer's Development. Ph.D. diss., London, 1980.

Leatherbarrow, W. J. The Force of Circumstances: A Study of the Hero and His Environment in the Works of

N. S. L. Ph.D. diss., Exeter, 1972.

Lottridge, Stephen S. Nikolaj Semënovič L's *Prolog* Tales. Ph.D. diss., Columbia, 1970.

McLean, Hugh. Studies in the Life and Art of L. Ph.D. diss., Harvard, 1956.

Russell, James. L and Folklore. Ph.D. diss., Princeton, 1971.

Allisandratos, Julia. A Stylization of Hagiographical Composition in L's "Singlethought" (Odnodum). *SEEJ* 27 (1983):416-32.

Aman, Thomas L. L's First Series of Sketches. *SEEJ* 12 (1968):424-34.

Ansberg, Aleksej B. Frame Story and First Person Story in N. S. L. *Scando-Slavica* 3 (1957):49-73.

Benjamin, Walter. The Story Teller: Reflections on the Works of Nikolai L. *Chicago Review* 16, 1 (1963):80-101.

Bowers, Catherine D. Nikolay L's Reminiscences of Kiev: Examples of His Memoir Style. *Harvard Ukrainian Studies* 6, 4 (1982):477-84.

Bridgman, Richard. L under the Bushel of Translation. *Texas Quarterly* 9, 3 (1966): 80-88.

Edgerton, William B. L and Gogol. In *American Contributions to the Ninth International Congress of Slavists.* Columbus: Slavica, 1983, vol. 2, pp. 135-48.

——.L and Russia's Slavic Brethren. In *American Contributions to the Fourth International Congress of Slavists.* 's-Gravenhage: Mouton, 1958, pp. 51-75.

—— L and Tolstoy: Two Literary Heretics. *ASEER* 12 (1953):524-34.

—— L on Quakers in Russia. *Bulletin of Friends Historical Association* 40 (1951): 3-15.

—— L's Trip Abroad in 1875. *ISS* 4 (1967): 88-99.

—— Missing Letters to L: An Unsolved Puzzle. *SlavR* 25 (1966):120-32.

Eekman, T. A. The Genesis of L's *Soborjane. CalSS* 2 (1963):121-40.

—— N. S. L's *At Daggers Drawn* Reconsidered. In *Miscellanea Slavica: To Honour the Memory of Jan M. Meijer,* ed. B. J. Amsenga, et al. Amsterdam: Rodopi, 1983, pp. 195-221.

Eikhenbaum, Boris. L and Contemporary Prose. Tr. Martin P. Rice. *RLT* 11 (1975):211-29.

Heir, Edmund. L and Meščerskij on Radstockism and Paškovism *Wiener Slavistisches Jahrbuch* 15 (1969):23-36.

Hopkins, W. H. Lermontovian Elements in L's Story "Deception." *NZSJ* 1 (1977):23-34.

Isenberg, Charles. Deconstructing Domna Platonova: Narrative Figures in Voitel'nitsa. *RusR* 43 (1984):339-53.

Keenan, W. L's "Left-Handed Craftsman" and Zamyatin's "Flea": Irony into Allegory. *FMLS* 16 (1980):66-78.

Lantz, K. L's "At The Edge of the World": The Search for an Image of Christ. *SEEJ* 25 (1981):34-43.

Lottridge, S. L's Moral Vision in the "Prolog" Tales. *SEER* 18 (1974):252-58.

——. Solzhenitsyn and L. *RLT* 6 (1973): 478-89.

McLean, Hugh. *Cathedral Folk:* Apotheosis of Orthodoxy or Its Doomsday Book? In *Slavic Forum: Essays in Linguistics,* ed. M. S. Flier. The Hague: Mouton, 1974, pp. 130-48.

——. A Contribution to the Revival of L. *SlavR* 22 (1963):745-50.

——. L and His Enigmatic Man. *HSS* 4 (1957):203-24.

——. L and Ioann of Kronstadt: On the Origins of "Polunoščniki." *ASEER* 12 (1953):93-108.

——. L and the Russian Superman. *Midway* 8, 4 (1968):105-23.

——. On the Style of a Leskovian "Skaz." *HSS* 2 (1958):297-322.

——. The Priest and the Sorcerer: L's First Short Story. In *Languages and Areas: Studies Presented to George V. Bobrinskoy on the Occasion of His Academic Retirement.* Chicago, 1967, pp. 90-99.

——. Russia, The Love-Hate Pendulum and the *Sealed Angel.* In *To Honor Roman Jakobson.* The Hague: Mouton, 1967, vol. 2, pp. 1328-39.

——. Theodore the Christian Looks at Abraham the Hebrew: L and the Jews. *CalSS* 7 (1973):65-98.

Muckle, James. The Author as Editor: L's

"The Musk-Ox." *SEEJ* 24 (1980):349-61.

——. Nikolay L: Educational Journalist and Imaginative Writer. *NZSJ* (1984):81-110.

——. Scholars, Critics and N. Leskov. *JRS* 36 (1978):35-42.

O'Connor, Katherine Tiernan. The Specter of Political Corruption: L's "White Eagle." *RLT* 8 (1974):393-408.

O'Toole, L. M. L: "The Man on Sentry Duty." In his *Structure, Style and Interpretation in the Russian Short Story.* New Haven: Yale UP, 1982, pp. 14-20.

Pritchett, V.S. L. *OSP* 10 (1962):18-24.

Russell, James. L and His Quarrel with the Men of the Sixties. *CSP* 12 (1970):108-27.

Schwencke, C. G. Some Remarks on the Use of Dialects in L's Prose. *SEER* 46 (1968):333-52.

——. Some Remarks on the Use of the Structural and Linguistic Devices in L's Prose. *SEER* 50 (1972):546-57.

Stammler, H. Conrad's Novel *Victory* and L's Chronicle *Soboriane:* Affinities and Resemblances. *Wiener Slavistiches Jahrbuch* 25 (1979):125-39.

Wehrle, A. J. Paradigmatic Aspects of L's "The Enchanted Pilgrim." *SEER* 20 (1976):371-78.

Wigzell, F. The *Staraya skazka* of L's *Soboryane:* Archpriest Tuberozov and Avvakum. *SEER* 63 (1985):321-36.

DMITRI MAMIN-SIBIRYAK

Translations

The Privalov Fortune. Tr. V. Shneerson. Moscow: Foreign Languages Publishing House, 1958.

Tales for Alyonushka. Moscow: Progress, 1978.

Verotchka's Tales. NY: Dutton, 1922.

NIKOLAI MIKHAILOVSKY

Translations

Dostoevsky: A Cruel Talent. Tr. S. Cadmus. Ann Arbor: Ardis, 1978.

Criticism

Billington, James. *Mikhailovsky and Russian Populism.* Oxford: Oxford UP, 1958.

NIKOLAI NADEZHDIN

Criticism

McCarthy, Sheila Margaret. The Literary Criticism of Nikolai Ivanovich Nadezhdin. Ph.D. diss., Cornell, 1980.

——. The Legacy of N. I. N's Critique of Romanticism. *SEEJ* (1984):164-79.

NIKOLAI NEKRASOV

Translations

Poems. Tr. J. Soskice. Intro. L. Abercrombie. London: Oxford UP, 1929. Reprinted with a foreword by Lord Stow Hill. Wilmington, DE: Scholarly Resources, 1974.
[Part I: Russian Women (Grandmother's Memoirs)—Princess Troubetzkoy; Princess Volkonskaya. Part II: The Pedlars; Peasant Children; Poems Dedicated to Russian Children: Uncle Jake, Nightingales, Grandad Marzay and the Hares, General Toptiggin, The Bees; Red-Nose Frost; Vlass; A Sleepless Night; On the Road; The Mother; The Railway; The Svat and the Bridegroom.]
Who Can Be Happy and Free in Russia? Tr. J. M. Soskice. Intro. by D. Soskice. London: Oxford UP, 1917.

Obolensky, Dmitri, ed. *The Heritage of Russian Verse.* Bloomington: Indiana UP, 1976.
[5 lyrics]
Raffel, Burton, ed. *Russian Poetry under the Tsars.* Albany: SUNY P, 1971.
[Self-Hate; Muse of Vengeance, Muse of Sorrow; I Feel So Low; A Black Day.]
Reeve, F. D. and Helen, tr. Poet and Citizen. *RLT* 17 (1982):153-60.
Zheleznova, Irina, ed. *Russian 19th-Century Verse.* Moscow: Raduga, 1983.
[38 lyrics]

Criticism

Birkenmayer, Sigmund S. *Nikolaj N: His Life and Poetic Art.* The Hague: Mouton, 1968.
Chukovsky, Kornei. *The Poet and the Hangman: Nekrasov and Muravyov.* Tr. W. Rotsel. Ann Arbor: Ardis, 1977.

Marullo, Thomas Catton. The Poet as Critic: The Literary Criticism of Nikolai N. Ph.D. diss., Cornell, 1976.
Perkins, Ann Weiler. N's Prose and Russian Popular Fiction of the 1840s. Ph.D. diss., Harvard, 1979.
Reeve, Helen. N's Poems of 1856: A Study of the Lyrical "I". Ph.D. diss., Columbia, 1976.

Birkenmayer, Sigmund S. N. A. N: A Glimpse of the Man and the Poet. *Slavic and East European Studies* 12 (1968):188-200.
——. The Peasant Poems of Nikolaj N. *SEEJ* 11 (1967):159-67.
——. Polish Themes in the Poetry of N. In *Studies in Honor of Xenia Gasiorowska,* ed. L. Leighton. Columbus: Slavica, 1983, pp. 44-54.
Brinton, C. Work of N. *Critic* 37 (1900): 423-25.
Gregg, Richard. A Brackish Hippocrene: N, Panaeva, and the "Prose in Love." *SlavR* 34 (1975):731-51.
——. Dar'ia's Secret; Or What Happens in *Moroz, krasnyi nos. SlavR* 45

(1986):38-48.

Kader, B. Nikolai N, Poet of the Russian People. *Books Abroad* 21 (1947):393-95.

Lojkine, A. K. N's Anapests. *MelbSS* 9-10 (1975):54-63.

Marullo, T. Demystifying the Literary Salon: N's "Sketches of Life" and "How Great I Am." *RLT* 17 (1982): 161-84.

——. N's "Chinovniki": A New Look at Russia's "Little Men." *SEEJ* 21 (1977): 483-94.

——. Reviving Interest in Verse: The Critical Efforts of Nikolai N, 1848-54. *CSP* 22 (1980):247-59.

Ransome, M. G. The Pessimism of N. A. N's *Moroz, krasnyy nos. JRS* 45 (1984):9-18.

Reeve, Helen. The Lyrical Stance in "Poet and Citizen. *RLT* 17 (1982):141-53.

——. An Unexpected Portrait of N; Preface to Borozdin's "N's Father." *RLT* 17 (1982):205-13.

Soskice, P. Esenin's "Anna Snegina": A Comparison with N's Poem "Korobeyniki" and Some Comments on its Relevance as a Social Document. *NZSJ* 9 (1972):38-49.

——. Imagery in Esenin and Some Comparisons with Koltsov and N. *NZSJ* 2 (1968):41-49.

——. N and Esenin: A Study of "Korobeyniki" and "Anna Snegina." *NZSJ* 2 (1968):41-49.

——. Video meliora proboque... A Study in the Psychology of N. *NZSJ* 10 (1972):2-10.

Trensky, P. I. Neruda and N: A Confrontation. *Czechoslovakia, Past and Present*, ed. M. Rechcigl. The Hague: Mouton, 1968, vol. 2, pp. 928-39.

Ware, R. J. A Russian Journal and Its Public: *Otechestvennye zapiski* [Fatherland Notes]. *OSP* 14 (1981):121-46.

VLADIMIR ODOEVSKY

Translations

Russian Nights. Tr. O. Koshansky-Olienikov and R. Matlaw. Intro. R. Matlaw. NY: Dutton, 1965.

Eyre, J., tr. The Improvisor. *SEER* 22 (1944):97-109.

Fetzer, Leland, ed. *Pre-Revolutionary Russian Science Fiction*. Ann Arbor: Ardis, 1982.
[The Year 4338. Letters from Petersburg]

Korovin, Valentin, comp. *Russian 19th-Century Gothic Tales*. Moscow: Raduga, 1984.
[4338 A.D.; The Sylphide; The Ghost; The City Without a Name; The Living Corpse.]

Proffer, Carl R., ed. *Russian Romantic Prose*. Ann Arbor: Translation Press, 1979.
[The Live Corpse; Princess Mimi; The Sylph.]

Rydel, Christine, ed. *The Ardis Anthology of Russian Romanticism*. Ann Arbor: Ardis, 1984.
[A Tale of Why it is Dangerous for Young Girls to Go Walking in a Group Along Nevsky Prospect; Princess Mimi.]

Criticism

Cornwell, Neil. *The Life, Times, and Milieu of V. F. O*. Athens: Ohio UP, 1986. [Bibliography.]

Cornwell, Neil John. The Life and Works of V. F. O (1804-1869). Ph.D. diss., Queen's, Belfast, 1983.

Ilyinsky, Oleg P. V. F. O's Prose within the Framework of Russian Romanticism. Ph.D. diss., New York, 1970.

Linburn, Jo Ann H. A Would-Be Faust: Vladimir Fyodorovich O and His Prose Fiction, 1830-1845. Ph.D. diss., Columbia, 1970.

Nanney, James Stanford. Prince Vladimir F. O: His Contribution to Russian Nationalism and Russian Philosophy. Ph.D. diss., Vanderbilt, 1975.

Bagby, L. V. F. O's *Knjažna Zizi. RusL* 12 (1985):221-42.

Brown, William Edward. Vladimir O. In his *A History of Russian Literature of the Romantic Period.* Ann Arbor: Ardis, 1986, vol. 2, pp. 219-40.

Cornwell, Neil. Belinsky and V. F. O. *SEER* 62 (1984):6-24.

——. A Note on Aristidov's Mistresses in "The Live Corpse." *Quinquereme* 3, 1 (1980):118-20.

——.Perspectives on the Romanticism of V. F. O. In *Problems of Russian Romanticism,* ed. Robert Reid. Brookfield, VT: Gower, 1986, pp. 169-208.

——. Utopia and Dystopia in Russian Fiction: The Contribution of V. F. O. *Renaissance and Modern Studies* 28 (1984):59-71.

——. V. F. O's Ridiculous Dream about That: Themes and Ideas in Works by V. F. O, Dostoevsky and Mayakovsky. *Quinquereme* 2, 1-2 (1979):75-86; 246-55.

——. V. F. O's *Russian Nights:* Genre, Reception and Romantic Poetics. *Essays in Poetics* 8, 2 (1983):19-55.

Ilgner, R Goethe's "Geist, der stets Verneint" and Its Emergence in the Faust Works of O, Lunacharsky and Bulgakov. *Germano-Slavica* 2 (1977): 169-80.

Ingham, Norman W. [O.] In his *E.T.A. Hoffmann's Reception in Russia.* Würzburg: Jal-Verlag, 1974, pp. 177-93.

Karlinsky, Simon. A Hollow Shape: The Philosophical Tales of Prince Vladimir O. *Studies in Romanticism* 5, 3 (1966):169-82.

Lang, Olga. Two Visions of the Future: Russia and China as Pictured in Two 19th-Century Russian Tales. In *Perspectives on a Changing China,* ed. J. A. Fogel. Boulder: Westview, 1979, pp. 7-31.

Lowe, David. Vladimir O as Opera Critic. *SlavR* 41 (1982):306-15.

Matlaw, Ralph. Introduction to *Russian Nights.* NY: Dutton, 1965.

Proffer, Carl R. Vladimir O. In his *Russian Romantic Prose.* Ann Arbor: Translation Press, 1979, pp. 23-24.

ALEXANDER OSTROVSKY

Translations

Even A Wise Man Stumbles. Tr. David Magarshack. In his *Easy Money and Two Other Plays.* London: Allen-Unwin, 1944.
[Even a Wise Man Stumbles; Easy Money; Wolves and Sheep.]

Five Plays. Tr. & ed. Eugene Bristol. NY: Pegasus, 1969.
[It's a Family Affair—We'll Settle It Ourselves; The Poor Bride; The Storm; The Scoundrel; The Forest.]

Plays. Ed., & intro. G. R. Noyes. NY: Scribners, 1917.
[A Protégé of the Mistress; Poverty Is No Crime; Sin and Sorrow Are Common to All; It's a Family Affair—We'll Settle It Ourselves.]

Plays. Tr. M. Wettlin. Moscow: Progress, 1974.
[Poverty Is No Crime; The Storm; Even the Wise Can Err; More Sinned Against than Sinning.]

Without a Dowry & Other Plays. Tr. Norman Henley. Ann Arbor: Ardis, forthcoming.
[Without a Dowry; A Profitable Position; Ardent Heart; Talents and Admirers.]

Bondwomen. A Comedy in Four Acts. Tr. S. Kurlandzik & G. Noyes. *Poet Lore* 36 (1925):475-541.

Career Woman. Artistes and Admirers. Tr. E. Hanson. NY: Barnes & Noble, 1976.

A Cat Has Not Always Carnival, Scenes from Moscow Life. Tr. J. Campbell & G. Noyes. *Poet Lore* 40 (1929):317-72.

The Diary of a Scoundrel. In *The Modern Theatre,* ed. Eric Bentley. Garden City: Doubleday, 1955, vol. 2, pp. 37-144.

Easy Money. Tr. David Magarshack. London: Allen-Unwin, 1944.

Fairy Gold. A Comedy in Five Acts. Tr. C. Winslow & G. Noyes. *Poet Lore* 40

(1929):1-80.

The Forest. Comedy in Five Acts. Tr. C. Winslow & G. Noyes. NY: French, 1926.

The King of Comedy. Tr. J. McPetrie. London: Stockwell, 1937.

A Last Sacrifice. A Comedy in Five Acts. Tr. E. Korvin-Krankovsky & G. Noyes. *Poet Lore* 39 (1928):317-410.

The Storm. Tr. C. Garnett. London: Duckworth, 1930.

The Storm. English version by G. Holland & M. Morley. London: Allen-Unwin, 1930.

The Storm. Tr. D. Magarshack. Ann Arbor: Ardis, 1988.

The Storm. Tr. F. Reeve. In *Nineteenth-Century Russian Plays,* ed. F. Reeve. NY: Norton, 1973.

The Thunderstorm. Drama in Five Acts. Tr. F. Whyte and G. Noyes. NY: French, 1927.

We Won't Brook Interference. Tr. G. Noyes & J. Seymour. San Francisco: Banner, 1938.

Wolves and Sheep. Tr. I. Colby & G. Noyes. *Poet Lore* 37 (1926):159-253.

You Can't Live Just as You Please. Tr. G. Noyes. *Poet Lore* 49 (1943):203-40.

Criticism

Hoover, Marjorie. *Alexander O.* Boston: Twayne, 1981.

Beasley, I. M. The Dramatic Art of O. Ph.D. diss., London, 1931.

Cox, Lucy. Form and Meaning in the Plays of Alexander O. Ph.D. diss., Pennsylvania, 1975.

Grylack, B. R. The Function of Proverbs in the Dramatic Works of A. N. O. Ph.D. diss., New York, 1975.

Kaspin, Albert. O and the *Raznochinets* in His Plays. Ph.D. diss., California, 1957.

Manheim, Martha. O and Vaudeville. Ph.D. diss., Columbia, 1978.

Wan, Ning. Female Characters in A. O's *The Storm* and Cao Yu's *The Thunderstorm.* Ph.D. diss., Pittsburgh, 1985.

Beasley, I. The Dramatic Art of O. *SEER* 6 (1927):603-17.

Dobrolyubov, N. A. *Selected Philosophical Essays.* Moscow: Foreign Languages Publishing House, 1956. [A Ray of Light in the Realm of Darkness; Realm of Darkness. The Works of A. O.]

Esam, I. An Analysis of O's *Ne ot mira sego* and the Play's Significance in Relation to the Author's Other Works. *NZSJ* 4 (1969):68-91.

——. Folkloric Elements as Communication Devices. *NZSJ* 2 (1968):67-88.

——. A Study of the Imagery Associated with Beliefs, Legends and Customs in *Bednost' ne porok. NZSJ* 11 (1973): 102-22.

——. The Style of *Svoi liudi sochtemsia. NZSJ* 10 (1972):79-105.

Henley, Norman. O's Play-Actors, Puppets, and Rebels. *SEEJ* 14 (1970):317-25.

Kaspin, Albert. Character and Conflict in O's *Talents and Admirers. SEEJ* 8 (1964):26-36.

——. Dostoevsky's Masloboyev and O's Dosuzhev: A Parallel. *SEER* 39 (1961): 222-27.

——. A Re-Examination of O's Character Lyubim Tortsov. In *Studies in Russian and Polish Literature in Honor of W. Lednicki,* ed. Z. Folejewski. The Hague: Mouton, 1962, pp. 185-91.

——. A Superfluous Man and an Underground Man in O's *The Poor Bride. SEEJ* 6 (1962):312-21.

Magarshack, D. He Created Russia's National Theatre. *Anglo-Soviet Journal* 9, 2 (1948):6-10.

Manning, Clarence. O and the "Kingdom of Darkness." *Sewanee Review* 38 (1930): 30-41.

Matual, David. O in the Background of Tolstoj's *Vlast' t'my. RLJ* 121-22 (1981): 125-31.

Patrick, George. A. N. O: Slavophile or Westerner. In *Slavic Studies,* ed. A. Kaun & E. Simmons. Ithaca: Cornell UP, 1943, pp. 117-31.

Rudnitsky, Konstantin. [Meyerhold's productions of O's plays.] In his

Meyerhold the Director. Ann Arbor: Ardis, 1981, pp. 34-35, 217-24, 323-26, 329-31, 342-43, 349-52.

Varneke, B. V. O. In his History of the Russian Theatre. NY: Macmillan, 1951, pp. 319-50.

Van Holk, André. The Key Scene in O's The Thunderstorm: On the Analysis of Modal Profiles. IJSLP 31-32 (1985): 481-93.

—— The Syntax of the Slovo-er: On the Thematic Composition of A. N. O's An Advantageous Job. Russian Linguistics 8, 3 (1984):215-50.

—— Thematic Analysis of O's Poverty is no Crime. Essays in Poetics 3, 2 (1978):41-76.

Zohrab, Irene. F. M. Dostoevsky and A. N. O. MelbSS 14 (1980):56-78.

——. Problems of Style in the Plays of O. MelbSS 12 (1977):35-46.

——. Problems of Translation. The Works of A. N. O in English. MelbSS 16 (1982):43-88.

IVAN
PANAEV

Criticism

Keynes, John L. Ivan Ivanovich P: A Literary Figure from the Background of Nineteenth-Century Russian Literature. Ph.D. diss., Pennsylvania, 1954.

AVDOTYA
PANAEVA

Criticism

Gregg, Richard. A Brackish Hippocrene: Nekrasov, P, and the "Prose in Love." SlavR 34 (1975):731-51.

Ledkovsky, Marina. Avdotya Panaeva: Her Salon and Her Life. RLT 9 (1974):423-32.

NIKOLAI
PAVLOV

Criticism

Shepard, Elizabeth Colvin. Nikolaj P: His Role in the Development of the Russian Short Story. Ph.D. diss., California, Berkeley, 1972.

Mersereau, John, Jr. Nikolai P. In his Russian Romantic Fiction. Ann Arbor: Ardis, 1983, pp. 240-46.

Shepard, Elizabeth Colvin. P's "Demon" and Gogol's "Overcoat." SlavR 33 (1974): 288-301.

KAROLINA
PAVLOVA

Translations

A Double Life. Tr. with an intro. by Barbara Heldt Monter. Ann Arbor: Ardis, 1978; 2d ed.: Tr. Barbara Heldt. Oakland: Barbary Coast Books, 1986.

Bowra, C. M., ed. A Second Book of Russian Verse. London: MacMillan, 1948.
[While in Dark and Deadly Places]

Obolensky, Dimitri, ed. The Heritage of Russian Verse. Bloomington: Indiana UP, 1976, pp. 147-49.
[The silent thought of what is past and old and perished; Rome.]

Sendich, Munir. Twelve Unpublished Letters to Alexey Tolstoy. RLT 9 (1974): 541-48.

Criticism

Ostrorog, Ludmilla Ignatievna. A Classification of Pavlova's and Benediktov's Rhymes. Ph.D. diss., Washington, Seattle, 1969.

Sendich, Munir. The Life and Works of Karolina Pavlova. Ph.D. diss., New York, 1968.

Briggs, A. D. Twofold Life: A Mirror of Karolina P's Shortcomings and

Achievement. *SEER* 49 (1971):1-17.

Green, Diana. Karolina P's "Tri dushi": The Transfiguration of Biography. *Proceedings of the Kentucky Foreign Language Conference: Slavic Section* 2, 1 (1984):15-24.

Monter, Barbara Heldt. From an Introduction to P's *A Double Life. RLT* 9 (1974):337-54.

Sendich, Munir. Boris Utin in P's Poems and Correspondence: P's Unpublished Letters (17) to Utin. *RLJ* 100 (1974): 63-88.

——. Karolina Jaenisch (P) and Adam Mickiewicz. *Polish Review* 14, 3 (1967):68-78.

——.Karolina P: A Survey of Her Poetry. *RLT* 3 (1972):229-48.

——. *Ot Moskvy do Drezdena:* P's Unpublished Memoirs. *RLJ* (1975):57-78.

——.Two Unknown Writings of Karolina P. *Die Welt der Slaven* 16 (1971):47-60.

ALEXANDER PISAREV

Translations

Bazarov. In *A Documentary History of Russian Thought,* tr. & ed. W. J. Leatherbarrow & D. C. Offord. Ann Arbor: Ardis, 1987, pp. 240-43.

The Struggle for Life. In *Crime and Punishment and the Critics,* ed. E. Wasiolek. Belmont, CA: Wadsworth Publishing House, 1961, pp. 134-41.

"Three Deaths": A Story by Count L. N. Tolstoi. Tr. Edmund Yarwood. *RLT* 11 (1975): 186-94.

Criticism

Lentulay, Rudy J. A Nihilist's Nihilist: A Study of D. I. P's Interpretation of *Fathers and Sons.* Ph.D. diss., Bryn Mawr, 1970.

Barghoorn, Frederick C. Nihilism, Utopia, and Realism in the Thought of P. *HSS* 4 (1957):225-37.

Brown, E. J. P and the Transformation of Two Russian Novels. In *Literature and*

Society in Imperial Russia, ed. W. M. Todd. Stanford: Stanford UP, 1978, pp. 151-72.

Brumfield, W. C. Bazarov and Rjazanov. The Romantic Archetype in Russian Nihilism. *SEEJ* 21 (1977):495-505.

Forsyth, J. P. Belinsky and Yevgenij Onegin. *SEER* 48 (1970):163-81.

Moser, Charles A. *Antinihilism in the Russian Novel of the 1860s.* The Hague: Mouton, 1964.

ALEXEI PISEMSKY

Translations

Nina, The Comic Actor and An Old Man's Sin. Tr. & intro. Maya Jenkins. Ann Arbor: Ardis, 1988.

One Thousand Souls. Tr. Ivy Litvinov. NY: Grove Press, 1959.

The Simpleton. Tr. Ivy Litvinov. Moscow: Foreign Languages Publishing House, 1959.

Baal. A Play. Tr. A. Donskov. *RLT* 9 (1974):160-219.

A Bitter Fate. Tr. Alice Kagan & G. Noyes. In *Masterpieces of the Russian Theater,* ed. G. Noyes. NY: Appleton, 1933, vol. 1, pp. 407-56.

Criticism

Moser, Charles A. *P: A Provincial Realist.* Cambridge: Harvard UP, 1969.

Jenkins, Maya. A Study of A. F. P and His Fate in Russian Literature. Ph.D. diss., London, 1977.

Pearson, Michael Manning Lane. A Comparative Study of the Art of A. F. P: *Tysjača duš* and the Novels of the Last Period. Ph.D. diss., California, Los Angeles, 1974.

Brown, Deming. P: The Aesthetics of Scepticism. In *American Contributions to the Fifth International Congress of Slavists.* The Hague:

Mouton, 1963, vol. 2, pp. 7-20.

Donskov, Andrew. P's Talent as a Playwright. *RLT* 9 (1974):486-95.

Jenkins, Maya. P's *Bitter Fate:* The First Outstanding Drama of Russian Peasant Life. *CSP* 3 (1958):76-88.

Moser, Charles A. P's Literary Protest: An Episode from the Polemics of the 1860's in Russia. *SEES* 8 (1963):60-72.

Steussy, R. E. The Bitter Fate of A. F. P. *RusR* 25 (1966):170-83.

Woodhouse,J. A.F.P: The Making of a Russian Novelist. *FMLS* 20 (1984):49-69.

___. A Realist in a Changing Reality: A. F. P and *Vzbalamuchennoie more. SEER* 64 (1986):489-505.

ANTONY POGORELSKY (PEROVSKY)

Translations

The Double, or My Evenings in Little Russia. Tr. & intro. Ruth Sobel. Ann Arbor: Ardis, 1988.

The Convent Girl. In *Ardis Anthology of Russian Romanticism,* ed. C. Rydel. Ann Arbor: Ardis, 1984, pp. 267-80.

Criticism

Frantz, Philip Edward. A. A. Perovskij (Pogorel'skij): Gentleman and Literateur. Ph.D. diss., Michigan, 1981.

Brown, William Edward. Antony Pogorelsky. In his *A History of Russian Literature of the Romantic Period.* Ann Arbor: Ardis, 1986, vol. 2, pp. 264-67.

Passage, Charles E. Pogorel'skij, the First Russian Hoffmannist. *ASEER* 15 (1956): 247-64.

NIKOLAI POMYALOVSKY

Translation

Seminary Sketches. Tr. & intro. by Alfred Kuhn. Ithaca: Cornell UP, 1973.

Criticism

Flath, Carol Apollonio. N. G. P's *Seminary Sketches:* Context and Genre. Ph.D. diss., North Carolina, 1987.

KOZMA PRUTKOV

Translations

Monter, Barbara Heldt. Twenty Translations from Koz'ma P. Appendix to her *Koz'ma P.* The Hague: Mouton, 1972, pp. 120-38.

Senelick, L., tr. Project: Towards Creating Uniformity of Opinion in Russia. The Fruits of Meditation: Thoughts and Aphorisms. *RLT* 14 (1976):297-301.

Criticism

Monter, Barbara Heldt. *Koz'ma P: The Art of Parody.* The Hague: Mouton, 1972.

Ingram, Frank LeQuellec. Koz'ma P: His Emergence and Development as a Classic of Russian Literature. Ph.D. diss., Indiana, 1967.

Monter, Barbara Heldt. Koz'ma P and the Theory of Parody. Ph.D. diss., Chicago, 1968.

Ingram, Frank. Koz'ma P Is More "Alive" Than Ever. *RLJ* 25 (1971):3-9.

___. Koz'ma P: The Dean of Russian Burlesque Satire. *RLJ* 119 (1980):67-88.

ALEXANDER PUSHKIN

Bibliographies

Fomichev, S. A. Soviet P Scholarship of the Past Decade. *CASS* 11 (1977):141-54.

Pachuta, J. E. A Bibliography of P Bibliographies. *CASS* 11 (1977):134-40.

Sendich, Munir. P's *Malen'kie tragedii:* A

Bibliography. *RLJ* 120 (1981):175-87.

Shaw, J. Thomas. Non-Periodical Serials on P. Review article. *CASS* 11 (1977):134-40.

Wreath, P. J. & A. I. P: A Bibliography of Criticism in English, 1920-1975. *CASS* 10 (1976):279-304.

Yarmolinsky, A. P in English: A List of Works by and about Him, 1799— 1837—1937. *Bulletin of the New York Public Library* July 1937: 530-59.

Translations

The Bakhchesarian Fountain by Alexander Pooshkeen. And Other Poems, By Various Authors. Tr. William D. Lewis. Philadelphia: C. Sherman, 1849; rpt. Ann Arbor: Ardis, 1987.

Boris Godunov. Russian Text with Translation. Ed. Philip L. Barbour. NY: Columbia Slavic Studies, 1953; Oxford: Oxford UP, 1953.

The Bronze Horseman: Selected Poems of Alexander P. Tr. D. M. Thomas. NY: Viking, 1982.

The Captain's Daughter and Other Stories. Tr. Natalie Duddington. NY: Dutton, 1935.

The Captain's Daughter and The Negro of Peter the Great. London: N. Spearman, 1958.

Collected Narrative and Lyrical Poetry. Tr. Walter Arndt. Ann Arbor: Ardis, 1983.
[100 lyric poems; Ruslan and Liudmila; The Gabriliad; Tsar Nikita and His Forty Daughters; The Fountain of Bakhchisaray; The Gypsies; The Bridegroom; Count Nulin; Poltava; Tsar Saltan; The Little House in Kolomna; The Golden Cockerel; The Bronze Horseman; Eugene Onegin (excerpts).]

Complete Prose Fiction. Tr. Paul Debreczeny. Stanford: Stanford UP, 1983.

Complete Prose Tales of Alexander Sergeyevitch P. Tr. Gillon R. Aitken. NY: Norton, 1967.

Count Nulin. Tr. Anthony Briggs. *SlavR* 26 (1967):286-94.

The Critical Prose of Alexander P, with Critical Essays by Four Russian Romantic Poets. Ed. & tr. Carl R.

Proffer. Bloomington: Indiana UP, 1970.

Dubrovsky. Tr. Ivy Litvinova. Moscow: Foreign Languages Publishing House, 1954.

Epigrams and Satirical Verse. Ed. & tr. Cynthia Whittaker. Ann Arbor: Ardis, 1984.

Eugene Onegin. Tr., intro. & notes by Walter Arndt. 2d, revised ed, NY: Dutton, 1981.

Eugene Onegin. Tr. Babette Deutsch. Baltimore: Penguin, 1965.

Eugene Onegin. Tr. Charles Johnston. NY: Viking, 1978.

Eugene Onegin. Tr. M. Kayden. Yellow Springs, OH: Antioch, 1964.

Eugene Onegin. Tr. with a commentary by Vladimir Nabokov. 4 vols. Revised ed., Princeton: Princeton UP, 1975.

Gabriel [The Gavriiliad]. Tr. Max Eastman. Illustrated by Rockwell Kent. NY: Covici-Friede, 1929.

The History of Pugachev. Tr. Earl Sampson. Ann Arbor: Ardis, 1983.

A Journey to Arzrum. Tr. Birgitta Ingemanson. Ann Arbor: Ardis, 1974.

The Letters of Alexander P. Tr. J. Thomas Shaw. 3 vols. Bloomington: Indiana UP, 1963. Reprinted in one volume: Madison: U Wisconsin P, 1967.

Little Tragedies. Tr. Eugene M. Kayden. Yellow Springs, OH: Antioch, 1965.

Mozart and Salieri: The Little Tragedies. Tr. Antony Wood. London: Angel Books, 1983.

Poems. Tr. Henry Jones. NY: Citadel, 1965.

The Poet and the Publisher: A Dialogue. Tr. W. G. Carey. *CSP* 12 (1965):189-94.

Pushkin on Literature. Ed. & tr. Tatiana Wolff. NY: Barnes and Noble, 1971; revised edition with an introduction by John Bayley—Stanford: Stanford UP, 1986.

Pushkin Threefold: Narrative, Lyric, Polemic and Ribald Verse. Tr. Walter Arndt. NY: Dutton, 1972.

The Queen of Spades and Other Tales. Tr. Tatiana Litvinov. NY: New American Library, 1961.

Ruslan and Liudmila. Tr. Walter Arndt. Ann Arbor: Ardis, 1974.

Secret Journal, 1836-1837. Tr. M. Armalinsky. Minneapolis: MIP, 1986.

Selected Verse with Introduction and Prose Translations. Tr. John Fennell. Baltimore: Penguin, 1967.

Six Poems from Pushkin. Tr. Jacob Krup. NY: The Galleon Press, 1936. [Includes Ruslan and Ludmila; Poltava; The Prisoner of the Caucasus.]

Tales of Belkin with The History of the Village of Goryukhino. Tr. G. Aitken & D. E. Budgen. London: Angel Books, 1983.

Three Comic Poems. Tr. William Harkins. Ann Arbor: Ardis, 1977. [Gavriiliada; Count Nulin; The Little House in Kolomna.]

Three Russian Poets (P, Lermontov, Tyutchev). Tr. Vladimir Nabokov. Forest Hills, NY: Transatlantic Press, 1949. [Exegi Monumentum; The Upas Tree; The Covetous Knight; The Feast During the Plague; Mozart and Salieri.]

The Works of Alexander P. Lyrics, Narrative Poems, Folk Tales, Prose. Ed. Avrahm Yarmolinsky. NY: Random House, 1936. [50 lyrics; Poltava; The Bronze Horseman; Eugene Onegin; The Tale of the Pope and His Workman Balda; The Tale of the Golden Cockerel; Boris Godunov; Mozart and Salieri; The Stone Guest; The Tales of Belkin; The Queen of Spades; Kirdjali; The Captain's Daughter; The Negro of Peter the Great; Dubrovsky; Egyptian Nights.]

Criticism

Andronikov, Irakly. *The Last Days of P. From Unpublished Contemporary Letters*. Moscow: Foreign Languages Publishing House, 1957.

Bayley, John. *P: A Comparative Commentary*. NY: Cambridge UP, 1971.

Briggs, A. D. P. *Alexander P: A Critical Study*. London: Croom Helm; Totowa, NJ: Barnes & Noble, 1983.

Clayton, J. Douglas. *Iced Flame: Aleksandr P's "Eugene Onegin."* Toronto: U Toronto P, 1985.

Cross, S.H. & E. J. Simmons, eds. *Centennial Essays for P*. Cambridge: Harvard UP, 1937; rpt. NY: Russell & Russell, 1967.

Debreczeny, Paul. *The Other P. A Study of Alexander P's Prose Fiction*. Stanford: Stanford UP, 1983.

Hoisington, Sona Stephan, tr. & intro. *Russian Views of P's "Eugene Onegin."* Bloomington: Indiana UP, 1988.

Jakobson, Roman. *P and His Sculptural Myth*. Tr & ed. John Burbank. The Hague: Mouton, 1975.

Kodjak, Andrej. *P's I. P. Belkin*. Columbus: Slavica, 1979.

——— and K. Taranovsky, eds. *Alexander P: A Symposium*. NY: New York UP, 1976.

———, K. Pomorska, K. Taranovsky, eds. *Alexander P: Symposium II*. Columbus: Slavica, 1980.

Lavrin, Janko. *P and Russian Literature*. London: Hodder & Stoughton, 1947.

Lednicki, Waclaw. *Bits of Table Talk on P, Mickiewicz, Goethe, Turgenev and Sienkiewicz*. The Hague: Martinus Nijhoff, 1956.

——— *P's "Bronze Horseman": The Story of a Masterpiece*. Berkeley & Los Angeles: U California P, 1955.

Lezhnev, Abram. *Pushkin's Prose*. Tr. Roberta Reeder. Intro. Paul Debreczeny. Ann Arbor: Ardis, 1983.

Magarshack, David. *P*. NY: Grove Press, 1969.

Meijer, Jan M. *The Tales of Belkin by A. S. P*. The Hague: Mouton, 1968.

Mirsky, D. S. *P*. NY: Dutton, 1963.

Nabokov, Vladimir. *Notes on Prosody, from the Commentary to his Translation of P's Eugene Onegin*. London: Routledge and Kegan Paul, 1965.

O'Bell, Leslie. *P's "Egyptian Nights." The Biography of a Work*. Ann Arbor: Ardis, 1984.

Pauls, John P. *P's "Poltava."* NY: Shevchenko Scientific Society, 1963.

Richards, D. J. & C. R. S. Cockrell, eds. & tr. *Russian Views of P*. Oxford: W. A. Meeuws, 1976.

Russian Language Journal. No. 120 (1981). Special P issue.

Simmons, Ernest J. *P*. Gloucester, MA: P. Smith, 1965.

Todd, William Mills III. *Fiction and*

Society in the Age of P. Cambridge: Harvard UP, 1986.

Troyat, Henri. *P.* Tr. Nancy Amphoux. Garden City: Doubleday, 1970.

Vickery, Walter N. *Alexander P.* NY: Twayne, 1970.

——. *P: Death of a Poet.* Bloomington: Indiana UP, 1968.

Brown, James Edwin. The Verse Epistles of A. S. P. Ph.D. diss., Wisconsin, 1983.

Browning, Olga. A. S. P, *The Songs of the Western Slavs:* A Study in Creative Folklorization. Ph.D. diss., Northwestern, 1973.

Brun-Zejmin, Julia. Chaadaev and P. Ph.D. diss., Texas, 1973.

Burnett, L. P. Dimensions of Truth: A Comparative Study of the Relationship between "Language" and "Reality" in the Works of Wordsworth, Coleridge, Zhukovsky, P and Keats. Ph.D. diss., Essex, 1976.

Burns, Virginia Marie. P's "Poltava": A Literary Interpretation. Ph.D. diss., Toronto, 1977.

Clayton, John Douglas. Parody and Burlesque in the Work of A. S. P: A Critical Study. Ph.D. diss., Illinois, 1971.

Connell, James Goodman, Jr. Freedom and the Don Juan Tradition in Selected Narrative Poetic Works and *The Stone Guest* of Alexander P. Ph.D. diss., Ohio State, 1973.

Cooke, Leighton Brett. Poet: Aleksandr P and the Creative Process. Ph.D. diss., California, Berkeley, 1983.

Cosman, Tatiana M. The Letter as a Literary Device in the Fiction of P, Lermontov and Gogol. Ph.D. diss., New York, 1973.

Emerson, Caryl Geppert. Boris Godunov and a Poetics of Transposition: Karamzin, P, Mussorgsky. Ph.D. diss., Texas, 1980.

Fehsenfeld, Nancy Kanach. P's Prose in Nikolaevan Russia: 1826-1827. Ph.D. diss., Cornell, 1980.

Frenkel, Monika Dudli. *V malen'koj ramke:* Fragmentary Structures in P's Poetry and Prose. Ph.D. diss., Yale, 1984.

Garnett, Sherman Wesley, Jr. P's Political Views as a Problem of Poetics. Ph.D. diss., Michigan, 1982.

Grad, Stephen. P's *Gavriiliada.* Ph.D. diss., California, Berkeley, 1972.

Gutsche, George J. The Elegies of Aleksandr P. Ph.D. diss., Wisconsin, 1972.

Hoisington, Sona S. Early Critical Responses to *Evgenij Onegin:* 1825-1845. Ph.D. diss., Yale, 1971.

Ingemanson, Birgitta Maria. On P and Travel Literature: *Puteshestvie v Arzrum.* Ph.D. diss., Princeton, 1974.

Johnson, D. J. L. The Sources of P's *Songs of the Western Slavs.* Ph.D. diss., Birmingham, 1954.

Kandel, Michael Anthony. Tuwim as P's Translator: Analytic Approaches to "P's Lyre." Ph.D. diss., Indiana, 1971.

Konick, Willis A. A Study of P's "Little Tragedies." Ph.D. diss., Washington, Seattle, 1964.

Levitt, Marcus C. The P Celebration of 1880 and the Politics of Literature in Russia. Ph.D. diss., Columbia, 1984.

Mikkelson, Gerald E. P and the History of the Russian Nobility. Ph.D. diss., Wisconsin, 1971.

O'Bell, Leslie Claff. The Problematics of P's *Egipetskie noči* in the Creative History of His Work. Ph.D. diss., Harvard, 1978.

Prednewa, Ludmila. P's *Captain's Daughter:* Historical Outlook. Ph.D. diss., Pennsylvania, 1982.

Reeder, Roberta F. Antiquity in the Lyric Poetry of P. Ph.D. diss., Wisconsin, 1970.

Sandler, Stephanie. The Problem of History in P: Poet, Pretender, Tsar. Ph.D. diss., Yale, 1981.

Senderovich, Savely. P's Elegy "Vospominanie." Ph.D. diss., New York, 1978.

Umrichin, Svetlana. The Style of P's Letters. Ph.D. diss., New York, 1974.

Vincent, Julie. P in France. Ph.D. diss., Pittsburgh, 1964.

Wynne, Lorraine. The Multiple Unity of P's Little Tragedies. Ph.D. diss., New York, 1984.

Criticism—Articles on Works other than "Eugene Onegin"

Akhmatova, Anna. Benjamin Constant's *Adolphe* in the Work of P. *RLT* 10 (1974):157-79.

Alexander, V. E. Correlations in P's *Malen'kie tragedii. CSP* 20 (1978):176-93.

Anderson, Roger B. A Study of Pëtr Grinëv as the Hero of P's *Kapitanskaya Dochka. CSS* 5 (1971):477-86.

Andrew, Joe. Alexander P. In his *Writers and Society during the Rise of Russian Realism.* Atlantic Highlands, NJ: Humanities Press, 1980, pp. 1-41.

Anikine, A. The Contribution of P to the History of Economic Thought. *Diogenes* 107 (1979):65-85.

Arndt, Walter. "Ruslan i Ljudmila": Notes from Ellis Island. In *Alexander P: A Symposium on the 175th Anniversary of His Birth,* ed. A. Kodjak & K. Taranovsky. NY: New York UP, 1976, pp. 155-66.

Bachtin, Nicholas. P. *OSP* 11 (1964):38-45.

Baker, J. Bodenstedt and P. *Anglo-Russian Literary Society Proceedings* 32 (1901):5-28.

Banerjee, M. P's *The Bronze Horseman:* An Agnostic Vision. *MLS* 8 (1978):47-64.

Barker, Adele. P's *Queen of Spades*: A Displaced Mother Figure. *American Imago* 41, 2 (1984):201-9.

Barksdale, E. C. P and the Non-Encoded Engram. In his *Daggers of the Mind,* pp. 76-83.

Barratt, Glynn R. V. Eighteenth-Century Neo-Classical Influences on E. A. Baratynsky and P. *CLS* 6 (1969): 435-61.

——. P's America: A Survey of the Sources. *CSP* 15, 3 (1973):274-97.

Bayley, John. P's Secret of Distance. *OSP* 1 (1968):74-84.

Beaumont, C. W. P and His Influence on Russian Ballet. *Ballet* 4 (Dec. 1947):56-60.

Beckworth, M. W. P's Relation to Folklore. In *P: The Man and the Artist.* NY: Paisley Press, 1937, pp. 187-204.

Bely, Andrei. An Unpublished Essay on P. Tr. A. Humesky. *RLT* 11 (1975):488-89.

Bethea, David M. & Sergei Davydov. *The History of the Village of Gorjuxino:* In Praise of P's Folly. *SEEJ* 28, 3 (1984):291-309.

——. P's Saturnine Cupid: The Role of the Narrator in *The Tales of Belkin. CASS* 11 (1977):75-90.

Blok, Alexander. On the Mission of the Poet. In *Modern Russian Poets on Poetry,* ed. Carl R. Proffer. Ann Arbor: Ardis, 1976, pp. 71-80.

Blustain, Jonah. *Boris Godunov:* For the Descendents of the Orthodox. *RusR* 27 (1968):177-94.

Bocharov, S. G. "The Queen of Spades." *New Literary History* 9 (1978):314-32.

Boehm, A. The Universal Significance of P. *Vassar Review* February 1937:31-35.

Borker, D. Annenskii and P's "Osen'." *SEEJ* 22 (1978):34-38.

Bowra, C. M. P. *OSP* 1 (1950):1-15.

Briggs, A. D. P. Alexander P: A Possible Influence on Henry James. *FMLS 8 (1972):522-60.*

——. The Hidden Forces of Unification in *Boris Godunov. NZSJ* 1 (1974):43-54.

——. Hidden Qualities of P's *Mednyi vsadnik. CASS* 10 (1976):228-41.

——. "Pikovaya dama" and "Taman": Questions of Kinship. *JRS* 37 (1979):13-20.

Bristol, Evelyn. The P "Party" in Russian Poetry. *RusR* 40 (1981):20-34.

Brody, Ervin C. "The People Remain Speechless": *Vox populi* in P's *Boris Godunov. Acta Litteraria Academiae Scientiarum Hungaricae* 27, 3-4 (1985): 245-79.

——. P's *Boris Godunov:* The First Modern Russian Historical Drama. *MLR* 72 (1977):857-75.

Brown, Clarence. Nabokov's P and Nabokov's Nabokov. *Wisconsin Studies in Comparative Literature* 8 (1967):280-93.

Brown, E. J. Nabokov and P (with Comments on New Translations of

Eugene Onegin). SlavR 24 (1965):688-701.

_____. Round Two: Nabokov versus P. *SlavR* 36 (1977):101-5.

Brown, William Edward. Alexander P. In his *A History of Russian Literature of the Romantic Period.* Ann Arbor: Ardis, 1986. [Byronic Poems and Minor Verse: pp.11-64; Major Narrative Poems: 65-104; Dramatic Works: 105-40; Lyric Verse: 141-88; Prose: 189-241.]

Brum-Zejmis, Julia. *Malen'kie Tragedii* and *Povesti Belkina:* Western Idolatry and Puškinian Parodies. *RLJ* 32, 111 (1978).

Burgi, R. P and the "Deipnosophists." *HSS* (1954):265-70.

Burgin, Diana L. The Mystery of "Pikovaya dama": A New Interpretation. In *Mnemozina,* ed. J. Baer & N. Ingham. Munich: Fink Verlag, 1974, pp. 46-56.

Burnett, L. *Obval:* P's "Kubla Khan." *Essays in Poetics* 6, 1 (1981):22-38.

Burns, V. M. The Narrative Structure of P's *Poltava:* Toward a Literary Interpretation. *CSP* 22 (1980):15-27.

Burton, Dora. The Theme of Peter as Verbal Echo in *Mednyj vsadnik. SEEJ* 26 (1982):12-26.

Burton, R. T. Two Russian Poets (P and Lermontov). *National Review* 108 (1937): 341-43.

Burtsev, V. On New Translations of P: How Should P Be Translated? *SEER* 15 (1936):305-09.

Call, Paul. P's *Bronze Horseman:* A Poem of Motion. *SEEJ* 11 (1967):137-44.

Campbell, S. The "Mavras" of P, Kochno and Stravinsky. *Music and Letters* 58 (1977):304-17.

Carus, P. Poet P. *Open Court.* 30 (1916):362-66.

Clark, A. F. B. Alexander S. P, 1799-1837. *University of Toronto Quarterly* 6 (1937): 174-88.

Claverton, F. B. The Cultural Barometer. *Current History* 46 (1937):87-92.

Clayton, J. Douglas. P, Faust and the Demons. *Germano-Slavica* 3 (1980): 165-88.

_____. "Spadar Dame," "Pique-dame" and "Pikovaia dama." *Germano-Slavica* 4

(1974):5-10.

_____The Theory and Practice of Poetic Translation in P and Nabokov. *CSP* 25 (1983):90-100.

Coleman, A. P. P and Mickiewicz. In *Centennial Essays for P,* ed. S. H. Cross & E. J. Simmons. Cambridge: Harvard UP, 1937.

Colton, R. E. A Note on Juvenal and P. *Classical World* 75, 2 (1981):118-20.

Connolly, Julian W. The Structure and Imagery of P's "Imitations of the Koran." In *New Studies in Russian Language and Literature,* ed. A. Crone & C. Chvany. Columbus: Slavica, 1986, pp. 59-72.

Conrad, Peter. The Characters of Artifice: Pushkinian Criticism. *Encounter* 41 (1973):74-77.

Cooper, B. P and the Anacreonta. *SEER* 52 (1974):182-87.

Cooper, M. P and the Opera in Russia. *Opera* 22 (1971):96-100.

Costello, D. P. P and Roman Literature. *OSP* 11 (1964):46-55.

Cournos, J. Golden Age and Twilight. *Virginia Quarterly Review* 13 (1937):440-42.

_____ P: 1837-1937. *Poetry* 49 (1937):328-31.

Cross, Anthony. P's Bawdy; or, Notes from the Literary Underground. *RLT* 10 (1974):203-36.

Davis, M. W. Democratic Chords in the Poetry of Alexander S. P. Black Russian Writer. *College Language Association Journal* 21 (1977):212-17.

Davydov, Sergei. P's Merry Undertaking and "The Coffinmaker." *SlavR* 44, 1 (1985):30-48.

_____ The Sound and Theme in the Prose of A. S. P: A Logo-Semantic Study of Paronomasia. *SEEJ* 27 (1983):1-18.

Debreczeny, Paul. The Beginnings of Mass Literature in Russia: Early Imitations of P's Narrative Poems. *CSS* (1971):1-21.

_____ "The Blackamoor of Peter the Great": P's Experiment with a Detached Mode of Narration. *SEEJ* 18 (1974):119-31.

_____ The Execution of Captain Mironov: A Crossing of the Tragic and Comic Modes. In *Alexander P: Symposium*

II, ed. A. Kodjak et al. Columbus: Slavica, 1980, pp. 67-78.

——. Poetry and Prose in "The Queen of Spades." *CASS* 11 (1977):91-113.

——. P's Use of His Narrator in "The Stationmaster." *RusL* 4 (1976):149-66.

——. The Reception of P's Poetic Works in the 1920's: A Study of the Critic's Role. *SlavR* 28 (1969):394-415.

——. The Three Styles of *Dubrovskii. CASS* 10 (1976):264-78.

Donchin, G. P. In *Russian Literary Attitudes,* ed. Richard Freeborn. NY: Harper, 1976, pp. 19-38.

Dostoevsky, Fyodor. Speech on P, June 8, 1880. In *P: The Man and the Artist.* NY: Paisley Press, 1937, pp 58-79. [Also printed in Dostoevsky's *The Diary of a Writer,* ed. B. Brasol.]

Downes, Olin. P and Russian Music. In *P: The Man and the Artist.* NY: Paisley Press, 1937, pp. 80-88.

Driver, Sam. On a Source for P's "The Lady Peasant." *SEEJ* 26 (1982):1-11.

——. P and Politics: The Later Works. *SEEJ* 25,3 (1981):1-23.

Dvoichenko-Markoff, E. P and the Rumanian Historical Legend. *ASEER* 7 (1948):144-49.

Edgerton, William B. P, Mickiewicz, and a Migratory Epigram. *SEEJ* 10 (1966):1-8.

Emerson, Caryl. Grinev's Dream: *The Captain's Daughter* and a Father's Blessing. *SlavR* 40 (1981):60-76.

Erlich, Victor. P's Moral Realism as a Structural Problem. In *Alexander P: A Symposium on the 175th Anniversary of His Birth,* ed. A. Kodjak & K. Taranovsky. NY: New York UP, 1976, pp. 167-77.

Etkind, Efim. Freedom and Law: Note on the Theme "P and Our Contemporaneity." *RLJ* 120 (1981):1-24.

Falchikov, M. The Outsider and the Number Game: Some Observations on "Pikovaya dama." *Essays in Poetics* 2, 2 (1977):96-106.

Faletti, Heidi. Remarks on Style as Manifestation of Narrative Technique in "Pikovaia dama." *CASS* 11 (1977):114-33.

Farsolas, Demetrios J. Alexander P: His Attitude Toward the Greek Revolution. *Balkan Studies* 12 (1971):57-80.

——. The Greek Revolution in the Principalities as Seen by Alexander P. *Neo-Hellenika* 2 (1975):98-119.

Fennell, John. P. In his *Nineteenth-Century Russian Literature: Studies of Ten Russian Writers.* Berkeley & Los Angeles: U California P, 1973, pp. 13-68.

Fiene, D. M. P's "Poor Knight": The Key to Perceiving D's *Idiot* as Allegory. *BulDS* 8 (1978):10-21.

Fiske, John C. The Soviet Controversy Over P and Washington Irving. *CL* 7 (1955):1-14.

Frank, John G. P and Goethe. *SEER* 26 (1948):146-56.

Fredericks, A. P for Americans. *RusR* 5, 2 (1946):83-89.

Gasparov, Boris. Encounter of Two Poets in the Desert: P's Myth. In *Myth in Literature,* ed. A Kodjak, et al. Columbus: Slavica, 1985, pp. 124-53.

Genereux, G. Botkin's Collaboration with Belinsky on the P Articles. *SEEJ* 21 (1977):470-82.

Gibian, George. Love by the Book: P, Stendhal, Flaubert. *CL* 8 (1956):97-109.

——. *Measure for Measure* and P's *Angelo. PMLA* 66 (1951):426-31.

——. Narrative Technique and Realism: Evgeny Onegin and Madame Bovary. *Langue et littérature,* 1962, 339.

Giergielewicz, M. Two Slavic Poets at the Czar's Court. In *Studies in Russian and Polish Literature in Honor of Waclaw Lednicki,* ed. Z. Folejewski, et al. s'Gravenhage: Mouton, 1962, pp. 127-41. [P and Krasiński.]

Gifford, Henry. P's "Feast in Time of Plague" and Its Original. *ASEER* 8 (1949):37-46.

——. Shakespearean Elements in *Boris Godunov. SEER* 26 (1948):152-61.

Glasberg, V. Marginalia Pushkiniana: Selected Documents. *SEER* 14 (1935):432-37.

Glasse, Antonia. "P" or "R" [Ryleev]; Who Wrote the *Mnemosyne* Review. *RLT* 10 (1974):274-78.

Gogol, Nikolai. A Few Words about P. In

Arabesques, tr. A. Tulloch. Ann Arbor: Ardis, 1982, pp. 109-14.

——. A Few Words about P. Tr. Mark Dillen. *RLT* 10 (1974):180-84.

——. On the Essence of Russian Poetry. In *Selected Passages from Correspondence with Friends.* Tr. J. Zeldin. Nashville: Vanderbilt UP, 1969, pp. 213-19.

Goller, Nina, comp. The P Memorial Museums (P's Last Days). In *Muzei-kvartira A. S. Pushkina.* Leningrad: Aurora, 1976, pp. 89-117.

Goscilo, Helena. Feet P Scanned, or Seeming Idée Fixe as Implied Aesthetic Credo. *SEEJ* 32, 4 (1988):562-73.

Green, Michael. *Boris Godunov: A Classical Tragedy in Disguise?* A Glance at P's Boris in Comparison with Kheraskov's. *Study Group on Eighteenth-Century Russia: Newsletter* 6 (1978):36-40.

Greene, Militsa. P and Sir Walter Scott. *FMLS* 1 (1965):207-15.

Gregg, Richard A. Balzac and the Women in *The Queen of Spades. SEEJ* 10 (1966):279-82.

——. The Eudaemonic Theme in P's "Little Tragedies." In *Alexander P: A Symposium on the 175th Anniversary of His Birth,* ed. A. Kodjak & K. Taranovsky. NY: New York UP, 1976, pp. 178-95.

——. The Nature of Nature and the Nature of Eugene in *The Bronze Horseman. SEEJ* 21 (1977):167-79.

——. P and Shenstone: The Case Reopened. *CL* 17 (1965):109-16.

——. A Scapegoat for All Seasons: The Unity and Shape of *The Tales of Belkin. SlavR* 30 (1971):748-61.

Gregory, Anne. Loose Ends: Position and Possession in "The Shot." *Cherez,* 1977.

Gronicka, A. von. Alexander P's View of Goethe. *CL* 12 (1960):243-55.

Grossman, Leonid. The Art of the Anecdote in P. Tr. Sam Cioran. *RLT* 10 (1974):129-48.

Gustafson, Richard F. The Upas Tree: P and Erasmus Darwin. *PMLA* 75 (1960): 101-9.

Gutsche, George J. P's "Andrei Shen'e" and Poetic Genres in the 1820's. *CASS*

10 (1976):189-204.

——. P's Boldino "Elegija." *RLJ* 120 (1981):115-26.

——. P's Revisions of His Lyceum Poems for His First Collection of Poems. *SEEJ* 20 (1976):103-20.

Harkins, William. The Place of "Domik v Kolomne" in P's Creation. In *Alexander P: A Symposium on the 175th Anniversary of His Birth,* ed. A. Kodjak & K. Taranovsky. NY: New York UP, 1976, pp. 196-205.

Hayes, A. P's *Boris Godunov. Proceedings of the Anglo-Russian Literary Society* 82 (1918):29-42.

Hayward, Max. P, Gogol, and the Devil. In his *Writers in Russia: 1917-1978.* NY: Harcourt, 1983, pp. 284-95.

Hereford, C. H. A Russian Shakespearean: A Centenary Study. *Bulletin of the John Rylands Library* 9 (1925):453-80.

Hoisington, S. S. P's Belkin and the Mystifications of Sir Walter Scott. *CL* 33 (1981):342-57.

Holloway, J. The Elegiac Note in Tennyson, Arnold, P, and Leopardi. In *The Modern World: II. Realities,* ed. D. Daiches & A. Thorlby. London: Albus Books, 1972, pp. 181-202.

Hope, A. D. P's Don Juan. *MelbSS* 1 (1967):5-10.

Huntley, David G. On the Source of P's *Nerukotvornyj. Die Welt der Slaven* 15 (1970):361-62.

Ingemanson, Birgitta. Between Poetry and Fictional Prose: Aleksandr P's *Journey to Arzrum. Selecta* 4 (1983):101-7.

——. The Movable Mountain: P's Ararat Scene and Other Fiction in *A Journey to Arzrum. Research Studies* 52 (1983):127-37.

Ingram, Frank L. P's "Skazka o zolotom petuške" and Washington Irving's "The Legend of the Arabian Astrologer." *RLJ* 84 (1969):3-18.

Jackson, Robert L. Miltonic Imagery and Design in P's *Mozart and Salieri:* The Russian Satan. In *American Contributions to the Seventh International Congress of Slavists,* vol. 2, ed. V. Terras. The Hague: Mouton, 1973, pp. 261-70.

Jacob, M. The Semantic Role of Metre in

P's *Zimnyi vecher:* A Suitable Case for Analysis? *Essays in Poetics* 10, 1 (1985):81-98.

Jocelyn, Michael. P and Barclay de Tolly. *RLT* 10 (1974):237-44.

Johnson, C. A. P: A Personal View. *Contemporary Review* 207 (1965):254-60.

Johnson, D. J. L. P and Serbian Tradition. *SEER* 34 (1956):388-407.

Johnson, Rod. Measures of Vocabulary Diversity. In *Advances in Computer-Aided Literary and Linguistic Research,* ed. D. E. Ager, et al. Birmingham: Department of Modern Languages, University of Aston, 1979, pp. 213-27.

Jones, L. G. Pervasive Structures in P's Rhymes. In *Alexander P: Symposium II,* ed. A. Kodjak, K. Pomorska, K. Taranovsky. Columbus: Slavica, 1980, pp. 27-38.

Jones, R. G. Linguistic and Metrical Constraints in Verse—Iambic and Trochaic Tetrameters of P. In *Linguistic and Literary Studies in Honor of Archibald A. Hill,* ed. M. A. Jazayery, E. C. Polomé, W. Winter. The Hague: Mouton, 1979, vol. 4, pp. 87-101.

Karlinsky, Simon. Two P Studies. 1. P, Chateaubriand and the Romantic Pose; 2. The Amber Beads of Crimea (P and Mickiewicz). *CalSS* 2 (1963):96-120.

Karpiak, R. P's *Little Tragedies:* The Controversies in Criticism. *CSP* 22 (1980):80-91.

———. The Sequel to P's *Kamennyi gost':* Russian Don Juan Versions by Nikolai Gumilev and Vladimir Korvin-Piotrovskii. In *Studies in Honour of Louis Shein,* ed. S. D. Cioran. Hamilton, Ont.: McMaster UP, 1983, pp. 79-92.

Karpovich, M. P as a Poet. *Transactions of the Connecticut Academy of Arts & Sciences* 33 (1937):37-46.

Katz, Michael R. Dreams in P. *CalSS* 11 (1980):71-104.

———. P's Creative Assimilation of Zhukovsky and Irving. In *The Old and New World Romanticism of Washington Irving,* ed. S. Brodwin. Westport, CT: Greenwood, 1986, pp. 81-89.

———. P's Literary Ballads. In his *Literary Ballad in Early Nineteenth-Century Russian Literature.* Oxford: Oxford UP, 1976, pp. 139-65.

Kaun, A. P's Sense of Measure. In *Centennial Essays for P,* ed. S. H. Cross & E. J. Simmons. Cambridge: Harvard UP, 1937.

Keefer, L. P and Goethe. *MLN* 56 (1941):24-34.

Ketchian, S. Vehicles for Duality in P's "The Bronze Horseman": Similes and Period Lexicon. *Semiotica* 25 (1979):111-21.

Khodasevich, Vladislav. The Shaken Tripod. Tr. Alexander Golubov. *RLT* 10 (1974):149-56.

Kireevsky, I. On the Nature of P's Poetry. In *Literature and National Identity: Nineteenth-Century Russian Critical Essays,* tr. & ed. P. Debreczeny & J. Zeldin. Lincoln: Nebraska UP, 1970, pp. 3-16.

Kirtley, B. F. National Character and Folklore in P's *Skazki. West Virginia University Philological Papers* 11 (1958): 22-32.

Kjetsaa, G. A Quantitative Norm for the Use of Epithets in the Age of P. In *Russian Romanticism,* ed. N. A. Nilsson. Stockholm: Alqvist, 1979, pp. 204-22.

Kodjak, A. P's Utopian Myth. In *Alexander P: Symposium II,* ed. A. Kodjak, et al. Columbus: Slavica, 1980, pp. 117-30.

———. "The Queen of Spades" in the Context of the Faust Legend. In *Alexander P: A Symposium on the 175th Anniversary of His Birth,* ed. A. Kodjak & K. Taranovsky, NY: New York UP, 1976, pp. 87-118.

———. The Semiosis of the Sequence of Signs in a Narrative. In *Semiotics 1980,* ed. Michael Herzfell & Margot D. Lenhart. NY: Plenum, 1982, pp. 267-74.

———. and L. Wynne. P's "Kirdžali": An Informational Model. *RusL* 7 (1979):45-63.

Koehler, Ludmila. The Identity of P's "Sublime Gaul." *SEER* 49 (1971):487-99.

Konick, W. Categorical Dreams and Compliant Reality: The Role of the Narrator in *The Tales of Belkin. CASS* 11 (1977):75-90.

Kopelev, Lev. P. Tr. D. Lapeza. *RLT* 10 (1974):185-92.

Kostich, G. On P's "Pesni zapadnykh slavjan'." *RLJ* 120 (1981):101-14.

Kostka, Edmund. P's Debt to Schiller. *Rivista di Letterature Moderne e Comparate* 20 (1967):85-100.

——. P's Third Dimension: The German Influence. In *Glimpses of Germanic-Slavic Relations from P to Heinrich Mann.* Lewisburg: Bucknell UP, 1975, pp. 101-21.

Krzyzanowski, J. Mickiewicz and P. *SEER* 6 (1927):635-45.

Kučera, H. P and Don Juan. In *For Roman Jakobson: Essays on the Occasion of His 60th Birthday,* comp. M. Halle, et al. The Hague: Mouton, 1956, pp. 273-84.

Kuk, Z. Premonition or Vanity? Remarks on P's *Pamiatnik. Michigan Academician* 11 (1979):263-73.

Lang, David M. A Note on the Slayer of P. *ASEER* 8 (1949):316-16.

Lanz, Henry. P from an International Point of View. *Slavia* 16 (1941):34-38.

Leatherbarrow, W. J. P and Dostoevsky. *MLR* 74 (1979):368-85.

Lednicki, W. Bits of "Table Talk" on P. *ASEER* 5, 12-13 (1946):93-110; 14-15 (1946):72-98.

——. Bits of Table Talk on P, III: *The Snowstorm. ASEER* 6, 18-19 (1948): 110-33.

——. Ex Oriente Lux. [P and Mickiewicz.] *Semitic and Oriental Studies* 11 (1950): 243-61.

——. Grammatici certant: P's "Aleksandrijskij stolp." *HSS* 2 (1954):241-64.

——. Mickiewicz's Stay in Russia and His Friendship with P. In *Mickiewicz in World Literature: A Symposium,* ed. W. Lednicki. Berkeley: California UP, 1956, pp. 13-104.

——. The Prose of P. *SEER* 28 (1949):105-22, 377-91.

——. P, Tyutchev, Mickiewicz and the Decembrists: Legend and Facts. *SEER* 29 (1951):375-401.

——. Some Doubts about the Identity of P's Polonophil. *SEER* 30 (1952):206-12.

——. Some Notes on the Translation of Poetry (P's Lyrics). *ASEER* 11 (1952):304-11.

Leighton, Lauren G. Gematria in "The Queen of Spades": A Decembrist Puzzle. *SEEJ* 21 (1977):455-69.

——. Numbers and Numerology in "The Queen of Spades." *CSP* 19 (1977):417-43.

——. P and Marlinskij: Decembrist Allusions. *RusL* 14, 4 (1983):351-82.

Liapunov, Vadim. Mnemosyne and Lethe: P's "Vospominanie." *Alexander P: A Symposium on the 175th Anniversary of His Birth,* ed. A. Kodjak & K. Taranovsky. NY: New York UP, 1976, pp. 27-41.

Little, Edmund. The Peasant and the Stationmaster: A Question of Realism. *JRS* 38 (1979):23-31.

Little, T. E. P. A. Viazemskii as a Critic of P. In *Russian and Slavic Literature: Papers from the 1st International Slavic Conference (Banff, 1974),* ed. R. Freeborn, R. Milner-Gulland, C. A. Ward. Cambridge: Slavica, 1976, pp. 1-16.

Loewenson, Leo. Sir Roger Manley's History of Muscovy. *The Russian Impostor* (1674). *SEER* 31 (1953):232-40. [Refers to *Boris Godunov.*]

Lotman, Yury. *Analysis of the Poetic Text.* Tr. D. B. Johnson. Ann Arbor: Ardis, 1976, pp. 148-70.

——. Point of View in a Text. Tr. L. M. O'Toole. *New Literary History* 6, 2 (1975):339-52.

——. The Theme of Cards and the Card Game in 19th-Century Russian Literature. *PTL: A Journal for Descriptive Poetics and Theory* 3, 3 (1978):455-92.

Maagdenberg, Frida van den. Towards a Diagnosis of Literary Irony, A. S. P's *Putešestvie v Arzrum.* In *Russische Erzählung—Russian Short Story: Utrechter Symposium zur Theorie und Geschichte der russichen Erzählung im 19. und 20. Jahrhundert,* ed. R. Grübel. Amsterdam: Rodopi, 1984, pp. 119-51.

McConnell, A. P's Literary Gamble.

ASEER 19 (1960):577-93.

Maguire, Robert A. A.S.P: Notes on French Literature. *ASEER* 17 (1957):101-9.

Maloff, N. Musorgskii's *Boris Godunov:* P's Drama Resurrected. *CSP* 19 (1977):1-15.

Mandelstam, Osip. P and Scriabin. In his *Complete Critical Prose and Letters,* ed. J. G. Harris. Ann Arbor: Ardis, 1979, pp. 90-95.

Manning, C. A. Alexander Sergyeyevich P. *South Atlantic Quarterly* 25 (1926): 76-88.

____ The Centenary of P. *Modern Language Journal* 21 (1937):242-43.

____ P in World Literature. In *Centennial Essays for P,* ed. S. H. Cross & E. J. Simmons. Cambridge: Harvard UP, 1937.

____ Russian Versions of Don Juan (P and A. K. Tolstoy). *PMLA* 38 (1923):479-93.

____ Shevchenko and P's "To the Slanderers of Russia." *MLN* 59 (1944):495-97.

Marshall, H. B. & E. C. Barksdale. P, Kleist and the Minamilist Position in Literature. *Revue Belge de Philologie et d'Histoire* 3 (1983):571-77.

Masing-Delic, I. Three Poems about Two Meetings (P's "K," Tiutchev's "K. B." and Blok's "O doblestjach." *RusL* 9 (1975):37-54.

Matlaw, Ralph E. Poetry and the Poet in Romantic Society as Reflected in P's *Egyptian Nights. SEER* 33 (1954):102-19.

Mersereau, John, Jr. P's Concept of Romanticism. *Studies in Romanticism* 3 (1963):24-41.

Meyerson, E. F. and Jack Weiner. Cervantes' "Gypsy Maid" and P's "The Gypsies." *ISS* 4 (1967):209-14.

Mikkelson, Gerald E. The Mythopoetic Element in P's Historical Novel *The Captain's Daughter. CASS* 7 (1973): 296-313.

____ P's "Arion": A Lone Survivor's Cry. *SEEJ* 24 (1980):1-13.

____ P's "Geroj": Adverse Dialogue on Truth. *SEEJ* 18 (1974):367-72.

Mirsky, D. S. P *SEER* 2 (1923):71-84.

Mocha, F. Polish and Russian Sources of

Boris Godunov. Polish Review 25 (1980): 45-51.

Montagu-Nathan, M. P and the Russian Opera. *Adelphi* 27, 3 (1951):216-21.

____ . P's Debt to English Literature. *Contemporary Review* 183 (1953):303-7.

Monter, Barbara Heldt. Love and Death in P's Little Tragedies. *RLT* 3 (1972):206-14.

Morrison, R. H. Colours and Tone in *The Bronze Horseman. MelbSS* 17 (1983): 112-17.

Moser, Charles A. Introduction: P and the Russian Short Story. In *The Russian Short Story: A Critical History,* ed. C. Moser. Boston: Twayne, 1986, pp. xi-xxiv.

Nabokoff, C. Alexander P. *Contemporary Review* 128 (1925):621-27.

Nabokov, Vladimir. P and Gannibal. *Encounter* 19 (1962):11-26.

____ . P, or the Real and the Plausible. Tr. & intro. Dmitri Nabokov. *New York Review of Books,* March 31, 1988, pp. 38-42.

Naydan, Michael M. P's Lyric Memory. *SEEJ* 28 (1984):1-14.

Nelson, A. S. Aleksandr S. P. *New Century Review* 7 (1900):7-12.

Newman, John K. P's *Bronze Horseman* and the Epic Tradition. *CLS* 9 (1972):173-95.

O'Bell, Leslie. In P's Library. *CASS* 16 (1982):207-26.

____ The Poetic Logic of P's "Egipetskie noči." *RLJ* 120 (1981):89-100.

____ Young P: "Ruslan and Liudmila" in Its Lyric Content. *RusR* 44, 2 (1985):139-55.

Olcott, Anthony. Parody as Realism: *The Journey to Arzrum. RLT* 10 (1974): 245-59.

Osborne, E. A. Early Translations from the Russian: P and His Contemporaries. *Bookman* 82 (1932):264-68.

Pachmuss, T. & Victor Terras. The Shift of the Image of Napoleon in the Poetry of A. P. *SEEJ* 5 (1961):311-30.

Pankhurst, R. P's African Ancestry: A Question of Roots. *History Today* (Sept. 1980):44-46.

Parson, N. S. A Hostage to Art: The Portraits of Boris Godunov by P and A. K. Tolstoy. *FMLS* 16 (1980):237-55.

Pauls, John P. Historicity of P's "Poltava." *Ukrainian Quarterly* 17, 3 (1961): 230-46 and 4 (1961):342-61.

——. P's Dedication of "Poltava" and Princess Mariya Volkonskaya. *Marquette University Slavic Institute Papers,* no. 12 (1961).

——. Two Treatments of Mazeppa: Ryleev's and P's. *Slavic and East European Studies* 8, 1-2 (1963):97-109.

——. & LaVerne R. Pauls. Marija in P's *Poltava:* The Character and the Person. In *Festschrift für Nikola R. Pribić,* ed. J. Matešić. Neuried: Hieronymus, 1983, pp. 245-57.

Pedrotti, Louis. Sekowski's Defense of P's Prose. *SEEJ* 7 (1963):18-25.

Phillips, D. Uedinennyj domik na Vasil'evskom ostrove: P and the Veiled Supernatural. *RLJ* 112 (1978):79-88.

Poltoratzky, M.A. A.S.P and the Contemporary Russian Literary Language. *RLJ* 69 (1964):3-12.

Pomar, Mark. The Question of Dramatic Form in P's *Boris Godunov. CASS* 16 (1982):63-72.

Pomorska, Krystyna. Structural Peculiarities in *Putešestvie v Arzrum.* In *Alexander P: A Symposium on the 175th Anniversary of His Birth,* ed. A. Kodjak & K. Taranovsky. NY: New York UP, 1976, pp. 119-25.

Ponomareff, C. V. Woman as Nemesis: Card Symbolism in Hebel, Esenin and P. *Germano-Slavica* 6 (1975):67-71.

Pritchett, V. S. P: Founding Father. In his *The Myth Makers.* NY: Random House, 1979, pp. 77-88.

Proffer, Carl R. ["The Gypsies" in *Lolita.*] In his *Keys to Lolita.* Bloomington: Indiana UP, 1968, pp. 49-53.

——. P and Parricide. *American Imago* 25 (1968):347-53.

——. P's Criticism. In *The Critical Prose of Alexander P,* ed. C. R. Proffer. Bloomington: Indiana UP, 1970, pp. 9-17.

——. The Similes of P and Lermontov. *RLT* 3 (1972):148-94.

——. Washington Irving in Russia: P, Gogol, Marlinsky. *CL* 20, 4 (1968:329-42.

Pursglove, M. Chronology in P's *Pikovaya dama. Irish Slavonic Studies* 6 (1985):5-10.

——. P's "Zima. Chto delat' nam v derevne?" *JRS* 20 (1970):21-25.

Raitch, Eugene. P's "Ode to the Old School Tie." With a Translation of "October 19, 1825." *RusR* 3 (1944):74-86.

Rancour-Laferriere, Daniel. "Ja vas ljubil" Revisited. In *Russian Poetics,* ed. T. Eekman & D. S. Worth. Columbus: Slavica, 1983, pp. 305-24.

Reeder, Roberta. The Greek Anthology and Its Influence on P's Poetic Style. *CASS* 10 (1976):205-27.

Reid, Robert. P Fivefold. *Irish Slavonic Studies* (1983):112-19.

Richardson, Robert. The Unnatural Perspective: P's Grotesque in *Ruslan i Ljudmila. RLJ* 101 (1974):55-66.

Roberts, C. P's *Pikovaya dama* and the Opera Libretto. *Canadian Review of Comparative Literature* 6 (1979):9-26.

Rosen, Nathan. The Magic Cards in "The Queen of Spades." *SEEJ* 19 (1975):255-75.

Sandler, Stephanie. The Poetics of Authority in P's "André Chénier." *SlavR* 42 (1983):187-203.

——. P, Baratynskii, and *Hamlet:* On Mourning and Poetry. *RusR* 42 (1983):73-90.

Schindler, K. Boris Godunoff. *North American Review* 197 (1913):256-67.

Schmid, Wolf. Three Diegetic Devices in P's *Tales of Belkin.* In *Language and Literary Theory: In Honor of Ladislav Matejka,* ed. I. R. Titunik & L. Dolezel. Ann Arbor: U Michigan, Dept. Slavic Languages and Literatures, 1984, pp. 505-25.

Schwartz, M. M. & A. "Queen of Spades": A Psychoanalytic Interpretation. *Texas Studies in Literature and Language* 17 (1975):275-88.

Seeley, F. F. The Problem of "Kamennyj Gost'." *SEER* 41 (1963):345-67.

Senderovich, Savely. On P's Mythology: The Shade-Myth. In *Alexander P: Symposium II,* ed. A. Kodjak, et al. Columbus: Slavica, 1980, pp. 103-16.

—— The Problem of the Text of P's "Vospominanie." *RLJ* 36, 123-24 (1982): 55-65.

Serman, I. A. Paradoxes of the Popular

Mind in P's *Boris Godunov. SEER* 64 (1986):25-39.

Shapiro, Michael. Journey to the Metonymic Pole: The Structure of P's "Little Tragedies." In *From Los Angeles to Kiev,* ed. V. Markov & D. S. Worth. Columbus: Slavica, 1983, pp. 169-206.

____. P's Modus Significandi: A Semiotic Exploration. In *Russian Romanticism: Studies in the Poetic Codes,* ed. N. A. Nilsson. Stockholm: Almqvist & Wiksell, 1979, pp. 110-34.

____. Social Codes and Arbiters of Elegance in P's *Little Tragedies. RLJ* 120 (1981):75-82.

Shaw, J. Thomas. The "Conclusion" of P's *Queen of Spades.* In *Studies in Russian and Polish Literature in Honor of W. Lednicki,* ed. Z. Folejewski. The Hague: Mouton, 1962, pp. 114-26.

____. Form and Style in the Letters of Aleksandr P. *SEEJ* 4 (1959): 147-57.

____. Large Rhyme Sets and P's Poetry. *SEEJ* 18 (1974):231-52.

____. The Problem of Persona in Journalism: P's Feofilakt Kosičkin. In *American Contributions to the Fifth International Congress of Slavists. Vol. 2: Literary Contributions.* The Hague: Mouton, 1963, pp. 301-26.

____. P on America: His *John Tanner. Orbis Scriptus,* 1966, pp. 739-56.

____. P's "The Shot." *ISS* 3 (1963):113-29.

____. P's "The Stationmaster" and the New Testament Parable. *SEEJ* 21 (1977):3-29.

____. Recent Soviet Scholarly Books on P: A Review Article. *SEEJ* 10 (1966):66-84.

____. Theme and Imagery in P's "Ja pomnju čudnoe mgnoven'e." *SEEJ* 14 (1970): 135-44.

____. Vertical Enrichment in P's Rhymed Poetry. In *American Contributions to the Eighth International Congress of Slavists,* vol. 1, ed. H. Birnbaum. Columbus: Slavica, 1978, pp. 637-64.

Shein, Louis J. P's Political Weltanschauung. *CSP* 10 (1968):68-78.

Sidiakov, L. S. Problems of Periodizing P's Art. *Soviet Studies in Literature* 20, 1 (1983-84):67-86.

Simmons, E. J. P's "Avaricious Knight" and Shenstone. *MLN* 45 (1930):454-57.

____. A. S. P: "The Avaricious Knight." *HSS* 15 (1933):329-44.

Singh, N. P: His Life and Its Relevance Today. *Commonwealth Quarterly* 4, 13 (1980):125-35.

Slonimsky, Alexander. On P. In *The Complection of Russian Literature,* ed. Andrew Field. NY: Atheneum, 1971, pp. 42-48.

Sorenson, Robert. P's *Gavriiliada:* From Style to Meaning. *RLJ* 120 (1981):59-74.

Starling, W. The Conversation of a Poet and a Miserly Knight. *RLT* 3 (1972):215-28.

Stenbock-Fermor, Elisabeth. French Medieval Poetry as a Source of Inspiration for P. In *Alexander P: A Symposium on the 175th Anniversary of His Birth,* ed. A Kodjak & K. Taranovsky. NY: New York UP, 1976, pp. 56-70.

____. Some Neglected Features of the Epigraphs in *The Captain's Daughter* and Other Stories of P. *IJSLP* 8 (1964):110-23.

Stephenson, Robert C. The English Source of P's Spanish Themes. *University of Texas Studies in English* 18 (1938):85-111.

____, tr. P's *Count Nulin. Studies in English* 33 (1954):67-79.

Strakhovsky, Leonid I. P and the Emperors Alexander I and Nicholas I. *CSP* 1 (1956):16-30.

Striedter, J. Poetic Genre and the Sense of History in P. *New Literary History* 8, 2 (1977):295-310.

Strought, M. From Folklore to Footlights. *Southern Folklore Quarterly* 24 (1960): 272-81.

Struve, Gleb. Marginalia Puschkiniana: P's "Only Intelligent Atheist." *MLN* 65 (1950):300-6.

____. P and His Place in Russian Literature. *SEER* 15 (1936):298-304.

____. P in Early English Criticism (1821-1838). *ASEER* 8 (1949):296-314.

____. Unpublished P Documents in the British Museum. *SEER* 15 (1936):688-91.

____. Who Was P's "Polonophil?" *SEER* 29 (1951):444-56.

Suhadolc, Joseph. P and Serfdom. In *Literature and Society,* ed. Bernice Slote. Lincoln: U Nebraska P, 1964, pp. 85-111.

Terras, Victor. Dissonances and False Notes in a Literary Text. In *The Structural Analysis of Literary Texts,* ed. A. Kodjak. Columbus: Slavica, 1980, pp. 82-95.

____. P and Romanticism. In *Alexander P: Symposium II,* ed. A. Kodjak, et al. Columbus: Slavica, 1980, pp. 49-60.

____. P's "Feast During the Plague" and Its Original: A Structural Confrontation. *Alexander P: A Symposium on the 175th Anniversary of His Birth,* ed. A Kodjak & K. Taranovsky. NY: New York UP, 1976, pp. 206-20.

____. Some Observations on P's Image in Russian Literature. *RusL* 14, 4 (1983):299-316.

Thaler, R. P. The French Tutor in Radishchev and P. *RusR* 13 (1954): 210-12.

Thomson, A. The Final Agony of Alexander P. *NZSJ* 1 (1975):1-18.

Timmer, C. B. The History of a History: A. S. P and "The History of the Village of Goriukhino." *RusL* 1 (1971):113-31.

Todd, William Mills. *The Familiar Letter as a Literary Genre in the Age of P.* Princeton UP, 1976. [For extensive commentary, but no separate chapters, on P's letters, see the Index.]

Trensky, Paul I. Peter the Great in P. *Transactions of the Assn. Russian-American Scholars in USA* 7 (1973): 239-50.

Tsvetaeva, Marina. My P. In her *A Captive Spirit: Selected Prose,* tr. J. Marin King. Ann Arbor: Ardis, 1980, pp. 319-64.

____. P and Pugachev. In her *Captive Spirit,* ibid, pp. 372-403.

Turkevich, Ludmilla. P's Dreams and Their Aesthetic Function: A New Interpretation. *RLJ* 101 (1974):40-54.

Ugrinsky, A. Chateaubriand's *Atala* and P's *Prisoner of the Caucasus:* French and Russian Variations Upon a Theme by Guillaume Thomas Reynard. *CLS* 17 (1980):469-76.

van Holk, A. G. F. The Open Message: On the Syntax of Envy in A. S. P's "Mozart and Salieri." *RusL* 5 (1980):1-54.

____. Thematic Composition in Russian Drama. The Theme of Envy in P's *Mozart and Salieri,* Turgenev's *A Month in the Country* and Chekhov's *Uncle Vanya. Essays in Poetics* 8, 1 (1984):53-73.

Vernadsky, G. P and His Time. *Transactions of the Connecticut Academy of Arts and Sciences* 33 (1937):18-36.

Vickery, Walter N. "Anchar": Beyond Good and Evil. *CASS* 10 (1976):175-88.

____. Anna Petrovna Kern: Let Us Be More Gallant. *SEEJ* 12 (1968):311-22.

____. "Arion": An Example of Post-Decembrist Semantics. *Alexander P: A Symposium on the 175th Anniversary of His Birth,* ed. A Kodjak & K. Taranovsky. NY: New York UP, 1976, pp. 71-86.

____. A Comparison of Samples of Lomonosov's and P's Four-Foot Iamb. *American Contributions to the Eighth International Congress of Slavists,* vol. 1, ed. H. Birnbaum. Columbus: Slavica, 1978, pp. 727-56.

____. "Ja vas ljubil": A Literary Source. *IJSLP* 15 (1972):160-67.

____. Lexical Similarities and Thematic Affinities: Three P Lyrics. *IJSLP* 28 (1983):137-48.

____. "Mednyj vsadnik" and the Eighteenth-Century Heroic Ode. *ISS* 4 (1967): 140-62.

____. On the Question of the Syntactic Structure of *Gavriiliada* and *Boris Godunov.* In *American Contributions to the Sixth International Congress of Slavists,* vol. 2, ed. W. E. Harkins. The Hague: Mouton: 1968, pp. 355-67.

____. Problems in P's Four-Foot Iambs. In *Russian Poetics,* ed. T. Eekman & D.

S. Worth. Columbus: Slavica, 1983, pp. 457-80.

——. P: Russia and Europe. *Review of National Literatures* 3, 1 (1972):15-38.

——. Recent Soviet Research on the Events Leading to P's Death. *SEEJ* 14 (1970):489-502.

——. "Stambul gjaury nynče slavjat." In *Alexander P: Symposium II,* ed. A. Kodjak, et al. Columbus: Slavica, 1980, pp. 11-26.

——. Three Examples of Narrated Speech in P's *Poltava. SEEJ* 8 (1964):273-83.

——. Toward an Interpretation of P's "Podrazhaniia Koranu." *CASS* 11 (1977): 61-74.

——. "The Water-Nymph" and "Again I Visited...": Notes on an Old Controversy. *RLT* 3 (1972):195-205.

Vinogradov, V. V. The Language of P. In his *The History of the Russian Literary Language.* Madison: U Wisconsin P, 1969, pp. 127-57.

Walter, Starling. The Conversation of a Poet and a Miserly Knight. *RLT* 3 (1972):215-28.

Ward, D. The Structure of P's "Tales of Belkin." *SEER* 33 (1955):516-28.

Warner, E. A. P in the Russian Folk Plays. In *Oral Literature: Seven Essays,* ed. J. L. Duggan. Edinburgh: Scottish Academic Press, 1975, pp. 101-7.

Weber, Harry. "Pikovaja dama": A Case for Freemasonry in Russian Literature. *SEEJ* 12 (1968):435-47.

Weil, Irwin. Onegin's Echo. *RLT* 10 (1974):260-73.

Weiner, J. and E. F. Meyerson. Cervantes' "Gypsy Maid" and P's *The Gypsies. ISS* 4 (1967):209-14.

Wheeler, M. P and Mickiewicz: Two Types of "National" Poet. *JRS* 43 (1982):14-23.

Williams, Gareth. The Obsessions of Madness of Germann in *Pikovaya dama. Rus L* 14, 4 (1983):383-96.

Wilson, Edmund. Notes on P. *New York Review of Books* 15 (3 Dec. 1970):4-10.

——. Notes on Russian Literature. *Atlantic Monthly* 173 (1943):79-83.

Wolff, T. A. Shakespeare's Influence on P's Dramatic Works. *Shakespeare Survey* 5 (1952):93-105.

Woll, Josephine. *Mozart and Salieri* and the Concept of Tragedy. *CASS* 10 (1976):250-63.

Worth, Dean. Grammar in Rhyme: P's Lyrics. In *Russian Romanticism: Studies in Poetic Codes,* ed. N. A. Nilsson. Stockholm: Almqvist, 1979, pp. 135-43.

Wynne, Lorraine. Oscillation in the *Stone Guest.* In *Alexander P: Symposium II,* ed. A. Kodjak, et al. Columbus: Slavica, 1980, pp. 89-102.

——. The Poetic Function of the Stage Audience and Embedded Performance in Drama. In *Semiotics 1980,* ed. Michael Herzfeld and Margot D. Lenhart. NY: Plenum, 1982, pp. 571-76.

Zholkovsky, A. Invariants and the Structure of a Text: P's "I loved you." In *Themes and Texts.* Ithaca: Cornell UP, 1984, pp. 179-94.

——. The Literary Text—Thematic and Expressive Structure: An Analysis of P's Poem "Ya vas lyubil." *New Literary History* 9 (1978):263-78.

——. Notes on "Carosel'skaja statuja." *RLJ* 120 (1981):127-50.

——. P's "Poetic World." *Russian Poetics in Translation* 8 (1981):62-107.

Zissermann, N. Heinrich Heine and Russia: Random Notes on Heine and P. *NZSJ* 9 (1972):73-100.

Articles on "Eugene Onegin" (*EO*)

Bakhtin, Mikhail. Discourse in *EO.* In *Russian Views of P's EO,* trans. S. Hoisington. Bloomington: Indiana UP, 1988, pp. 115-21.

Belinsky, Vissarion. *EO:* An Encyclopedia of Russian Life. In *Russian Views of P's EO,* trans. S. Hoisington. Bloomington: Indiana UP, 1988, pp. 17-42.

Bocharov, Sergey. The Stylistic World of the Novel. In *Russian Views of P's EO,* trans. S. Hoisington. Bloomington: Indiana UP, 1988, pp. 122-68.

Borland, Helen. Theories and Problems of Translation with Special Reference to P's Novel in Verse *EO.* In *Russian*

Contributions II: Problemy perevoda. Melbourne: U Melbourne, n.d., pp. 1-32.

Bowra, C. M. Two Translations of *EO. Sewanee Review* 73 (1965):330-33.

Clayton, J. D. Emblematic and Iconographic Patterns in P's *EO.* A Shakespearean Ghost?" *Germano-Slavica* 6 (1975):53-66.

——. The Epigraph of *EO:* A Hypothesis. *CSS* 5 (1971):226-33.

——. *EO:* Symbolism of Time. *RLJ* 120 (1981):43-58.

——. New Directions in Soviet-American Criticism of *EO. CSP* 22 (1980):208-19.

Clipper-Sethi, Roberta. A Lesson for Novelists: Or, the Dramatic Structure of *EO. RusL* 14, 4 (1983):397-412.

Crookes, David Z. A Contextual Study of the Musical Instruments in P's *EO. NZSJ* (1984): 1-13.

Dostoevsky, Fyodor. P. In *Russian Views of P's EO,* trans. S. Hoisington. Bloomington: Indiana UP, 1988, pp. 56-67.

England, D. P and *EO. Contemporary Review* (January 1951):28-33.

Fanger, Donald. Influence and Tradition in the Russian Novel. In *The Russian Novel from Pushkin to Pasternak,* ed. G. Garrard. New Haven: Yale UP, 1983, pp. 29-41.

Forsyth, J. Pisarev, Belinsky and *EO. SEER* 48 (1970):163-81.

Gerschenkron, Alexander. Review of *EO: A Novel in Verse,* tr. Vladimir Nabokov. *Modern Philology* 63, 4 (1967):336-47.

Gibian, George. Narrative Technique and Realism: *EO* and *Madame Bovary. Langue et littérature* (1962):339.

Gregg, L. Slava Snabokovu. *RLT* 3 (1972):313-29.

Gregg, Richard. Rhetoric in Tat'jana's Last Speech: The Camouflage that Reveals. *SEEJ* 25 (1981):1-12.

——. Tat'jana's Two Dreams: The Unwanted Spouse and the Demonic Lover. *SEER* 48 (1970):492-505.

Gustafson, R. F. The Metaphor of the Seasons in *EO. SEEJ* 6 (1962):6-20.

Hoisington, Sona. *EO:* An Inverted Byronic Poem. *CL* 27 (1975):136-52.

——. *EO:* Product of or Challenge to *Adolphe?" CL* 15 (1977):205-13.

——. The Hierarchy of Narrators in *EO. CASS* 10 (1976):242-49.

Johnson, D. B. Contrastive Phono-Aesthetics, or, Why Nabokov Gave Up Translating Poetry as Poetry. In *A Book of Things about Vladimir Nabokov,* ed. Carl R. Proffer. Ann Arbor: Ardis, 1974, pp. 28-41.

——. Nabokov's *Ada* and P's *EO. SEEJ* 15 (1971):316-23.

Katz, Michael R. Love and Marriage in P's *EO. OSP* (1984):77-89.

Kliuchevskii, V. *EO* and His Ancestors. Tr. M. Shatz. *CASS* 16 (1982):227-46.

Leighton, L. Marlinskij's "Ispytanie": A Romantic Rejoinder to *EO. SEEJ* 13 (1969):200-16.

Little, E. Onegin at School and University. *JRS* 41 (1981):33-41.

Little, T. E. P's Tatyana and Onegin: A Study in Irony. *NZSJ* 1 (1975):19-28.

Lotman, Yury. Point of View in a Text. Tr. L. M. O'Toole. *New Literary History* 6 (1975):339-52.

——. The Structure of *EO.* In *Russian Views of P's EO,* trans. S. Hoisington. Bloomington: Indiana UP, 1988, pp. 91-114.

——. The Transformation of the Tradition Generated by *Onegin* in the Subsequent History of the Russian Novel. In *Russian Views of P's EO,* trans. S. Hoisington. Bloomington: Indiana UP, 1988, pp. 169-77.

McLean, Hugh. Eugene Rudin. In *Literature and Society in Imperial Russia, 1800-1914,* ed. W. M. Todd III. Stanford: Stanford UP, 1978, pp. 259-66.

——. The Tone(s) of *EO. CalSS* 6 (1971):3-15.

Manson, Joseph P. P's *EO:* A Study in Literary Counter-Point. In *Studies Presented to Professor Roman Jakobson by His Students,* ed. C. E. Gribble. Cambridge: Slavica, 1968, pp. 201-6.

Matlaw, Ralph E. The Dream in *EO,* with a Note on *Gore ot uma. SEER* 37 (1959):487-503.

Meijer, Jan M. The Digressions in *EO.* In

Dutch Contributions to the Sixth International Congress of Slavists. The Hague: Mouton, 1968, pp. 122-52.

Mitchell, S. The Digressions of *EO: Apropos of Some Essays by Ettore Lo Gatto. SEER* 44 (1966):51-65.

——. Tatiana's Reading. *FMLS* 4 (1968):1-21.

Nabokov, Vladimir. Translator's Introduction to *EO.* Princeton: Princeton UP, 1975, vol. 1, pp. 3-88.
[Description of the Text; The *EO* Stanza; The Structure of *EO*; P on *EO*; The Publication of *EO*; P's Autographs; Bibliography.]

——. Commentary on *EO.* Ibid., vols 2-3 (547 + 540 pp.).
[Appendices: Abram Gannibal; Notes on Prosody.]

——. Nabokov's Reply (On His Edition of *EO). Encounter* 26 (Feb. 1966):80-89.

——. Pounding the Clavichord & Reply to My Critics. In his *Strong Opinions.* NY: McGraw-Hill, 1973, pp. 231-40; 241-67.

——. Problems of Translation: *Onegin* in English. *Partisan Review* 22 (1955): 495-512.

Nesaule, Valda. Tatiana's Dream in P's *EO. ISS* 3 (1963):119-24.

Peer, Larry H. P and Goethe Again: Lensky's Character. *Papers on Language and Literature* 5 (1969):267-72.

Picchio, Riccardo. Dante and J. Malfilâtre as Literary Sources of Tat'jana's Erotic Dream. In *Alexander P: A Symposium on the 175th Anniversary of His Birth,* ed. A. Kodjak & K. Taranovsky. NY: New York UP, 1976, pp. 42-55.

Pisarev, Dmitry. P and Belinsky: *EO.* In *Russian Views of P's EO,* trans. S. Hoisington. Bloomington: Indiana UP, 1988, pp. 43-55.

Rowe, W. W. Onegin Up-To-Date. *RLT* 3 (1972):452-53.

——. Pushkinian Impatient Expectation and Its Function in *EO.* In his *Nabokov and Others.* Ann Arbor: Ardis, 1979, pp. 15-26.

Shaw, J. Thomas. The Problem of Unity of Author-Narrator's Stance in P's *EO. RLJ* 120 (1981):25-42.

——. Translations of *Onegin. RusR* 24 (1965):111-27.

Shklovskii, Viktor. *EO* (P and Sterne). Tr. Richard Sheldon. *Review of Contemporary Fiction* 3, 1 (1983):225-36.

Simmons, E. J. English Translations of *EO. SEER* 17 (1938):198-208.

Stilman, Leon. Problems of Literary Genres and Traditions in P's *EO.* In *American Contributions to the Fourth International Congress of Slavists.* 's-Gravenhage: Mouton, 1958, pp. 365-68.

Todd, W. M. III. *EO:* Life's Novel. In *Literature and Society in Imperial Russia, 1800-1914,* ed. W. M. Todd III. Stanford: Stanford UP, 1978, pp. 203-36.

Tynyanov, Yury. On the Composition of *EO.* In *Russian Views of P's EO,* trans. S. Hoisington. Bloomington: Indiana UP, 1988, pp. 71-90.

Vickery, Walter N. Byron's *Don Juan* and P's *EO:* The Question of Parallelism. *ISS* 4 (1967):181-91.

Weil, I. Onegin's Echo. *RLT* 10 (1974): 260-73.

Weintraub, W. Norwid—P: Norwid's "Spartacus" and the "Onegin" Stanza. *HSS* 2 (1954):271-86.

Wilson, Edmund. *EO:* In Honor of P, 1799-1837. *New Republic* 89 (1936): 165-71.

——. P; Notes on P; The Strange Case of P and Nabokov. In his *A Window on Russia.* NY: Farrar, Strauss, Giroux, 1972, pp. 15-27; 185-96; 209-37.

Worth, Dean. Grammatical Rhyme Types in *EO.* In *Alexander P: A Symposium on the 175th Anniversary of His Birth,* ed. A. Kodjak & K. Taranovsky. NY: New York UP, 1976, pp. 39-48.

——. Rhyme Enrichment in *EO.* In *Miscellanea Slavica: To Honour the Memory of Jan M. Meijer,* ed. B. J. Amsenga, et al. Amsterdam: Rodopi, 1983, pp. 535-42.

KONDRATY RYLEEV

Translations

The Poems of K. F. Relaieff. Tr. T. Hart-Davies. London: Remington, 1887.
Voinarovsky and Other Poems. Tr. T. Davies. Calcutta, 1879.

Bannikov, Nikolai, comp. *Three Centuries of Russian Poetry.* Moscow: Progress, 1980, pp. 139-43.
[The Citizen; Voinarovsky; Nalivaiko's Testament.]
Frere, T., tr. Artemon Matveiev. Sviatopolk. *Anglo-Russian Literary Society Proceedings* 63 (1912):101-4.
——. Poems. *Anglo-Russian Literary Society Proceedings* 57 (1910):83-107.
Rydel, Christine, ed. *The Ardis Anthology of Russian Romanticism.* Ann Arbor: Ardis, 1984, pp. 81-82.
[Ivan Susanin; The Citizen.]

Criticism

O'Meara, Patrick. *K. F. R: A Political Biography of the Decembrist Poet.* Princeton: Princeton UP, 1984.

Persen, William. Kondratii R, the Poet and the Revolutionary. Ph.D. diss., Harvard, 1953.

Glasse, A. "P" or "R"; Who Wrote the *Mnemosyne* Review. *RLT* 10 (1975): 274-78.
O'Meara, P. J. Mediaeval and Eighteenth-Century Themes in the Work of R. *Study Group on Eighteenth-Century Russia: Newsletter* 8 (1980):17-20.
Pauls, John P. The Treatments of Mazeppa: R's and Pushkin's. *Slavic and East European Studies* 8 (1963):97-109.
——. Ukrainian Themes in R's Works. *Wiener Slavistisches Jahrbuch* 17 (1972): 228-42.
Pauls, LaVerne R. & John. R and the Ukraine. *Ukrainian Review* 16, 4

(1969): 33-40; 17, 1 (1970):49-60.
Walker, Franklin. K. F. R: A Self-Sacrifice for Revolution. *SEER* 47 (1969):436-46.

MIKHAIL SALTYKOV-SHCHEDRIN

Bibliography

Bibliography, secondary sources in English, French and German. Translations in English, French and German. Complete list of short works in English. In *M. E. Saltykov-Shchedrin, The Golovlyov Family.* Ann Arbor: Ardis, 1977, pp. 249-51.

Translations

Fables by Shchedrin. Tr. V Volkhovsky. London: Chatto & Windus, 1931.
The Golovlyov Family. Tr. Samuel Cioran. Ann Arbor: Ardis, 1977.
The Golovyovs. Tr. Andrew R. MacAndrew. NY: New American Library, 1961.
The History of a Town, or, The Chronicle of Foolov. Tr. & ed. Susan Brownsberger. Ann Arbor: Ardis, 1982. [Preface, Background notes, Glossary of Names & Terms, Illustrations by L. Lamm.]
The History of a Town. Tr. & intro. I. P. Foote. Oxford: Meeuws, 1980.
The Pompadours. Tr. David Magarshack. Ann Arbor: Ardis, 1984.
Tales. Moscow: Foreign Languages Publishing House, 1956. [Inferior in quality and number to the fables in Volkhovsky's book of translations—see above.]
Tchinovnicks. Sketches of Provincial Life. Tr. F. Aston. London: L. Booth, 1861.
The Village Priest and Other Stories. Tr. B. Tollemache. London: Unwin, 1918.

Boy in Pants and Boy Without. Tr. G. Struve. *SEER* 18 (1939):18-28.
The Old Governor's Favourite. *Twentieth-Century Russia* 1, 3 (1916):188-207.
Pazukhin's Death. Tr. L. Senelick. *RLT* 14 (1976):321-76.

Porfiry Petrovich. Tr. W. E. Brown. *RLT* 10 (1974):79-91.

Zubatov. Tr. David Lapeza. *RLT* 10 (1974):67-76.

Criticism

Kaye, S. E. S's Theory and Practice of Writing: An Analysis of the Work of M. Ye. S, 1868-1884. Ph.D. diss., London, 1975.

Kulešov, Catherine. S, *Istorija odnogo goroda:* An Annotated Edition with an Introduction. Ph.D. diss., Indiana, 1969.

Strelsky, Nikander. S and the Russian Squire. Ph.D. diss., Columbia, 1941.

Walker, S. E. S's Theory and Practice of Writing: An Analysis of the Work of M. Ye. S, 1868-84. Ph.D. diss., London School of Slavonic Studies, 1976.

Bartholomew, F. M. S, Miliutin and Maikov: A Forgotten Circle. *CSP* 26 (1984):283-95.

Ehre, Milton. A Classic of Russian Realism: Form and Meaning in *The Golovlyovs. Studies in the Novel* 9 (1977):3-16.

Foote, I.P. M.E.S: *The Golovlyov Family. FMLS* 4 (1968):53-63.

——. Quintessential S: "Uzbezhishche Monrepo." *OSP* 12 (1979):84-103.

——. Reaction or Revolution: The Ending of S's *History of a Town. OSP* 1 (1968):105-25.

Grishin, D. The Problem of Dictatorship in Dostoevsky and S. *Australian Quarterly* 31, 3 (1959):82-91.

Kramer, Karl D. Satiric Form in S's *Gospoda Golovlevy. SEEJ* 14 (1970): 453-64.

Lednicki, Waclaw. S and the Russian Squire. *SEER* 20 (1941):347-54.

Naumoff, S. S on Germany. *Twentieth-Century Russia* 1, 4 (1916):312-16.

Neuhäuser, R. The Early Prose of S and Dostoevsky: Parallels and Echoes. *CSP* 22 (1980):372-87.

Proffer, Carl R. S and the Russian Novel. In S, *The Golovlyov Family,* tr. S. D. Cioran. Ann Arbor: Ardis, 1979, pp. ix-xxxiv.

Todd, W. M. III. The Anti-Hero with a Thousand Faces: S's Porfiry Golovlev.

Studies in Literary Imagination 9, 1 (1976):87-105.

OSIP SENKOVSKY

Criticism

Pedrotti, Louis. *Genesis of a Literary Alien (Osip I. S.).* Berkeley: U California P, 1965.

Zilber, V. S (Baron Brambeus). In *Russian Prose,* ed. B. Eikhenbaum & Yu. Tynyanov, tr. Ray Parrott. Ann Arbor: Ardis, 1985, pp. 127-49.

VLADIMIR SOLLOGUB

His Hat and Cane. A Comedy in One Act. Tr. by members of the Bellevue Dramatic Club of Newport. Boston: Baker, 1902.

The Tarantas:Traveling Impressions of Young Russia. London: Chapman-Hall, 1850.

The Tarantas. Impressions of a Journey. Tr. & afterword by William Edward Brown. Ann Arbor: Ardis, 1989.

The Snowstorm. Tr. W. E. Brown. In *Russian Romantic Prose: An Anthology,* ed. C. Proffer. Ann Arbor: Ardis, 1975, pp. 265-77.

OREST SOMOV

Translation

Mommy and Sonny. Tr. & intro. John Mersereau, Jr. *RLT* 8 (1974):259-77. Reprinted in *Russian Romantic Prose,* ed. C. R. Proffer. Ann Arbor: Translation Press, 1979, pp. 212-30.

Criticism

Mersereau, John Jr. *Orest S. Russian Fiction between Romanticism and Realism.* Ann Arbor: Ardis, 1989.

Barratt, Glynn. S, Kozlov and Byron's Russian Triumph. *Canadian Review of Comparative Literature* 1 (1974):104-22.

Mersereau, John, Jr. Orest Mikhailovich S: Life and Literary Activities. In *Papers in Slavic Philology*, ed. B. Stolz. I (1977):198-224.

___ Orest S: An Introduction. *SEER* 43 (1965):354-71.

___ Orest S and the Illusion of Reality. In *American Contributions to the Sixth International Congress of Slavists*, vol. 2, ed. W. E. Harkins. The Hague: Mouton: 1968, pp. 307-31.

___. S: The Supernatural Tale; The Physiological Sketch and Society Tale; S's Novellas of Manners. In his *Russian Romantic Fiction*. Ann Arbor: Ardis, 1983.

Brodiansky, N. S, 1817-1903. *SEER* 24 (1946):110-21.

Curran, Michael A. S's *Smert' Tarelkina.* In *Studies Presented to Professor Roman Jakobson by His Students*, ed. C. E. Gribble. Cambridge: Slavica, 1968, 84-90.

Rudnitsky, Konstantin. *Meyerhold the Director.* Ann Arbor: Ardis, 1981. [Meyerhold productions of *The Case, The Death of Tarelkin,* and *Krechinsky's Wedding* (see index).]

Segal, Harold. Introduction. In his translation of *The Trilogy of Alexander S.* NY: Dutton, 1969, pp. xiii-xlix.

Wilson, Edmund. S: Who Killed the French Woman. In his *A Window on Russia.* NY: Farrar, 1972, pp. 148-60.

ALEXEI TOLSTOY

ALEXANDER SUKHOVO-KOBYLIN

Translations

The Trilogy of Alexander Sukhovo-Kobylin. Tr. & intro. by Harold Segal. NY: Dutton, 1969. [Krechinsky's Wedding; The Case; The Death of Tarelkin.]

Krechinsky's Wedding. Tr. R. Magidoff. Ann Arbor: U Michigan P, 1961.

Criticism

Fortune, Richard. *Alexander S.* Boston: Twayne, 1982.

Adrianow, Gennadij Yakovlevich. The Importance of Lexical and Socio-Cultural Symbolism in A. V. S's Trilogy. Ph.D. diss., McGill, 1976.

Curran, M. A. The Theater of S and the Tradition of Russian Grotesque Satire. Ph.D. diss., Harvard, 1968.

Smith, Melissa Trimble. A. V. S's *Krečinskij's Wedding* on the Russian and Soviet Stage. Ph.D. diss., Pittsburgh, 1984.

Translations

Czar Fedor Ivanovich. Tr. A. Hayes. London: Paul, 1924.

The Death of Ivan the Terrible. A Drama in Verse. Tr. A. Hayes. Preface C. Nabokoff. London: Trubner, 1926.

The Death of Ivan the Terrible. Tr. G. R. Noyes in his *Masterpieces of the Russian Drama.* NY: Dover, 1961, vol. 2, pp. 457-546.

A Prince of Outlaws. Tr. C. Manning. NY: Knopf, 1927.

Prince Serebrenni. Tr. M. Galitzine. London: Chapman-Hall, 1874.

Tsar Fyodor Ivanovitch. Tr. G. Coran. In *The Moscow Art Theater Series of Russian Plays*, ed. O. M. Sayler. NY: Brentanos, 1922, pp. 1-91.

On the Mount. Tr. N. Zharintsova. *Englishwoman* 27 (1915):67-81.

T's Parody History of the Russian State. Tr. W. Harkins. *SlavR* 27 (1968):459-69.

Tugar and the Dragon. Tr. J. Posin. *Pacific Spectator* (Stanford) 10 (1956): 184-88.

Vassili Shibanov. Tr. N. Shishkoff. *Anglo-*

Russian Literary Society Proceedings 55 (1909):90-93.

For a complete listing of translations of T's poems, see Lewanski, pp. 367-69. The following are selected recent translations:

Bannikov, Nikolai, comp. *Three Centuries of Russian Verse.* Moscow: Progress, 1980, pp. 275-79.
[Native land, fair land of mine!; By chance once, amidst all the bustle; It happened in the early spring; Clearer than the skylark's singing.]

Obolensky, D., ed. *The Heritage of Russian Verse.* Bloomington: Indiana UP, 1976, pp. 172-85.
[Prince Michael Repin; I have killed; Along the rough and bumpy causeway; The Troparian from *John Damascene;* It was in the early spring; Ballad of the Chamberlain Delarue.]

Raffel, Burton, ed. *Russian Poetry under the Tsars.* Albany: State University of New York Press, 1971, pp. 134-38.
[My Carriage Bumps and Rumbles; When All the World Trembles; Sometimes, in the Middle of Daily Things.]

Criticism

Berry, Thomas E. *A. K. T: Russian Humorist.* Bethany, WV: Bethany College P, 1971.

Dalton, Margaret. *A. K. T.* NY: Twayne, 1972.

Graham, S. D. *The Lyric Poetry of A. K. T.* Amsterdam: Rodopi, 1985.

Berry, Thomas Edwin. Satire in the Works of A. K. T. Ph.D. diss., Texas, 1967.

Dalton, Margaret. Alexej Konstantinovich T: A Study of His Life and Work. Ph.D. diss., Harvard, 1964.

Ivancin, Michael Walter. Aleksej Konstantinovič T and Russian Romanticism. Ph.D. diss., Illinois, 1983.

Lee, Edward Seymour. A. K. T: Life and Lyric Poetry. Ph.D. diss., Pittsburgh, 1985.

Padro, Joan E. A. K. T's Trilogy of Historical Plays: *The Death of Ioann the Terrible, Tsar Fyodor Ioannovich,*

Tsar Boris. Ph.D. diss., Columbia, 1970.

Bernard, J. Notes on Alexei T's "Harold Svenholm." *ASEER* 6 (1947):79-91.

Graham, S. Rhyme and Reason: An Aspect of A. K. T's Poetic Technique. *Essays in Poetics* 4, 1 (1979):86-92.

Harkins, William E. A. K. T's Parody History of the Russian State. *SlavR* 27 (1969):459-69.

Kjellberg, Lennart. Aleksej K. T's *Tropar':* A Study in the Art of Paraphrase. *Studia Slavica Gunnarsson* (1960):43-63.

Manning, Clarence. Count Aleksyey Konstantinovich T. *South Atlantic Quarterly* 28 (1929):59-70.

——. The Humorous Poems of Count Aleksyey K. T. *RusR* 2 (1943):88-96.

——. Russian Versions of Don Juan (Pushkin and A. K. T). *PMLA* 38 (1923):479-93.

Parsons, N. A Hostage to Art: the Portraits of Boris Godunov by Pushkin and A. K. T. *FMLS* 16 (1980):237-55.

Pavlova, K. Twelve Unpublished Letters to Alexey T. Comp. M. Sendich. *RLT* 9 (1974):541-58.

Simmons, J.S.G. F.M. Dostoevsky and A. K. T: Two Letters. *OSP* 9 (1960):64-72.

Thompson, E. M. Henryk Sienkiewicz and Alexey K. T: A Creative Borrowing. *Polish Review* 17, 3 (1972):52-66.

(See also the bibliography for Koz'ma Prutkov—T was one of the inventors of Prutkov.)

LEO TOLSTOY

Bibliographies

Egan, David R. & Melinda A. Egan. *Leo T: An Annotated Bibliography of English-Language Sources to 1978.* Metuchen, NJ: Scarecrow Press, 1979.

Donskov, A. Most Recent Soviet Publications on T: A Survey. In *Les Littéra-*

tures de langues européenes au tournant du siècle: lecteurs d'aujoud'hui. Série D, Perspective critique soviétique, ed. P. Varnai. Ottawa: Carleton UP, 1984, pp. 1-22.

Terry, G. M. T Studies in Great Britain: A Bibliographical Survey. In *New Essays on T,* ed. M. V. Jones. Cambridge: Cambridge UP, 1978, pp. 223-50.

Wreath, P. J. and A. I. Leo T: A Bibliography of Criticism in English from the Late Nineteenth Century through 1979. *CASS* 14 (1980):466-512.

Translations—Collections

The Works. Tr. L. & A. Maude. 21 vols. Oxford: Milford, 1928-37.
[1-3: Childhood, Boyhood & Youth; 4: Tales of Army Life; 5: 9 Stories; 6-8: War and Peace; 9-10: Anna Karenina; 11: Confession and Gospel in Brief; 12: On Life, and Essays on Religion; 13: 23 Tales; 14: What Then Must We Do?; 15: Ivan Ilyich, and Hadji Murad; 16: The Devil and Cognate Tales; 17: Plays; 18: What is Art? and Essays on Art; 19: Resurrection; 20: The Kingdom of God is within You; 21: Recollections and Essays.]

Darkness and Light: Three Short Works by T. Ed. P. Rudy. NY: Holt, Rinehart & Winston, 1965.
[The Death of Ivan Ilyich; The Power of Darkness; The Fruits of Enlightenment.]

The Death of Ivan Ilych and Other Stories. Tr. J. D. Duff & A. Maude. Afterword by D. Magarshack. NY: New American Library, 1960.
[Family Happiness; The Death of Ivan Ilych; The Kreutzer Sonata; Master and Man.]

Great Short Works of Leo T. In the translations by Louise and Aylmer Maude with an intro. by John Bayley. NY: Harper & Row, 1967.
[Family Happiness; The Cossacks; The Death of Ivan Ilych; The Devil; The Kreutzer Sonata; Master and Man; Father Sergius; Hadji Murat; Alyosha the Pot.]

The Kreutzer Sonata and Other Stories. Tr. Louise & Aylmer Maude. Franklin Center, PA: Franklin Library, 1983.
[The Wood-Felling; Two Hussars; Albert; Polikushka; God Sees the Truth, But Waits; What Men Live By; How Much Land Does a Man Need; Strider, The Story of a Horse; The Death of Ivan Ilych; The Kreutzer Sonata; Master and Man.]

The Portable Tolstoy. Ed. John Bayley. NY: Penguin, 1978.
[The Power of Darkness; A Confession; I Cannot Be Silent; God Sees the Truth; The Kreutzer Sonata; Master and Man; How Much Land; Memoirs of a Madman; The Raid; The Wood-Felling; Two Hussars; Strider; excerpts from other works.]

A Prisoner in the Caucasus and Other Stories. Tr. Yu. Zelenkov. Moscow: Raduga, 1983.
[The Raid; The Wood-Felling; A Prisoner in the Caucasus; Yardstick.]

Short Novels. Selected & intro. by E. J. Simmons. 2 vols. NY: Modern Library, 1965-66.

Short Stories. Tr. M. Wettlin & H. Altschuler. Moscow: Progress, 1969.
[Two Hussars; Yardstick; The Death of Ivan Ilyich; The Kreutzer Sonata; Father Sergius; After the Ball.]

Tolstoy on Art. Ed. Aylmer Maude. Boston: Small, Maynard & Co., 1924.
[Schoolboys and Art; The Last Supper; On Truth in Art; What Is Truth; Introduction to Amiel's Journal; Introduction to Semenov's Peasant Stories; Introduction to Maupassant; On Art; An Introduction to What Is Art?; Preface to What Is Art?; What Is Art?; Shakespeare and the Drama; A Talk on the Drama; Two Kinds of Mental Activity; Preface to Orlov's Album of Russian Peasant; Afterword to Chekhov's The Darling; and other writings on art.]

Tolstoi on Education. Tr. Leo Wiener, intro. Reginald D. Archambault. Chicago: U Chicago P, 1967.

Translations—Fiction

Anna Karenina. Tr. R. Edmonds. Baltimore: Penguin, 1953.

Anna Karenina. The Maude Translation.

Backgrounds and Sources; Essays in Criticism. Ed. G. Gibian. NY: Norton, 1970.

The Cossacks. Tr. Vera Traill. NY: Pantheon, 1949.

The Death of Ivan Ilyich. Tr. Carl R. Proffer in his *From Karamzin to Bunin.* Bloomington: Indiana UP, 1969, pp. 229-83.

Fables and Fairy Tales. Tr. Ann Dunnigan. NY: New American Library, 1962.

Family Happiness. Tr. A. Fitzlyon. London, 1953.

Hadji Murat. Tr. A. Maude. NY: Dodd Mead, 1912.

The Kreutzer Sonata. Tr. I. Kamen. NY: Random House, 1956.

Resurrection. Tr. L. Maude. NY: Grosset, 1927.

Resurrection. Tr. L. Maude with 33 illustrations by L. Pasternak. London: F. R. Henderson, 1900.

The Sebastopol Sketches. Tr. David McDuff. NY: Penguin, 1986.

War and Peace. The Maude Translation. Backgrounds and Sources; Essays in Criticism. Ed. George Gibian. NY: Norton, 1960.

Translations—Non-Fiction

T's Diaries. Ed. & tr. R. F. Christian. NY: Scribners, 1985. 2 vols.

The Diaries of Leo T. Youth, 1847-1852. Tr. C. J. Hogarth. NY: Dutton, 1918.

The Last Diaries of Leo T. Tr. L. Weston-Kesich. NY: Putnam, 1960.

The Private Diary of Leo T, 1853-1857. Tr. L. & A. Maude. NY: Doubleday, 1927.

Essays and Letters. Tr. A. Maude. NY: Funk-Wagnalls, 1909.

Essays from Tula. Intro. Nicolas Berdyayev. London: Sheppard Press, 1948. [Bethink Yourself; The Slavery of Our Times; An Appeal to Social Reformers; True Criticism; I Cannot Be Silent; Thou Shalt Kill No One; A Letter on the Peace Conference; The End of the Age; Love One Another.]

The Four Gospels Harmonized and Translated. Tr. Leo Wiener. Boston: Estes, 1904, 2 vols.

A History of Yesterday. Tr. G. L. Kline.

RusR 8, 2 (1949):142-60.

The Kingdom of God Is within You. Tr. Constance Garnett. Foreword Martin Green. Lincoln: U Nebraska P, 1984.

Letters of T and His Cousin Countess A. A. Tolstoy (1857-1903). Tr. L. Islavin. NY: Dutton, 1929.

Letters. Ed. R. F. Christian. NY: Scribners, 1978, 2 vols.

Literary Fragments, Letters and Reminiscences Not Previously Published. Ed. R. Fülöp-Miller. Tr. P. England. NY: MacVeagh, 1931.

On Civil Disobedience and Non-Violence. NY: Berman Publishers, 1967.

T on Education: T's Educational Writings 1861-62. Ed. A. Pinch & M. Armstrong. Rutherford, NJ: Fairleigh Dickinson UP, 1982.

T's Love Letters. Tr. V. Woolf & S. Koteliansky. London: Hogarth, 1923.

T's Writings on Civil Disobedience and Non-Violence. NY: New American Library, 1968.

What Is Art? Tr. A. Maude. NY: Funk-Wagnalls, 1904.

What Is Art? Tr. A. Maude. Intro. V. Tomas. NY: Bobbs-Merrill, 1960.

Why Do Men Stupefy Themselves and Other Writings by Leo T. Tr. A. Maude. Ed. M. Murray and the editors of *24 Magazine.* Hankins, NY: Strength Books, 1975.

Criticism

Abraham, Gerald. *T.* London: Duckworth, 1935.

Aitken, Eleanor, ed. *Leo T: Master and Man.* NY: Cambridge UP, 1970.

Asquith, Cynthia. *Married to T.* Boston: Houghton Mifflin, 1961.

Baudouin, Charles. *T the Teacher.* Tr. F. Rothwell. NY: Dutton, 1923.

Bayley, John. *T and the Novel.* NY: Viking Press, 1968.

Behrs, Stepan A. *Recollections of Count Leo T Together with a Letter to the*

Women of France on "The Kreutzer Sonata." Tr. C. Turner. London Heinemann, 1896.

Benson, Ruth C. *Women in T: The Ideal and the Erotic.* Urbana: U Illinois P, 1973.

Berlin, Isaiah. *The Hedgehog and the Fox: An Essay on T's View of History.* NY: Simon & Schuster, 1953.

Biriukov, Paul. *Leo T: His Life and Work.* NY: Scribner's, 1906.

___. *The Life of T.* London: Cassell, 1911.

Bloom, Harold, ed. *Leo T.* NY: Chelsea House, 1986.

Bodde, Derk. *T and China.* Princeton: Princeton UP, 1950.

Borras, F. M. *Maxim Gorky and Lev T: An Inaugural Lecture.* Leeds: Leeds UP, 1968.

Brinker, Menachem, ed. *"Anna Karenina"—T.* Jerusalem: Keter, 1984.

Bulgakov, Valentin F. *The Last Year of Leo T.* Tr. Ann Dunnigan, intro. George Steiner. NY: Dial, 1971.

Cain, Thomas. *T.* NY: Harper & Row, 1977.

Canadian-American Slavic Studies. Special T issue: L. N. T: 1828-1910-1978. Vol. 12, no. 4, 1978.

Canadian Slavonic Papers. Special T issue. Vol. 11, no. 3, 1979.

Carroll, Sara N. *The Search: A Biography of Leo T.* NY: Harper & Row, 1973.

Chebotarevskaya, Y., et al. *T's Moscow Home.* Moscow: Foreign Languages Publishing House, 1957.

Chertkov, Vladimir G. *The Last Days of T.* Tr. N. Duddington. Millwood, NY: Kraus, 1973 (reprint of 1922 ed.).

Christian, R. F. *T: A Critical Introduction.* NY: Cambridge UP, 1970.

___. *T's "War and Peace": A Study.* NY: Clarendon, 1962.

Collis, J. S. *Marriage and Genius: Strindberg and T; Studies in Tragi-Comedy.* London: Cassell, 1963.

Coming, Andrew G. *T's "Anna Karenina": The Problem of Form.* Athens: Ohio UP, 1973.

Crankshaw, Edward. *T: The Making of a Novelist.* NY: Viking, 1974.

Craufurd, Alexander H. *The Religion and Ethics of T.* London: Unwin, 1912.

Crosby, Ernest H. *T and His Message.* London: Fifield, 1904.

___. *T as a Schoolmaster.* Chicago: Hammersmark, 1904.

Daniel, C. W. *T's Teaching.* London: C. W. Daniel, 1919.

Darrow, Clarence & Arthur Lewis. *Marx versus T: A Debate.* Chicago: Kerr, 1911.

Davis, Helen E. *T and Nietzsche: A Problem in Biographical Ethics.* Intro. J. Dewey. NY: New Republic, 1929.

Diffey, T. J. *T's "What Is Art?"* London: Croom Helm, 1985.

Dillon, Emile J. *Count Leo T. A New Portrait.* London: Hutchinson, 1934.

Dole, Nathan H. *The Life of Lyof N. T.* Intro. Ilya Tolstoy. NY: Scribner's, 1923.

Duffield, Holley G. & M. Bilsky, eds. *T and the Critics: Literature and Aesthetics.* Chicago: Scott Foresman, 1965.

Eikhenbaum, Boris. *T in the Seventies.* Tr. A. Kaspin. Ann Arbor: Ardis, 1982.

___. *T in the Sixties.* Tr. Duffield White. Ann Arbor: Ardis, 1982.

___. *The Young T.* Tr. G. Kern. Ann Arbor: Ardis, 1972.

Eiloart, Arnold. *Shakespere & T.* Letchworth: Garden City Press, 1909.

Fausset, Hugh I'Anson. *T: The Inner Drama.* NY: Russell & Russell, 1968.

Feitlowitz, Marguerite. *Leo T's "Anna Karenina."* Woodbury, NY: Barron's Educational Series, 1985.

Fodor, Alexander. *T and the Russians.* Ann Arbor: Ardis, 1984.

Forbes, Neville. *T.* London: H. Frowde, 1911.

Fowler, Austin. *Leo T's "War and Peace."* NY: Simon & Schuster, 1965.

Garnett, Edward. *T: His Life and Writings.* Boston: Houghton-Mifflin, 1914; rpt. NY: Haskell House, 1974.

Garrod, H. W. *T's Theory of Art.* Oxford: Clarendon, 1935.

Gibelli, V. *The Life and Times of T.* Tr. from Italian by R. Rudoff. NY: Hamlyn, 1970.

Gibian, George, ed. *Anna Karenina. The Maude Translation: Backgrounds and Sources; Essays in Criticism.* NY: Norton, 1970.

———. *T and Shakespeare.* The Hague: Mouton, 1957.

———. *War and Peace. The Maude Translation: Backgrounds and Sources; Essays in Criticism.* NY: Norton, 1966.

Gifford, Henry, ed. *Leo T. A Critical Heritage.* Harmondsworth: Penguin, 1971.

———. *T.* NY: Oxford UP, 1983.

Goldenweiser, Alexander S. *Crime a Punishment and Punishment a Crime: Leading Thoughts of T's "Resurrection."* Washington, D.C., 1909.

Goldenweizer, A. B. *Talks with T.* Tr. S. Koteliansky & V. Woolf, intro. H. Finch. NY: Horizon, 1969.

Gorky, M. *Reminiscences of T, Chekhov and Andreev.* Tr. K. Mansfield, S. S. Koteliansky & L. Woolf. London: Hogarth Press, 1948.

Gottschling, A. *Tsar and T Played Out.* London, 1899.

Green, K. R. *Leo T.* London: Commercial Press, 1935.

Green, Martin. *The Origins of Non-Violence: T and Gandhi in Their Historical Settings.* University Park: Pennsylvania State UP, 1986.

———. *T and Gandhi: Men of Peace.* NY: Basic Books, 1983.

Greenwood, E. B. *T: The Comprehensive Vision.* NY: St. Martin's Press, 1975.

Gudzii, N. K. *Leo T. 1828-1910.* N.p., n.p., 1953.

Gunn, Elizabeth. *A Daring Coiffeur: Reflections on "War and Peace" and "Anna Karenina."* Totowa, NJ: Rowman & Littlefield, 1971.

Gustafson, Richard. *Leo T: Resident and Stranger: A Study in Fiction and Theology.* Princeton: Princeton UP, 1986.

Harrison, I. H. *T as Preacher.* London: W. Scott, 1895.

Hayman, Ronald. *T.* NY: Humanities, 1970.

Hoffman, Modest & Andre Pierre. *By Deeds of Truth: The Life of Leo T.* Tr. R. Fermaud. NY: Orion, 1958.

Holmes, John Haynes. *Leo T: A Sermon.* NY: Church of the Messiah, 1911.

Jamosky, Edward. *T's "Cossacks": An Analysis.* Ames: Iowa State U, 1985.

Jones, Malcom, ed. *New Essays on T.* Cambridge: Cambridge UP, 1978.

Jones, P. *Philosophy and the Novel: Philosophical Aspects of "Middlemarch," "Anna Karenina," "The Brothers Karamazov," "A la recherche du temps perdu."* Oxford: Clarendon Press, 1975.

Juhasz, Leslie A. *T's "War and Peace."* NY: Barrister, 1966.

Kamakhya-Natha, Mitra. *The New Pilgrim's Progress; or, T, the Man and the Meaning of Life.* Bankipur, 1909.

Kenworthy, John. *A Pilgrimage to T.* London: Brotherhood, 1896.

———. *T: His Life and Works.* NY: Haskell, 1971 (rpt. of 1902 ed.).

Kerr, Walter B. *The Shabunin Affair: An Episode in the Life of Leo T.* Ithaca: Cornell UP, 1982.

Knight, George W. *Shakespeare and T.* London: English Association, 1934.

Knowles, A. V. *T: The Critical Heritage.* London: Routledge Kegan Paul, 1978.

Knowlson, T. Sharper. *Leo T. A Biographical and Critical Study.* London: Warne, 1904.

Koelb, Clayton, ed. *Thomas Mann's "Goethe and T": Notes and Sources.* University, AL: U Alabama P, 1984.

Kuzminskaya, Tatyana A. *T as I Knew Him: My Life at Home and at Yasnaya Polyana.* Tr. N. Sigersit, et al., intro. E. J. Simmons. NY: Macmillan, 1948.

Kvitko, David. *A Philosophic Study of T.* NY: Columbia UP, 1927.

Lacey, R., ed. *"War and Peace": A Full Guide to the Serial.* London: BBC, 1972.

Lavrin, Janko. *T: A Psycho-Critical Study.* London: Collins, 1924.

———. *T: An Approach.* NY: Russell and Russell, 1968.

Lednicki, Waclaw. *T between "War and Peace."* The Hague: Mouton, 1965.

Lehrman, Edgar. *A Guide to the Russian Texts of T's "War and Peace."* Ann Arbor: Ardis, 1979.

Lenin, V. *Lenin on Leo T.* Moscow: Novosti, 1972.

Leon, Derrick. *T: His Life and Work.* London: Routledge, 1944.

Lloyd, J. A. T. *Two Russian Reformers: Ivan Turgenev, Leo T.* London: Paul, 1912.

Lubbock, Percy. *The Craft of Fiction.* NY: Viking, 1964.

Lukacs, Gyorgy. *Studies in European Realism.* Tr. E. Bone. London: Hillway, 1950; NY: Grosset & Dunlap, 1964.

Matlaw, Ralph E., ed. *T. A Collection of Critical Essays.* Englewood Cliffs, NJ: Prentice-Hall, 1967.

Matual, D. *T's Interpretation and Translation of the Gospel.* Belmont, MA: Nordland House, 1982.

Maude, Aylmer. *Family Views of T.* London: Allen & Unwin, 1926.

___. *The Life of T.* 2 vols. Oxford: Oxford UP, 1930.

___. *T on Art and Its Critics.* London: Milford, 1925.

Merezhkovski, Dmitri. *T as Man and Artist, with an Essay on Dostoevski.* Westport, CT: Greenwood Reprint, 1970.

Micek, Eduard. *The Real T.* Austin, TX: Czech Literary Society, 1958.

___. *T, the Artist and Humanist: Impressions and Evaluations.* Austin, TX: Czech Literary Society, 1961.

Mishchenko, A. I. *Yasnaya Polyana.* Tr. A. Weise. Tula, 1966.

Mittal, Sarla. *T: Social and Political Ideas.* Meerut, India: Meenakshi Prakashan, 1966.

Mooney, Harry J. *T's Epic Vision: A Study of "War and Peace" and "Anna Karenina."* Tulsa: U Tulsa P, 1968.

Morson, Gary Saul. *Hidden In Plain View.* Stanford: Stanford UP, 1987.

Nazaroff, Alexander I. *T, The Inconstant Genius: A Biography.* NY: Stokes, 1929.

Newton, William Wilberforce. *A Run through Russia: The Story of a Visit to Count T.* Hartford, CT: Student Publishing Co., 1894.

Noyes, George R. *T.* NY: Dover, 1968.

Perris, George H. *The Life and Teaching of T.* London: Richards, 1904.

___. *Leo T, the Grand Mujik: A Study in Personal Evolution.* London: Unwin, 1898.

Philipson, Morris. *The Count Who Wished He Were a Peasant.* NY: Random House, 1967.

Polner, Tikhon. *T and His Wife.* Tr. N. Wreden. NY: Norton, 1945.

Rappoport, Angelo Solomon. *T: His Life, Works, and Doctrine.* London: New Age Press, 1908.

Reaske, Herbert E. *Leo T's "Anna Karenina."* NY: Simon & Schuster, 1965.

Redfern, P. *T: A Study.* London: Fifield, 1907.

Redpath, Theodore. *T.* NY: Hillary House, 1960.

Rolland, Romain. *T.* Tr. Bernard Miall. NY: Dutton, 1911; rpt. Port Washington, NY: Kennikat, 1972.

Rothkopf, Carol Z. *Leo T.* NY: Franklin Watts, 1968.

Rowe, William W. *Leo T.* Boston: Twayne, 1986.

Salaman, E. *The Great Confession: From Aksakov and De Quincey to T and Proust.* London: Allen Lane, 1973.

Sampson, R. V. *T: The Discovery of Peace.* London: Heinemann, 1973.

Sarolea, Charles. *Count Leo T: Life and Work.* London, 1912.

Schultze, Sydney. *The Structure of "Anna Karenina."* Ann Arbor: Ardis, 1982.

Seltzer, Thomas. *T: A Critical Study of Him and His Works.* NY: Werner, 1901.

Sergyeenko, P. A. *How Count L. N. Lives and Works.* Tr. I. F. Hapgood. NY: Crowell, 1899.

Shklovsky, Viktor. *Lev T.* Moscow: Progress, 1978.

Silbajoris, Frank R. *T's Esthetics and the Modern Idiom in Art.* Occasional paper no. 197. Washington, D.C.: Woodrow Wilson International Center for Scholars, Kennan Institute, 1985.

Simmons, Ernest J. *Introduction to T's Writings*. Chicago: U Chicago P, 1968.

——. *Leo T.* Boston: Little Brown, 1946; rpt. NY: Vintage, 1961, 2 vols.

——. *T.* Boston: Routledge & Kegan Paul, 1972.

Sorokin, Boris. *T in Prerevolutionary Russian Criticism*. Columbus: Published by Ohio State University Press for Miami University, 1979.

Speirs, Logan. *T and Chekhov*. Cambridge: Cambridge UP, 1971.

Spence, G. W. *T the Ascetic*. NY: Barnes & Noble, 1968.

Stanoyevich, Milivoy S. *T's Theory of Social Reform: His Doctrine of Law, Money and Property*. NY: Columbia UP, 1926.

Steiner, Edward A. *T, The Man*. NY: Outlook, 1904.

——. *T, The Man and His Message*. NY: Revell, 1908.

Steiner, George. *T or Lostoevsky. An Essay in the Old Criticism*. NY: Random House, 1959.

Stenbock-Fermor, E. *The Architecture of "Anna Karenina": A History of Its Writing, Structure and Message*. Lisse: P. de Ridder Press, 1975.

Stockham, Alice B. *T: A Man of Peace*. Chicago: Stockham, 1900.

Sturman, Marianne. *"Anna Karenina": Notes*. Lincoln: Cliff's Notes, 1965.

——. *"War and Peace": Notes*. Lincoln: Cliff's Notes, 1967.

Sukhotin-Tolstoy, Tatiana. *The T Home*. Tr. A. Brown. NY: AMS, 1966.

Tchertkoff, Vladimir. *The Last Days of T.* Tr. Nathalie A. Duddington. NY: Kraus, 1973.

Tolstoy, Alexandra. *The Real T: A Critique and Commentary on the Book "T" by Henri Troyat*. Morristown, NJ: H. S. Evans, 1968.

——. *T. A Life of My Father*. Tr. Elizabeth R. Hapgood. NY: Octagon, 1973.

——. *The Tragedy of T.* Tr. E. Varneck. New Haven: Yale UP, 1933.

Tolstoy, Ilya. *Reminiscences of T by His Son Count Ilya T.* Tr. G. Calderon. London: Chapman & Hall, 1914.

——. *T, My Father: Reminiscences*. Tr. A. Dunnigan. Chicago: Cowles, 1971.

Tolstoy, Leo L. *The Truth about My Father*. London: Murray, 1924.

Tolstoy, Sergei. *T Remembered by his Son Sergei T.* Tr. M. Budberg. NY: Atheneum, 1962.

Tolstoy, Sofia. *The Autobiography of Countess Sophie T.* Tr. S. Koteliansky & L. Woolf. London: Hogarth, 1922.

——. *The Countess T's Later Diary, 1891-1897*. Tr. & intro. A. Werth. Freeport, NY: Books for Libraries, 1971 (rpt. of 1929 ed.).

——. *The Diary of T's Wife, 1860-1891*. Tr. A. Werth. London: Gollancz, 1928.

——. *The Final Struggle, Being Countess T's Diary for 1910*. Intro. by A. Maude & S. Tolstoy. NY: Oxford, 1936.

Townsend, R. S. *T for the Young*. London: Paul, 1916.

Troyat, Henri. *Firebrand: The Life of T.* Tr. Norbert Guterman. NY: Roy, 1946.

——. *T.* Tr. Nancy Amphoux. Garden City: Doubleday, 1969.

Turberville, A. C. *Leo T.* London: E. Dalton, 1908.

Turner, Charles E. *Count T as Novelist and Thinker*. NY: Haskell, 1974 (rpt. of 1888 ed.).

Waleffe, Pierre. *Leo T.* Tr. A. Negro. Geneva: Minerva, 1969.

Walsh, Walter. *T's Emblems, Collected by Walter Walsh*. London: Daniel, 1909.

Wasiolek, Edward. *T's Major Fiction*. Chicago: U Chicago P, 1978.

——, ed. & intro. *Critical Essays on T.* Boston: G. K. Hall, 1986.

Winstanley, Lilian. *T.* London: T. C. & E. C. Jack, 1914.

Zweers, Alexander F. *Grown-Up Narrator and Childlike Hero: An Analysis of the Literary Devices Employed in T's Trilogy "Chilhood, Boyhood and Youth."* The Hague: Mouton, 1971.

Dissertations

Abcarian, Gilbert. Political Romanticism: Coleridge and T. Ph.D. diss., California, 1957.

Adams, Eleanora Karpinicz. Franz Werfel and L. N. T: Affinities and Contrasts. Ph.D. diss., Pennsylvania, 1973.

Ater, Leroy Early, Jr. An Examination of Three Major Novels in World Literature in the Light of Critical Precepts Derived from T's *What Is Art?"* Ph.D. diss., Southern California, 1964.

Bakalar, Paul Francis. A Critique of Leo T's *What is Art?* Ph.D. diss., Northwestern, 1976.

Bakst, James. A Comparative Study of the Philosophies of Music in the Works of Schopenhauer, Nietzsche and T. Ph.D. diss., New York University, 1942.

Benson, Ruth Crego. The Ideal and the Erotic: T's Heroines in Love and Marriage. Ph.D. diss., Yale, 1969.

Boyd, Joan. Patterns of Imagery in T's Major Fiction: A Phenomenological Study. Ph.D. diss., Chicago, 1985.

Bradshaw, David Gerald. The Aesthetic Treatment of Historical, Moral, and Philosophical Themes in L. N. T's *Vojna i mir* and Victor Hugo's *Les Misérables*. Ph.D. diss., North Carolina, 1974.

Brown, Leon. T and Flaubert as Inner Monologuists and Creative Portraitists in Their Major Novels. Ph.D. diss., New York, 1981.

Buyniak, Victor. Leo Nikolaevich T and the Early English Victorian Novelists: William Makepeace Thackeray, Charles Dickens, Anthony Trollope and George Eliot. Ph.D. diss., Ottawa, 1970.

Cohen, Elliot Franklin. The Genre of the Autobiographical Account of Childhood—Three Test Cases: The Trilogies of T, Aksakov, and Gorky. Ph.D. diss., Yale, 1973.

Csicsery-Ronay, Istvan, Jr. The Realistic Historical Novel and the Mythology of Liberal Nationalism: Scott, Manzoni, Eötvös, Kemény, T. Ph.D. diss., Princeton, 1982.

Davis, Helen E. T and Nietzsche: A Problem in Biographical Ethics. Ph.D. diss., Columbia, 1929.

Eros, Carol Carbone. T's Tales of the Caucasus and Literary Tradition. Ph.D. diss., Wisconsin, 1973.

Feuer, Kathryn. The Genesis of *War and Peace*. Ph.D. diss., Columbia, 1965.

Fleetwood, Janet Rye. The Spiderweb and the Beehive: A Study of Multiplicity in George Eliot's *Middlemarch* and T's *Anna Karenina*. Ph.D. diss., Indiana, 1977.

Girona, Ilse. T on Art: A Study of His Fiction and His Essays in Criticism. Ph.D. diss., Chicago, 1984.

Grimes, William H. The Critical Reception of T in England, 1880-1910. Ph.D. diss., Chicago, 1982.

Gubler, Donworth V. A Study of Illness and Death in the Loves and Representative Works of Leo T and Thomas Mann. Ph.D. diss., Brigham Young, 1971.

Guffee, Ruth Meyer. The Yasnaya Polyana School 1859-1862: Its Place in Leo T's Development as a Writer and Thinker. Ph.D. diss., Yale, 1980.

Gurley, Robert Eugene. The Diaries of Leo T: Their Literariness and Relationship to His Literature. Ph.D. diss., Pennsylvania, 1979.

Hamblin, Ellen N. Adulterous Heroines in Nineteenth-Century Literature: A Comparative Literature Study. Ph.D. diss., Florida State, 1977.

Hecht, Leo. Freedom for the Individual: T's Struggle Against Authority. Ph.D. diss., Columbia, 1974.

Hogan, Rebecca S. H. The Wisdom of Many, the Wit of One: The Narrative Function of the Proverbs in T's *Anna Karenina* and Trollope's *Orley Farm*. Ph.D. diss., Colorado, 1984.

Jahn, Gary Robert. L. N. T's Stories for the People on the Theme of Brotherly Love. Ph.D. diss., Wisconsin, 1972.

Kornman, William Raymond. T and the Drama. Ph.D. diss., Stanford, 1973.

Krzyzanowski, Jerzy Roman. Turgenev, T and W. D. Howells. Ph.D. diss., Michigan, 1965.

Kuk, Zenon Michael. T's *War and Peace* and Zeromski's *Ashes:* A Comparative Study. Ph.D. diss., Ohio State, 1973.

Kvitko, David. A Philosophic Study of T. Ph.D. diss., Columbia, 1927.

Lewis, Robert Peter. Deception and Revelation: A Study of Three Systems of Characterization in T's *War and Peace*. Ph.D. diss., Columbia, 1972.

Low, Frederick. The Troubled Heroine: Flaubert's Emma, T's Anna, Goethe's Gretchen and the Condition of Feminine Fulfillment. Ph.D. diss., CUNY, 1972.

Matual, David Michael. T's *Vlast' t'my:* History and Analysis. Ph.D. diss., Wisconsin, 1971.

Mitchell, Paul MacArthur, Jr. Lev Nikolaevich T in Pre-Soviet Russian Literary Criticism. Ph.D. diss., Indiana, 1977.

Moore, A. Ulrich. Art, Community and Theatre: A Study of the Theories of Five Nineteenth-Century Artists: T, Wagner, Nietzsche, Appia, Rolland. Ph.D. diss., Cornell, 1936.

Murphy, Terry Wade. Dostoevsky and T on Dickens' Christianity. Ph.D. diss., Kent State, 1973.

Naginski, Isabelle Hoog. Stendhal and T: A Study in Literary Kinship. Ph.D. diss., Columbia, 1982.

Orwin, Donna Louise Tussing. The Relationship of Nature and Morality in the Early Works of Lev T. Ph.D. diss., Harvard, 1979.

Patterson, David Alan. The Literary and Philosophical Expressions of Existential Faith: A Study of Kierkegaard, T and Shestov. Ph.D. diss., Oregon, 1978.

Rempel, Margareta. Leo T, Gerhart Hauptmann and Maxim Gorky: A Comparative Study. Ph.D. diss., Iowa, 1960.

Rudy, Peter. Young Leo T and Laurence Sterne. Ph.D. diss., Columbia, 1957.

Schultze, Sydney Patterson. *Anna Karenina:* A Structural Analysis. Ph.D. diss., Indiana, 1974.

Silberman, Marsha. T and America: A Study in Reciprocal Influence. Ph.D. diss., CUNY, 1979.

Smith, J. Allan. T's Fiction in England and America. Ph.D. diss., Illinois, 1939.

Sorokin, Boris. Lev T in Pre-Revolutionary Russian Criticism. Ph.D. diss., Chicago, 1974.

Tumas, Elena Valiute. The Literary Kinship of Leo N. T and Romain Rolland: A Comparative Study of the Epic Dimensions of *War and Peace* and *Jean Christophe.* Ph.D. diss., Southern California, 1964.

Zborilek, Vladimir. T and Rousseau: A Study in Literary Relationship. Ph.D. diss., California, Berkeley, 1969.

Zimmerman, John F. Leo T and the Period of Liberation, 1894-1910. Ph.D. diss., Harvard, 1961.

Critical Articles

For additional entries see *Leo T: An Annotated Bibliography of English-Language Sources to 1978,* compiled by David R. Egan and Melinda A. Egan.

Adamovitch, G. T as an Artist. *RusR* 19 (1960):140-49.

Addams, Jane. A Visit to T. *McClure's* 36 (1911):295-302.

Aldanov, Mark A. New Light on T. *Slavonic Review* 6 (1927):162-67.

_____. Some Observations on T. *Slavonic Review* 5 (1926):305-14.

_____. Some Reflections on T and Tolstoyism. *Slavonic Review* 7 (1929):482-92.

Alexandrov, Vladimir E. Relative Time in *Anna Karenina. RusR* 41 (1982):159-68.

Allisandratos, J. Leo T's "Father Sergius" and the Russian Hagiographical Tradition. *Cyrillomethodianum* 8-9 (1984-85): 146-64.

Alter, Robert. The Novel and the Sense of the Past. *Salmagundi* 68-69 (1985-86):91-106.

Anschuetz, C. The Young T and Rousseau's *Discourse on Inequality. RusR* 39 (1980):401-25.

Anzulic, Branimir. T and the Novel. *Genre* 3 (1970):1-16.

Arkhangelskaya, T. In the Yasnaya Polyana Library. *Soviet Literature* 10 (1975):127-30.

Armstrong, Judith. *The Novel of Adultery.* London: Macmillan, 1976. [See index for extensive commentary on *Anna Karenina* and other works by T.]

_____. T's Lost Childhood. *Journal of the Australasian Universities Modern Languages and Literatures Association* 65 (1986):16-35.

Arnold, Matthew. *Anna Karenina* as Life, Not Literature. In *Anna Karenina. The Maude Translation,* ed. George Gibian. NY: W. W. Norton, 1970, pp. 798-801.

___. Count Leo T. In his *Essays in Criticism* (2d series). London: Macmillan, 1896, pp. 253-99. Also in *Critical Essays on T,* ed. Edward Wasiolek. Boston: G. K. Hall & Co., 1986, pp. 134-43.

Auchincloss, Louis. James and the Russian Novelists. In his *Reflections of a Jacobite.* Boston: Houghton Mifflin, 1961, pp. 157-71.

Baeza, Richard. Talks with T. *Living Age* 319 (1923):70-75.

Bagby, Lewis & Pavel Sigalov. The Semiotics of Names and Naming in T's *The Cossacks. SEEJ* 31, 4 (1987):473-89.

Bailey, L. T as a Playwright. *Drama* 110 (1973):50-55.

Baring, Maurice. T and Dostoevsky. In his *An Outline of Russian Literature.* NY: Holt, 1915, pp. 196-225.

___. T and Tourgeniev. In his *Landmarks of Russian Literature.* NY: Barnes & Noble, 1960, pp. 50-73.

___. T's Last Play. In *Punch and Judy and Other Essays.* Garden City, NY: Doubleday, 1924, pp. 327-32.

Barksdale, E. C. T: Consciousness Expanded. In his *Daggers of the Mind.* Lawrence, KS: Coronado Press, 1979, pp. 109-21.

Barrett, William. Existentialism as a Symptom of Man's Contemporary Crisis. In *Spiritual Problems in Contemporary Literature,* ed. S. Hopper. NY: Harper, 1952, pp. 139-52.

Bartell, James. The Trauma of Birth in *The Death of Ivan Ilich:* A Therapeutic Reading. *Psychocultural Review* 2 (1978): 97-117.

Baudouin, Charles. T and the Realist Faith. In *Contemporary Studies.* Freeport, NY: Books for Libraries, 1969, pp. 24-27.

Baumgarten, Murray. Irtenev, Olenin, Levin: Three Characters in Search of Nature. *Centennial Review* 14 (1970): 188-200.

Bayley, John. Family versus Group as Formal Techniques of the Novelist. *Arizona Quarterly* 36 (1980):21-34.

___. The Worlds of Love. In *The Characters of Love: A Study in the Literature of Personality.* NY: Basic Books, 1960, pp. 22-26. [*Anna Karenina.*]

___. and Timothy Binyon. War and Peace: An Exchange. *Essays in Criticism* 18 (1968):100-4.

Beach, Joseph Warren. Dramatic Interest: Thackeray, T. In *The Twentieth Century Novel: Studies in Technique.* NY: Century, 1932.

Bellman, Harold. Leo T. In *Architects of the New Age.* London: Sampson Low, Marston, 1929, pp. 141-61.

Berenson, B. The Writings of T. *Harvard Monthly* 3 (1887):138-49.

Berlin, Isaiah. The Dilemma of History. In *Critical Essays on T,* ed. Edward Wasiolek. Boston: G. K. Hall & Co., 1986, pp. 104-7.

___. T and Enlightenment. *Encounter* 16 (1961):29-40; reprinted in his *Russian Thinkers.* NY: Penguin, 1978, pp. 238-60; also in *T: A Collection of Critical Essays.* Englewood Cliffs, NJ: Prentice-Hall, 1967, pp. 28-51.

Bernstein, Herman. Leo T. In *Celebrities of Our Time.* Freeport, NY: Books for Libraries, 1968, pp. 3-16.

Beveridge, Albert J. Three Russians of World Fame. In *The Russian Advance.* NY: Harper & Brothers, 1904, pp. 426-62.

Bidney, Martin. Water, Movement, Roundness: The Epiphanic Pattern in T's *War and Peace. Texas Studies in Language and Literature* 23 (1981): 232-47.

Bier, Jesse. A Century of *War and Peace*— Gone, Gone with the Wind. *Genre* 4 (1971):107-41.

Birkett, G. A. Official Plans for T's Funeral in 1902. *SEER* 30 (1951):2-6.

Black, Michael. Anna Karenina and the Cost of Self-Fulfillment. In his *The Literature of Fidelity.* London: Chatto & Windus, 1975, pp. 103-24.

Blackmur, R. P. The Dialectic of Incarnation: T's *Anna Karenina.* In his *Eleven Essays in the European Novel.* NY: Harcourt Brace, 1964, pp. 3-26.

Bloom, Harold. Homer, Virgil, T: The Epic Hero. *Raritan* 6, 1 (1986):1-25.

Blumberg, Edwina J. T and the English Novel: A Note on *Middlemarch* and *Anna Karenina. SlavR* 30 (1971):561-69.

Bondanella, Peter F. Rousseau, the Pastoral Genre, and T's *The Cossacks. Southern Humanities Review* 3 (1969): 288-92.

Borker, David. Sentential Structure in T's "Smert' Ivana Il'icha." In *American Contributions to the Eighth International Congress of Slavists,* vol. 1, ed. H. Birnbaum. Columbus: Slavica, 1978, pp. 180-94.

Borras, F. M. A Common Theme in T, Andreyev and Bunin. *SEER* 32, 78 (1953):230-35.

Boyd, Alexander F. An Anatomy of Marriage: Leo T and *Anna Karenina.* In *Aspects of the Russian Novel.* London: Chatto & Windus, 1972, pp. 87-108.

Briggs, A. D. P. "Hadji Murat": The Power of Understatement. In *New Essays on T,* ed. M. V. Jones. Cambridge: Cambridge UP, 1978, pp. 109-27.

Brostrom, K. N. Ethical Relativism in *Anna Karenina. American Contributions to the Eighth International Congress of Slavists,* vol. 2, ed. V. Terras. Columbus: Slavica, 1978, pp. 96-124.

Brown, E. K. Interweaving Themes. In *Rhythm in the Novel.* Toronto: U Toronto P, 1963, pp. 78-85.

Browning, Gary L. The Death of Anna Karenina: Anna's Share of the Blame. *SEEJ* 30 (1986):327-39.

Buck, Philo M. The Perplexed Spirit—T. In *The World's Great Age: The Story of a Century's Search for a Philosophy of Life.* NY: Macmillan, 1936, pp. 166-96.

Bullitt, M. M. Rousseau and T: Childhood and Confession. *Comparative Literature Studies* 16, 1 (1979):12-20.

Bunin, Ivan A. Leo T. In his *Memoirs and Portraits.* Garden City, NY: Doubleday, 1951, pp. 17-30.

——. My Meetings with T. *Contemporary Review* 145 (1934):591-99.

——. My Reminiscences of T. *Dial* 83 (1927):271-82.

Burgin, Diana L. Jungian Dactyls on Death and T: Verse Burlesque with Notation in Earnest. In *New Studies in Russian Language and Literature,* ed.

A. Crone. Columbus: Slavica, 1986, pp. 27-38.

Bychkov, S. O. The Social Bases of *Anna Karenina.* In *Anna Karenina. The Maude Translation,* ed. G. Gibian. NY: Norton, 1970, pp. 822-35.

Cahan, Abraham. Posthumous Works of T. In *Critical Essays on T,* ed. Edward Wasiolek. Boston: G. K. Hall & Co., 1986, pp. 168-73.

Cain, T. T's Use of *David Copperfield. Critical Quarterly* 15 (1973):238-46.

Cairns, Huntington, et al. Leo T, *War and Peace.* In *Invitation to Learning.* NY: New Home Library, 1942, pp. 154-66.

Calder, Angus. Man, Woman and Male Woman: T's *Anna Karenina* and After. In *Russia Discovered: Nineteenth-Century Fiction from Pushkin to Chekhov.* NY: Harper & Row, 1976, pp. 209-36.

Calderon, George L. The Wrong T. *Monthly Review* 3, 8 (1901):129-41.

Call, Paul. Anna Karenina's Crime and Punishment: The Impact of Historical Theory Upon the Russian Novel. *Mosaic* 1 (1967):94-102.

Carden, Patricia. Career in *War and Peace. Ulbandus Review* 2 (1982):23-38.

——. The Recuperative Powers of Memory: T's *War and Peace.* In *The Russian Novel from Pushkin to Pasternak,* ed. J. Garrard. New Haven: Yale UP, 1983, pp. 81-102.

Carr, E. H. Two Russians: T and Turgenev. *Fortnightly Review* 132 (1929): 823-26.

Castro, Dominador C. Constantine Dimitrich Levin: A Contemporary Christian Agnostic Poor in Spirit. *St. Louis University Research Journal of Arts and Sciences* 6 (1975):306-24.

Chandler, Frank W. Exponents of Russian Realism: T and Gorky. In his *Modern Continental Playwrights.* NY: Harper & Row, 1931, pp. 64-78.

Chapple, Richard L. The Role and Function of Nature in L. N. Tolstoy's *War and Peace. NZSJ* 11 (1973):86-101.

Chernyshevsky, N. G. *Childhood* and *Boyhood,* and *Army Tales* by Count L. N. T. In *Leo T: A Critical Anthology,* ed. H. Gifford. Harmondsworth: Penguin, 1971, pp. 30-34.

——. T's *Childhood*. In *Critical Essays on T,* ed. Edward Wasiolek. Boston: G. K. Hall & Co., 1986, pp. 39-44.

Chertkova, Anna. The Question of T's Posthumous Works. *RusR* 3, 2 (1914): 165-70.

Christian, R. F. The Later Stories. In *Critical Essays on T,* ed. Edward Wasiolek. Boston: G. K. Hall & Co., 1986, pp. 179-91.

——. The Passage of Time in *Anna Karenina. SEER* 44, 104 (1967):207-10.

——. The Problem of Tendentiousness in *Anna Karenina. CSP* 21 (1979):276-88.

——. Style in *War and Peace*. In *T: A Collection of Critical Essays,* ed. R. Matlaw. Englewood Cliffs, NJ: Prentice-Hall, 1967, pp. 102-10.

——. The Theme of Art of *War and Peace.* In *War and Peace. The Maude Translation* ed. G. Gibian. NY: Norton, 1966, pp. 1456-80.

——. T's Letters. A Portrait of the Writer, Thinker and Man. *Scottish Slavonic Review* (1985):89-107.

Clayre, Alasdair. Levin in the Fields. In his *Work and Play: Ideas and Experiences of Work and Leisure.* NY: Harper & Row, 1974, pp. 147-50.

Clifford, E. *War and Peace* and the Dynasts. *Modern Philology* 54 (1956): 33-44.

Clive, G. T and the Varieties of the Inauthentic. In his *The Broken Icon.* NY: Macmillan, 1970, pp. 86-127.

Cockerell, Sydney. Count Leo T. In *Friends of a Lifetime,* ed. V. Meynell. London: Cape, 1940, pp. 78-86.

Cockrell, C. R. S. and D. J. Richards. T: *War and Peace*. In *The Voice of a Giant: Essays on Seven Russian Prose Classics,.* ed. R. Cockrell & D. Richards. Exeter: U. Exeter, 1985, pp. 81-102.

Cockrell, R. The Bayreuth Connection: T as a Wagnerophile. *JRS* 44 (1982):34-42.

Cook, Albert. The Moral Vision: T. In *The Meaning of Fiction.* Detroit: Wayne State UP, 1960, pp. 179-201.

——. The Unity of *War and Peace*. In *War and Peace. The Maude Translation,* ed.

G. Gibian. NY: Norton, 1966, pp. 1398-1411.

Crawford, Virginia M. *War and Peace*. In her *Studies in Foreign Literature.* Port Washington, NY: Kennikat, 1970.

Creelman, James. The Avatar of Count T. T and His People. In his *On the Great Highway.* Boston: Lothrop, 1901, pp. 120-56.

Cruise, Edwina. The Ideal Woman in T's *Resurrection. CASS* 11 (1977):281-86.

Curtis, James. Anticipations of *War and Peace* in T's Early Fiction. *Ulbandus Review* 2 (1982):52-78.

——. The Function of Imagery in *War and Peace. SlavR* 29 (1970):460-80.

——. Notes on Spatial Form in T. *Sewanee Review* 78 (1970):517-30.

Darrow, Clarence. Leo T. In *Verdicts Out of Court.* Chicago: Quadrangle, 1963, pp. 186-200.

Dataller, Roger. The Historical Novel. In *The Plain Man and the Novel.* London: Nelson, 1940, pp. 47-62.

Debreczeny, Paul. The Device of Conspicuous Silence in T, Čexov and Faulkner. *American Contributions to the Eighth International Congress of Slavists,* vol. 2, ed. V. Terras. Columbus: Slavica, 1978, pp.125-44.

——. Freedom and Necessity: A Reconsideration of *War and Peace. Papers on Language and Literature* 7 (1971):185-98.

De Haard, Eric. L. N. T's "Metel'" (The Snowstorm). In *Russische Erzählung—Russian Short Story: Utrechter Symposium zur Theorie und Geschichte der russischen Erzählung im 19. und 20. Jahrhundert,* ed. R. Grübel. Amsterdam: Rodopi, 1984, pp. 239-59.

——. On Narration in *Vojna i mir. RusL* 7 (1979):95-120.

——. T's "Zapiski markera" and the Russian Prose Tradition. In *Dutch Contributions to the Ninth International Congress of Slavists, Kiev, Sept. 6-14, 1983,* ed. A. G. F van Holk. Amsterdam: Rodopi, 1983, pp. 83-109.

Donnelly, John. Death and Ivan Ilych. In *Language. Metaphysics and Death,* NY: Fordham UP, 1978, pp. 116-30.

Donskov, Andre. L. N. T's Sources for His Play *The First Distiller. CSP* 15 (1973):

375-81.

___. Most Recent Soviet Publications on T: A Survey. *Les Littératures de langues européenes au tournant du siècle: lecteurs d'aujourd'hui, Serie D.,* ed. Paul Varnai. Ottawa: Carleton UP, 1984, pp. 1-22.

___. A Note on "Schwere Fragen" in T. *Germano-Slavica* 3 (1986):107-16.

___. The Peasant in T's Thought and Writings. *CSP* 21 (1979):183-96.

___. T and Galsworthy: Similarities and Parallels. *Germano-Slavica* 2 (1977): 157-68.

___. T's Peasant Plays—The Peasant as the Natural Educator. In *The Changing Image of the Peasant in Nineteenth-Century Russian Drama.* Helsinki: Finnish Academy of Sciences, 1972, pp. 117-58.

___. T's Use of Proverbs in *Power of Darkness. RusL* 9 (1974-75):67-80.

Dostoevsky, F. *Anna Karenina.* In his *The Diary of a Writer.* NY: Scribners, 1949, pp. 783-95. Also in In *Critical Essays on T,* ed. Edward Wasiolek. Boston: G. K. Hall & Co., 1986, pp. 127-33.

Dragomirov, M. I. Count T's *War and Peace* from a Military Standpoint. In *Leo T: A Critical Anthology,* ed. H. Gifford. Harmondsworth: Penguin, 1971, pp. 42-44.

Dubbink, J. H. L. Šestov and L. T. In *Dutch Contributions to the Sixth International Congress of Slavists.* The Hague: Mouton, 1968, pp. 33-50.

Ducusin, Dionisio S. The Experience of Nothingness in *Anna Karenina:* A Study of the Essential Differences of Anna and Alexandrovitch. *St. Louis University Research Journal of Arts and Sciences* 6 (1975):293-305.

Dukas, Vytas & Glenn A. Sandstorm. Taoistic Patterns in *War and Peace. SEEJ* 14, 2 (1970):182-93.

Dukes, Ashley, T and Gorky. In his *Modern Dramatists.* Freeport, NY: Books for Libraries, 1967, pp. 181-89.

Dupuy, Ernest. Lyof T. In his *Great Masters of Russian Literature.* NY: Crowell, 1886, pp. 215-338.

Dworsky, Nancy. *Hadji Murat:* A Summary and a Vision. *Novel* 8 (1975):138-46.

Dyck, J. W. Aspects of Nihilism in German and Russian Literature: Nietzsche-T. *Humanities Association Review* 25 (1974):187-96.

Edel, Leon. Portrait of the Artist as an Old Man. In *Aging, Death and the Completion of Being,* ed. D. D. van Tassel. Philadelphia: U Pennsylvania P, 1979, pp. 193-214.

Edgerton, William B. The Artist Turned Prophet: Leo T after 1880. In *American Contributions to the Sixth International Congress of Slavists,* vol. 2, ed. W. E. Harkins. The Hague: Mouton, 1968, pp. 61-85.

___. The Critical Reception Abroad of T's *What Is Art?* In *American Contributions to the Eighth International Congress of Slavists,* vol. 2, ed. V. Terras. Columbus: Slavica, 1978, pp. 146-64.

___. T, Immortality and Twentieth-Century Physics. *CSP* 21 (1979):289-300.

Eikhenbaum, Boris. *Anna Karenina* and the Literary Tradition. In *Anna Karenina. The Maude Translation,* ed. G. Gibian. NY: Norton, 1970, pp. 810-11.

___. The Composition of *Anna Karenina:* Its Russian and Western Antecedents. In *Anna Karenina. The Maude Translation,* ed. G. Gibian. NY: Norton, 1970, pp. 812-15.

___. Experiments in the Novel. In *Critical Essays on T,* ed. Edward Wasiolek. Boston: G. K. Hall & Co., 1986, pp. 44-58.

___. The Genre of *War and Peace* in the Context of Russian Literary History. In *War and Peace. The Maude Translation,* ed. G. Gibian. NY: Norton, 1966, pp. 1442-45.

___. On Lev T. Tr. Ray J. Parrott, Jr. & Philip E. Frantz. *RLT* 10 (1974):198-202.

___. The Puzzle of the Epigraph, N. Schopenhauer. In *Anna Karenina. The Maude Translation,* ed. G. Gibian. NY: Norton, 1970, pp. 815-21.

___. T's Essays as an Element of Structure. In *War and Peace. The Maude Translation,* ed. G. Gibian. NY: Norton, 1966, pp. 1444-45.

Elliott, George P. A Piece of Lettuce. In his *A Piece of Lettuce and Other Essays.* NY: Random House, 1957, pp. 246-70.

Ellis, Havelock. T. In *My Confessional. Questions of Our Day.* Boston: Houghton Mifflin, 1934, pp. 122-25.

——. T. In *The New Spirit.* Washington, D.C.: National Home Library Foundation, 1935, pp. 167-218.

Ellis, K. Ambiguity and Point of View in Some Novelistic Representations of Jealousy. *MLN* 86 (1971):891-909.

Fadiman, Clifton. *War and Peace.* In his *Party of One: The Selected Writings of Clifton Fadiman.* NY: World Pub. Co., 1955, pp. 176-202.

——. *War and Peace* Fifteen Years After. In his *Any Number Can Play.* NY: World Pub. Co., 1957, pp. 361-70.

Fanger, Donald. Nazarov's Mother: On the Poetics of T's Late Epics. *CASS* 12 (1978):571-82.

Farrell, James T. History and War in T's *War and Peace;* Leo T and Napoleon Bonaparte; T's Portrait of Napoleon; T's *War and Peace* as a Moral Panorama of the Tsarist Feudal Nobility. In his *Literature and Morality.* NY: Vanguard, 1946, pp. 185-266.

Fausett, Hugh I'Anson. The Testimony of T. In his *Poets and Pundits.* Port Washington, NY: Kennikat, 1967, pp. 13-30.

Feiler, Lily. The T Marriage: Conflict and Illusions. *CSP* 23 (1981):245-60.

Feuer, Kathryn. Alexis De Tocqueville and the Genesis of *War and Peace. CalSS* 4 (1967):92-118.

——. *August 1914:* Solzhenitsyn and T. In *Aleksandr Solzhenitsyn: Critical Essays and Documentary Materials,* ed. J. Dunlop, et al. Belmont: Nordland, 1973, pp 372-81.

——. Book That Became *War and Peace. Reporter* 20 (1959):33-36.

——. Stiva. In *Russian Literature and American Critics: In Honor of Deming Brown,* ed. K. N. Brostrom. Ann Arbor: U Michigan, 1984, pp. 347-56.

——. T and Stendhal: Human Freedom and Artistic Determinism. In *Russia: Essays in History and Literature,* ed. L. H. Legters. Leiden: Brill, 1972, pp. 117-34.

Fichter, Joseph. T and the Class Struggle. In his *Roots of Change.* NY, 1939, pp. 265-89.

Findlater, J. H. T as Novelist. *Living Age* 230 (1901):488-96.

Flint, Martha M. The Epigraph of *Anna Karenina. PMLA* 80 (1965):461-62.

Fodor, Alexander. The Acceptance of Leo T in the United States. *Research Studies* 45 (1977):73-81.

——. Changes in the Evaluation of Čertkov's Impact on the Tolstojs. *RLJ* 136-37 (1986):181-200.

Folejewski, Z. T's Problems with Literary Genres. *CSS* 11 (1979):301-13.

Forster, E. M. [Great Chords and *War and Peace.*] In *Critical Essays on T,* ed. Edward Wasiolek. Boston: G. K. Hall & Co., 1986, pp. 99-100.

——. Three Stories by T. In his *Two Cheers for Democracy.* NY: Harcourt, 1951, 208-12.

Forsyth, J. T the Writer. *FMLS* 7 (1971):28-35.

Freeborn, R. T. In his *Russian Literary Attitudes from Pushkin to Solzhenitsyn.* London: Macmillan, 1976, pp. 60-78.

——. T's "Upstairs, Downstairs": Some Thoughts on His Comedy *The Fruits of Enlightenment. JRS* 40 (1980):13-22.

——. *War and Peace.* In his *The Rise of the Russian Novel.* Cambridge: Cambridge UP, 1972, pp. 208-66.

French, A. L. *Anna Karenina:* T's Toryism. *Critical Review* 22 (1980):21-31.

Friedberg, Maurice. The Comic Element in *War and Peace. ISS* 4 (1967):100-18.

Friedman, Simon. Detail and Accident in *Anna Karenina. Proceedings of the Pacific Northwest Conference on Foreign Languages* 26 (1975):164-66.

Fülöp-Miller, R. T the Apostolic Crusader. *RusR* 19 (1960):99-121.

Furbank, Phillip N. *Anna Karenina.* In *The Nineteenth-Century Novel and Its Legacy.* London: Open UP, 1973.

Futrell, Michael. Levin, the Land, and the Peasants. *CSS* 11 (1979):314-23.

——. T and History. *RLT* 17 (1982):63-73.

Galsworthy, John. Six Novelists in Profile: An Address, 1924. In his *Castles in Spain and Other Screeds.* London:

Heinemann, 1927 pp. 145-71.

Ganz, Hugo. A Visit to Count T. In *The Downfall of Russia: Under the Surface in the Land of Riddles*. London: Hodder & Stoughton, 1905, pp. 274-320.

Garnett, Edward. T's Place in European Literature. In *Critical Essays on T,* ed. Edward Wasiolek. Boston: G. K. Hall & Co., 1986, pp. 15-18.

Garrod, H. W. T's Theory of Art. In his *The Study of Good Letters*. Oxford: Clarendon, 1963, pp. 37-54.

Geduld, Harry M. Bernard Shaw and Leo T. *The California Shavian* 4, 2 (1962): 1-9.

Geiger, Don. T as a Defender of a "Pure Art" That Unwraps Something. *Journal of Aesthetic Art and Criticism* 20 (1961):81-89.

Gibian, George, ed. Two Kinds of Understanding and the Narrator's Voice in *Anna Karenina*. In *Orbis Scriptus: Dmitrij Tschižewskij zum 70. Geburtstag*. Munich: W. Fink, 1966, pp. 315-22.

Gifford, Henry. Anna, Lawrence and the Law. *Critical Quarterly* 1 (1959):203-6; rpt. *Russian Literature and Modern English Fiction,* ed. D. Davie. Chicago: U Chicago P, 1965, pp. 148-52.

——. Further Notes on *Anna Karenina*. *Critical Quarterly* 2 (1960):158-60; rpt. *Russian Literature and Modern English Fiction,* ed. D. Davie. Chicago: U Chicago P, 1965, pp. 160-63.

——. On Translating T. In *New Essays on T,* ed. M. V. Jones. Cambridge: Cambridge UP, 1978, pp. 17-38.

——. T: Art and Conscience. In his *The Novel in Russia from Pushkin to Pasternak*. London: Hutchinson, 1964, pp. 85-96.

Glicksberg, Charles I. T and *The Death of Ivan Ilyitch*. In his *The Ironic Vision in Modern Literature*. The Hague: Nijhoff, 1969, pp. 81-86.

Golding, William G. T's Mountain. In his *The Hot Gates and Other Occasional Papers*. NY: Harcourt, Brace & World, 1965, pp. 121-25.

Gorin, Bernard. Feminine Types in T's Works. *Sewanee Review* 16, 4 (1908): 442-51.

Gorki, Maxim. Leo T. In *Critical Essays on T,* ed. Edward Wasiolek. Boston: G. K. Hall & Co., 1986, pp. 26-31.

——. Lev T. In his *Literary Portraits*. Moscow: Foreign Languages Publishing House, 1958, pp. 9-102.

Gorodetzky, Nadezhda. *Anna Karenina*. *SEER* 24, 63 (1946):121-26.

——. Literature of Questions. *CSS* 2 (1968):100-10.

Goscilo-Kostin, Helena. Tolstoyan Fare: Credo à la carte. *SEER* 62, 4 (1984): 481-95.

Goubert, D. Did T Read "East Lynne"? *SEER* 58 (1980):22-39.

Goy, E. D. The Role of Topic and Question in *Anna Karenina*. *Annali* (Istituto Universitario Orientale, Sezione Slava, Napoli) 6 (1963):51-84.

Green, Dorothy. *The Kreutzer Sonata:* T and Beethoven. *MelbSS* 1 (1967):11-23.

Green, M. Morality of *Lolita*. *Kenyon Review* 28 (1966):352-77.

——. T, Keats and Shakespeare. *Yale Review* 72 (1983):206-24.

Greene, Gayle. Women, Character and Society in T's *Anna Karenina*. *Frontiers: A Journal of Women Studies* 2, 1 (1979):106-25.

Greenspan, E. T: Colossus in the Classroom. *English Journal* 57, 7 (1968): 965-71.

Greenwood, E. B. Eikhenbaum, Formalism and T. *Essays in Criticism* 23 (1973):372-87.

——. T and Religion. In *New Essays on Tolstoy,* ed. M. V. Jones. Cambridge: Cambridge UP, 1978, pp. 149-74.

——. T, Wittgenstein, Schopenhauer. *Encounter* 36, 4 (1971):60-72.

——. T's Poetic Realism in *War and Peace*. *Critical Quarterly* 11 (1969):219-33.

——. The Unity of *Anna Karenina*. *Landfall* 15, 2 (1961):124-33.

Griffiths, F. T. & S. J. Rabinowitz. T and Homer. *CL* 35 (1983):97-125.

Grigoriev, A. The Literary Work of Count L. Tolstoi. Tr. P. Mitchell. *RLT* 17 (1982):7-18.

Gromeka, M. S. The Epigraph and the Meaning of the Novel. In *Anna Karenina. The Maude Translation,* ed. G. Gibian. NY: Norton, 1970, p. 801.

Grossman, Joan Delaney. T's Portrait of Anna: Keystone in the Arch. *Criticism* 18, 1 (1976):1-14.

Gustafson, Richard. Levin's Mowing and the Task of Life. *Ulbandus Review* 2 (1982):96-111.

——. The Three Stages of Man. *CASS* 12 (1978):481-518.

Guthrie, Anna M. B. Wordsworth and T. In her *Wordsworth and T and Other Papers.* London: Constable, 1922, pp. 1-36.

Haard, Eric. T's *Zapiski Markera* and the Russian Prose Tradition. In *Dutch Contributions to the Ninth International Congress of Slavists.* Amsterdam: Rodopi, 1983, pp. 83-109.

Hagan, John. Ambivalence in T's "The Cossacks." *Novel* 3 (1969):28-47.

——. Detail and Meaning: T's "Master and Man." *Criticism* 11 (1969):31-58.

——. On the Craftsmanship of *War and Peace. Essays in Criticism* 13 (1963):17-49.

——. A Pattern of Character Development in T's *War and Peace:* P'er Bezuxov. *Texas Studies in Literature and Language* 11 (1969):985-1011.

——. A Pattern of Character Development in *War and Peace:* Prince Andrej. *SEEJ* 13 (1969):164-90.

——. Patterns of Character Development in T's *War and Peace:* Nicholas, Natasha, and Mary. *PMLA* 84 (1969):235-44.

Hajnády, Zoltán. Ivan Ilyich and Existence Compared to Death: Lev T and Martin Heidegger. *Acta Litteraria Academiae Scientiarum Hungaricae* 27, 1-2 (1985):3-15.

——. The Starry Heavens Above and the Moral Law Within. T's Moral Philosophy. *Acta Litteraria Academiae Scientiarum Hungaricae* 27, 3-4 (1985): 281-94.

Halperin, George. Count Leo T. In *T, Dostoevsky, Tourgenev: Three Great Men of Russia's World of Literature.* Chicago: Chicago Literary Club, 1946, pp. 3-30.

Halperin, Irving. The Structural Integrity of *The Death of Ivan Il'ich. SEEJ* 5 (1961):334-40.

Halperine-Kaminsky, E. T on the Music of Wagner. *Music* 14 (1898):345-56.

Hamburger, Kate. The Technique of Decentralization. In *War and Peace. The Maude Translation,* ed. G. Gibian. NY: Norton, 1966, pp. 1480-81.

Hamilton, Clayton M. Two Plays by Count Leo T: *The Living Corpse* and *The Power of Darkness.* In his *Seen on the Stage.* NY: Holt, 1920, pp. 144-53.

Hanak, M. Dostoevsky Versus T: A Struggle Against Subjective Idealism. *CASS* 12 (1978):371-76.

Hardwick, Elizabeth. Seduction and Betrayal; part 2. *New York Review of Books* 20, 10 (14 June 1973):6-10. [*The Kreutzer Sonata* and *Resurrection.*]

Hardy, Barbara. Form and Freedom: T's *Anna Karenina.* In her *The Appropriate Form: An Essay on the Novel.* London: Athlone, 1964, pp. 174-211.

——. Forms and Themes. In her *Tellers and Listeners: The Narrative Imagination.* London: Athlone Press, 1975, pp. 150-54.

——. A Note on Certain Revisions in *Anna Karenina.* In her *The Appropriate Form: An Essay on the Novel.* London: Athlone, 1964, pp. 212-16.

Hare, Richard. Did T Correctly Diagnose the Disease of "Modern Art?" *SEER* 36 (1957):181-88.

——. T after *War and Peace.* In his *Portraits of Russian Personalities between Reform and Revolution.* London: Oxford UP, 1959, pp. 196-244.

——. T and Dostoevsky. In his *Russian Literature from Pushkin to Present Day.* London: Methuen, 1947, pp. 104-42.

——. T's Motives for Writing *War and Peace. RusR* 15, 2 (1956):110-21.

Harkins, William E. A Note on the Use of Narrative and Dialogue in *War and Peace. SlavR* 29 (1970):86-92.

Harvey, John R. T in England. *Critical Quarterly* 5 (1970):115-33.

Hearn, Lafcadio. T's Theory of Art. In his *Life and Literature.* Freeport, NY: Books for Libraries, 1969, pp. 288-99.

——. T's Vanity of Wisdom. In *Essays in European and Oriental Literature,* ed. A. Mordell. NY: Dodd, Mead, 1968, pp. 195-99.

Heier, Edmund. *Hadji Murat* in the Light

of T's Moral and Aesthetic Theories. *CSS* 21, 3 (1979):324-35.

——. T and Nihilism. *CSP* 11, 4 (1969):454-65.

Heim, M. H. *Master and Man: Three Deaths* Redivivus. In *American Contributions to the Eighth International Congress of Slavists,* vol. 2, ed. V. Terras. Columbus: Slavica, 1978, pp. 260-70.

Heller, Otto. Leo T: A Study in Revivalism. In his *Prophets of Dissent: Essay on Maeterlinck, Strindberg, Nietzsche, and T.* NY: Knopf, 1918, pp. 161-216.

Hichens, R. T the Novelist. *English Review* 47 (1928):306-13.

Hirschberg, W. R. T's *The Death of Ivan Ilich. Explicator* 28 (1969), item 26.

Holderness, G. T and Art. *Durham University Journal* 42, 2 (1981):135-46.

Holland, C. T's Eightieth Birthday and His English Colony. *Pall Mall Magazine* 42 (1908):311-20.

Holman, M. J. de K. L. N. T's *Resurrection:* Eighty Years of Translation into English. *SEER* 61 (1983):125-38.

——. The Purleigh Colony: Tolstoyan Togetherness in the Late 1890s. In *New Essays on Tolstoy,* ed. M. V. Jones. Cambridge: Cambridge UP, 1978, pp. 194-222.

Holquist, J. M. Did T Write Novels? *American Contributions to the Eighth International Congress of Slavists,* vol. 2, ed. V. Terras. Columbus: Slavica, 1978, pp. 272-79.

——. Resurrection and Remembering. The Metaphor of Literacy in Late T. *CASS* 12 (1978):549-70.

Howe, Irving. Leo T: "The Death of Ivan Ilyich." In his *Classics of Modern Fiction.* NY: Harcourt Brace Jovanovich, 1972, pp. 113-78.

Howell, R. Fictional Objects: How They Are and How They Aren't. *Poetics* 8 (1979):129-77.

Howells, William Dean. The Philosophy of T. In *Criticism and Fiction and Other Essays,* ed. W. Gibson. NY: New York UP, 1965, pp. 165-79.

——. T. In his *My Literary Passions.* NY: Harper, 1895, pp. 250-58.

Hrushovski, Benjamin. Segmentation and

Motivation in the Text Continuum of Literary Prose: The First Episode of *War and Peace.* In *Russian Poetics: Proceedings of the International Colloquium at UCLA, September 22-26, 1975,* ed. T. Eekman & D. S. Worth. Columbus: Slavica, 1982, pp. 117-46.

Humboldt, C. T and Art. *Masses and Mainstream* 3 (1950):69-84.

Huneker, James. Dostoievsky and T, and the Younger Choir of Russian Writers. In his *Ivory Apes and Peacocks.* NY: Scribner's, 1915, pp. 52-88.

Jackson, Robert Louis. The Archetypal Journey: Aesthetic and Ethical Imperatives in the Art of T: *The Cossacks. RusL* 11, 4 (1982):389-99.

——. Chance and Design in *Anna Karenina.* In *The Disciplines of Criticism: Essays in Literary Theory, Interpretation and History,* ed. P. Demetz, et al. New Haven: Yale UP, 1968, pp. 315-29.

——. The Second Birth of Pierre Bezukhov. *CASS* 12 (1978):535-42.

——. T's "Kreutzer Sonata" and Dostoevsky's *Notes from the Underground. American Contributions to the Eighth International Congress of Slavists,* vol. 2, ed. V. Terras. Columbus: Slavica, 1978, pp. 281-91.

Jahn, Gary R. The Aesthetic Theory of Leo T's *What Is Art? Journal of Aesthetics* 34, 1 (1975):59-65.

——. *The Death of Ivan Ilič*—Chapter One. In *Studies in Honor of Xenia Gasiorowska,* ed. Lauren Leighton. Columbus: Slavica, 1983, pp. 37-43.

——. The Image of the Railroad in *Anna Karenina. SEEJ* 25, 2 (1981):1-11.

——. L. N. T's "Narodnye rasskazy." *RLJ* 109 (1977):67-78.

——. A Note on the Concept of the Artist in Thomas Mann and Dmitry Merezhkovsky. *Germano-Slavica* 2 (1978): 451-54.

——. A Note on the Organization of Part I of *Anna Karenina. CASS* 16 (1982):82-86.

——. The Role of the Ending in Lev T's *The Death of Ivan Ilich. CSP* 24 (1982):229-38.

——. T and Kant. In *New Perspectives on*

Nineteenth-Century Russian Prose, ed. G. J. Gutsche & L. G. Leighton. Columbus: Slavica, 1982.

———. T's Vision of the Power of Death and "How Much Land Does a Man Need." *SEEJ* 22 (1978):442-63.

———. The Unity of *Anna Karenina. RusR* 41 (1982):144-58.

James, Henry. The Tragic Muse. In his *The Art of the Novel.* NY: Scribner's, 1962, pp. 70-97.

James, William. The Divided Self. In his *The Varieties of Religious Experience.* NY: Random House, 1929, pp. 180-85.

———.The Sick Soul. In his *The Varieties of Religious Experience.* NY: Random House, 1929, pp. 146-54.

Jepsen, L. To Kill Like a Cossack. *South Atlantic Bulletin* 43, 1 (1978):86-94.

Johnson, Doris. The Autobiographical Heroine in *Anna Karenina. University of Hartford Studies in Literature* 12 (1979): 111-22.

Jones, Malcolm V. An Aspect of T's Impact on Modern English Fiction: *The Kreutzer Sonata* and Joyce Carey's *The Moonlight. SEER* 56 (1978):97-105.

———. Dostoevsky, T, Leskov and *Redstokizm. JRS* 23 (1972):3-20.

———. Problems of Communication in *Anna Karenina.* In *New Essays on T,* ed. M. V. Jones. Cambridge: Cambridge UP, 1978, pp. 85-108.

Jones, Peter. Action and Passion in *Anna Karenina. FMLS* 7 (1971):1-27.

Jones, T. Robert. *Anna Karenina* and the Tragic Genre. *MelbSS* 4 (1970):57-67.

Jones, W. Gareth. George Eliot's *Adam Bede* and T's Conception of *Anna Karenina. MLR* 61, 3 (1967):473-81.

———. A Man Speaking to Men: The Narratives of *War and Peace.* In *New Essays on T,* ed. M. V. Jones. Cambridge: Cambridge UP, 1978, pp. 63-84.

———. The Nature of the Communication between Author and Reader in T's *Childhood. SEEJ* 55 (1977):506-16.

Karpman, B. *The Kreutzer Sonata:* A Problem in Latent Homosexuality and Castration. *Psychoanalytic Review* 24 (1938):20-48.

Karpovich, Michael. T and Dostoevsky: Two Spokesmen for Russia. In *World Literatures,* ed. J. Remenyi. Pittsburgh: U Pittsburgh P, 1956, pp. 241-52.

Kaufmann, Walter. T versus Dostoevsky. In his *Existentialism, Religion and Death: Thirteen Essays.* NY: Meridan, 1976, pp. 15-27.

Kaun, Alexander. T and Andreyev. *California University Chronicle* 26 (1924): 176-81.

———. T and Gorky. *California University Chronicle* 32 (1930):351-75.

Kestner, Joseph A. T and Joyce: "Yes." *James Joyce Quarterly* 9 (1973):484-86.

Ketchian, S. Linguo-Stylistic Devices in the Temporal Structure of Lev T's *Childhood, Boyhood and Youth. Die Welt der Slaven* 23 (1978):140-52.

Khodasevich, Vladislav. T's Departure. *TriQuarterly* 27 (1973):71-82.

Kirkland, Joseph. T and the Russian Invasion of the Realm of Fiction. *Dial* 7 (1886):79-81; rpt. in *Critical Essays On T,* ed. E. Wasiolek. Boston: G. K. Hall & Co., 1986, pp. 67-71.

Kisseleff, N. Idyll and Ideal: Aspects of Sentimentalism in T's *Family Happiness. CSP* 21, 3 (1979):336-46.

Klimenko, Michael. *Anna Karenina* Seen as an Expression of Schopenhauer's *Wille zum Leben. Pacific Northwest Conference on Foreign Languages. Proceedings* 22 (1970):271-78.

Knapp, Shoshana. T's Reading of George Eliot: Visions and Revisions. *SEEJ* 27 (1983):318-26.

Knight, George W. Shakespeare's Spiritual Experience Compared to that of T. *Occult Review* (Feb.-Mar. 1930):103-7, 177-80.

Knowles, A. Russian Views of *Anna Karenina,* 1875-1878. *SEEJ* 22 (1978): 301-12.

———. Some Aspects of L. N. T's Visit to London in 1861. An Examination of the Evidence. *SEER* 56 (1978):106-14.

———. War over *War and Peace:* Prince Andrey Bolkonsky and Critical Literature of the 1860s and Early 1870s. In *New Essays on T,* ed. M. V. Jones.

Cambridge: Cambridge UP, 1978, pp. 39-62.

Kodjak, Andrej. T's Personal Myth of Immortality. In *Myth in Literature,* A. Kodjak, et al. Columbus: Slavica, 1985, pp. 188-207.

Kolesnikoff, N. and J. Leo T and the Doukhobors. In *Canadian Contributions to the VIII International Congress of Slavists, Zagreb-Ljubljana, 1978,* ed. Z. Folejewski, et al. Ottawa: Canadian Association of Slavists, 1978, pp. 37-44.

Konick, W. The Shock of the Present: Levin's Role in *Anna Karenina.* In *American Contributions to the Eighth International Congress of Slavists,* vol. 2, ed. V. Terras. Columbus: Slavica, 1978, pp. 375-90.

___ T's Underground Woman: A Study of *Anna Karenina.* In *Russian and Slavic Literatures. Selected Papers,* ed. Richard Freeborn. Cambridge: Slavica, 1974, pp. 92-112.

Krasnov, Vladislav. Wrestling with Lev T: War, Peace and Revolution in Aleksandr Solzhenitsyn's New *Avgust Chetyrnadtsatogo. SlavR* 45, 4 (1986): 707-19.

Kumar, P. Four Figures in Love: Anna Karenin, Emma Bovary, Constance Chatterly, and Chitralekha. *Journal of South Asian Literature* (Rochester, MI) 12, 3-4 (1977):73-80.

Lamm, Martin. Leo T. In his *Modern Drama.* NY: Philosophical Library, 1953, pp. 182-93.

Lampert, E. The Body and Pressure of Time. In *New Essays on T,* ed. M.V. Jones. Cambridge: Cambridge UP, 1978, pp. 131-48.

___ On T, Prophet and Teacher. *SlavR* 25 (1966):604-14.

___ T. In *Nineteenth-Century Russian Literature,* ed. John Fennell. Berkeley: U California P, 1973, pp. 261-92.

Larkin, Maurice. Experience versus the Intellect: T. In *Man and Society in Nineteenth-Century Realism: Determinism and Literature.* Totowa, NJ: Rowman & Littlefield, 1977, pp. 111-20.

Lavrin, Janko. Dostoevsky and T. In his *Russian Writers, Their Lives and Literature.* NY: Van Nostrand, 1954, pp. 176-201.

___ T and Nietzsche. In his *Studies in European Literature.* Port Washington, NY: Kennikat, 1970.

Lawrence, D. H. The Novel. In his *Reflections on the Death of a Porcupine and Other Essays.* Bloomington: Indiana UP, 1969, pp. 103-23.

Layton, Susan. Imagining the Caucasian Hero: T vs. Mordovcev. *SEEJ* 30, 1 (1986):1-17.

___ The Mind of the Tyrant: T's Nicholas and Solženicyn's Stalin. *SEEJ* 23 (1979):479-90.

Leavis, F. R. *Anna Karenina.* Thought and Significance in a Great Creative Work. *Cambridge Quarterly* 1 (1965-66):5-27. Reprinted in his *"Anna Karenina" and Other Essays.* London: Chatto & Windus, 1967, pp. 9-32.

___ and Q. D. Leavis. Dickens and T: The Case for a Serious View of *David Copperfield.* In *Dickens: The Novelist.* NY: Random House, 1970, pp. 34-105.

Ledkovsky, Marina. Dolly Oblonskaia as a Structural Device in *Anna Karenina. CASS* 12, 4 (1978):543-48.

___ The Interior Monologue in T's Works. *Mid-Hudson Language Studies* 1 (1977):113-24.

Lednicki, Waclaw. T Between *War and Peace. CalSS* 4 (1967):73-91.

___ T Through American Eyes. *SEER* 25 (1948):455-77.

Lee, C. N. Dreams and Daydreams in the Early Fiction of T. In *American Contributions to the Seventh International Congress of Slavists,* vol. 2, ed. V. Terras. The Hague: Mouton, 1973, pp. 373-92.

___ Ecological Ethics in the Fiction of L. N. T. *American Contributions to the Eighth International Congress of Slavists,* vol. 2, ed. V. Terras. Columbus: Slavica, 1978, pp. 422-37.

___ Philosophy and Artistic Devices in the Historical Fiction of L. N. T and M. A. Aldanov. *American Contributions to the Sixth International Congress of Slavists,* vol. 2, ed. W. E. Harkins. The Hague: Mouton: 1968, pp. 239-59.

Lee, Vernon. T as a Prophet: Notes on the Psychology of Asceticism. In *Gospels of Anarchy.* NY: Brentano's, 1909, p. 103-32.

Lehman, Kristin. T's Fables: Tools for a Vision. *Children's Literature Association Quarterly* 9, 2 (1984):68-70.

Lehrman, Edgar H. T's *Vojna i mir* in English. *RLJ* 36, 123-124 (1982):257-66.

Leighton, Lauren G. Denis Davydov and *War and Peace.* In *Studies in Honor of Xenia Gasiorowska,* ed. L. Leighton. Columbus: Slavica, 1983, pp. 22-36.

Lengyel, József. Marginal Notes on T's *War and Peace. Mosaic* 6, 2 (1973):85-102.

Leontiev, K. The Novels of Count L. N. T: Analysis, Style and Atmosphere. In *Essays in Russian Literature,* ed. S. Roberts. Athens: Ohio UP, 1968, pp. 225-356.

Levin, Y. D. T, Shakespeare, and Russian Writers of the 1860s. *OSP* 1 (1968):85-104.

Levitsky, Ihor. The T Gospel in the Light of the Jefferson Bible. *CSP* 21, 3 (1979):347-55.

Lindstrom, T. S. From Chapbooks to Classics: The Story of *The Intermediary. ASEER* 16, 2 (1957):190-201.

Low, Frances H. *Anna Karenina,* An Appreciation. *Fortnightly Review* 96 (1911):728-44.

Lubbock, Percy. [Craft in *War and Peace.*] In *Critical Essays On T,* ed. E. Wasiolek. Boston: G. K. Hall & Co., 1986, pp. 92-99.

Lukacs, Georg. The Social Background of the Parallel Plots in *Anna Karenina. In Anna Karenina. The Maude Translation,* ed. G. Gibian. NY: Norton, 1970, pp. 821-22.

———. T. In his *Studies in European Realism.* London, 1964, pp. 126-205, 242-64.

Lyngstad, Alexandra H. T's Use of Parentheses in *War and Peace. SEEJ* 16, 4 (1972):403-13.

Lyons, J. Pronouns of Address in *Anna Karenina.* The Stylistics of Bilingualism and the Impossibility of Translation. In *Studies in English Linguistics,* ed. Sidney Greenbaum, et al. NY:

Longman, 1980, pp. 235-49.

Lytle, Andrew N. The Image as a Guide to Meaning on the Historical Novel. *Sewanee Review* 61 (1953):408-26.

McLaughlin, S. Some Aspects of T's Intellectual and Social Development: T and Schopenhauer. *CalSS* 5 (1970): 187-240.

McLean, Hugh. Leskov and Ioann of Kronstadt: On the Origins of Polunoščniki. *ASEER* 12 (1953):93-108.

———. The Shabunin Affair. *RussR* 42, 2 (1983):191-95.

MacMaster, Robert E. No Peace without War—T's *War and Peace* as Cultural Criticism. In *American Contributions to the Eighth International Congress of Slavists,* vol. 2, ed. V. Terras. Columbus: Slavica, 1978, pp. 438-84.

———. Tsarism Right Side Up in T's *Polikuška. American Contributions to the Ninth International Congress of Slavists,* vol. 2, ed. Paul Debreczeny. Columbus: Slavica, 1983, pp. 285-304.

Makovitsky, D. My Years with T. *Unesco Courier* (Jul. 1978):14-23.

Malia, M. E. Adulthood Refracted: Russia and Leo T. *Daedalus* 105 (1976):-169-83.

Mann, Thomas. *Anna Karenina.* In his *Essays by Thomas Mann.* NY: Vintage, 1957, pp. 180-96.

———. Goethe and T. In his *Essays of Three Decades.* NY: Knopf, 1947, pp. 93-115.

Manning, C. Significance of T's War Stories. *PMLA* 52 (1937):1161-69.

———. Thoreau and T. *New England Quarterly* 16 (1943):234-43.

———. T and *Anna Karenina. PMLA* 42 (1927):505-21.

Massey, Irving. Escape from Fiction: Literature and Didacticism. *Georgia Review* 32 (1978):611-30.

Matlaw, Ralph E. Mechanical Structure and Inner Form: A Note on *War and Peace* and *Dr. Zhigago.* In *War and Peace. The Maude Translation,* ed. G. Gibian. NY: Norton, 1966, pp. 1416-23.

Matual, David. *The Confession* as Subtext in *The Death of Ivan Il'ich. International Fiction Review* 8 (1981):124-28.

——— Echoes of Renan's "Vie de Jésus" in T's "Soedinenie i perevod chetyrekh

Evangelii. *St. Vladimir's Theological Quarterly* 25, 2 (1981):85-94.

———. L. N. T's "Vlast' t'my": An Explanation of Two Titles. *RLJ* 109 (1977):61-65.

———. T's Translation of John 1:1-18. *CASS* 13 (1979):271-82.

Maude, Aylmer. Leo T. *RusR* 1, 1 (1912):27-31.

———. Misinterpretation of T. *Open Court* 16 (1902):590-601.

———. My Last Visit to T. *Bookman* 24 (1906):108-14.

———. Non-Resistance. *Humane Review* 4 (1903):193-208.

———. Recollections of T. *Slavonic Review* 7 (1929):475-81.

———. A Talk with Miss Jane Addams and Leo T. *Humane Review* 2 (1902):203-18.

———. Talks with T. *New Century Review* 7 (1900):404-18.

———. T Contra Socialism. *Millgate Monthly* 2 (1907):577-82.

———. T's Character. *Queens Quarterly* 40 (1933):530-40.

Maugham, William Somerset. T and *War and Peace.* In *An Introduction to Ten Novels and Their Authors.* NY: Greenwood, 1968, pp. 273-99.

Merezhkovsky, Dmitri S. [Body Imagery in T.] In *Critical Essays On T,* ed. E. Wasiolek. Boston: G. K. Hall & Co., 1986, pp. 85-91.

———. Dostoevsky and T. In *Russian Literature and Modern English Fiction,* ed. D. Davie. Chicago: U Chicago P, 1965, pp. 75-98.

———. T's Physical Descriptions. In *Anna Karenina. The Maude Translation,* ed. G. Gibian. NY: Norton, 1970, pp. 802-10.

Mersereau, John, Jr. Thackeray, Flaubert, T and Psychological Realism. *American Contributions to the Eighth International Congress of Slavists,* vol. 2, ed. V. Terras. Columbus: Slavica, 1978, pp. 499-522.

Mihajlov, M. A New Approach to *Anna Karenina.* In his *Underground Notes.* Kansas City: Sheed Andrews, 1976, pp. 153-68.

Mikhaylovsky, N. K. *Master and Man* and

The Death of Ivan Ilych. In *Critical Essays On T,* ed. E. Wasiolek. Boston: G. K. Hall & Co., 1986, pp. 175-79.

Miliukov, Paul. The Classical Period. In his *Outlines of Russian Culture: Part II, Literature.* Philadelphia: U Pennsylvania P, 1942, pp. 25-49.

Mitchell, Paul. Cartoons, Captions and Captiousness: *Iskra (The Spark)* on T's *War and Peace. RLT* 17 (1982):74-84.

Monter, Barbara Heldt. T's Path Towards Feminism. In *American Contributions to the Eighth International Congress of Slavists,* vol. 2, ed. V. Terras. Columbus: Slavica, 1978, pp. 523-35.

Moore, George. Turgenev and T. In *Russian Literature and Modern English Fiction,* ed. D. Davie. Chicago: U Chicago P, 1965, pp. 31-46.

More, Paul. T; or, the Ancient Feud between Philosophy and Art. In *Shelburne Essays* (1st series). NY: Putnam, 1906, vol. 1, pp. 139-224.

Morgan, Charles. T: The Second Epilogue; T: *War and Peace.* In his *Reflections in a Mirror.* NY: Macmillan, 1945, pp. 199-216.

Morson, Gary Saul. The Reader as Voyeur: T and the Poetics of Didactic Fiction. *CASS* 12 (1978):465-80.

———. T's Absolute Language. *Critical Inquiry* 7 (1981):667-87.

Mossman, Elliott. Metaphors of History in *War and Peace* and *Doctor Zhivago.* In *Literature and History: Theoretical Problems and Russian Case Studies,* ed. G. S. Morson. Palo Alto: Stanford UP, 1986, pp. 247-62.

Muchnic, Helen. Sholokhov and T. *RusR* 16, 2 (1957):25-34.

———. The Steeplechase in *Anna Karenina.* In her *Russian Writers: Notes and Essays.* NY: Random House, 1971, pp. 126-38.

Muir, Edwin. The Chronicle. In *Critical Essays On T,* ed. E. Wasiolek. Boston: G. K. Hall & Co., 1986, pp. 100-3.

Murry, John M. Keats and T. In his *Selected Criticism,* ed. R. Rees. London: Oxford UP, 1960, pp. 195-206.

Nabokoff, C. T's *Power of Darkness* and Alexander III. *Spectator* 138 (May 14,

1927):841-42.

Nabokov, Vladimir. Leo T. In his *Lectures on Russian Literature*. NY: Harcourt Brace, 1981, pp. 137-244.

Naginski, Isabelle. T's *Childhood:* Literary Apprenticeship and Autobiographical Obsession. *Ulbandus Review* 2 (1982): 191-208.

Nagorny, Vera. The Original of Natasha in *War and Peace. In Family Views of T,* ed. A. Maude. London: Allen & Unwin, 1926, pp. 25-70.

Naumann, M. T. Tolstoyan Reflections in Hemingway: *War and Peace* and *For Whom the Bell Tolls. American Contributions to the Eighth International Congress of Slavists*, vol. 2, ed. V. Terras. Columbus: Slavica, 1978, pp. 550-69.

Neatrour, Elizabeth. The Role of Platon Karataev in *War and Peace. Madison College Studies and Research* (March 1970):19-30.

Nilsson, N. A. T-Čechov-Babel'. "Shortness" and "Syntax" in the Russian Short Story. *Scando-Slavica* 28 (1982): 91-108.

Nolan, Paul T. T's *Power of Darkness:* Genre as Meaning. *Educational Theatre Journal* 17 (1965):1-9.

Nordau, Max. Tolstoism. In his *Degeneration*. NY: Appleton, 1895, pp. 144-71.

Novak, D. An Unpublished Essay on Leo T by Peter Kropotkin. *CSP* 3 (1958):7-26.

Noyes, George R. The Essential Elements in T's Ethical System. In *Anniversary Papers by Colleagues and Pupils of George Lyman Kittredge*. Boston: Ginn, 1913, pp. 295-303.

——. T's Literary Technique in *The Cossacks. Proceedings of the American Philological Association* 39 (1908): 52-58.

Ober, Warren. The Three Bears from Southey to T. *Bulletin of the New York Public Library* 73 (1968):659-66.

O'Connor, Frank. T and the Surrender of Will. In his *The Mirror in the Roadway*. NY: Knopf, 1956, pp. 148-64.

O'Faolain, S. Greatest of War Books: T's *War and Peace. Yale Review* n.s. 30, 1 (1940):141-49.

Olney, James. Experience, Metaphor, and Meaning: "The Death of Ivan Ilych." *Journal of Aesthetics and Art Criticism* 31 (1972):101-14.

Orwell, George. Lear, T, and the Fool. In his *Shooting an Elephant and Other Essays*. NY: Harcourt, 1950, pp. 32-52.

Orwin, Donna. Freedom, Responsibility and the Soul: The Platonic Contribution to T's Psychology. *CSP* 25 (1983):501-17.

——. Prince Andrei: The Education of a Rational Man. *SlavR* 42, 4 (1983):620-32.

——. The Riddle of Prince Nexljudov. *SEEJ* 30, 4 (1986):473-86.

——. The Unity of T's Early Works. *CASS* 12 (1978):449-63.

O'Toole, L. M. The Scythian Factor: Non-Verbal Interaction in T and Dostoevsky. *MelbSS* 17 (1983):1-20.

——. T: "Father Sergius." In his *Structure, Style and Interpretation in the Russian Short Story*. New Haven: Yale UP, 1982, pp. 62-83.

Pachmuss, Temira. The Theme of Love and Death in T's *The Death of Ivan Ilyich. ASEER* 20, 1 (1961):72-83.

Parker, David. "Social Being" and "Innocence" in *Anna Karenina. Critical Review* 27 (1985):110-23.

Parkin, C. J. F. T's *What is Art?" NZSJ* 4 (1969):54-67.

Parry, Albert. T at Sevastopol. In his *Russian Cavalcade, A Military Record*. NY: Washburn, 1944, pp. 75-90.

Parthé, Kathleen. Death Masks in T. *SlavR* 41 (1982):297-305.

——. Masking the Fantastic and the Taboo in T's "Polikushka." *SEEJ* 25 (1981): 21-33.

——. The Metamorphosis of Death in T. *Language and Style* 18 (1985):205-14.

Pasternak, Leonid. My Meetings with T. *RusR* 19 (1960):122-31.

——. Working with T. *Adam* nos. 284-86 (1960):23-31.

Patterson, David. The Movement of Faith as Revealed in T's *Confession. Harvard Theological Review* 71 (1978):227-43.

——. T's "Ispoved'" as a Confluence of Existential Philosophy and Literature. *Proceedings of the Pacific Northwest*

Conference of Foreign Languages 28, 1 (1977):124-26.

Pavlov, P. T's Novel *Family Happiness*. *Slavonic Review* 7 (1929):492-510.

Peace, R. Dostoevsky and T as Novelists of Ideas. *Transactions of the Association of Russian-American Scholars in the USA* 14 (1981):231-38.

Pearson, Irene. The Social and Moral Roles of Food in *Anna Karenina*. *JRS* 48 (1985):10-20.

Pergosa, Sergio. James, T and the Novel. *Revue de littérature comparée* 57, 3 (1983):359-68.

Pervushin, N.V. T, Rousseau, G. Sand and Dostoevsky. *Transactions of the Association of Russian-American Scholars in the USA* 11 (1978):164-73.

Phelps, Gilbert. The Rousseau of His Time: The Impact of T on English Thought and Fiction. In his *The Russian Novel in English Fiction*. London: Hutchinson, 1956, pp. 138-55.

Phelps, William L. T. In *Essays on Russian Novelists*. NY: Macmillan, 1917, pp. 170-214.

Pickford, R. W. Déjà vu in Proust and T. *International Journal of Psychoanalysis* 25 (1944):155-65.

Pisarev, Dmitri. The Old Gentry. In *War and Peace. The Maude Translation,* ed. G. Gibian. NY: Norton, 1966, pp. 1377-80.

Pizer, Donald. Stephen Crane's "The Monster" and T's *What to Do?* A Neglected Allusion. *Studies in Short Fiction* 20 (1982):127-29.

Plekhanov, George. T and Nature. In *Leo T: A Critical Anthology,* ed. H. Gifford. Harmondsworth: Penguin, 1971, pp. 137-40.

Poggioli, Renato. Lev T as Man and Artist. *OSP* 10 (1962):25-37.

——. A Portrait of T as Alceste. In his *The Phoenix and the Spider*. Cambridge: Harvard UP, 1957, pp. 49-108.

——. T's *Domestic Happiness:* Beyond Pastoral Love. In his *The Oaten Flute: Essays on Pastoral Poetry and the Pastoral Idea*. Cambridge: Harvard UP, 1975, pp. 265-82.

Poltoratzky, Nikolai P. Lev T and *Vekhi*. *SEER* 42, 99 (1964):332-52.

——. Soviet Literary Criticism on Lev T and *Vekhi. SEEJ* 8, 2 (1964):141-48.

Pomar, Mark G. T's *Anna Karenina*. *Explicator* 41, 3 (1983):32-33.

Pomorska, Krystyna. T—Contra Semiosis. *IJSLP* 25-26 (1982):383-90.

——. T's "Triplets": An Approach to Biography and Creativity. In *Semiosis: Semiotics and the History of Culture: In Honorem Georgii Lotman,* ed. M. Halle, et al. Ann Arbor: U Michigan, 1984, pp. 176-80.

——. and M. Drazen. T's Rotary System. *Ricerche Slavistiche* 17-19 (1970-72):453-65.

Price, Martin. T and the Forms of Life. In his *Forms of Life: Character and Moral Imagination in the Novel*. New Haven: Yale UP, 1983.

Pritchett, V. S. T. In his *Books in General*. London: Chatto & Windus, 1953, pp. 148-54.

Proffer, Carl R. T's "The Death of Ivan Ilych." In his *From Karamzin to Bunin*. Bloomington: Indiana UP, 1969, pp. 25-31.

Proust, Marcel. T. In his *On Art and Literature*. London: Chatto & Windus, 1957, pp. 378-80.

Pursglove, Michael. The Smiles of *Anna Karenina*. *SEEJ* 17 (1973):42-48.

Radford, C. The Essential Anna. *Philosophy* 54 (1979):390-94.

——. On Being Moved by Anna Karenina and *Anna Karenina*. *Philosophy* 52 (1977):344-47.

Rahv, Philip. *The Death of Ivan Ilyich* and Joseph K. In his *Image and Idea: Twenty Essays on Literary Themes*. NY: New Directions, 1949, pp. 121-40.

——. T: The Green Twig and the Black Trunk. In his *Image and Idea: Twenty Essays on Literary Themes*. NY: New Directions, 1949, pp. 87-104; reprinted in his *Literature and the Sixth Sense*. Boston: Houghton-Mifflin, 1969, pp. 134-49.

Rajakrishnan, V. T's *The Death of Ivan Ilyich:* Illness as Motif and Metaphor. In *Studies in Russian Literature,* ed. J. V. Paul. Hyderabad: Central Institute of English and Foreign Languages, 1984, pp. 28-35.

Raleigh, John Henry. Joyce and T. In *Literary Theory and Criticism Festschrift Presented to René Wellek in Honor of His Eightieth Birthday,* ed. J. P. Strelka. NY: P. Lang, 1984, vol. 2, pp. 1137-57.

——. T and Sight: The Dual Nature of Reality. *Essays in Criticism* 21 (1971): 170-79.

Rascoe, Burton. T: The Painter. In *Titans of Literature from Homer to the Present.* Freeport, NY: Books for Libraries Press, 1970, pp. 411-20.

Reeve, F. D. *Anna Karenina.* In his *The Russian Novel.* London: Mullen, 1967, pp. 236-73.

Remizov, Alexey. The Miraculous in T. *Slavonic Review* 7 (1929):473-75.

Richards, D. J. Wit and Worship—Two Impulses in Modern Russian Literature. *RLT* 14 (1976):7-19.

Rogers, Philip. Lessons for Fine Ladies: T and George Eliot's *Felix Holt, the Radical. SEEJ* 29, 4 (1985):379-92.

Roosevelt, Theodore R. T. In his *The Works of Theodore Roosevelt.* NY: Scribners, 1924, vol. 14, pp. 411-17.

Rosenberg, Brian. *Resurrection* and *Little Dorrit:* T and Dickens Reconsidered. *Studies in the Novel* 17, 1 (1985):27-37.

Roubiczek, Paul. T: The Struggle for Virtue. In his *The Misinterpretation of Man: Studies in European Thought of the Nineteenth Century.* Port Washington, NY: Kennikat, 1968, pp. 199-226.

Rougle, Charles. Structure and Theme in L. N. T's "Posle Bala." *RLJ* 38, 129-30 (1984):79-92.

Rowe, W. W. Some Fateful Patterns in T. In his *Nabokov and Others.* Ann Arbor: Ardis, 1979, pp. 47-60.

Royce, Josiah. T and the Unseen Moral Order. In *The First Book of the Author's Club. Liber Scriptorum.* NY: Author's Club, 1893, pp. 488-97.

Ruckman, J. A. The Philosophy of T's Novels. *Lamar Journal of the Humanities* 5, 2 (1979):16-27.

Rudy, Peter. Lev T's Apprenticeship to Laurence Sterne. *SEEJ* 15 (1971):1-21.

——. T on Shakespeare. *SEEJ* 14 (1970):92.

——. Young Lev T's Acquaintance with Sterne's *Sermons* and Griffith's *The Koran. SEEJ* 4 (1960):119-26.

Russell, R. From Individual to Universal: T's "Smert' Ivana Il'icha." *MLR* 79 (1981):629-42.

Rzhevsky, N. Shape of Chaos: Herzen and *War and Peace. RusR* 34 (1975):367-81.

Saintsbury, G. Turgenev, Dostoievsky, and T. In *Russian Literature and Modern English Fiction: A Collection of Critical Essays,* ed. D. Davie. Chicago: Chicago UP, 1965, pp. 23-30.

Salaman, Esther. T. In her *The Great Confession from Aksakov and De Quincey to T and Proust.* London: Penguin, 1973, pp. 67-195.

Salys, Rima. Signs on the Road of Life: "The Death of Ivan Il'ič." *SEEJ* 30, 1 (1986):18-28.

Scanlan, J. P. L.N.T as Philosopher of Art. *American Contributions to the Eighth International Congress of Slavists,* vol. 2, ed. V. Terras. Columbus: Slavica, 1978, pp. 146-65.

Ščeglov, Ju. K. & A. K. Žolkovskij. The Eclipsing Construction and Its Place in the Invariant Structure of Lev T's Children's Stories. *RusL* 7 (1979):121-58.

Schaarschmidt, G. Time and Discourse Structure in "The Death of Ivan Il'ich." *CSP* 21, 3 (1979):356-66.

Schefski, Harold K. Leo T's Short Sketch "Three Deaths." *Studies in Short Fiction* 16 (1979):349-50.

——. Margaret Mitchell: *Gone with the Wind* and *War and Peace. Southern Studies* 19 (1980):243-60.

——. T and the Jews. *RusR* 41 (1982):1-10.

——. T's Case Against Doctors. *SEEJ* 22 (1978):569-73.

Schultze, Sydney. The Chapter in *Anna Karenina. RLT* 10 (1974):351-59.

——. Meaning in "The Snowstorm." *MLS* 17, 1 (1987):67-74.

——. Notes on Imagery and Motifs in *Anna Karenina. RLT* 1 (1971):366-74.

——. Structure in the 1873 Edition of *War and Peace. CASS* 19, 1 (1985):44-53.

——. The Tradition of the Drowning Woman in the Background of *Anna Karenina. RLJ* 123-24 (1982):75-87.

Schulz, Robert K. Lev Nikolayevich T. In his *The Portrayal of the German in*

Russian Novels: Goncharov, Turgenev, Dostoevskij, T. Munich: Sagner, 1969, pp. 155-82.

Scott, William T. The Paradoxes in the Life and Writings of T. In his *Chesterton and Other Essays.* NY: Eaton & Mains, 1912, pp. 123-44.

Seeley, F. F. T's Philosophy of History. In *New Essays on T,* ed. M. V. Jones. Cambridge: Cambridge UP, 1978, pp. 175-93.

Sen, S. State Dignitaries, Liberal Landlords and Peasants: The Political World of *Anna Karenina.* In *Studies in Russian Literature,* ed. J. V. Paul. Hyderabad: Central Institute of English and Foreign Languages, 1984, pp. 36-46.

Shaw, George Bernard. T: Tragedian or Comedian. In his *Pen Portraits and Reviews.* London: Constable, 1932, pp. 260-66.

____. T on Art. In *Selected Non-Dramatic Writings of George Bernard Shaw,* ed. D. Laurence. Boston: Houghton Mifflin, 1965, pp. 427-32.

Shaw, Michael. *Anna Karenina:* A Double Dactyl. *RLT* 8 (1974):571.

Sherman, David J. Philosophical Dialogue and T's *War and Peace. SEEJ* 24 (1980):14-24.

Shestov, Lev. The Good in the Teaching of T and Nietzsche. In his *Dostoevsky, T and Nietzsche.* Athens: Ohio UP, 1969, pp. 1-140.

____. The Last Judgement: T's Last Works. In his *In Job's Balances.* Athens: Ohio UP, 1975, pp. 83-138. Reprinted in *Tolstoy: A Collection of Critical Essays,* ed. R. E. Matlaw. Englewood Cliffs, NJ: Prentice-Hall, 1967, pp. 157-72. [The Death of Ivan Ilich, Father Sergius, Master and Man.]

____. T's "Memoirs of a Madman." *Slavonic Review* 7 (1929):465-72.

Shklovsky, Victor. Art as Technique. In *Russian Formalist Criticism: Four Essays,* ed. L. Lemon & M. Reis. Lincoln: U Nebraska P, 1965, pp. 3-24.

____. Details in *War and Peace.* In *War and Peace. The Maude Translation,* ed. G. Gibian. NY: Norton, 1966, pp. 1429-42.

____. The Struggle Towards the Light. *Unesco Courier* (July 1978):24-26.

Siegel, George. The Fallen Woman in Nineteenth-Century Russian Literature. *HSS* 5 (1970):81-107.

Silbajoris, Rimvydas. Lev T: Esthetics and Art. *RLT* 1 (1971):58-72.

____. T's Aesthetics in Soviet Perspective. *Bucknell Review* 18 (1971):103-16.

____. T's Esthetics and the Modern Idiom in Art. Washington, D.C.: Woodrow Wilson International Center for Scholars, Kennan Institute, 1985. (Occasional Paper no. 197.)

Simmons, Ernest J. L. N. T: A Cadet in the Caucasus. *SEER* 20 (1941):13-27.

____. Soviet Scholarship and T. *American Review of the Soviet Union* 4 (1941): 52-61.

____. T: My Hero Is Truth. In his *Introduction to Russian Realism.* Bloomington: Indiana UP, 1965, pp. 135-80.

____. T's Dramatic Writings. *Midway* 8, 2 (1967):57-72.

____. The Writing of *War and Peace.* In *Slavic Studies,* ed. A. Kaun & E. J. Simmons. Freeport, NY: Books for Libraries, 1972, pp. 180-98.

Simonov, K. On Reading T: An Essay on the Centenary of the First Edition of *War and Peace. Partisan Review* 38, 2 (1971): 208-16.

Simpson, Mark. Dolokhov and Vronsky: Two of T's Officers and Their Background. *NZSJ* 2 (1980):49-58.

____. L. N. T and the Famine of 1891-1892. *MelbSS* 15 (1981):41-53.

Sisk, Jean. Leo T. In her *Lessons in Critical Reading and Writing. Three Masters of Russian Fiction.* NY: Harcourt Brace Jovanovich, 1970, pp. 85-176.

Slade, Tony. *Anna Karenina* and the Family Ideal. *Southern Review* 1 (1963): 85-90.

Slonim, Marc. Four Western Writers on T. *RusR* 19, 2 (1960):187-204.

Smith, Mack. T and the Conventions of Representation. *Renascence.* 37, 4 (1985): 220-37.

Smyrniw, Walter. Lev T's Unfinished Novel on the Epoch of Peter I: The

Enigma of Russia in an Enchanted Circle. *RLT* 17 (1982):102-16.

____. T's Depiction of Death in the Context of Recent Studies of the "Experience of Dying." *CSP* 21 (1979):367-79.

____. T's Response to Modern Utopian Theories. In *Studies in Honor of Louis Shein,* ed. S. Cioran, et al. Hamilton, Ontario: McMaster University, 1983, pp. 135-44.

Soloviev, Vladimir S. A Letter to Count Tolstoy on *Resurrection. Contemporary Review* 96 (1909):217-21.

Sorokin, Boris. Acute Conscience but Dulled Intelligence: A Famous Marxist (Plekhanov) Judges T. *North Dakota Quarterly* 46, 1 (1978):32-43.

____. Ivan Il'ich as Jonah: A Cruel Joke. *CSS* 5 (1971):487-507.

____. Moral Regeneration: N. N. Strakhov's Organic Critiques of *War and Peace. SEEJ* 20, (1976):130-47.

Spackman, W. M. Being Fair About Lyof Nikolayevich. *Canto* 1, 4 (1977):76-85.

Spanos, William V. Leo T's *The Death of Ivan Ilych:* A Temporal Interpretation. In *De-Structing the Novel: Essays in Applied Postmodern Hermeneutics,* ed. L. Orr. Troy, NY: Whitson Pub. Co., 1982, pp. 1-64.

Speirs, Logan. *Anna Karenina:* A Study in Structure. *Neophilologus* 50 (1966):3-28.

____. T and Chekhov: *The Death of Ivan Ilych* and *A Dreary Story.* Oxford Review 8 (1968):81-93.

Spence, G. W. Suicide and Sacrifice in T's Ethics. *RusR* (1963):157-67.

Stacy, Robert H. T or Dostoevsky. In *Russian Literary Criticism, A Short History.* Syracuse, NY: Syracuse UP, 1974, pp. 80-86.

Stakhovich, M. The Question of T's Posthumous Works. *RusR* 2, 2 (1913): 143-53.

Stanislavsky, Konstantin S. *Rubenstein and T.* Forum 71 (1924):437-47.

States, Bert O. The Hero and the World: Our Sense of Space in *War and Peace. MFS* 11, 2 (1965):153-64.

Steiner, George. The Beginning of *Anna Karenina.* In *Anna Karenina. The Maude Translation,* ed. G. Gibian. NY: Norton, 1970, pp. 865-75.

____. The Ending of *Anna Karenina.* In *Anna Karenina. The Maude Translation,* ed. G. Gibian. NY: Norton, 1970, pp. 875-77.

____. [T. and Homer.] In *Critical Essays On T,* ed. E. Wasiolek. Boston: G. K. Hall & Co., 1986, pp. 107-14.

Stenbock-Fermor, E. Elements of Folklore in an Early Work by T (The Wood-Felling). In *For Roman Jakobson: Essays on the Occasion of His 60th Birthday,* comp. M. Halle, et al. The Hague: Mouton, 1956, pp. 540-46.

Stepun, Fedor. The Religious Tragedy of T. *RusR* 19 (1960):157-70.

Stern, J. P. M. *Effi Briest: Madame Bovary: Anna Karenina. MLR* 52 (1957): 363-75; rpt. in *Anna Karenina. The Maude Translation,* ed. G. Gibian. NY: Norton, 1970, pp. 281-87.

____. The Social Code and the Moral Problem. In *Anna Karenina. The Maude Translation,* ed. G. Gibian. NY: Norton, 1970, pp. 856-65.

Stevens, Martin. A Source for Frou-Frou. *CL* 24, 1 (1972):63-71.

Stewart, David H. *Anna Karenina:*The Dialectic of Prophecy. *PMLA* 79 (1940): 266-82.

Strakhov, Nikolai. Critical Essays on I. S. Turgenev and L. N. T. In *Leo T: A Critical Anthology,* ed. H. Gifford. Harmondsworth: Penguin, 1971, pp. 56-57.

____. Levin and Social Chaos. In *Anna Karenina. The Maude Translation,* ed. G. Gibian. NY: Norton, 1970, pp. 794-98.

____. The Russian Idea in *War and Peace.* In *War and Peace. The Maude Translation,* ed. G. Gibian. NY: Norton, 1966, pp. 1382-87.

____. The Significance of the Last Part of *War and Peace.* In *War and Peace. The Maude Translation,* ed. G. Gibian. NY: Norton, 1966, pp. 1380-81.

____. T's *War and Peace.* In *Literature and National Identity,* ed. P. Debreczeny & J. Zeldin. Lincoln: U Nebraska P, 1970, pp. 119-68.

____. *War and Peace.* In *Critical Essays On T,* ed. E. Wasiolek. Boston: G. K. Hall & Co., 1986, pp. 75-85.

Stromberg, R. N. A Critique of Symbolism: Leo T, *What is Art?* In his *Realism, Naturalism and Symbolism: Modes of Thought and Expression in Europe, 1848-1914.* London: Macmillan, 1968, pp. 208-19.

Struve, Gleb. *Monologue intérieur:* The Origins of the Formula and the First Statement of Its Possibilities. *PMLA* 69 (1954):1101-11.

——. T in Soviet Criticism. *RusR* 19 (1960):171-80.

Symons, Arthur. The Russian Soul: Gorki and T. In his *Studies in Prose and Verse.* NY: Dutton, 1922.

——. T on Art. In his *Studies in Prose and Verse.* NY: Dutton, 1922, pp. 173-82.

Thale, J. *War and Peace:* The Art of Incoherence. *Essays in Criticism* 16 (1966):398-415.

Thompson, Ewa M. Dialectical Methodologies in the American Academy. *Modern Age* 28 (1984):9-22.

Thurber, A. T's Art. *Sewanee Review* 22, 3 (1914):329-40.

Thurston, G. J. Alexis de Tocqueville in Russia. *Journal of the History of Ideas* 37 (1976):289-306.

Tilby, M. T, Sterne and the Spurious *Koran. SEEJ* 29 (1986):325-29.

Timm, Leonora. Code Switching in *War and Peace.* In *Aspects of Bilingualism,* ed. M. Paraddis. Columbia, SC: Hornbeam, 1978, pp. 302-15.

Torgovnick, Mariana. "Open" and "Closed" Form in *War and Peace.* In her *Closure in the Novel.* Princeton: Princeton UP, 1981, pp. 61-79.

Trahan, Elizabeth. L. N. T's *Master and Man*—A Symbolic Narrative. *SEEJ* 7 (1963):258-68.

Trainor, Edward A. T: Novelist and Moralist. In *Six Novelists: Stendhal, Dostoevsky, T, Hardy, Dreiser, and Proust,* ed. W. Schutte, et al. Pittsburgh: Carnegie UP, 1959, pp. 29-40.

Trilling, Lionel. *Anna Karenina.* In his *The Opposing Self.* NY: Viking, 1955, pp. 66-75; rpt. in *Critical Essays on T,* ed. E. Wasiolek. Boston: G. K. Hall & Co., 1986, pp. 144-49.

Turkevich, L. B. T and Galdós: Affinities and Coincidences Reviewed. *American Contributions to the Eighth Interna-*

tional Congress of Slavists, vol. 2, ed. V. Terras. Columbus: Slavica, 1978, pp. 707-34.

Turner, C. T's *The Cossacks:* The Question of Genre. *MLR* 73 (1978):563-72.

——. The First Kind of "Novelistic Poetry." *CSP* 21 (1979):380-87.

——. The Language of Fiction: Word Clusters in T's *The Death of Ivan Ilyich. MLR* 65 (1970):116-21.

Urban, Wilbur M. T and the Russian Sphinx. *International Journal of Ethics* 28 (1939):220-39.

Van der Eng, J. "The Death of Ivan Il'ič": The Construction of the Theme; Some Aspects of Language and Time. *RusL* 7 (1979):159-92.

Van Kaam, Adrian & Katherine Healy. Anna in T's *Anna Karenina.* In their *The Demon and the Dove: Personality Growth through Literature.* Pittsburgh: Duquesne UP, 1967, pp. 169-96.

Vogue, E. M. de. Nihilism and Mysticism—T. In his *The Russian Novel.* NY: Doran, 1914, pp. 271-332.

Walsh, Harry. A Buddhistic Leitmotif in *Anna Karenina. CASS* 11 (1977):561-67.

——. Introspective Psychology in T. *SEEJ* 25, 2 (1981):11-29.

——. On the Putative Influence of Benjamin Franklin on T. *CASS* 13 (1979):306-9.

——. Schopenhauer's "On the Freedom of Will" and the Epilogue to *War and Peace. SEER* 57 (1979):572-75.

——. & Paul Alessi. The *Apophthegmata Patrum* and T's *Father Sergius. CLS* 19 (1984):1-10.

Wanamaker, M. and A. Comstock. T and *The Kreutzer Sonata. Forum* 10 (1890): 264-65.

Warner, Nicholas O. Character and Genre in *War and Peace:* The Case of Natasha. *MLN* 100 5 (1985):1012-24.

——. Shaw, T and Blake's Russian Reputation. *Blake* 17, 3 (1983-84):102-4.

——. The Texture of Time in *War and Peace. SEEJ* 28, 2 (1984):192-204.

Wasiolek, Edward. A Paradox in T's *What Is Art? CASS* 12 (1978):583-91.

——. The Theory of History in *War and*

Peace. Midway 9, 2 (1968):117-35.

——. T's *The Death of Ivan Ilyich* and Jamesian Fictional Imperatives. *MFS* 6 (1960):314-24; rpt. *T: A Collection of Critical Essays,* ed. R. E. Matlaw. Englewood Cliffs, NJ: Prentice-Hall, 1967, pp. 146-56.

——. Why Anna Kills Herself. In *Critical Essays on T,* ed. E. Wasiolek. Boston: G. K. Hall & Co., 1986, pp. 149-58.

Watt, Lewis. Nietzsche, T and the Sermon on the Mount. *Catholic World* 3 (1920): 577-87.

Weitz, Morris. *Anna Karenina:* Philosophy and the Word. In his *Philosophy in Literature: Shakespeare, Voltaire, T, Proust.* Detroit: Wayne State UP, 1963, pp. 24-39.

Wellek, René. Russian Conservative Critics: Leo T. In his *A History of Modern Criticism,* vol. 4. New Haven: Yale UP, 1965, pp. 280-91.

Wells, C. W. T as a Literary Artist. *California University Chronicle* 11 (1909): 315-24.

West, Ray B., Jr. & Robert W. Stallman. Leo T's *Three Arshins of Land, or How Much Land Does a Man Need?* In their *The Art of Modern Fiction.* NY: Rinehart, 1949, pp. 122-34.

Weston, Bruce. Leo T and the Ascetic Tradition. *RLT* 3 (1972):297-310.

Wexelblatt, Robert. The Higher Parody: Ivan Ilych's Metamorphosis and the Death of Gregor Samsa. *Massachusetts Review* 21, 3 (1980):601-28.

Wiener, Leo. The Genetics of T's Philosophy. *Russian Student* 5, 1 (1928):27-29.

——. T as a Novelist. *Hound and Horn* 2 (1921):132-39.

White, Peter T. The World of T. Sam Abell, photos. *National Geographic Magazine* 169, 6 (1986):758-92.

Wierzbicka, Anna. The Semantic Structure of Words for Emotions. In *Slavic Poetics: Essays in Honor of Kiril Taranovsky,* ed. R. Jakobson, et al. The Hague: Mouton, 1973, pp. 499-505.

Willcocks, Mary P. T. *English Review* 34 (1922):513-29.

Williams, Gareth. T's *Kavkazskij plennik. Essays in Poetics* 10, 2 (1985):58-74.

Williams, Michael V. T's *The Death of Ivan Il'ych:* After the Fall. *Studies in Short Fiction* 21, 3 (1984):229-34.

Williams, Raymond. Lawrence and T. *Critical Quarterly* 2, 1 (1960):33-39.

——. Social and Personal Tragedy: T and Lawrence. In his *Modern Tragedy.* Stanford, CA: U Stanford P, 1966, pp. 121-38.

——. Tolstoy, Lawrence and Tragedy. *Kenyon Review* 25 (1963):633-50.

Wilson, Edmund. Notes on T. In his *A Window on Russia.* NY: Farrar, Straus, Giroux, 1972, pp. 160-83.

——. The Original of T's Natasha. In his *Classics and Commercials: A Literary Chronicle of the Forties.* NY: Farrar, Straus, 1950, pp. 442-52.

Winner, Thomas G. "Glaubst zu schieben und wirst geschoben": Some Observations about T's Experiments with Children's Writing. In *Slavic Poetics: Essays in Honor of Kiril Taranovsky,* ed. R. Jakobson, et al. The Hague: Mouton, 1973, pp. 507-24.

Woodward, James B. T's *Hadji Murat:* The Evolution of Its Theme and Structure. *MLR* 68 (1973):870-82.

Woolf, Virginia. The Russian Point of View. In her *The Common Reader.* NY: Harcourt, Brace, 1925, pp. 243-56.

Woronzoff, A. T's *War and Peace* and the Historical Novel. *RLJ* 115 (1979):63-75.

Wright, A. C. Mikhail Bulgakov's Adaptation of *War and Peace. CASS* 15 (1981): 382-439.

Yakushev, H. The Trial Scenes in *The Brothers Karamazov* and *Resurrection* as a Reflection of the Authors' *Weltanschaaung. Forum International* 3 (1980): 119-32.

Yarmolinsky, Avrahm. T's *War and Peace* and *Anna Karenina.* In *Russian Literature.* Chicago: American Library Association, 1931, pp. 31-38.

——. Two Letters by L. T. *SEER* 8, 23 (1929):242-48.

Yarwood, E. T's "Three Deaths": The Maturation of Technique. *Proceedings of the Pacific Northwest Conference on Foreign Languages* 28, 1 (1977):121-33.

Youzovsky, Jozef. *Anna Karenina.* Theatre Arts Monthly 21 (Nov. 1937):852-

60.

Zborilek, Vladimir. Young T and Rousseau: The Birth of the Rousseauan Hero in T's Fiction. In *Medieval Epic to the Epic Theater of Brecht,* ed. R. Armato & J. Spalek. Los Angeles: U Southern California P, 1968, pp. 147-58.

Žekulin, Gleb. Echoes of *What Is Art?* in the Soviet Theory of Art. *CSP* 21 (1979):388-96.

Zenkovskii, V. V. N. N. Strakhov, L. N. T, and N. K. Mikhailovsky. In his *Russian Thinkers and Europe.* Ann Arbor: American Council of Learned Societies, 1953, pp. 114-35.

Zimmerman, Eugenia N. Death and Transfiguration in Proust and T. *Mosaic* 6 (1973):161-72.

Zirin, Mary. Prince Dmitri Nekhlyudov: A Synthetic Portrait. *RLT* 17 (1982):85-101.

Zohrab, Irene. Leo T from the Perspective of the New Zealand Born Linguist and Writer Harold W. Williams (With the Publication of a Forgotten Interview between Them of 20 January 1905). *MelbSS* 19 (1985):14-48.

Zucker, A. E. The Genealogical Novel. A New Genre. *PMLA* 43 (1928):551-60.

Zweers, A. F. Is There Only One Anna Karenina? *CSP* 11, 2 (1969):272-81.

—. Leo T's Role in Henriëtte Roland Holst's Quest for Brotherhood and Love. *Canadian Review of Comparative Literature* 7 (1980):1-21.

Zweig, Stefan. T. In his *Adepts in Self-Portraiture: Casanova, Stendhal, T.* London: Cassell, 1952, pp. 199-336.

IVAN TURGENEV

Bibliography

Urbanic, Allan J. & Barbara T. Urbanic, comps. Ivan T: A Bibliography of Criticism in English, 1960-83. *CASS* 17, 1 (1983):118-43.

Yachnin, R & David Stamm. *Turgenev in English. A Checklist.* NY: New York Public Library, 1962.

Žekulin, N. G. *A Bibliography of Books 1843-1982 by and about Ivan T.* Calgary: Calgary UP, 1985.

Translations

The Novels of Turgenev. Tr. Constance Garnett. NY: Macmillan (London: Heinemann), 1894-1899. 15 vols.
[Rudin; A House of Gentlefolk; On the Eve; Fathers and Children; Smoke; Virgin Soil; A Sportsman's Sketches; Dream Tales & Prose Poems; The Torrents of Spring, etc.; A Lear of the Steppes; The Diary of a Superfluous Man; A Desperate Character; The Jew; Two Friends & Other Stories; Knock, Knock, Knock & Other Stories.]

The Borzoi Turgenev. Tr. H. Stevens, intro. A. Yarmolinsky. NY: Knopf, 1950.
[On the Eve; Fathers and Sons; Rudin; Smoke; A Quiet Spot; First Love; Diary of a Superfluous Man.]

Fathers and Sons. Tr. Rosemary Edmonds. London: Penguin, 1975.

Fathers and Sons. Edited with a substantially new translation by Ralph E. Matlaw. NY: W. W. Norton & Co., 1966; 2d ed., 1989.]
[T: Apropos of *Fathers and Sons;* Excerpts from T's letters; criticism.]

Fathers and Sons. A Nest of the Gentry. Tr. Bernard Isaacs. Moscow: Progress, 1977.

First Love. Tr. Isaiah Berlin. Intro. V. S. Pritchett. NY: Penguin, 1977.

Home of the Gentry. Tr. Richard Freeborn. Harmondsworth: Penguin, 1970.

A Month in the Country. Tr. & intro. Isaiah Berlin. NY: Penguin, 1983.

A Month in the Country. Tr. Ariadne Nicolaeff. NY: Dramatists Play Service, 1976; rev. ed., 1980.

The Mysterious Tales. Tr. R. Dessaix. Canberra: Australian National University, 1979.
[Faust; Knock, Knock, Knock; The Dream; Song of Love Triumphant; Klara Milich.]

Selected Tales. Tr. & intro. David Magarschack. Garden City, NY: Doubleday, 1960.

[The Singers; Bezhin Meadow; Mumu; Assya; First Love; Knock, Knock, Knock; Living Relics; Clara Milich.]
Stories and Poems in Prose. Tr. Olga Shartse, et al. Moscow: Progress, 1982.
[Three Encounters; The Inn; Faust; Asya; First Love; A Steppeland King Lear; Clara Milich; Poems in Prose.]
Three Famous Plays. Tr. C. Garnett. NY: Scribners, 1951.
[A Month in the Country; A Provincial Lady; A Poor Gentleman.]
The Torrents of Spring. Tr. David Magarshack. NY: Vintage, 1959.

Flaubert and Turgenev: A Friendship in Letters: The Complete Correspondence. Ed. Barbara Beaumont. NY: W. W. Norton, 1985.
Letters in Two Volumes. Tr. & ed. David A. Lowe. Ann Arbor: Ardis, 1983.
Letters to an Actress. The Story of T and Savina. Tr. N. Gottlieb & R. Chapman. Athens: Ohio UP, 1973.
T's Letters. Tr. A. V. Knowles. NY: Scribners. 1983.
T's Letters: A Selection. Tr. Edgar H. Lehrman. NY: Knopf, 1961.
T's Literary Reminiscences. NY: Farrar, 1958.

Criticism

Berlin, Isaiah. *Fathers and Children.* Oxford: Clarendon P, 1972.
Berry, Thomas E. *Plots and Characters in Major Russian Fiction, I: Pushkin, Lermontov, T, Tolstoi.* Hamden, CT: Shoestring Press, 1977.
Canadian-American Slavonic Papers. Ivan T 1818-1883-1983. Special Issue. 17, 1 (1983). Ed. P. Debreczeny.
Dessaix, Robert. *T: The Quest for Faith.* Canberra: Australian National University, 1980.
Fitzlyon, April. *The Price of Genius: A Life of Pauline Viardot.* London: John Calder, 1964.
Freeborn, Richard. *T: The Novelist's Novelist.* NY: Oxford UP, 1960; rpt. Westport, CT: Greenwood Press, 1978.
Garnett, E. *Turgenev, A Study.* Pt. Washington, NY: Kennikat, 1966; rpt. NY: Haskill, 1975.

Gettmann, Royal A. *T in England and America.* Urbana: Illinois Studies in Language and Literature, 1941; rpt. Westport, CT: Greenwood, 1975.
Halperin, George. *Tolstoy, Dostoevskiy, T: The Three Great Men of Russia's World of Literature.* Chicago: Folcroft Library, 1971; rpt. Philadelphia: R. West, 1977.
Hellgren, Ludmila. *Dialogues in T's Novels: Speech-Introductory Devices.* Stockholm: Amlqvist, 1980.
Hershkowitz, Harry. *Democratic Ideas in T's Works.* NY: AMS, 1973.
Hubbard, E. D., ed. *Fathers and Sons: Chapter Notes and Criticism.* NY: American R.D.M., 1964.
Kagan-Kans, Eva. *Hamlet and Don Quixote. T's Ambivalent Vision.* The Hague: Mouton, 1975.
Lampert, Evgenii. *Sons against Fathers: Studies in Russian Radicalism and Revolution.* Oxford: Clarendon, 1965.
Ledkovsky, Marina. *The Other T: From Romanticism to Symbolism.* Würzburg: Jal-Verlag, 1973.
Lloyd, John A. T. *Ivan T.* NY, 1942; rpt. Pt. Washington, NY: Kennikat, 1972.
Lowe, David. *T's "Fathers and Sons."* Ann Arbor: Ardis, 1983.
Magarshack, David. *T. A Life.* NY: Grove, 1954.
Mainwaring, Marin, ed. *T: The Portrait Game.* London: Chatto & Windus, 1973.
Mlikotin, A. M. *The Genre of the "International Novel" in the Works of Henry James: A Critical Study.* Los Angeles: U Southern California P, 1971.
Moser, Charles A. *Ivan T.* NY: Columbia UP, 1972.
Moxom, P. S. *Two Masters: Browning and T.* Chicago: Folcroft Library, 1977.
New Zealand Slavonic Journal. 1983. Ed. Patrick Waddington. Special Turgenev issue.
Pahomov, G. S. *In Earthbound Flight: Romanticism in T.* Rockville, MD: Victor Kamkin, 1986.
Peterson, Dale L. *The Clement Vision: Poetic Realism in T and James.* Pt. Washington, NY: Kennikat, 1975.
Pritchett, V. S. *The Gentle Barbarian: The*

Life and Work of T. NY: Random House, 1977.

Ripp, Victor. *T's Russia: From "Notes of a Hunter" to "Fathers and Sons."* Ithaca: Cornell UP, 1980.

Russian Literature 16, 4 (1984). Special Turgenev issue.

Schapiro, Leonard. *T. His Life and Times.* Cambridge: Harvard UP, 1978.

Schulz, Robert K. *The Portrayal of the German in Russian Novels: Gončarov, T, Dostoevskij, Tolstoj.* Munich: O. Sagner, 1969.

Smyrniw, W. *T's Early Works.* Oakville, Ont.: Mosaic, 1980.

Soviet Literature. No. 12 (1983). Special Turgenev issue.

Tilley, W. H. *The Background of "The Princess Casamassima."* Gainesville: U Florida P, 1960.

Turgenev Commemorative Volume 1818-1883. NY: Association of Russian-American Scholars in the U.S.A., 1983. *(Transactions of the Assn. of Russian-American Scholars in USA,* vol. 16.)

Waddington, Patrick, ed. *The Dodillion Copies of Letters by T to Pauline and Louis Viardot.* Belfast: Queens UP, 1970,

⸺ *T and England.* London: Macmillan, 1980.

⸺ *T and George Sand: An Improbable Entente.* London: Macmillan, 1981.

Wilkinson, Myler. *Hemingway and T: The Nature of Literary Influence.* Ann Arbor: UMI Research P, 1986.

Worrell, N. *Nikolai Gogol and Ivan T.* London: Macmillan, 1982.

Yarmolinsky, Avrahm. *T. The Man, His Art and His Age.* NY: Octagon, 1977.

Zhitova, Vera. *The T Family.* London: Harvill Press, 1947.

Allen, Elizabeth Cheresh. The Poetics of Ivan S. T: A Study in Appollonian Art. Ph.D. diss., Yale, 1984.

Costlow, Jane Tussey. Worlds within Worlds: The Novels of Ivan T. Ph.D. diss., Yale, 1987.

Eliason, Lynn Russell. The Problem of the Generations in the Fiction of T and Theodor Fontane. Ph.D. diss., Colorado, 1970.

Gettman, Royal. T in England and America. Ph.D. diss., Illinois, 1937.

Hershkowtiz, Harry. Democratic Ideas in T's Works. Ph.D. diss., Columbia, 1932.

Howarth, Nina. Edmond de Goncourt and Ivan T: A Page in Franco-Russian Literary History. Ph.D. diss., SUNY, Albany, 1971.

Kagan-Kans, Eva. Archetypal Patterns in T's Fiction. Ph.D. diss., Berkeley, 1968.

Kappler, Richard G. T and the French. Ph.D. diss., Columbia, 1960.

Krzyzanowski, Jerzy Roman. T, Tolstoy and W. D. Howells. Ph.D. diss., Michigan, 1965.

Ledkovsky, Marina. The Other T: From Romanticism to Symbolism. Ph.D. diss., Columbia, 1969.

Lowe, David Allan. T's *Fathers and Sons.* Ph.D. diss., Indiana, 1977.

Matlaw, Ralph E. The Composition of T's Novels. Ph.D. diss., Harvard, 1954.

Mlikotin, Anthony Matthew. The International Theme in the Novels of T and Henry James. Ph.D. diss., Indiana, 1961.

Ozdrovsky, Marina. The Plays of T in Relation to Nineteenth-Century European and Russian Drama. Ph.D. diss., Columbia, 1972.

Pahomov, George Serge. Romanticism in T: T as the Inheritor of the Themes and Concerns of Russian Romanticism. Ph.D. diss., New York, 1973.

Peterson, Dale E. One Much-Embracing Echo: Henry James' Response to Ivan T. Ph.D. diss., Yale, 1971.

Porter, Richard N. T's Critical History of Russian Literature. Ph.D. diss., Indiana, 1968.

Ripp, Victor. The Structure of Sincerity: T's Novels in the Context of the Cultural Movement, 1855-62. Ph.D. diss., Columbia, 1973.

Rosenstreich, Susan Lepawsky. A Scythian Among the French: The Role of Ivan T in the Société Cinq. Ph.D. diss., CUNY, 1981.

Schwaebel, Willi Hans. The Influence of T on the Narrative Technique of Fontane. Ph.D. diss., Michigan State, 1981.

Sherman, David James. Concepts of Self in T's Novels: *Rudin, A Nobleman's*

Nest, and *Fathers and Sons.* Ph.D. diss., Cornell, 1985.

Sly, Gerlinde. The Role of Social Consciousness and Fatalism in the Works, Life, and Letters of Georg Büchner and the Younger Ivan Sergeyevich T (Two Types of Literary Reactions to Social Conditions). Ph.D. diss., New York, 1966.

Smyrniw, Walter. Character Types in Ivan T's Early Works. Ph.D. diss., Toronto, 1974.

Turton, L. G. T and the Context of English Literature, 1850-1900. Ph.D. diss., Warwick, 1984.

Critical Articles

Ahnebrink, L. The Influence of T. In his *The Beginnings of Naturalism in American Fiction (1891-1903).* NY: Russell & Russell, 1961, pp. 315-42.

Alexeyev, M. P. William Ralston and Russian Writers of the Later Nineteenth Century. *OSP* 11 (1964):83-93.

Andrew, Joe. Ivan T. In his *Russian Writers and Society in the Second Half of the Nineteenth Century.* Atlantic Highlands, NJ: Humanities Press, 1982. pp. 1-43.

Annan, N. Novelists-Philosophers III: T. *Horizon* 11 (1945):152-63.

Annenkov, P. V. The Literary Type of the Weak Man: Apropos of T's Story "Asya." Tr. T. Goerner. *Ulbandus Review* (1977): 90-104; (1978):74-58.

Armstrong, Judith. T's Novella "The Diary of a Superfluous Man." *NZSJ* (1983):1-20.

Arndt, Walter. The Mold and Modernity of T. *Boston University Journal* 26 (1978):20-31.

Bachman, Charles R. Tragedy and Self-Deception in T's *Fathers and Sons. Revue des Langues Vivantes* 34, 3 (1968):269-76.

Ball, David. T's Dialectic. *Massachusetts Review* 20 (1979):145-60.

Baring, Maurice. Tolstoy and T. The Place of T. In his *Landmarks in Russian Literature.* NY: Barnes & Noble, 1960, pp. 50-73, 74-79.

Barratt, Glynn R. T's Article on E. A. Baratynsky. *Etudes slaves et est-euro-péennes* 13 (1968):62-67.

Berlin, Isaiah. An Episode in the Life of Ivan T. *London Monthly* 4, 7 (1957):14-24.

—— "Fathers and Children." *New York Review of Books* 20, No. 16 (Oct. 18 1973):39-44; No. 17, (Nov. 1, 1973):22-29; No. 18 (Nov. 15, 1973):9-11.

——"Fathers and Children:" T and the Liberal Predicament. In his *Russian Thinkers.* NY: Penguin, 1978, pp. 261-305.

Blair, Joel. The Architecture of T's *Fathers and Sons. MFS* 19 (1973-74):555-63.

Bortnes, Jostein. The Poetry of Prose: The Art of Parallelism in T's *Ottsy i deti. Scando-Slavica* 30 (1984):31-55.

Bowen, C. M. T and the Russian Revolution. *Englishwoman* (June 1917):211-21.

Boyd, Alexander F. A Landscape with Figures: Ivan T and *Fathers and Sons.* In his *Aspects of the Russian Novel.* London: Chatto & Windus, 1972, pp. 68-86

Brang, P. T and the Isms. *RusL* 16 (1984):305-22.

Briggs, Anthony D. Ivan T and the Workings of Coincidence. *SEER* 58 (1980):195-211.

—— Someone Else's Sledge: Further Notes on T's *Virgin Soil* and Henry James's *The Princess Casamassima. OSP* 5 (1972):52-60.

Brodiansky, N. T's Short Stories: A Revaluation. *SEER* 32 (1954):70-92.

Brostrom, Kenneth N. The Heritage of Romantic Depictions of Nature in T. In *American Contributions to the Ninth International Congress of Slavists,* vol. 2, ed. Paul Debreczeny. Columbus: Slavica, 1983, pp. 81-96.

—— The Journey as Solitary Confinement in *Fathers and Children.* In *Ivan T, 1818-1883-1983,* ed. P. Debreczeny. Special issue of *CASS* 17 (1983), pp. 13-38.

Brown, A. T. *Shenandoah* 6 (1954):17-30.

Brown, E. J. Pisarev and the Transformation of Two Russian Novels. In *Literature and Society in Imperial Russia,* ed. W. M. Todd III. Stanford: Stanford UP, 1978, pp. 151-72.

[*Fathers and Sons* and *Crime and Punishment*]

——. T's "Notes on Stankevich" and *Rudin*. In his *Stankevich and His Moscow Circle, 1830-1840*. Stanford: Stanford UP, 1966, pp. 26-31.

Brumfield, William C. Bazarov and Rjazanov: The Romantic Archetype in Russian Nihilism. *SEEJ* 21, 4 (1977):495-505.

——. Invitation to a Beheading: T and Troppmann. In *Ivan T, 1818-1883-1983*, ed. P. Debreczeny. Special issue of *CASS* 17 (1983), pp. 79-88.

Burns, Virginia M. The Structure of the Plot in "Otcy i deti." *RusL* 6 (1974):33-53.

Cadot, Michel. The Role of I. S. T and Louis Viardot in the Promulgation of Russian Literature in France. In *Turgenev Commemorative Volume 1818-1883*. NY: Association of Russian American Scholars in the USA, 1983, pp. 225-39.

Calder, Angus. Fiction and Politics: The Art of T. In his *Russia Discovered: 19th Century Fiction from Pushkin to Chekhov*. NY: Barnes & Noble, 1976, pp. 73-107.

Carden, Patricia. Finding the Way to "Bezhin Meadow": T's Intimation of Mortality. *SlavR* 36 (1977):455-64.

Carr, E. H. T and Dostoyevsky. *SEER* 8 (1929):156-63.

——. Two Russians (Tolstoi and T). *Fortnightly Review* (Dec. 1929):823-26.

Cecil, Lord D. T. *Fortnightly Review* (July 1948):42-49.

Chamberlain, Lesley. The Opening Chapter of *Nakanune*: Some Thoughts on Possible German Origins. *Journal of European Studies* 8 (1978):93-108.

Chamberlain, W. H. T—The Eternal Romantic. *RusR* 5, 2 (1946):10-23.

Chamberlin, Vernon A. & Jack Weiner. Galdós' *Dona Perfecta* and T's *Fathers and Sons*: Two Interpretations of Conflict Between Generations. *PMLA* 86, 1 (1971):19-24.

Chances, Ellen B. On the Road to Ideology: Herzen, T and Goncharov. In her *Conformity's Children: An Approach to the Superfluous Man in Russian Literature*. Columbus: Slavica, 1978, pp. 50-90.

Chernov, Nikolai. Ivan T's Story "First Love" and Its Actual Sources. Tr. P. Mann. *Soviet Literature* 10 (1975):61-72.

Chyzhevskyi, Dmytro. T. In his *History of Nineteenth-Century Russian Literature*, vol. 2, The Age of Realism. Tr. R. N. Porter. Nashville: Vanderbilt UP, 1974, pp. 26-46.

——. Manuscripts of Dostoevsky and T at Harvard. *Harvard Library Bulletin* 9 (1955):410-15.

Clardy, Jesse V. & Betty Clardy. Goncharov and T. In their *The Superfluous Man in Russian Letters*. Washington, D.C.: University Press of America, 1980, pp. 23-30.

Clayton, J. Douglas. The Hamlets of T and Pasternak: On the Role of Poetic Myth in Literature. *Germano-Slavica* 2 (1978):455-61.

——. Night and Wind: Images and Allusions as the Source of the Poetic in T's *Rudin*. *CSP* 26, 1 (1984):10-14.

Christa, Boris. Vestimentary Markers in T's *Fathers and Sons*. *NZSJ* (1983):21-36.

Clive, Geoffrey. Romanticism and Anti-Romanticism in the Nihilism of Bazarov. *Christian Scholar* 45 (1962):215-29.

Colum, P. Maria Edgeworth and Ivan T. *British Review* (July 1915):109-13.

Conrad, Joseph. Joseph Conrad on Ivan T. In *Novelists on Novelists: An Anthology*, ed. L. Kronenberger. NY: Doubleday, 1962, pp. 158-60.

Conrad, Joseph L. T's "Asja": Ambiguous Ambivalence. *SEEJ* 30, 2 (1986):215-29.

——. T's *Asja*: An Analysis. *SEEJ* 8 (1964):391-400.

Costlow, J. Death of Rhetoric in *Rudin*. *RusL* 16 (1984):375-84.

Crosfield, H. T's Novels and Russian Revolution. *Westminster Review* 168 (1907):523-36.

Cross, A. G. The Breaking Strings of Chekhov and T. *SEER* 47 (1969):510-13.

Culianu-Georgescu, C. T's *A Month in the Country* and Balzac's *La Marâtre*. *RusL* 16 (1984):385-410.

Dalton, M. Reflections of I. S. T in Eduard V. Keyserling: An Analysis of *Pervaia liubov'* and *Schwüle Tage*. *Germano-Slavica* 2 (1978):397-410.

Danilova, Galina. A Story of Love and Friendship. *Soviet Literature* 5 (1977):169-73.

Daugherty, Sarah B. The Psychological Novelists: Eliot, Trollope, and T. In her *The Literary Criticism of Henry James*. Athens, OH: Ohio UP, 1981, pp. 71-86.

Davie, David. T in England, 1850-1950. *Studies in Russian and Polish Literature in Honor of Waclaw Lednicki*, ed. Z. Folejewski, et al. 's-Gravenhage: Mouton, 1962, pp. 168-84.

Davies, Ruth. T: The Nihilists and *Virgin Soil*. In her *The Great Books of Russia*. Norman, OK: U Oklahoma P, 1968, pp. 64-100.

Debreczeny, Paul. Ivan T and Henry James: The Function of Social Themes in *Fathers and Sons* and *The Princess Casamassima*. In *American Contributions to the Ninth International Congress of Slavists*, vol. 2, ed. Paul Debreczeny. Columbus: Slavica, 1983, pp. 113-23.

Delaney, Consolata, Sister. T's Sportsman: Experiment in Unity. *SEEJ* 8 (1964):17-25.

Delaney, Joan. Edgar Allan Poe and I. S. T. *Studia Slavica Academiae Scientiarum Hungaricae* 15, 3-4 (1969):349-54.

Delany, Paul & Dorothy E. Young. T and the Genesis of "A Painful Case." *MFS* 20, 2 (1974):217-21.

Delbaere-Garant, Jeanne. Henry James's Divergences from his Russian Model in *The Princess Casamassima*. *Revue des langues vivantes* 37, 5 (1971):535-44.

Dessaix, Robert. The Concept of Ideal Love in the Works of T and Tolstoi. *Melbourne Slavonic Studies* 11 (1976):52-64.

_____ T and Maupassant as Fantasts. *RusL* 5, 4 (1977):325-37.

Donskov, A. T and Drama. *RLJ* 131 (1984):103-12.

_____ T's *Iskusheniye svyatogo Antoniya:* A Reassessment. *NZSJ* (1985): 33-46.

Dukas, Vytas and Richard H. Lawson. *Werther* and *Diary of a Superfluous Man*. *CLS* 21 (1969):146-54.

De Maegd-Soëp, Carolina. Women's Emancipation in the Works of T. In her *The Emancipation of Women in Russian Literature and Society*. Ghent: Ghent State University, 1978, pp. 197-260.

Edel, Leon. *Henry James: The Conquest of London, 1870-81*. NY: Lippincott, 1962. [Ivan Sergeyevich, pp. 201-7; The Lesson of the Master, pp. 207-14.]

Eikhenbaum, Boris. The *Sportman's* [sic] *Sketches:* An Introductory Essay. Tr. & ed. Sona & Thomas Hoisington. In *Ivan T, 1818-1883-1983*, ed. P. Debreczeny. Special issue of *CASS* 17 (1983), pp. 7-12.

Eliason, Lynn R. A Nineteenth-Century Solution to the Problem of Generations—T and Theodor Fontane. *Germano-Slavica* 2 (1973):29-34.

Feuer, Kathryn. *Fathers and Sons:* Fathers and Children. In *The Russian Novel from Pushkin to Pasternak*, ed J. Garrard. New Haven: Yale UP, 1983, pp. 67-80.

Feuer, Lewis S. *The Conflict of Generations: The Character and Significance of Student Movements*. NY: Basic Books, 1969.

Field, Andrew, comp. *The Complection of Russian Literature*. NY: Atheneum, 1971. [Ivan Goncharov on Ivan T, pp. 131-47; Leonid Grossman on T, pp. 147-52.]

Fischler, Alexander. The Garden Motif and the Structure of T's *Fathers and Sons*. *Novel* 9 (1976):243-55.

Fiszman, S. Ivan T's Unknown Letter and His Stay in Russia, 1879. *SlavR* 40, 1 (1981):77-83.

FitzLyon, April. T and the "Woman

Question." *NZSJ* (1983):161-74.

___ An Unpublished Novel by T? In *Turgenev Commemorative Volume 1818-1883*. NY: Association of Russian American Scholars in the USA, 1983, pp. 213-24.

___ A Weekend in the Country. *Listener* 74 (Dec. 9, 1965):951-53.

Folejewski, Zbigniew. The Recent Storm around T as a Point in Soviet Aesthetics. *SEEJ* 6, 1 (1962):21-27.

___ T and Prus. *SEER* 29 (1951):132-39.

Forbes, N. T. *RusR* 1, 3 (1912):116-40.

Ford, Ford Maddox. John Galsworthy. In *Russian Literature and Modern English Fiction*, ed. D. Davie. Chicago: Chicago UP, 1965, pp. 54-71.

___ T, The Beautiful Genius. *American Mercury* 39 (1936):41-50.

Foxcroft, E. The Spirit of an Age as Reflected in *Fathers and Sons* and *The Possessed*. *Unisa English Studies* 19, 2 (1981):11-16.

Frank, Joseph. Fathers and Sons. *Sewanee Review* 73 (1969):699-708.

Freeborn, Richard. Bazarov as a Portrayal of the Doomed Revolutionary. *NZSJ* (1983):71-84.

___ A Centenary Tribute to T. *Journal of European Studies* 14, 3 (1984):155-71.

___ The Hunter's Eye in *Zapiski okhotnika*. *NZSJ* 2 (1976):1-9.

___ T and Revolution. *SEER* 61 (1984): 518-27.

___ T at Ventnor. *SEER* 51, 124 (1973): 387-412.

___ T, The Dramatist. In *Turgenev Commemorative Volume 1818-1883*. NY: Association of Russian American Scholars in the USA, 1983, pp. 57-74.

Frost, Edgar L. The Function of Music in *Dvorjanskoe gnezdo* [Nest of Gentlefolk]. *RLJ* 100 (74):8-17.

Garnett, D. T, Madame Viardot, and *A Month in the Country*. *Adelphi* 27 (1951):346-50.

Gassner, John. Past and Present: Reviving T's *A Month in the Country*. In his *Theatre at the Crossroads: Plays and Playwrights of the Mid-Century American State*. NY: Holt, Rinehart, 1960, pp. 193-94.

Gershenzon, M. O. A Sketch of T. *Living Age* 318 (1923):513-16.

Gifford, Henry. T. In *Nineteenth-Century Russian Literature*, ed. J. Fennell. Berkeley & Los Angeles: U California P, 1973, pp. 145-67.

___ T in *Fathers and Sons*. In his *The Novel in Russia: From Pushkin to Pasternak*. NY: Harper, 1965, pp. 63-72.

Glicksberg, C. I. T and Bazarov. In *The Literature of Nihilism*. Lewisburg: Bucknell UP, 1975, pp. 77-82.

Goncharov, Ivan. A Literary Quarrel: T as "Plagiarist." *Encounter* (June 1971): 24-32.

Goy, E. D. The Attitude of the Serbs to T's Works in the 19th Century. *SEER* 36 (1958):123-50.

Grey, R. T and Nature: A Centenary Note. *Englishwoman* (Nov. 1918):75-80.

Gribble, F. T. *Fortnightly Review* 94 (1910):1071-81.

Grigorev, A. *A Nest of the Gentry* by Ivan T. In *Literature and National Identity: Nineteenth-Century Russian Critical Essays*, tr. & ed. P. Debreczeny & J. Zeldin. Lincoln: U Nebraska P, 1970, pp. 65-118.

Gronicka, Andre von. Goethe's Influence on I. S. T's "Faust" and "Asia." In *Aufnahme—Weitergabe: Literarische Impulse um Lessing und Goethe*, ed. John A. McCarthy. Hamburg: Buske, 1982, pp. 193-204.

___ Ivan S. T's Faust Essay. *Germano-Slavica* 3 (1979):17-32.

Grossman, J. D. *Edgar Allen Poe in Russia: A Study in Legend and Literary Influence*. Chapter 3: Poem and the Romantic Realists. Würzburg: Jal-Verlag, 1973.

Guerney, B. G. T: A Novel Aspect. *University of Kansas City Review* 14, 1 (1947):75-77.

Hamilton, Eunice C. Henry James's *The Princess Casamassima* and Ivan T's *Virgin Soil*. *South Atlantic Quarterly* 61, 3 (1962):354-64.

Harper, Kenneth E. Text Progression and Narrative Style. *American Contributions to the Eighth International Congress of Slavists*, vol. 2, ed. V. Terras. Columbus: Slavica, 1978, pp.

223-35.

Harrison, Royden J. & Joseph Strmecki. T's Later Political Commitments: Six Letters to Beesley, 1880. *SEEJ* 9, 4 (1965):400-19.

Hart, Pierre. Nature as the Norm in *Otcy i deti. RLJ* 110 (1977):55-64.

——. The Passionate Page: T's "First Love" and Dostoevsky's "The Little Hero." *New Perspectives on Nineteenth-Century Russian Prose,* ed. G. J. Gutsche & L. G. Leighton. Columbus: Slavica, 1982, pp. 111-20.

Harvie, J. A. T's Swan-Song "Klara Milich." *NZSJ* (1983):105-22.

Heier, Edmund. Duty and Inclination in T's *Faust.* In *Crisis and Commitment: Essays in Honour of J. W. Dyck,* ed. J. Whiton & H. Loewen. Waterloo, Ontario: U Waterloo P, 1983, pp. 78-86.

Henry, Peter. I. S. T: *Fathers and Sons* (1862). In *The Monster in the Mirror: Studies in Nineteenth-Century Realism,* ed. D. A. Williams. Oxford: Oxford UP, 1978, pp. 40-74.

Hermann, Lesley S. George Sand and Ivan T. In *George Sand Papers: Conference Proceedings, 1976,* ed. N. Datlof, et al. NY: AMS, 1980, pp. 162-73.

——. Woman as Hero in T, Goncharov, and George Sand's *Mauprat. Ulbandus Review* 2, 1 (1979):128-38.

Hindus, M. The Duels in Mann and T. *CL* 11 (1959):308-12.

Hollingsworth, B. I. S. T and *Kolokol. SEER* 41 (1963):89-100.

Holman, C. Hugh. Of Everything the Unexplained and Irresponsible Specimen: Notes on How to Read American Realism. *Georgia Review* 18 (1964):316-24.

Holquist, M. Bazarov and Sečenov: The Role of Scientific Metaphor in *Fathers and Sons. RusL* 16 (1984):359-74.

Howe, Irving. T: The Politics of Hesitation. In his *Politics and the Novel.* NY: Horizon, 1967, pp. 117-41.

——. T: The Virtues of Hesitation. *Hudson Review* 8 (1956):533-51.

Hubbard, E. D., ed. *Fathers and Sons: Chapter Notes and Criticism.* NY: American R.D.M., 1964.

Ingham, Norman W. T in the Garden. In *Mnemozina: Studia Litteraria Russica in Honorem Vsevolod Setchkarev,* ed. J. T. Baer & N. W. Ingham. Munich: Fink, 1974, pp. 209-28.

Ingram, Forrest L. American Short Story Cycles: Foreign Influences and Paralells. In *Modern American Fiction: Insights and Foreign Lights,* vol. 5 of *Proceedings of the Comparative Literature Symposium,* ed. W. Zyla & W. Aycock. Lubbock, TX: Texas Tech UP, 1972, pp. 19-38.

Jackson, Robert Louis. The Root and the Flower: Dostoevsky and T. *Yale Review* 63 (1973):228-50.

——. T's "The Inn": A Philosophical Novella. *RusL* 16 (1984):411-20.

Jahn, G. R. Character and Theme in *Fathers and Sons. College Literature* 4 (1977):80-91.

Jakobson, Roman. Supraconscious T. Tr. S. Rudy. In *On Signs,* ed. Marshall Blonsky. Baltimore: John Hopkins UP, 1985, pp. 303-7.

James, Henry. Ivan T. In his *French Poets and Novelists.* London, 1884; rpt. NY: Grosset & Dunlap, 1964.

——. Ivan T (1884). In his *Partial Portraits.* London: Macmillan, 1888; rpt. Westport, CT: Greenwood, 1970.

——. Ivan T (1818-1883). In *Russian Literature and Modern English Fiction,* ed. Donald Davie. Chicago: Chicago UP, 1965, pp. 31-43.

——. Ivan T's *Virgin Soil.* In his *Literary Reviews and Essays,* ed. Albert Mordell. NY: Twayne, 1957.

——. T and Tolstoy. In his *The House of Fiction,* ed. Leon Edel. London: R. Hart-Davis, 1957.

Johanson, Christine. T's Heroines: A Historical Assessment. *CSP* 26, 1 (1984): 15-23.

Justus, James H. *Fathers and Sons:* The Novel as Idyll. *Western Humanities Review* 15 (1961):259-65.

Kagan-Kans, Eva. Fate and Fantasy: A Study of T's Fantastic Stories. *SlavR* 28 (1969):543-60.

——. Ivan T and Henry James: "First Love" and "Daisy Miller." *American Contributions to the Ninth International*

Congress of Slavists, vol. 2, ed. Paul Debreczeny. Columbus: Slavica, 1983, pp. 251-66.

———. T, The Metaphysics of an Artist, 1818-1883. *Cahiers du Monde Russe et Soviétique* 13, 3 (1972):382-405.

Kappler, Richard G. Ivan S. T as a Critic of French Literature. *CL* 20, 2 (1968): 133-41.

———. T and George Sand. *Research Studies* (Washington State Univ) 34, 1 (1966): 37-45.

Karp, C. George Sand and T: A Literary Relationship. *Studies in Literary Imagination* 12, 2 (1979):73-81.

Kaspin, Albert. *Uncle Tom's Cabin* and "Uncle" Akim's Inn: More on Harriet Beecher Stowe and T. *SEEJ* 9, 1 (1965):47-55.

Kaun, A. T in England and America. *Journal of English and Germanic Philology* 41 (1942):112-15.

———. T Rerambled. *Bookman* 55 (1922): 308-11.

Keefer, Lubov. The Operetta Librettos of Ivan T. *SEEJ* 10, 2 (1966):134-54.

Kelley, Cornelia. T. In her *The Early Development of Henry James.* Chapter 14, part 6. Urbana, U Illinois P, 1965.

Kennedy, Eileen. Genesis of a Fiction: The Edgeworth-T Relationship. *English Language Notes* 6, 4 (1969):271-73.

———. T and George Moore's *The Untilled Field. English Literature in Transition (1880-1920)* 18, 3 (1975);145-59.

Kochan, L. Russian History in T's Novels. *History Today* 14 (1964):25-33.

Korn, David. T in Nineteenth-Century America. *RusR* 27 (1968):461-67.

Kropotkin, P. T; Tolstoy. In his *Russian Literature.* NY: B. Blom, 1967, pp. 88-109.

Lainoff, Seymour. The Country Doctors of Kafka and T. *Symposium* 16 (1962):130-35.

Landor, Mikhail. *A Hunter's Sketches* as Read Today. *Soviet Literature* 12 (1983): 160-67.

Lee, Nicholas. Exposure to European Culture and Self-Discovery for Russians and Americans in the Fiction of Ivan T and Henry James. *American Contributions to the Ninth International Congress of Slavists,* vol. 2, ed.

Paul Debreczeny. Columbus: Slavica, 1983, pp. 267-84.

Lerner, D. The Influence of T on Henry James. *SEER* 20 (1941):28-55.

Levin, Iu. D. T's Project for a Historical Novel. *CASS* 17, 1 (1983):49-78.

Lloyd, J. A. T. Charm of T. *Fortnightly Review* 112 (1919):297-307.

Loewen, Harry. Human Involvement in T's and Kafka's Country Doctors. *Germano-Slavica* 3, (1974):47-54.

Long, Robert E. James's *Roderick Hudson:* The End of the Apprenticeship: Hawthorne and T. *American Literature* 48, 3 (1976):312-26.

Lowe, David. *Comedy and Tragedy in Fathers and Sons:* A Structural Analysis. *CASS* 13 (1979):283-94.

———. Doubling in *Fathers and Sons. Essays in Literature* 9 (1982):240-50.

———. *Otcy i deti* and T's Correspondence: A Study in Reciprocity. *RLJ* 33, 114 (1979):55-62.

———. T and *Besy. RLJ* 121-22 (1981):67-77.

Mabie, H. W. Appreciation of T. *Outlook* 88 (1908):223-6.

McLean, H. Eugene Rudin. In *Literature and Society in Imperial Russia, 1800-1914,* ed. William Todd. Stanford: Stanford UP, 1978, pp. 259-66.

Manning, Clarence Augustus. Ivan Sergeyevich T. *South Atlantic Quarterly* 30 (1931):366-81.

Marsh, Cynthia. T and Corot: An Analysis of the Comparison. *SEER* 61, 1 (1983): 107-17.

Masing-Delic, I. Schopenhauer's Metaphysics of Music and T's *Dvorjanskoe gnezdo. Die Welt der Slaven* 31 (1986):183-96.

Mathewson, R. W. Rebuttal II: Hamlet and Don Quixote. In his *The Positive Hero in Russian Literature,* 2d ed.. Stanford: Stanford UP, 1975, pp. 126-46.

Matlaw, Ralph E. T's Art in *Spring Torrents.* SEER 35 (1957):157-71.

———. T's Novels: Civic Responsibility and Literary Predilection. *HSS* 4 (1957): 249-62.

Matthews, Roy T. Bazarov and Hans: Archetypes of Student Attitudes. *Intellect* 103, no. 2356 (1974):365-67.

Maurois, A. The Art of T. In his *The Art of*

Writing, tr. G. Hopkins. NY: Dutton, 1960, pp. 295-315.

Maxwell, J. C. Conrad and T: A Minor Source of *Victory. Notes and Queries* n.s. 10 (1963):372-73.

Mersereau, John Jr. Don Quixote-Bazarov-Hamlet. *American Contributions to the Ninth International Congress of Slavists,* vol. 2, ed. Paul Debreczeny. Columbus: Slavica, 1983, pp.345-56.

Michnik, Adam. Rudin: The Superfluous Man. Tr. Wanda Rapaczynski. *Formations* 2 (1986):95-105.

Mills, Judith O. Theme and Symbol in "First Love." *SEEJ* 15 (1971):433-40.

Mlikotin, Anthony M. The Genre of "The International Novel" in the Works of T. In *Texte und Kontexte: Studien zur Deutschen und Vergleichenden Literaturwissenschaft,* ed. M. Durzak, et al. Bern: Francke, 1973, pp. 131-47.

——. The "International Theme" In the Novels of Ivan T. *Research Studies* (Washington State Univ.) 35, 1 (1967): 1-10.

Moller, P. U. The Relation of the Description of Nature and the Description of Man in the Prose of I. S. T. In *VII Międzynarodowy Kongres Slawistów w Warszawie 1973: Streszczenia Referatów i Komunikatów.* Warsaw: PAN, 1973, p. 404.

Moore, G. Avowals, Being the Second of a New Series of "Confessions of a Young Man" (T and Balzac). *Lippincott's Monthly Magazine* 72 (1903):481-88.

——. T and Tolstoy. In *Russian Literature and Modern English Fiction,* ed. D. Davie. Chicago: U Chicago P, 1965, pp. 31-43.

Moser, Charles A. T: The Cosmopolitan Nationalist. *Review of National Literatures* 3, 1 (1972):56-88.

——. T and the Esthetics of the Whole Man. In *T Commemorative Volume 1818-1883.* NY: Association of Russian-American Scholars in the USA, 1983, pp. 19-30.

Moss, W. G. Why the Anxious Fear: Aging and Death in the Works of T. In *Aging and the Elderly: Humanistic Perspectives in Gerontology,* ed. S. F. Spicket, et al. Atlantic Highlands, NJ:

Humanities Press, 1978, pp. 241-60.

Mostovskaia, N. N. Soviet T Scholarship of the Last Decade. *CASS* 17, 1 (1983):89-108.

Motola, Gabriel. The Mountains of *The Waste Land. Essays in Criticism* 19 (1969):67-69.

Moulik, Achala. Ivan T. In his *Silhouettes of Russian Literature.* Mysore: Prasaranga, Univ. of Mysore, 1976, pp. 58-67.

Moxom, P. S. T: The Man. *North American Review* 196 (1912):394-405.

Muchnic, Helen. T: The Music of His Face. In *T Commemorative Volume 1818-1883.* NY: Association of Russian-American Scholars in the USA, 1983, pp. 3-17.

Murphy, A. B. T and Flaubert: A Contrast in Styles. *NZSJ* (1983):143-60.

Nabokov, Vladimir. Ivan T: *Fathers and Sons.* In his *Lectures on Russian Literature.* NY: Harcourt, Brace, Jovanovich, 1981, pp. 63-96.

Nilsson, Nils A. The Use of Preterite + *Bylo* in T. *Scando-Slavica* 13 (1967): 39-58.

O'Connor, Frank. Hamlet and Quixote. In his *The Lonely Voice: A Study of the Short Story.* Cleveland: World, 1963, pp. 46-61.

Oliver, D. E. Russian Literature: T. *Papers of the Manchester Literary Club* 43 (1917):172-90.

Osborne, E. A. Russian Literature and Translations: Ivan S. T, 1818-1883. *Bookman* 83 (1932):198-202.

O'Toole, L. M. T's "Asya" and "Bezhin Meadow." In his *Structure, Style and Interpretation in the Russian Short Story.* New Haven: Yale UP, 1982, pp. 142-60, 180-203.

Page, S. W. Lenin, T, and the Russian Landed Gentry. *CSP* 18 (1976):442-56.

Pahomov, George S. Nature and the Use of Paradox in T. In *T Commemorative Volume 1818-1883.* NY: Association of Russian-American Scholars in the USA, 1983, pp. 47-56.

——. T's "Lyrical" Perception. *Forum at Iowa on Russian Literature* 1, 1 (1976):83-90.

Passage, Charles E. T. In his *The Russian Hoffmannists.* The Hague: Mouton, 1963, pp. 192-94.

Peace, R. A. *Russian Literature and the Fictionalization of Life.* Hull: U Hull P, 1976, pp. 10-12.

Peterson, D. E. The Origin and End of T's *Sportsman's Notebook:* The Poetics and Politics of Precarious Balance. *RusL* 16 (1984):347-58.

Porter, Richard N. The Criteria of T's Literary Criticism. *RusR* 28 (1969): 441-52.

Posin, Jack A. *A Sportsman's Sketches* by T versus *Uncle Tom's Cabin* by Beecher Stowe: A Study in Understatement. *CL* 9, 2 (1960):455-62.

Powers, Lyall H. *Henry James and the Naturalist Movement.* East Lansing: Michigan State UP, 1971, passim.

Pribić, Rado. Keyserling's "Schwüle Tage" and T's "First Love": A Comparison. In *Probleme der Komparatistik und Interpretation: Festschrift für André von Gronicka,* ed. W. Sokel, et al. Bonn: Bouvier, 1978, pp. 142-52.

Priestly, J. B. The Novelists. In his *Literature and Western Man.* NY: Harper, 1960, pp. 222-73.

Pritchett, V. S. Hero of Our Time? *London Mercury* 36 (1937):359-64.

——. The Russian Day. In his *The Living Novel and Later Appreciations.* NY: Random House, 1964, pp. 383-89.

——. T and *Virgin Soil. New York Review of Books,* 24, 4 (Mar. 17, 1977):37-39.

——. T in Baden. *New York Review of Books,* 24, 2 (Feb. 17, 1977):40-42.

Reed, T. J. Mann and T: A First Love. *German Life and Letters* 17 n.s., no. 4 (1964):313-18.

Reeve, F. D. Fathers and Children. In his *The Russian Novel.* NY: McGraw-Hill, 1966, pp. 119-58.

Rexroth, Kenneth. Fathers and Sons. In his *The Elastic Retort: Essays in Literature and Ideas.* NY: Seabury, 1973, pp. 112-15.

Rinkus, Jerome J. Reflections on T's "Hamlet and Don Quixote." In *Perspectives on Hamlet: Collected Papers of the Bucknell-Susquehana Colloquium on Hamlet (April 27-28, 1973),* ed. W. Holzberger & P. Waldeck. Lewisburg, PA: Bucknell UP, 1975, pp. 74-99.

Ripp, Victor. Ideology in T's *Notes of a Hunter:* The First Three Sketches. *SlavR* 38 (1979):75-88.

——. T as a Social Novelist: The Problem of the Past and the Whole. In *Literature and Society in Imperial Russia, 1800-1914,* ed. W. M. Todd III. Stanford: Stanford UP, 1978, pp. 237-57.

Ritchie, A. T. Concerning T. *Living Age* 257 (1908):214-20.

Ropp, S. de. Ivan Sergeyevich T, 1818-1888. In his *Changing Patterns of Russian Art and Letters.* [Syracuse?]: n.p. 1968, pp. 144-55.

Rowland-Brown, L. T and Girlhood. *Nineteenth Century* 90 (1921):230-44.

Russell, Bertrand R. The Romance of Revolt. In his *Fact and Fiction.* London: George Allen, 1961, pp. 17-22.

Saintsbury, G. E. B. T, Dostoievsky and Tolstoy. In *Russian Literature and Modern English Fiction,* ed. Donald Davie. Chicago: U Chicago P, 1965, pp. 23-30.

Sandwich, H. Hamlet the Lover: Thoughts on Ivan T's Essay "Hamlet and Don Quixote." *Proceedings of the Anglo-Russian Literary Society* 85 (1919):33-41.

Sayler, O. M. The Intellectual in Strindberg and T. *Texas Review* 7 (1922):215-35.

——. T as a Playwright. *New American Review* 214 (1921):398-400.

Schapiro, Leonard. *Spring Torrents:* Its Place and Significance in the Life and Work of Ivan Sergeevich T. In *T's Spring Torrents,* tr. L. Schapiro. London: Methuen: 1972, pp. 159-212.

Schefski, H. K. *Nouvelle* Structure in T's *Spring Torrents. Studies in Short Fiction* (1985): 431-35.

Seed, D. Two Contributions to Henry James' Bibliography. *Notes and Queries* n.s. 23 (Jan. 1976):11-12. [James's article on T.]

Seeley, Frank F. Thematic Counterpoint in "Poezdka v Poles'e." *Annali (Istituto Universitario Orientale. Sezione Slava, Napoli)* 16-17 (1973-74):13-20.

——. Oblomov. *SEER* 54, 3 (1976):335-54. [Goncharov and T's *On the Eve.*]

Sergievsky, N. N. The Tragedy of a Great Love. T and Pauline Viardot. *ASEER* 5, 14-15 (1946):55-71.

Seyersted, Per E. T's Interest in America, as Seen in His Contacts with H. H. Boyesen, W. D. Howells and Other American Authors. *Scando-Slavica* 11 (1965):25-39.

Silbajoris, Rimvydas. Images and Structures in T's *Sportsman's Notebook*. *SEEJ* 28 (1984):180-91.

Simmons, J.S.G. T and Oxford. *Oxoniensia* 31 (1966):146-51.

Slawinska, Irena. Two Concepts of Time in Dramatic Structure: T and Norwid. In *For Wiktor Weintraub: Essays in Polish Literature, Language and History*, ed. V. Erlich, et al. The Hague: Mouton, 1975, pp. 479-92.

Slonim, Marc. T Revisited. *Bulletin of the New York Public Library* 65 (1961): 570-76.

Smyrniw, Walter. I. S. T's and Bettina von Arnim's Depictions of Nature: Creative Affinities and Divergencies. *CSP* 25 (1983):13-24.

___. T's Emancipated Women. *MLR* 80 (1985):97-105.

Spalding, P. A. A Re-Reading of T. *Congregational Quarterly* (July 1953): 253-63.

Stephens, Robert O. Cable and T: Learning How to Write a Modern Novel. *Studies in the Novel* 15, 3 (1983):237-48.

Strauss, W. A. T in the Role of Publicity Agent for Flaubert's *La tentation de Saint Antoine*. *Harvard Library Bulletin* 2 (1948):405-10.

Struc, Roman. The Doctor's Predicament: A Note on T and Kafka. *SEEJ* 9, 2 (1965):174-80.

___. Kafka and the Russian Realists. *Newsletter of the Kafka Society of America* 1 (1979):11-15.

___. Thomas Mann and T. *CSP* 26, 1 (1984):35-41.

Strunsky, S. T and the Moderns. *Nation* 85 (1907):488-90.

Tammi, Pekka. Nabokov's *Lolita:* The T Subtext. *Notes on Modern American Literature* 5, 2 (1981):item 10.

Tedford, Barbara W. The Attitudes of Henry James and Ivan T toward the Russo-Turkish War. *Henry James Review* 1, 3 (1980):257-61.

___. Of Libraries and Salmon-Colored Volumes: James's Reading of T through 1873. *Resources for American Literary Study* 9 (1979):39-49.

Terras, Victor. T's Aesthetic and Western Realism. *CL* 22 (1970):19-35.

Tilley, W. H. *The Background of "The Princess Cassamassima."* Gainesville, FL: U Florida P, 1960. [T's *Virgin Soil* and James's novel.]

Todd, William Mills. "Artistizm T-a" as a Structural Principle: Rudin and Cultural Grouping. *RusL* 16 (1984):323-32.

Tucker, C. M. Russian Novelist's Estimate of the Russian Intellectual. *Sewanee Review* 24 (1916):61-68.

Tumas, Elena. The Non-Hero in Nineteenth-Century Russian Fiction. In *Medieval Epic to the Epic Theater of Brecht,* ed. R. Armato & J. Spalek. Los Angeles: U Southern California P, 1968, pp. 171-83.

Varnai, Paul. A New Addition to T's Works. *CSP* 14, 1 (1972):102-04.

Vidan, Ivo. James's Novel of "Looming Possibilities." In *Renaissance and Modern Essays Presented to Vivian de Sola Pinto.* NY: Barnes & Noble, 1966, pp. 137-45. [*Virgin Soil* and *On the Eve* and James's *The Princess Casamassima.*]

Vladiv, Slobodanka. The Origin and Meaning of the Term "Superfluous Man." *AULLA: Australasian Universities Languages and Literatures Association: Proceedings and Papers of the Twelfth Congress* (Feb. 5-11, 1969), ed. A. P. Treweek. Sydney: AULLA, 1970, p. 129.

Vucinich, Alexander. *Social Thought in Tsarist Russia: The Quest for a General Science of Society, 1861-1917.* Chicago: U Chicago P, 1976. [T's nihilism.]

Waddington, Patrick. A Bibliography of the Writings of W. R. S. Ralston (1829-89). *NZSJ* 1 (1980):1-15.

___. A Catalog of Letters by T to Pauline and Louis Viardot. *NZSJ* (1983):249-84.

____. Dickens, Pauline Viardot, T: A Study in Mutual Admiration. *NZSJ* 1 (1974): 55-73.

____. Document: Some Letters from A. I., I. S., and N. I. T to Richard Monckton Milnes (Lord Houghton). *NZSJ* 2 (1975): 61-83.

____. Document: Some Unpublished Letters by T, Addressed to Various Correspondents. *NZSJ* 1 (1975):57-76.

____. Henry Chorley, Pauline Viardot and T: A Musical and Literary Friendship. *Musical Quarterly* 67 (1981):165-92.

____. More Material By and Concerning T. *NZSJ* (1985):47-80.

____. More Unpublished Documents By and Concerning T. *NZSJ* 2 (1981):7-26.

____. Pauline Viardot as T's Censor. *TLS* (Jan. 1, 1970):16-17.

____. Some New Light on T's Relations with His French Publisher, Pierre-Jules Hetzel. *SEER* 55 (1977):328-47.

____. Some Salient Phases of T's Critical Reception in Britain. Part I: 1853-70. *NZSJ* 2 (1980):17-48. Part II: *NZSJ* 1 (1981):21-52.

____. Still More Letters of T. *NZSJ* 1 (1979):1-27.

____. The Strange History of Dr. F. and the Dismantling of Courtavenel. *MLR* 65, 2 (1970):333-54.

____. T and George Eliot: A Literary Friendship. *MLR* 66, 4 (1971):751-59.

____. T and Gounod: Rival Strangers in the Viardots' Country Nest. (Part I). *NZSJ* 2 (1976):11-32.

____. T and Pauline Viardot: An Unofficial Marriage. *CSP* 26, 1 (1984):42-64.

____. T and the Translator of *Virgin Soil*. *NZSJ* 1 (1977):35-76.

____. T and Trollope: Brief Crossings of Paths. *AULLA: Journal of the Australasian Universities Languages and Literatures Association* 42 (1974):199-201.

____. T's Relations with Henry Fothergill Chorley (With an Unpublished Letter). *NZSJ* 2 (1978):27-40.

____. T's Scenario for Brahms. *NZSJ* 1 (1982):1-16.

____. T's Sketches for *Ottsy i deti* (Fathers and Sons). *NZSJ* (1984):33-76.

____. Two Months in the Country: A Critical Episode in the Life and Career

of T. *NZSJ* 11 (1973):29-50.

____. Two Unpublished Letters from T to the Buloz Family. *SEER* 51, 124 (1973): 439-44.

____. An Unpublished Letter of T to Pauline Viardot. *SEER* 49, 115 (1971): 272-75.

Walicki, A. T and Schopenhauer. *OSP* 10 (1962):1-17.

Wasiolek, Edward. Bazarov and Odintsova. In *Ivan T 1818-1883-1983,* ed. Paul Debreczeny. Special issue of *CASS* 17, 1 (1983):39-48.

Wellek, René. Fathers and Sons. In *World Masterpieces,* vol. 2, ed. M. Mack. NY: Norton, 1965, pp. 658-62.

Wheeler, Marcus. T and Conrad. *JRS* 38 (1979):33-37.

____. T and Corot: An Analysis of the Comparison. *SEER* 61 (1983):107-17.

Whibley, C. Literary Sketch. *North American Review* 174 (1902):212-21.

Willcocks, M. P. T. *English Review* 33 (1921):175-89.

Wilson, Edmund. T and the Life-Giving Drop. *New Yorker* 33 (19 Oct. 1957): 150-200; reprinted in *Turgenev's Literary Reminiscences and Autobiographical Fragments,* tr. D. Magarshack. London, 1959; rpt. in his *Window on Russia.* NY: Farrar, Straus, 1972, pp. 68-146.

Winegarten, Renée. The Liberal Dilemma: T. In her *Writers and Revolution: The Fatal Lure of Action.* NY: New Viewpoints, 1974, pp. 183-95.

Woodcock, George. The Elusive Ideal: Notes on T. *Sewanee Review* 69, 1 (1961):34-47.

Woodward, James B. Aut Caesar aut nihil: The "War of the Wills" in T's *Ottsy i deti. SEER* 64 (1986):161-88.

____. The Symbolism and Rhythmic Structure of T's "Italian Pastiche." *Die Welt der Slaven* 18 (1973):368-85.

____. T's "New Manner": A Reassessment of His Novel *Dym. CSP* 26, 1 (1984): 65-80.

____. T's "Phantoms": A Reassessment. *SEER* 50 (1972):530-45.

____. Typical Images in the Later Tales of T. *SEEJ* 17 (1973):18-32.

Woolf, Virginia. The Novels of T. In her *The Captain's Deathbed and Other*

Essays. NY: Harcourt, Brace, 1950. [First published in *Yale Review,* 1933.]

Yarmolinsky, Avrahm. T—A Revaluation. In his *The Russian Literary Imagination.* NY: Funk & Wagnalls, 1969, pp. 57-81.

Žekulin, Nicholas G. Humour in T's Operetta *Le dernier sorcier. RusL* 16 (1984):421-36.

_____ T and Anglo-Irish Writers: 1. Maria Edgeworth. *CSP* 25 (1983):25-40.

_____ T in Scotland. *SEER* 54, 3 (1976):355-70.

_____ Two Unpublished Letters of Ivan T. *SEER* 53, 133 (1975):558-65.

Zohrab, Irene. T and Dostoevsky: A Reconsideration and a Suggested Attribution. *NZSJ* (1983):123-42.

Zöldhelyi-Deák, Zsuzsánna. The Chevalier des Grieux of the Russian Province. In *Ivan T 1818-1883-1983,* ed. Paul Debreczeny. Special issue of *CASS* 17, 1 (1983):1-6.

Zweers, A. F. First Love. Ivan T's Description of Dawning Love. In *Signs of Friendship. To Honour A. G. F. van Holk,* ed. J. J. van Baak. Amsterdam: Rodopi, 1984, pp. 569-89.

_____ The Influence of Ivan T on Marcellus Emants: A Suffering versus a Dogmatic Pessimist. *CSP* 25 (1983):41-53.

Kayden. Boulder: U Colorado P, 1974.

Versions from Fyodor T, 1803-1873. Tr. Charles Tomlinson. London: Oxford UP, 1960.

Bannikov, Nikolai, comp. *Three Centuries of Russian Poetry.* Moscow: Progress, 1980, pp. 223-35. [14 poems.]

Gregg, Richard A. *Fedor T: The Evolution of a Poet.* NY: Columbia UP, 1965. [Contains translations of 87 poems.]

Ignatieff, L. I. F. I. T (1803-18783): Selected Poems. *CSS* (1968):259-63.

Kayden, E. M., tr. [14 poems.] *Colorado Quarterly* 19 (1971):404-12.

Nabokov, Vladimir. *Three Russian Poets.* Forest Hills, NY: Transatlantic Press, 1949. [Nightfall; Tears; the Journey; Silentium; Last Love; Dusk; The Abyss; Autumn; Appeasement; Tears.]

Obolensky, Dimitri, ed. *The Heritage of Russian Verse.* Bloomington: Indiana UP, 1976, pp. 129-42. [16 poems.]

Pratt, Sarah. *The Semantics of Chaos in T.* Munich: Sagner, 1983. [Includes 19 poems.]

Rydel, Christine, ed. *The Ardis Anthology of Russian Romanticism.* Ann Arbor: Ardis, 1984, pp. 91-94. [12 poems.]

Zheleznova, Irina, ed. *Russian 19th-Century Verse.* Moscow: Raduga, 1983, pp. 179-227. [82 poems.]

FYODOR TYUTCHEV

Bibliography

Lane, Ronald C. Bibliography: T in English Translation, 1873-1974. *Journal of European Studies* 2 (1975):153-75.

Translations

Poems and Political Letters of F. I. T. Tr., intro. & notes by Jesse Zeldin. Knoxville: U Tennessee P, 1973.

Poems of Night and Day. Tr. Eugene M.

Criticism

Bilokur, Borys. *A Concordance to the Russian Poetry of F. I. T.* Providence: Brown UP, 1975.

Conant, Roger. *The Political Poetry and Ideology of F. I. T.* Ann Arbor: Ardis, 1983.

Gregg, Richard A. *Feodor T: The Evolution of a Poet.* NY: Columbia UP, 1965.

Pratt, Sarah. *Russian Metaphysical Romanticism. The Poetry of T and Boratynskii.* Stanford: Stanford UP, 1984.

_____. *The Semantics of Chaos in T.* Munich: Sagner, 1983.

Bilokur, Borys. Lexical Elements of T's Poetry. Ph.D. diss., Illinois, 1968.

Coates, William A. T and Germany: The Relationship of His Poetry to German Literature and Culture. Ph.D. diss., Harvard, 1950.

Gregg, Richard A. The Evolution of T. Ph.D. diss., Columbia, 1962.

Pratt, Sarah Claflin. The Metaphysical Poetry of F. I. T and E. A. Boratynskij: Alternatives in Russian Romanticism. Ph.D. diss., Columbia, 1978.

Rydel, Christine A. A Formal Analysis of the Poems of Fedor Ivanovič T. Ph.D. diss., Indiana, 1976.

Webb, M. P. The Life and Poetry of T. Ph.D. diss., London, 1927.

Wehrle, Albert James. Tensions in the Poetry of F. I. T. Ph.D. diss., Ohio State, 1974.

Barabtarlo, Gennadi. T's Poem "Zdes' negoda, mogučij i prekrasnyj...": Textology and Exegesis of the Bogatyrev Manuscript. *SEEJ* 30, 3 (1986):420-30.

Bidney, M. The Aeolian Harp Reconsidered: Music of Unfulfilled Longing in T, Mörike, Thoreau and Others. *CLS* 22 (1985):329-43.

Bilokur, Borys. On T's Archaisms. *SEEJ* 18 (1974):373-76.

——.Statistical Observations on T's Lexicon. *SEEJ* 14 (1970):302-16.

Binyon, T. J. Lermontov, T and Fet. In *Nineteenth-Century Russian Literature: Studies of Ten Russian Writers,* ed. J. Fennell. Berkeley & Los Angeles: U California P, 1973, pp. 168-224.

Brown, William Edward. Fyodor T (Before 1841). In his *A History of Russian Literature of the Romantic Period.* Ann Arbor: Ardis, 1986, vol. 4, pp. 11-35.

Byrns, R. Temporal and Spatial Enclosures in the Poetry of T. *SEEJ* 21 (1977):180-90.

Chopyk, D. B. Schelling's Philosophy in F. I. T's Poetry. *RLJ* 27 (1973):17-23.

Conant, R. The Political Poetry and Ideology of Fedor Ivanovich T: A Study in Compensatory Nationalism. *Slavic and Soviet Studies* 2, 2 (1977):61-94.

Ferrell, James. On the Problem of Unity in Stanzaic Poetry with Special Reference to T's Solutions. In *Orbis Scriptus,* ed. D. Gerhardt. Munich: W. Fink, 1966, pp. 202-10.

Florovsky, G. Historical Premonitions of T. *SEER* 3 (1924):337-49.

Gifford, Henry. The Evolution of T's Art. *SEER* 37 (Dec. 1958-Jan. 1959):378-86.

Gregg, Richard A. Dream at Sea: T and Pascal. *SlavR* 23 (1964):526-30.

Gustafson, R. F. T's Imagery and What It Tells Us. *SEEJ* 4 (1960):1-16.

Kjetsaa, Geir. T's Vocabulary: A Quantitative Approach. In *Russian Poetics,* ed. T. Eekman & D. Worth. Columbus: Slavica, 1983, pp. 209-26.

Lane, Ronald C. Anniversaries in T's Poetry. *SSR* (1983):125-36.

——. Russia and the Revolution in T's Poetry: Some Poems of 1828-1830. *SEER* 51 (1973):214-30.

——. Russia and the West in T's Poetry: On the Origins of Some Poems of 1830. In *VII Międzynarodowy Kongres Slawistów w Warszawie 1973: Streszczenia Referatów i Komunikatów.* Warsaw: PAN, 1973, pp. 491-92.

——. T in Russian Fiction. *NZSJ* 2 (1975): 17-32.

——. T in the 1820s-1840s: An Unpublished Correspondence of 1874-75. *Irish Slavonic Studies* 3 (1982):2-13.

——. T in the 1820s-1840s: An Unpublished Letter of F. I. T to Prince P. B. Kozlovsky. *NZSJ* 1 (1982):17-28.

——. T's Place in the History of Russian Literature. *MLR* 71 (1976):344-56.

——. T's Role as Mediator between the Government and M. N. Katkov (1863-66). *RusL* 12 (1985):111-26.

Lednicki, W. Pushkin, T, Mickiewicz and the Decembrists: Legend and Facts. *SEER* 29 (1951):375-402.

Liberman, Anatoly. The Structure of T's Poem "Pesok sypučij po koleni." In *Semiosis: Semiotics and the History of Culture: In Honorem Georgii Lotman,* ed. M. Halle, et al. Ann Arbor: U Michigan, 1984, pp. 165-68.

Masing-Delic, I. Three Poems about Two Meetings. (Pushkin's "K," T's "K.B."

and Blok's "O doblestjach.") *RusL* 9 (1975):37-54.

Matlaw, Ralph E. The Polyphony of T's "Son na more." *SEER* 36 (1958):198-203.

——. T's Punctuation and T's Texts. In *Orbis Scriptus,* ed. D. Gerhardt. Munich: W. Fink, 1966, pp. 524-35.

Pratt, Sarah. Antithesis and Completion: Zabolotskii Responds to T. *SEEJ* 27, 2 (1983):211-27.

——. The Metaphysical Abyss: One Aspect of the Bond Between T and Schelling. *Germano-Slavica* 4 (1982):71-88.

——. Points of Contact: Two Russian Poets and Their Links to Schelling. *Germano-Slavica* 4 (1982):3-16.

Safonov, Sidonie H. The Metaphors in T's Philosophical System. *Bulletin of the Rocky Mountain Modern Language Association* 26 (1972):55-64.

Weeks, Andrew. T, Schelling and the Question of Influence. *Germano-Slavica* 3, (1981):307-17.

Wehrle, Albert. T and Writing. *RLJ* 116 (1979):69-84.

Wilson, Edmund. Notes on Russian Literature: T. *Atlantic Monthly* (Jan 1944):78-80.

GLEB USPENSKY

Translations

Concerning One Old Woman. *Monthly Review* 17 (1904):106-22.

Voynich, E. L., ed. *The Humor of Russia.* London: Scott, 1895.
[The Steam Chicken; A Trifling Defect.]

Wiener, Leo, ed. *Anthology of Russian Literature,* vol. 2. NY: Putnam, 1902-3, pp. 408-17.
[The Power of the Land (excerpt).]

Criticism

Prutskov, Nikita I. *Gleb U.* NY: Twayne, 1972.

ALEXANDER VELTMAN

Translation

Travel Impressions and, Among Other Things, a Pot of Geraniums. Tr. J. Gebhard. In *Russian Romantic Prose,* ed. Carl R. Proffer. Ann Arbor: Translation Press, 1979, pp. 102-36.

Criticism

Gabara, Uliana Fischbein. A. F. V's *Salomeja:* A Case for the Nineteenth-Century Picaresque Novel. Ph.D. diss., Virginia, 1982.

Gebhard, James J. The Early Novels of A. F. V. Ph.D. diss., Indiana, 1968.

Lapeza, David. Kaleidoscope: The Poetics of Alexander V's Early Novels. Ph.D. diss., Michigan, 1986.

Ward, Charles Alexander. The Later Novels of A. F. V. Ph.D. diss., Chicago, 1974.

Brown, William Edward. Alexander V. In his *A History of Russian Literature of the Romantic Period.* Ann Arbor: Ardis, 1986, vol. 2, pp. 241-58.

Bukhshtab, B. V's Earliest Novels. In *Russian Prose,* ed. B. Eikhenbaum & Yu. Tynyanov, tr. Ray Parrott. Ann Arbor: Ardis, 1985, pp. 151-80.

Mersereau, John, Jr. V. In his *Russian Romantic Fiction.* Ann Arbor: Ardis, 1983, pp. 230-40.

DMITRI VENEVITINOV

Translations

Complete Poetry. 35 poems. Tr. Donald R. Boucher & Larry Andrews. *RLT* 8 (1974):84-130.

A Critique on an Essay on *Eugene Onegin* Published in *The Telegraph.* In *The Critical Prose of Alexander Pushkin,* ed. & tr. Carl R. Proffer. Bloomington:

Indiana UP, 1969, pp. 290-97; rpt. *Ardis Anthology of Russian Romanticism,* ed. C. Rydel. Ann Arbor: Ardis, 1984, pp. 419-22.

Three Essays. Tr. Larry Andrews. *RLT* 11 (1975):179-85.
[Sculpture, Painting and Music; Morning, Midday, Evening and Night; Anaxagoras: A Platonic Dialogue.]

Criticism

Andrews, Larry B. The Complete Poetry of D. V. V: Translation with Critical Introduction: V's Romantic Image of the Poet. Ph.D. diss., Rutgers, 1971.

Brkich, Lazar. D. V. Venevitinov (1805-1827): Poet-Thinker of the Liubomudry Circle. Ph.D. diss., Wisconsin, 1974.

Javorsky, Kaleria. The Dictionary of D. V. V's Language. Ph.D. diss., New York, 1973.

Andrews, Larry B. D.V.V: A Sketch of His Life and Works. *RLT* 8 (1974):373-84.

Brown, William Edward. Dmitry V. In his *A History of Russian Literature of the Romantic Period.* Ann Arbor: Ardis, 1986, vol. 3, pp. 347-63.

McMillin, A. B. Byron and V. *SEER* 53 (1975):188-201.

Mersereau, John, Jr. V. In his *Baron Delvig's "Northern Flowers."* Carbondale: Southern Illinois UP, 1967, pp. 96-97, 148-49.

PYOTR
VYAZEMSKY

Translations

Myers, A., tr. [Poems.] *Modern Poetry in Translation* 40 (1980):29-32.

Rydel, Christine, ed. *The Ardis Anthology of Russian Romanticism.* Ann Arbor: Ardis, 1984, pp. 412-15.
[In Place of a Foreword to *The Fountain of Bakhchisarai.*]

Criticism

Ivask, George. V's Literary Criticism. Ph.D. diss., Harvard, 1955.

Brown, William Edward. The Younger Innovators: Prince Pyotr V. In his *A History of Russian Literature of the Romantic Period.* Ann Arbor: Ardis, 1986, vol. 2, pp. 59-83.

Leighton, Lauren G. The Anecdote in Russia: Puškin, V and Davydov. *SEEJ* 10 (1966):155-66.

Little, E. Eighteenth-Century Russian Literature as Seen Through the Eyes of Prince P. A. V. *Study Group on Eighteenth-Century Russia: Newsletter* 1 (1973):7-10.

Little, T. E. P. A. V as a Critic of Gogol. *NZSJ* 1 (1978):47-58.

——. V as a Critic of Pushkin. In *Russian and Slavic Literature,* ed. R. Freeborn, et al. Cambridge: Slavica, 1976, pp. 1-16.

Meijer, J. M. V and Romanticism. In *Dutch Contributions to the Seventh International Congress of Slavists,* ed. A. van Holk. The Hague: Mouton, 1973, pp. 271-304.

Mersereau, John, Jr. [V.] In his *Baron Delvig's "Northern Flowers."* Carbondale: Southern Illinois UP, 1967, pp. 11-16, 27-37, 42-47, 72-75.

Todd, William Mills III. [V.] In his *The Familiar Letter as a Literary Genre in the Age of Pushkin.* Princeton: Princeton UP, 1976, pp. 8-9, 132-33, 187-88, 168-69; also see index.

NIKOLAI
YAZYKOV

Translations

Bannikov, Nikolai, comp. *Three Centuries of Russian Poetry.* Moscow: Progress Publishers, 1980, pp. 165-67.
[Song; The Mariner.]

Obolensky, Dimitri, ed. *The Heritage of Russian Verse.* Bloomington: Indiana UP, 1976, pp., 124-25.
[Elegy; To the Rhine.]

Rydel, Christine, ed. *The Ardis Anthology of Russian Romanticism.* Ann Arbor: Ardis, 1984, pp. 73-74.
[Songs; Elegy; A Prayer; The Colt.]

Criticism

Leong, Albert. The Poetics of N. M. Y. Ph.D. dissertation, Chicago, 1970.

Bristol, E. I. Y: His Lyric, Narrative and Dramatic Verse. *CalSS* 7 (1973):41-64.
Dees, Benjamin. Y's Lyrical Poetry. *RLT* 10 (1975):316-29.
___ Y's Unpublished Erotica. *RLT* 10 (1975):408-13.
Humesky, Assya. Grammatical Rhymes in N. Y's Poetry. In *Papers in Slavic Philology,* vol. 1, ed. B. Stolz. Ann Arbor: Michigan Slavic Publications, 1977, pp. 121-41.
Lilly, Ian K. N. M. Y as a Slavophile Poet. *SlavR* 31 (1972):797-804.
___ The Stanzaic Forms of N. M. Y. In *Russian Poetics,* ed. T. Eekman & D. S. Worth. Columbus: Slavica, 1983, pp. 227-34.

MIKHAIL ZAGOSKIN

Translations

Tale of Three Centuries. Tr. J. Curtin. Boston: Little-Brown, 1891.
[An Evening on the Hopyor; The Three Suitors; Kuzma Roshchin.]
The Young Muscovite, or the Poles in Russia. Ed. F. Chamier. NY: Harper, 1834, 2 vols.

Rydel, Christine, ed. *The Ardis Anthology of Russian Romanticism.* Ann Arbor: Ardis, 1984, pp. 252-68.
[Yury Miloslavsky (excerpts).]

Criticism

Schwartz, Miriam Golin. M. N. Z as a Historical Novelist. Ph.D. dissertation, Ohio State, 1979.

Brown, William Edward. Nikolai Z. In his *A History of Russian Literature of the Romantic Period.* Ann Arbor: Ardis, 1986, vol. 2, pp. 280-87.
Christian, R. F. An Unpublished Letter by M. N. Z. *SEER* 50 (1972):434-35.
Mersereau, John, Jr. The Historical Novel—Z. In his *Russian Romantic Fiction.* Ann Arbor: Ardis, 1983, pp. 102-11.

VASILY ZHUKOVSKY

Translations

Bannikov, Nikolai, comp. *Three Centuries of Russian Poetry.* Moscow: Progress, 1980, pp. 93-97.
[Svetlana (excerpt); Friendship; Remembrance; The Sea.]
Obolensky, Dimitri, ed. *The Heritage of Russian Verse.* Bloomington: Indiana UP, 1976.
[To Her; Song; 19 March 1823; The Night.]
Rydel, Christine, ed. *The Ardis Anthology of Russian Romanticism.* Ann Arbor: Ardis, 1984, pp. 50-52.
[The Sea. An Elegy; March 19, 1823; Song; Spring Feeling; Night Review.]

Criticism

Semenko, Irina. *Vasily Z.* Boston: Twayne, 1976.

Burnett, L. P. Dimensions of Truth: A Comparative Study of the Relationship between "Language" and "Reality" in the Works of Wordsworth, Coleridge, Z, Pushkin and Keats. Ph.D. diss., Essex, 1976.

Brown, William Edward. The Older Innovators: Vasily Z. In his *A History of Russian Literature of the Romantic Period.* Ann Arbor: Ardis, 1986, vol. 1, pp. 185-226.
___ Vasily Andreevich Z. *RLT* 8 (1974): 295-328.

Gogol, Nikolai. The *Odyssey* in Z's Translation. In his *Selected Passages from a Correspondence with Friends*. Nashville: Vanderbilt UP, 1969, pp. 32-41.

____ On the Essence of Russian Poetry. In his *Selected Passages from a Correspondence with Friends*. Nashville: Vanderbilt UP, 1969, pp. 208-13.

Gronicka, A. von. Goethe and his Russian Translator-Interpreter. *PMLA* 70 (1955): 145-65.

Hewton, Ainslie. A Comparison of Sir Walter Scott's *The Eve of St. John* and Z's Translation of the Ballad. *NZSJ* 11 (1973):145-50.

Jensen, K. B. Meaning in a Poem: An Analysis of V. A. Z's "19 marta 1823." *Scando-Slavica* 27 (1981):5-14.

Johnson, Doris. The Simile in Batyushkov and Z. *RLT* 7 (1973):407-22.

Katz, Michael. Polemics, Z's Literary Ballads. Z's Imitators. In his *The Literary Ballad in Early 19th-Century Russian Literature*. Oxford: Oxford UP, 1976, pp. 37-138.

Matenko, P. Tieck's Russian Friends: Kiukhel'beker and Z. *PMLA* 55 (1940): 1129-45.

Ober, K. H. & W. U. Percy's Nancy and Z's Nina: A Translation Identified. *SEER* 57 (1979):396-402.

____. Z and Southey's Ballads: The Translator as Rival. *Wordsworth Circle* 5 (1974):76-88.

____ Z's Early Translations of the Ballads of Robert Southey. *SEEJ* 9 (1965):181-90.

____ Z's First Translation of Gray's Elegy. *SEEJ* 10 (1966):167-72.

____ Z's Translation of Campbell's "Lord Ullin's Daughter." *Germano-Slavica* 2 (1977):295-305.

____ Z's Translation of Oliver Goldsmith's "The Deserted Village." *Germano-Slavica* 1 (1973):19-28.

____ Z's Translation of "The Prisoner of Chillon." *SEEJ* 17 (1973):390-98.

Passage, Charles. The Influence of Schiller in Russia: 1800-1840 (Schiller and Z). *ASEER* 5 (1956):111-37.

Senderovich, S. Z's World of Fleeting Visions. *RusL* 12 (1985):203-20.

Turgenev, Ivan. Z. In his *Literary Reminiscences*. NY: Farrar, 1958, pp. 171-75.